A Behavioral Approach to Education of Children and Youth

SCHOOL PSYCHOLOGY

A series of volumes edited by
  Thomas R. Kratochwill and James E. Ysseldyke

A Behavioral Approach to Education of Children and Youth

Edited by

CHARLES A. MAHER AND SUSAN G. FORMAN

LEA LAWRENCE ERLBAUM ASSOCIATES, PUBLISHERS
1987   Hillsdale, New Jersey   London

Lawrence Erlbaum Associates, Inc., Publishers
365 Broadway
Hillsdale, New Jersey 07642

Library of Congress Cataloging in Publication Data
Main entry under title:
A Behavioral approach to education of children and
    youth.
  Bibliography: p.
  Includes index.
  1. Behavior modification—Addresses, essays,
lectures.   2. Teaching—Addresses, essays, lectures.
I. Maher, Charles A., 1944-   .   II. Forman,
Susan G.
LB1060.2.B44   371.1'024   85-32561
ISBN 0-89859-634-3

Printed in the United States of America
10 9 8 7 6 5 4 3 2 1

Contents

Contributors

Charles A. Maher
Department of School Psychology
Graduate School of Applied and
  Professional Psychology
Rutgers University
Piscataway, NJ 08854

Susan G. Forman
Department of Psychology
University of South Carolina
Columbia, SC 29208

Anthony Cancelli
School of Education at Lincoln Center
Fordham University
New York, NY 10023

Roland K. Yoshida
School of Education at Lincoln Center
Fordham University
New York, NY 10023

Wayne C. Piersel
Department of Educational Psychology
University of Nebraska-Lincoln
Lincoln, Nebraska 68588

Robert J. Illback
Department of Student Services
Ft. Knox Community Schools
Ft. Knox, KY 40121

Bruce A. McClenahagn
Department of Physical Education
College of Health
University of South Carolina
Columbia, SC 29208

Diane S. Ward
Department of Physical Education
College of Health
University of South Carolina
Columbia, SC 29208

Frank M. Gresham
Department of Psychology
Louisiana State University
Baton Rouge, LA 70803-5501

Kathleen L. Lemanek
Department of Psychology
Louisiana State University
Baton Rouge, LA 70803-5501

Jason K. Feld
Department of Educational Psychology
College of Education
University of Arizona
Tucson, AZ 85721

John R. Bergan
Department of Educational Psychology
College of Education
University of Arizona
Tucson, AZ 85721

Clement A. Stone
Department of Educational Psychology
College of Education
University of Arizona
Tucson, AZ 85721

Susan A. Cook
Department of School Psychology
Graduate School of Applied and Professional
   Psychology
Rutgers University
Piscataway, NJ 08854

Louis J. Kruger
Department of Education
Tufts University
Medford, MA

Thomas R. Kratochwill
Department of Educational Psychology
University of Wisconsin-Madison
Madison, WI 53706

F. Charles Mace
School of Education
Lehigh University
Bethlehem, PA 18015

Mary S. Bissel
Department of Educational Psychology
College of Education
University of Arizona
Tucson, AZ 85721

Susan L. Graham-Clay
Child Guidance Clinic of Greater Winnipeg
Winnipeg, Manitoba
Canada R3E 1B2

Daniel J. Reschly
Department of Psychology
Iowa State University
Ames, IA 50011

Preface

Professionals who provide services in schools, and related educational settings, particularly those involved with special needs students, are becoming increasingly interested in the field of behavior modification. Influenced by public concern over educational excellence and standards for effective practice, school psychologists, counselors, social workers, nurses, special services coordinators, and consultants are becoming more familiar with behavioral procedures and programs as means to enhance educational services delivery. In this regard, our observations and those of colleagues suggest that practitioners are learning more about behavioral technology through the reading of professional books and journal articles, as well as by attending professional conferences and in-service training workshops.

Empirical research has documented the value of behavioral procedures and programs in numerous ways and in various areas of educational services delivery. These ways and areas include:

- As a means of providing assessment services, whereby behavioral assessment procedures allow for trustworthy information to be gathered for individualized program planning and evaluation.
- As a means of providing instructional and related services, whereby academic achievement and functional living skills of students are improved through carefully designed programs and other interventions.
- As a means of providing personnel development services, whereby teachers are helped to become more proficient in educating children and youth.
- As a means of providing administrative services, including program evaluation and research, that support system operations.

Given the range of educational services that have been suggested by empirical research as benefiting from application of behavioral technology, it is only natural that practitioners, if aware of the possible benefits, would desire to apply such procedures and programs to their local circumstances. Translation of behavioral research results into effective procedures and programs, however, does not proceed in a straightforward manner, as those of us who practice and conduct research in schools have readily experienced. An important reason why "a research to practice initiative" does not occur quickly in schools and related educational settings is that empirical research results, to be used by practitioners, must be considered in light of organizational factors such as staff capabilities, community values, educational goals, and budget constraints. This kind of consideration, however, takes time, requires participation of many people, necessitates appreciation of the school as an organization, and involves understanding of effective behavioral procedures and programs.

This edited volume contains material of an informative and instructive nature about effective behavioral procedures and programs that can be applied in schools and related educational settings by school psychologists, counselors, social workers, nurses, curriculum consultants, and special services coordinators. Typically, these professionals are called upon to provide assessment, instructional, related, personnel development, and administrative services, as well as to evaluate effectiveness of these diverse service delivery efforts. In doing so, these practitioners and applied researchers routinely interact with a range of regular and special education teachers, parents, and community members. Hence, these practitioners and applied researchers are in good position to view the school as an organization, especially its readiness for behavioral technology, and they can be facilitators of incorporation of effective procedures and programs into school routines.

This volume also explicates a behavioral approach as seen in the 11 sequential, interrelated chapters, authored by individuals having considerable knowledge about and experience with behavioral technology in schools and related educational settings. The behavioral approach reflected in the chapters, however, is not to be viewed narrowly in a "cookbook" sense. Rather, and most fundamentally, this material advocates a framework for understanding the nature and scope of behavior and performance in schools, and how behavioral technology can be employed to improve student achievement and staff productivity. By reading this edited volume, we expect that practitioners, graduate students, and applied researchers in special education, remedial education, psychology, counseling, nursing, and social work will become more knowledgeable about and appreciative of a behavioral approach to education of children and youth that is practical and that can be effectively incorporated into school routines.

In undertaking and completing this book, we acknowledge the diligence, vigilance, and timeliness of the contributors in submitting one or more revisions of their manuscripts while graciously responding to editorial feedback. In addition, our sincerest appreciation is extended to Thomas R. Kratochwill and James Ysseldyke for their support as Series Editors as well as to Judy Cox and M. Kathryn Marion for considerable assistance in manuscript preparation.

Charles A. Maher
Piscataway, New Jersey
Susan G. Forman
Columbia, South Carolina

1 The Behavioral Approach to Education of Children and Youth: Overview and Orientation

Charles A. Maher
Susan G. Forman

Improvement of educational services for children and youth has become a priority concern for school professionals, parents, and other community members. A number of occurrences on national, state, and local levels have served to underscore the need for change in our schools and have provided the impetus for action.

National education reports, most notably "A Nation at Risk" (United States Office of Education [USOE] 1983) and Carnegie Foundation reports (Boyer, 1983), have identified the need to direct efforts at enhancing levels of student achievement, staff productivity, and quality of school life. Toward such ends, a number of states have increased funding for education and have passed legislation and regulations aimed at improving the effectiveness and efficiency of educational services. In addition, school and community task forces have been organized to address issues related to upgrading the ways educational services and programs are provided, and how students benefit from such offerings. Professional organizations whose members are employed in schools and related educational settings, such as the National Education Association, National Association of School Psychologists, and the American Personnel and Guidance Association, also have reflected interest in school improvement through refinement of standards and identification of the best educational practices. Similarly, business and industrial leaders have reflected the concern of the private sector for quality education by providing funding and assistance for programs aimed at ensuring the quality of future employees.

Concurrent with interest in and mandate for improving education has been increased concern about particular educational program matters. In some states, along with additional funding has come more explicit demands for monitoring student and staff performance to ensure the effective use of tax monies, Conversely, other states and local communities have had to decrease funding for education because of shrinking tax bases. In addition, federal financial support of educational services and programs has declined; federal budget deficit projections have indicated that such a trend may continue. These conditions, as well as the generally tenuous state of the economy, have focused attention on educational program cost effectiveness and staff accountability, and have resulted in a heightened awareness of the need to maximize returns on tax dollar investments. Such emphases also have been advanced by federal law, particularly Public Law 94-142, and derivative state laws and regulations regarding education of the handicapped. The cost effectiveness and accountability issues have likewise gained prominence in connection with a number of minimum competency testing programs that seek to upgrade the basic academic skills of high school graduates (Grise, in press).

The mandate to enhance educational excellence and effectiveness and maintain accountability points to the need for approaches to education with the following characteristics: (a) meaningful information about students serves as the basis for program design; (b) programs are targeted to specific educational goals; (c) evaluation of program operation and outcomes is an important part of the educational effort; and (d) programs are revised based on evaluation information.

The behavioral approach to education of children and youth, which is the focus of this book, provides a range of procedures, and programs that reflect the aforementioned characteristics. In order to place the chapters that follow into a contemporary perspective, this initial chapter provides an overview of the behavioral approach to the education of children and youth and orients the reader to the format and content of subsequent chapters.

THE BEHAVIORAL APPROACH

The behavioral approach to educating children and youth can be considered a broad-based notion, encompassing a range of perspectives, principles, processes, procedures, and programs. However, all of these elements have the following in common;

1. Focus on current behavior as it relates to school performance.
2. Emphasis on precision in assessing behavior and in setting goals.
3. Reliance on prior experimental research and evaluation information as a basis for program design.
4. Emphasis on specificity in defining programs and procedures.
5. Commitment to routine evaluation of program effectiveness.

Current Behavior and School Performance

The behavioral approach implies that efforts at improving school performance can best proceed with a focus on defining current behavior in the school setting (Sulzer-Azaroff & Mayer, 1977). As an initial step, the area of school performance to be addressed must be described in terms of operationally defined behavior. Operationally defined behavior is behavior that is measureable. Behaviors can be measured along a number of dimensions including: (a) frequency (e.g., number of times a student participates in class discussion); (b) duration (e.g., length of time a school psychologist spends writing a report); (c) intensity (e.g., voice volume of a verbal response of a "shy" student); (d) topography-form or shape (e.g., the type and sequence of movements necessary for skipping); and (e) accuracy (e.g., criteria for writing a complete sentence).

To be considered as measurable, a behavior must also be observable; in this regard, behaviors can be either overt or covert (Kendall & Butcher, 1982). Overt behavior is directly observable (e.g., number of times a student talks without permission). In contrast, covert behaviors, such as feelings or thoughts, are internal behaviors that cannot be observed by others (e.g., feelings of anxiety, self-talk—"Nobody likes me"). However, covert behaviors can be made observable through verbal or written communication (e.g., self-report measures).

Thus, with the behavioral approach, current observable, measureable behavior is used as a means of defining school performance. Moreover, in this approach, it is expected that the particular behaviors that are to be the target of behavioral procedures or programs are directly related to the mission and goals of the schools (Salvia & Ysseldyke, 1981). For students, these educational goals typically will reflect academic behaviors, affective and social behaviors, motor behaviors, health-related behaviors, and prevocational behaviors (Evans & Meyer, 1985). For school personnel, target behaviors will be those related to effective job performance (e.g., managing time, providing feedback to students, socially reinforcing students), as these can be seen as facilitating student learning (Allen & Forman, 1984; see also Chapter 9).

Precision in Assessing Behavior and Setting Program Goals

The behavioral approach to education emphasizes precision and specificity in assessing behavior for the purpose of defining specific program goals (Nelson, 1985; see also Chapter 2). Behavioral assessment places particular importance on use of methods that are valid and reliable (Cone, 1978, 1979). Valid methods are those that actually do measure what they are supposed to measure. Reliable methods yield standard results regardless of who uses them on a particular occasion.

As an emerging area, behavioral assessment encompasses a range of methods including direct observation of behavior in specified settings, judgments obtained through interviews, checklists, rating scales or questionnaires, and review of permanent products, such as reports or written tests (Haynes & Wilson, 1979). The behavioral assessment approach, particularly when multiple measures are used, can yield information that specifically defines an individual's current functioning (Nelson, 1985). This information can be utilized easily in the setting of specific goals and behavioral objectives, and in the design of school programs that are targeted to these outcomes (Maher & Bennett, 1984). Behavioral objectives include specification of the target behavior, the situation in which it is to occur, and the criterion level. Criterion levels typically include a requirement to increase, extend, or maintain a behavior, or to decrease or restrict a behavior. Criterion levels can be used to determine both individual and program success (Evans & Meyer, 1985). For example, a behavioral objective for a student who does not verbally participate in class might be: "Jane will raise her hand to volunteer to answer two questions asked by the teacher during the discussion session following silent reading."

In addition to information related to the individual's or group's behavior in the school setting, descriptive material about relevant contextual factors, such as individual or group cultural and linguistic characteristics, home factors, and organizational conditions in the school, are important to obtain (Salvia & Ysseldyke, 1981). These factors are important in that consideration of them will provide information that is essential in designing an effective behavioral program.

Reliance on Prior Experimental and Evaluation Research

The behavioral approach to education emphasizes utilization of previous empirical research and evaluation information in the design of programs (Barlow, Hayes, & Nelson, 1984; see also Chapter 10). Behavioral procedures have their origins in experimental psychology and learning theory. Four areas of psychological research have made a major impact on current behavioral technology (Kazdin & Wilson, 1978). These include research related to: (a) respondent conditioning, which involves changing the conditions under which an innate response takes place; (b) operant learning, which emphasizes the idea that behavior is a function of its consequences; (c) observational learning, which explores the influence of demonstration of behavior; and (d) cognitive processes and their influences on behavior.

The behavioral research base covers a broad range of literature in psychology, education, and related fields (Kazdin, 1978). Behavioral programs are designed based on principles and procedures that have been demonstrated to be effective in controlled basic and applied research, as well as in program evaluation efforts in a variety of applied settings. Consideration of information that demonstrates the effectiveness of particular procedures and/or programs, as well as information that identifies important individual and situational variables that impact on effectiveness, can lead to a high probability of success for those implementing behavioral programs in applied settings, such as schools (Kazdin, in press).

Specificity in Defining Programs and Procedures

The behavioral approach to education involves careful delineation of programs and procedures. Previously discussed anchor points for the design of behavioral programs are information arrived at from the assessment process, clearly specified goals and objectives, and information culled from previous empirical research and program evaluation efforts (Hersen, 1981; Sulzer-Azaroff & Mayer, 1977).

Behavioral assessment information concerning the target individual or group leads to the formulation of educational program goals and objectives that are considered educationally relevant and realistic (Kratochwill, 1982). Once these goals and objectives have been determined, attention can then be directed to designing methods, activities, and materials that can be reasonably organized and developed into a program targeted at those clearly described outcomes (Cunningham, 1982; Maher & Barbrack, 1985).

In the design of particular procedures and programs to be used to bring about behavioral change, contextual characteristics of the particular school setting in which the program is to be implemented must be considered. In addition, information gleaned from previous research and evaluation efforts must also be considered. All too often, these contextual characteristics are given little or no attention, resulting in program implementation problems (Marholin & Siegel, 1978). Contextual factors considered important to assure appropriate program implementation within the context of a behavioral approach to education include the following:

1. Adequate numbers of personnel must be available to implement the program. Additional staff or reallocation of existing staff may be necessary to ensure such things as appropriate use of reinforcement procedures, adequate rehearsal training, or adequate data collection (Evans & Meyer, 1985).
2. Appropriate materials (e.g., tangible reinforcers, instructional videotapes) must be made available (Johnson, Frederick, & Toews, 1983).
3. Time for program planning and program implementation is essential. Those involved in the program need to understand program goals, objectives, methods, materials, and activities, and how the program can be implemented within the context of other school operations (Kazdin, 1982).

4. Adequate staff training, which allows for observation and rehearsal, as well as didactic instruction, is necessary (Sulzer-Azaroff & Reese, 1982).
5. Consultative support and technical assistance during program implementation is needed to ensure the ability of staff to perform program responsibilities (Witt, Elliott, & Martin, 1984).
6. Continuous program monitoring and supervision is essential so that program implementation proceeds according to plan, and so that adaptations in the program can be made if problems arise (Barlow, Hayes, & Nelson, 1984).
7. Feedback mechanisms need to be developed so that information from program monitoring and supervisory efforts, as well as program changes, can be communicated to program staff in a timely manner. In this regard, a means of providing information to staff concerning their performance, as well as procedures for reinforcing exemplary performance, appear necessary (Mace, Cancelli, & Manos, 1983).
8. Decision-making procedures need to be developed so that periodic determinations can be made regarding continuing or revising current program operations (Nelson & Hayes, 1979).
9. Administrative sanction for program implementation is important because administrative support may increase the likelihood that the program will continue to be implemented as planned (Posovac & Carey, 1985).
10. The manner in which the program relates to broad-based educational goals and other school programs must be examined to ensure appropriate implementation within the complex school setting (Forman, 1984).

Routine Evaluation

The behavioral approach implies evaluation of program operations and effectiveness on a routine basis (see also Chapter 10). Because program objectives and procedures have been specified, information can be obtained easily concerning: (a) degree of program implementation; (b) attainment of program goals; and (c) reactions of individuals, such as teachers and parents. The continuous effort aimed at program evaluation provides information concerning possible needed revisions during program implementation, as well as information concerning final program outcome (Barlow & Hersen, 1984; Maher & Bennett, 1984).

THE RANGE OF BEHAVIORAL PROCEDURES

The contemporary behavioral approach to the education of children and youth encompasses a wide range of procedures. In their evaluation of behavior therapy, Kazdin and Wilson (1978) define four behavioral models that can be useful in conceptualizing the behavioral approach to education. These models subsume a number of theoretical positions about the nature of human behavior, a number of sets of empirical studies providing a research base, and various sets of intervention techniques.

The first model, applied behavior analysis (Baer, Wolf, & Risley, 1968), relies on techniques derived from operant conditioning (Skinner, 1953). This model assumes that learning involves the performance of behaviors that are controlled primarily by their consequences. An individual's behaviors are assumed to operate on the environment in terms of production of certain consequences, which will then increase or decrease the occurrence of the behavior. Applied behavior analysis intervention procedures are based on altering the relationship between specific overt behaviors and their consequences. They include a wide range of techniques based on reinforcement, punishment, extinction, and stimulus control (Sulzer-Azaroff & Mayer, 1977).

The mediational S-R model relies on the application of principles of classical conditioning and counterconditioning to behavior. According to the classical conditioning position (Pavlov, 1927), certain physical stimuli in the environment (e.g., food), called unconditioned stimuli (UCS), elicit certain reflex responses (e.g., salivation), called unconditioned responses (UCR). A neutral stimulus paired in time with a particular UCS can produce a response like that of the UCR. The neutral stimulus is called a conditioned stimulus (CS) and the response that is similar to the UCR is called a conditioned response (CR). A famous study that demonstrated the application of classical conditioning to children was performed by Watson and Rayner (1920) with an 11-month-old child called Little Albert. By pairing the presence of a live white rat (CS) with a loud noise (UCS) that produced a startle reaction (UCR), the experimenters taught Little Albert to become afraid (CR) of a live white rat.

The mediational S-R model presumes that underlying drives, such as anxiety, motivate an individual's observable behavior and that behavior is classically and operantly conditioned. For example, avoidance of a feared event is assumed to be motivated by anxiety that was classically conditioned through the pairing of a neutral CS and an aversive UCS (Morris & Kratochwill, 1983). The intervention technique of systematic desensitization (Wolpe & Lazarus, 1966) is most closely associated with this model. This technique is used to reduce fear reactions by conditioning a substitute activity (e.g., relaxation) that is incompatible with the fear response.

The social learning theory model (Bandura, 1977) assumes that human behavior is developed and maintained through operant conditioning processes, classical conditioning processes, and cognitive-mediational processes. Cognitive-mediational processes determine what environmental influences are attended to, how they are perceived, and if they affect future action. Modeling is the best known intervention technique derived from social-learning theory. With this procedure, the individual acquires a response by observing a model performing the behavior and acquiring a symbolic representation of the modeled event.

The most recently developed model related to the behavioral approach to education is cognitive behavior modification (Mahoney, 1974; Meichenbaum, 1977). Cognitive behavior modification techniques emphasize the importance of cognitive processes and private events as mediators of behavior change. Assumptions, interpretations, attributions, thoughts, images, self-statements, sets, and strategies of responding are considered to be the source of problem behavior. Restructuring these cognitions is the goal of cognitive-behavioral interventions, which include such procedures as rational-emotive therapy (Ellis, 1962), self-instructional training (Meichenbaum, 1977), social problem solving (Spivack & Shure, 1974) and stress inoculation.

OVERVIEW OF SUBSEQUENT CHAPTERS

The following chapters in this book further define and describe the behavioral approach to the education of children and youth. In these chapters, the behavioral approach can be viewed with respect to: (a) processes (assessment, program development and implementation, program evaluation); (b) instructional target areas for students (academic education, affective and social education, health and physical education, vocational education); and (c) human resources necessary for implementation of the behavioral approach to education (teachers, parents, administrators, special services personnel, paraprofessionals).

The first step in the behavioral approach is considered in Chapter 2, Behavioral Assessment. In that chapter, Anthony Cancelli and Roland Yoshida provide a broad-based and educationally relevant view of behavioral assessment methods, identify how they can be used in program design efforts, and discuss school organizational factors that need to be considered in the assessment effort.

Chapters 3 through 6 focus on program development and implementation issues relevant to use of the behavioral approach in four instructional target areas. In each of these chapters, the instructional target area is discussed with respect to behavioral principles, procedures, and programs. Included therein is information that describes procedures and programs, reflects relevant research, and identifies school organizational factors that impact on implementation of the behavioral approach.

Basic Skills Education is discussed by Wayne Piersel in Chapter 3. This instructional target area may be considered the "heart" of school education. It includes instructional domains such as reading, mathematics, and written communication. In Chapter 4, Susan Forman describes the behavioral approach to Affective and Social Education. This area focuses on development of social skills and behavioral self-control, as well as enhancement of emotional adjustment. Although behavioral affective and social education programs are often a component of classroom instruction, these programs may be provided by supportive school services personnel, such as school psychologists or counselors.

The area least developed in terms of behavioral technology, Vocational Education, is discussed in Chapter 5 by Robert Illback. This area includes programs of career awareness, vocational guidance, and job skill development. These programs may take place in classrooms, business, and industrial settings, or as part of guidance and counseling services. In Chapter 6, Bruce McClenaghan and Diane Ward present information about rapidly developing behavioral approaches to Health and Physical Education. Health education focuses on increasing student skill in maintaining a healthy life style and preventing health problems. Physical education has goals of improving student gross and fine motor skills, as well as recreational and leisure skills.

Chapters 7 through 9 focus on human resources necessary for implementation of a behavioral approach to education. These include school personnel and parents who may assist with or be instrumental in the implementation of behavioral programs. Alternatively, as part of efforts to enhance student growth and development, they may be the targets of behavioral programs.

In Chapter 7, Frank Gresham and Kathryn Lemanek address the area of Parent Education. This area includes programs aimed at improving parenting skills and directly involving parents in school programs that seek to improve student functioning. In Chapter 8, Jason Feld, John Bergan, and Clement Stone present the area of Behavioral Consultation. The focus of this chapter is on behavioral approaches to providing consultative services for teachers and other school personnel. Such services provide assistance in development, implementation, and evaluation of behavioral programs and procedures. In Chapter 9, Charles Maher, Susan Cook, and Louis Kruger consider the rapidly developing area of Human Resource Development. This chapter focuses on programs that aim to develop a school's human resources—administrators, staff, paraprofessionals—to perform their roles and functions more proficiently. Human resource development programs occur in many forms, such as staff supervision, teacher consultation, and inservice training. Goals of human resource development are increased knowledge about one's role in the school, improved capability to instruct and manage programs, and enhanced attitudes and job satisfaction.

The final process addressed in this book, and one that underlies all aspects of the behavioral approach to education, is Program Evaluation and Research. In Chapter 10, Thomas Kratochwill, F. Charles Mace, and Mary Bissell describe a wide variety of methods, procedures, and evaluation designs for use in making judgments about educational program outcomes so that more effective programs can be designed and implemented.

In Chapter 11, the last, but most important chapter, Susan Graham-Clay and Daniel Reschly present Legal and Ethical Issues relevant to the behavioral approach to education. The implications of legal influences and professional standards for use of the behavioral approach in schools is examined. Behavioral technology provides powerful methods for addressing educational needs and goals. The rights of clients and consumers of behavioral programs and procedures must be considered to ensure application of this technology in an appropriate, constructive manner.

REFERENCES

Allen, C. T., & Forman, S. G. (1984). Efficacy of methods of training teachers in behavior modification. *School Psychology Review, 13,* 26–32.

Baer, D. M., Wolf, M. M., & Risley, L. R. (1968). Current dimensions of applied behavior analysis. *Journal of Applied Behavior Analysis, 1,* 91–97.

Bandura, A. (1977). *Social learning theory.* Englewood Cliffs, NJ: Prentice-Hall.

Barlow, P. H., Hayes, S. C., & Nelson, R. O. (1984). *The scientist practitioner: Research and accountability in clinical and educational settings.* New York: Pergamon Press.

Barlow, D. H., & Hersen, M. (1984). *Single case experimental designs: Strategies for studying behavior change* (2nd ed.). New York: Pergamon Press.

Boyer, E. L. (1983). *High school: A report on secondary education in America.* New York: Harper & Row.

Cone, J. D. (1978). The Behavioral Assessment Grid (BAG): A conceptual framework and a taxonomy. *Behavior Therapy, 9,* 882–888.

Cone, J. D. (1979). Confounded comparisons in triple response mode assessment. *Behavioral Assessment, 1,* 85–96.

Cunningham, W. G. (1982). *Systematic planning for educational change.* Palo Alto: Mayfield.

Ellis, A. (1962). *Reason and emotion in psychotherapy.* New York: Lyle Stuart Press.

Evans, I. M., & Meyer, L. H. (1985). *An educative approach to behavior problems.* Baltimore: Brookes.

Forman, S. G. (1984). Behavioral and cognitive-behavioral approaches staff development. In C. A. Maher, R. J. Illback, & J. E. Zins (Eds.), *Organizational psychology in the schools: A sourcebook for professionals* (pp. 302–322). Springfield, IL: Charles C. Thomas.

Grise, P. (in press). Minimum competency testing and education of the handicapped. *Special Services in the Schools.*

Haynes, S. N., & Wilson, C. C. (1979). *Behavioral assessment: Recent advances in methods, concepts, and applications.* San Francisco: Jossey-Bass.

Hersen, M. (1981). Complex problems require complex solutions. *Behavior Therapy, 12,* 15–29.

Johnson, J., Frederick, H. D., & Toews, J. W. (1983). *The Teaching Research curriculum for mildly and moderately handicapped adolescents and adults.* Monmouth, OR: Teaching Research.

Kazdin, A. E. (1978). *History of behavior modification: Experimental foundations of contemporary research.* Baltimore: University Park Press.

Kazdin, A. E. (1982). *Single case research designs: Methods for clinical and applied settings.* New York: Oxford University Press.

Kazdin, A. E. (in press). *Behavior modification in applied settings* (3rd ed.). Homewood, IL: Dorsey.

Kazdin, A. E., & Wilson, G. T. (1978). *Evaluation of behavior therapy.* Lincoln, NE: University of Nebraska Press.

Kendall, P. C., & Butcher, J. N. (1982). *Handbook of research methods in clinical psychology.* New York: Wiley.

Kratochwill, T. R. (1982). Behavioral assessment. In C. R. Reynolds & T. R. Gutkin (Eds.), *Handbook of school psychology* (pp. 314–350). New York: Wiley.

Mace, F. C., Cancelli, A., & Manos, J. (1983). Increasing teacher delivery of continued praise and contingent materials using consultant feedback and praise. *School Psychology Review, 12,* 340–345.

Maher, C. A., & Barbrack, C. R. (1985). Evaluating individual counseling of conduct problem adolescents: The goal attainment scaling method. *Journal of School Psychology, 22*, 285–297.

Maher, C. A., & Bennett, R. E. (1984). *Planning and evaluating special education services.* Englewood Cliffs, NJ: Prentice-Hall.

Mahoney, M. J. (1974). *Cognition and behavior modification.* Cambridge, MA: Ballinger.

Marholin, D., & Siegel, L. (1978). Beyond the law of effect. In D. Marholin (Ed.), *Child behavior therapy* (pp. 397–415). New York: Gardner Press.

Meichenbaum, D. H. (1977). *Cognitive behavior modification.* New York: Plenum Press.

Morris, R. J., & Kratochwill, L. R. (1983). *Treating children's fears and phobias: A behavioral approach.* New York: Pergamon Press.

Nelson, R. O. (1985). Behavioral assessment in the school setting. In T. R. Kratochwill (Ed.), *Advances in school psychology,* (Vol. IV, pp. 45–87). Hillsdale, NJ: Lawrence Erlbaum Associates.

Nelson, R. O., & Hayes, S. C. (1979). Some current dimensions of behavioral assessment. *Behavioral Assessment, 1,* 1–16.

Pavlov, I. P. (1927). *Conditioned reflexes* (G. V. Anrep, Trans.). London: Oxford University Press.

Posovac, E. J., & Carey, R. C. (1985). *Program evaluation methods and case studies* (2nd ed.). Englewood Cliffs, NJ: Prentice-Hall.

Salvia J., & Ysseldyke, J. E. (1981). *Assessment in special and remedial education* (2nd ed.). Boston: Houghton-Mifflin.

Skinner, B. F. (1953). *Science and human behavior.* New York: Free Press.

Spivack, G., & Shure, M. B. (1974). *Social adjustment of young children: A cognitive approach to solving real-life problems.* San Francisco: Jossey-Bass.

Sulzer-Azaroff, B., & Mayer, G. R. (1977). *Applying Behavior analysis procedures with children and youth.* New York: Holt, Rinehart, & Winston.

Sulzer-Azaroff, B., & Reese, E. P. (1982). *Applying behavior analysis: A program for developing professional compliance.* New York: Holt, Rinehart, & Winston.

United States Office of Education. (1983). *A nation at risk: Imperatives for educational reform.* Washington, DC: Author.

Watson, J. B., & Rayner, R. (1920). Conditioned emotional reactions. *Journal of Experimental Psychology, 3,* 1–14.

Witt, J. C., Elliott, S. N., & Martin, B. K. (1984). Acceptability of behavioral intervention used in classrooms: The influence of amount of teacher time, severity of problem behavior, and type of intervention. *Behavior Disorders, 9,* 95–104.

Wolpe, J., & Lazarus, A. (1966). *Behavior therapy techniques.* New York: Pergamon Press.

2 Behavioral Assessment

Anthony A. Cancelli
Roland K. Yoshida

One aspect of behavioral technology that has recently begun to receive attention is behavioral assessment. Books on behavioral assessment (e.g., Ciminero, Calhoun, & Adams, 1977; Cone & Hawkins, 1977; Haynes, 1978; Hersen & Bellack, 1981; Marsh & Terdal, 1980) are published regularly and two journals dedicated to issues in behavioral assessment (i.e., *Behavioral Assessment, Journal of Behavioral Assessment*) are available.

Issues related to the psychometric properties of behavioral measurement procedures have captured much attention (see, for example, Cone 1981). The effective engineering of behavioral assessment technology to the various settings where it is employed has gone relatively unnoticed. Due to its complexity, one setting that requires detailed attention is the school.

There are a variety of decisions made in the schools that are aided by educational and psychological assessment data. One decision for which behavioral assessment has no equal is instructional planning. It is insufficient for assessment techniques used to plan instruction to have validity for predicting the need for intervention. This is the case for most of the traditional intrapersonal assessment techniques. Optimally, assessment strategies employed for instructional planning should have validity for predicting desired behavior change. The use of an assessment technique for instructional planning should offer data that are of importance in deciding the specific instructional content and strategies of the intervention. The inherent link between the assessment data collected in behavioral assessment and subsequent intervention strategies has an extensive research literature that supports the validity of behavioral technology for this purpose. Although certain assessment strategies related to behavioral assessment technology (e.g., criterion-referenced assessment) are used more frequently than they were in the past for planning educational programs in the schools, the full impact of behavioral assessment technology is not being felt.

NATURE OF BEHAVIORAL ASSESSMENT

Behavioral assessment is defined by Nelson and Hayes (1981) as "the identification and measurement of meaningful response units and their controlling variables (both environmental and organismic) for the purposes of understanding and altering human behavior" (p. 3). As with all forms of assessment, the "meaningful response units" (i.e., behavior) and the "controlling variables" of interest in behavioral assessment are influenced by the underlying assumptions that the approach adheres to in characterizing human performance. Behavioral assumptions are substantively different from those governing present day school assessment practice that is formally and functionally based on traditional perspectives for understanding human performance (Cancelli & Duley, 1985).

Several of the techniques employed in behavioral assessment are similar to those used in traditional school practice; for example, interviewing and the use of questionnaires are common to both. Yet, even in those techniques, the type of data collected and the interpretation of the data are different. These differences stem from the opposing views of behavior held by those who espouse behavioral and traditional conceptualizations.

There are a variety of traditional conceptual models proposed for understanding human functioning (see Kratochwill, 1982, for a review) that form the present foundation of school practice. All models are based on the belief that human functioning can be most parsimoniously explained through an understanding of stable abilities, traits, or dispositions within the individual. Consequently, traditional conceptualizations may be classified as intrapersonal models (Cancelli & Duley, 1985).

Included in the class of intrapersonal models are the medical or disease model, the trait model, and the psychoeducational process model. Because, from an intrapersonal perspective academic and/or social behavior is the product of enduring dispositions, the focus of assessment is on the measurement of these dispositions. Behaviors observed during assessment are viewed as an index or sign of these dispositions (Goldfried & Kent, 1972; Goodenough, 1949). In and of themselves, the assessed behaviors are of little importance; however, the enduring nature of the disposition results in a view of behavior as consistent across time and settings. Perceptions of stability across settings is important because it translates into assessment practices that samples behaviors with little consideration of the setting in which they occur. For example, in the assessment of the trait of aggression, an intrapersonal assessment technique may include a self-report inventory that asks a child if he/she hits others. The setting in which the behavior occurs is not important because hitting is only conceived of as symptomatic of the disposition of aggression that is the responsible agent for this and other "aggressive type" behavior in a variety of settings.

Behavioral assumptions, on the other hand, result in a focus on what the person does rather than on what the person has (Mischel, 1968). From a behavioral perspective, the academic and(or) social behavior a child exhibits are of major importance. Behavior observed during assessment is viewed as a sample of how the individual responds in a given situation (Goldfried & Kent, 1972; Goodenough, 1949). The specific behaviors exhibited by a child are viewed in contemporary behavioral thought as controlled by an interaction between the individual's previous learning and the environment. Consequently, the setting in which the behavior occurs is of major importance. The individual's previous learning is linked to the environmental circumstances in which behavior occurs. Because from a behavioral perspective behavior is tied to the situation, previous learning does not necessarily influence performance across settings. In contemporary behavioral thought, previous learning is viewed as covert behavior usually in the form of statements individuals make to themselves or as images they have at the time the behavior is exhibited. Consequently, a major distinction between dispositions posited in intrapersonal models and previous learning advanced in a behavioral model is the generality of potential impact each is purported to control (Goldfried & Kent, 1972). Yet, there is no one model for behavioral assessment.

Behavioral Model

As mentioned previously, the focus of behavioral assessment is on the measurement of the specific behaviors of the individual and the surrounding circumstances hypothesized to be the current determinants of the behaviors. At a general level, there is agreement on the major purposes of assessment; differences exist regarding the controlling variables that are important to measure. The differences appear to reflect the various approaches to contemporary behavior therapy. Approaches tend to differ on the importance ascribed to previous learning. Traditional behavioral assessment models (e.g., those derived from applied behavior analysis) focus exclusively on environmental factors, the focus of more recent models includes the assessment of cognitive and physiological events (e.g., cognitive-behavior therapy) (see Kratochwill, 1982, for a review).

One contemporary model, the *SORC* model, proposed by Goldfried and Sprafkin (1976), can be viewed as generic, because it encompasses many of the variables customarily considered during present day behavior analysis (Nelson & Hayes, 1981). In the *SORC* model, the *R* represents the behavior or response of the individual; the *S, O,* and *C* represent the controlling variables of interest to the assessor. The *S* represents the stimuli or antecedent conditions present in the environment at the time the behavior occurs; the *O* represents organism variables, such as cognitions; and the *C* represents the consequences that follow the response.

Stimulus. As described previously, from a behavioral perspective, the behavior of an individual is perceived as specific to the situation in which it occurs. Consequently, a thorough behavioral assessment includes the measurement of immediate environmental variables. One of the major tasks for the behavioral assessor is to identify the salient environmental variable(s) that occasions a given response. For example, in the assessment of a child's hitting behavior in the classroom it is important to assess the stimuli present immediately preceding the hitting episode. The problem for the behaviorist is to identify a meaningful way to organize the environment for study (Nelson & Hayes, 1981). For example: Is the classroom the antecedent for a given behavior? or Should some specific setting variable within the classroom, such as the child's proximity to the teacher, who is sitting next to the child, or the teacher's use of reinforcement, be defined as the unit of analysis? Although the research literature has generally supported the hypothesis on the situation specificity of behavior (Mischel, 1968), it has provided little help in identifying generic criteria to evaluate settings, if, in fact, any exist, that can be useful as a general guide to assessment.

Because of the importance to ascribed situational factors, behavioral assessment should be conducted in the setting in which the behavior occurs or in an analog setting that is similar to the natural environment. A useful strategy employed by behavioral assessors to identify salient stimulus variables is sequence analysis (Goodwin, 1969). Sequence analysis is a procedure in which an observer records the description of events that precede and follow a response. The recordings occur over a period of time; therefore, the potential controlling variables can be determined by an analysis of several behavioral episodes.

Organism. In addition to stimulus or environmental events, the behavioral assessor is interested in measuring characteristics of the organism that interact with stimulus events to cause individual response differences. The past learning of an individual as represented in cognitions, the physiological state of the individual at the time the behavior occurs, and the individual's genetic predisposition are potential controlling variables of interest.

As described earlier, the measurement of private events has been the mainstay of traditional assessment. The effective measurement of cognitive constructs (e.g., intelligence and aggression) have been the subject of much discussion in the traditional psychometric literature. Hundreds of tests purported to measure these and numerous other organismic events are widely used in traditional school assessment. Because of the movement in behavioral thought toward the recognition of organismic factors as potentially important in control of behavioral re-

sponses, it is important to discuss the question regarding the distinction between behavioral and traditional measures of constructs.

As alluded to previously, the behavioral assessment of covert events, such as cognitions, can be perceived as qualitatively different from those measured in interpersonal assessment. For the most part, their differences lie in the scope and stability of the constructs postulated for measurement. For example, a behavioral assessor may be interested in assessing a child's expectations for his/her ability to perform a certain type of mathematics problem. Such expectations, identified by some as efficacy expectations (Bandura, 1977, 1982), are conceptualized as specific to a defined situation (e.g., performance on certain types of mathematics problems) and, although usually stable over time, they are susceptible to change with environmental manipulation. From an intrapersonal perspective, such expectations are considered to be stable across situations. For example, one's performance expectations in the intrapersonal literature. (e.g., self-esteem) are dynamic in the sense that they are a pervasive influence in an individual's life across a variety of situations (e.g., all school work). As a "personality" characteristic, they are highly resistant to change.

Although conceptually different, the behavioral methods for assessing cognitions bear a striking resemblance to traditional measures of constructs. For example, as in traditional assessment the measurement of cognitions in behavioral assessment employs introspective accounts of the way a person thinks. Nevertheless, a qualitative difference that holds critical implications for establishing the validity of these measures remains. The cognitions measured in behavioral assessment are often perceived as covert behaviors, not as constructs. A *construct* is a term used to classify situations, persons, or responses. The cognitions sampled in behavioral assessment are not perceived as representing anything other than themselves. In addition, they are not perceived as occurring in any situation other than the situation represented in the assessment, and for no one other than the person being assessed. Therefore, the notion of validity becomes bound to determinations of the accuracy of the measure: If the measure is accurate, it is valid.

Some behavioral measures, however, do intend to measure constructs. The cognitions measured are perceived as representing a class or domain of cognitions so interrelated that the occurrence of one cognition in a particular situation presupposes the existence of another cognition. For example, examine more closely a measure of self-efficacy in which an assessor, through self-report, identifies the self-referent statement or statements one might make during a problem solving task. If the assessor were to infer that such statements were present with other similar type problems, or that the statements represent a class of self-statements related to a more general notion of self-efficacy, the issue of construct validity would need to be addressed.

Even if the assessor did not draw an inference from the data, other than the existence of the cognition in this situation, the covert nature of the behavior raises a spectrum of reliability issues not raised in the measurement of overt behavior. These issues relate to the accuracy of the measure in representing a private event that can only be reported by the person experiencing it.

Consequences.   As with stimulus variables, consequences are typically conceived as environmental variables. The difference is that stimulus variables are antecedent to the response, and consequences occur after the response. Consequences are defined as environmental events that occur after the response and influence the probability of the occurrence of the response. The purpose of the assessment of consequences is to identify those that are maintaining present behavior and/or those that may be useful in developing and maintaining behavior. When the goal of the intervention following assessment is to reduce behavior, an assessment of the environmental events that contribute to the maintenance of the behavior is often conducted. When the goal is to increase behavior that occurs at a low frequency or is absent altogether, consequences that may be useful in developing and maintaining responses are important to assess. The sequence analysis strategy, mentioned in the stimulus assessment section, employs a direct observational method, a common procedure employed in the analysis of consequences.

Responses.   Responses that are identified as in need of modification are referred to as targeted behaviors, the behaviors against which the success of intervention is measured.

Contemporary behaviorists have adopted a very liberal interpretation of behavior. Early behaviorists defined behavior in terms of observable or overt motor responses; contemporary behaviorists, in addition to these observable responses, define cognition and physiological responses as behavior. Consequently, cognition and physiological responses are eligible to be targeted for intervention. It is generally the prerogative of the assessor to determine whether covert events are treated as responses to be targeted for intervention or as controlling variables that occasion subsequent overt behavior. Often, this decision is influenced by the specific behaviors in question and by the available treatment literature related to these behaviors. If treated as a target for intervention, subsequent overt behavior, where appropriate, is measured to demonstrate the utility of covert behavior change.

In standard behavioral practice, it is in the preliminary phase of assessment that identification of the behavior or behaviors to be targeted for intervention is accomplished. In the selection of the behavior or behaviors several decisions must be made. Nelson and Hayes (1979) review a variety of philosophical and empirical guidelines to determine what behaviors to assess and how to prioritize more than one behavior targeted for change.

Decisions about the behavior to be targeted can be classed as two types. The first type involves value judgments about the ethics of the behavior change being considered. Typical questions addressed include: "Will the client be the major beneficiary of the behavior change proposed?" and "Is the behavior significantly atypical to warrant intervention?" Decisions regarding these and other ethical questions have been the issue of serious discussion in behavioral and the general assessment literature and have become an important step in behavioral assessment practice (see, for example, Stoltz & Associates, 1978; Chapter 11). The second type of decision involves the identification of the specific behavior or behaviors to be targeted for assessment and intervention. Usually, initial referral problems provided to an assessor contain information about the general area in which a problem is occurring. In behavioral assessment one of the major tasks is to detail the specifics of the problem and choose a behavior or behaviors for intervention that address the major problem. For example, if the problem is a child's verbal abuse of other children, a major task in the behavioral assessment process is to identify the specific verbally abusive behaviors (i.e., precisely what the child says) and to determine the appropriate alternative behaviors the child does not engage in or engages in at too low a frequency.

In identifying the specific behavior or behaviors to target for intervention, the behavioral assessor must remain aware of the relationship between the specific behaviors being considered. This is particularly important in the assessment of academic behaviors in which the performance of one behavior may have to precede the performance of another behavior. Such relationships, often referred to as hierarchical relationships (Gagné, 1977), may have a significant bearing on the behaviors chosen for intervention. In such a case, a behavior in which a child cannot perform may be important to target before another behavior, if the former is prerequisite to the performance of the latter. For example, it may be determined that a child who cannot perform on subtraction problems that require regrouping should first be taught to perform on subtraction problems that do not require regrouping if unable to do so. From an assessment point of view, it is necessary to assess the various skills in the hierarchy of concern to determine the skills in the individual's repertoire.

Another highly related problem facing the behavioral assessor is to define the specific behaviors found in an individual's repertoire so that if one behavior is present, all are present. Conversely, if one behavior is absent, all behaviors representing that response class are absent. For example, a response class may be composed of behaviors useful in correctly performing on subtraction problems that require finding the difference between any two single digit numbers. That is, if the child can respond correctly to $5-3 = $ ___, he/she could correctly respond to $6-2 = $ ___. Thus, the importance of the assessment of response classes instead of discrete behavior becomes obvious. It would be highly impractical if an assumption regarding classes of behavior were not made and all possible behaviors of interest assessed. As with concerns for learning hierarchies, the potential difficulty in assessing response classes is more apparent with academic than social behaviors.

It may now be apparent that assessment to identify behaviors to target for intervention, especially academic behaviors, is an intricate and complex process. One procedure useful in the assessment of behaviors that may be hierarchically related or part of the same response class is task analysis (Gagné, 1977; Resnick, Wang, & Kaplan, 1973). Task analysis involves the ordering of tasks from the most to least complex based on rational analysis of the skills underlying the performance of the complex task. The component skills required to perform the complex task are identified; the process is then repeated with tasks representing each of the components identified. Once the hierarchy is rationally deduced, assessment can proceed to identify which of the tasks in the hierarchy the child can and cannot perform.

Path-Referenced Assessment.   As mentioned previously, task analysis is a procedure that employs rational judgments in the identification of response classes and learning hierarchies. However, such rational approaches yield a product that lacks empirical validation of the homogeneity of the responses hypothesized to form a response class and the hierarchical ordering of the response classes. Validation procedures have been time consuming and, consequently, have retarded efforts to develop empirically validated diagnostic instruments from which behavioral assessors can reliably draw inferences (Cancelli, Bergan, & Jones, 1982).

In recent years several mathematical techniques have become available (Bergan, 1980). These techniques hold promise for a cost efficient method of validating homogeneous item domains and learning hierarchies. Utilizing mathematical models to represent the relationships among tasks, this technology has been applied to the development of diagnostic assessment procedures known as path-referenced assessment (Bergan, 1981).

The potential applications of path-referenced assessment for screening, placement, diagnostic testing, and program evaluation have only recently been described (Bergan, 1981). The utilization of path-referenced assessment for school-related purposes, such as the development of individualized education programs (IEPs), seems tailor made. The use of path-referenced assessment has value to the behavioral assessor in the identification of specific target behaviors and prioritizing hierarchically-ordered tasks. It is not designed to provide information about the stimulus or about consequent circumstances controlling the behavior other than the stimulus materials present during assessment (see chapter 8, Behavioral Consultation, for more detailed discussion).

Criterion-Referenced Assessment.   The most popular type of school assessment linked both theoretically and practically to behavioral assessment is criterion-referenced assessment (Cancelli & Kratochwill, 1981). Building on assumptions of learning consistent with behavioral thought has resulted in criterion-referenced assessment that has evolved with theoretical support drawn from instructional psychology and technical support drawn from psychometry (Cancelli & Kratochwill, 1981).

The use of criterion-referenced tests (CRTs) first appeared in the 1960's because of the need to measure children's mastery of specific objectives in objective-based instructional programs. Before the inception of criterion-referenced tests, only norm-referenced tests of academic achievement were employed to measure student performance. Norm-referenced tests compare a student's performance to the performance of others; whereas, criterion-referenced tests compare a student's performance against an absolute predefined criterion. As stated by Popham and Husek (1969), criterion-referenced measures are "those which are used to ascertain an individual's status with respect to some criterion, (i.e., performance standard). It is because the individual is compared with some established criterion, rather than with other individuals that the measures can be described as criterion-referenced" (p. 2).

As with path-referenced assessment, criterion-referenced assessment focuses its attention on the measurement of responses (i.e., specific performance capabilities) and can be employed for the identification of target behaviors and the evaluation of the success of instruction. The technology that has evolved for developing and investigating the psychometric properties of criterion-referenced tests allows for comfortable inferences to predefined behavioral domains, the scope of which are explicated in domain specifications.

However, the domains of behaviors that items on a CRT represent are not necessarily consistent with the notion of a response class. The domains operationalized through the use of domain specifications often are designed as a matter of convenience (Cancelli & Kratochwill, 1981) instead of on assumptions about the homogeneous nature of the sets of items within each domain. This creates a problem for behavioral assessors who wish to employ CRTs to identify specific behavioral deficits in need of instructional attention (Cancelli & Kratochwill, 1981). For example, assume a domain represents more than one response class, and that the sample of items selected for assessment represents those response classes the child has already mastered. The child will be identified as a master of the domain even though there may be response classes in the domain that the child has not yet mastered. Such a circumstance is relatively unimportant when CRTs are employed to gauge a child's overall mastery in a subject area. However, when employed for diagnostic purposes, as would be the case when used in behavioral assessment, the heterogeneous nature of the domain structures or CRTs becomes problematic.

The hierarchical nature of the responses sampled in CRTs offer no greater advantage to the behavioral assessor than the task analysis strategies employed in the targeting of academic behaviors. Although the notion of hierarchical sequences has been either explicit or implicit in discussions of criterion-referenced assessment (Gray, 1978), no technology for empirically validating the implied hierarchical nature of the domain in CRTs has been delineated in the CRT literature.

As discussed earlier, criterion-referenced tests focus on response capabilities. They are not designed to measure stimulus or consequent circumstances that may be in control of the behavior other than the stimulus task presented in the test. Because CRTs are often administered in settings outside the natural environment, concerns associated with the use of analog behavioral assessment should be addressed (see Methods of Behavioral Assessment section of this chapter for a discussion of analog assessment).

What, then, does criterion-referenced assessment have to offer the behavioral assessor? Because CRTs focus on behavioral responses, they can be employed to gain information about areas of deficit academic functioning. Most CRTs are not designed to reflect domains composed of behavioral response classes; therefore, further analysis of a child's capabilities in domains not yet mastered and closely related domains the child may appear to have mastered should be undertaken. CRTs do not provide behavioral assessors with information about existing setting events (i.e., stimulus and consequent circumstances) that have been and/or will be employed to teach new skills. In addition, CRTs do not assess covert skills that may mediate performance. Therefore, the use of CRTs needs to be supplemented with an assessment of potentially important controlling variables.

METHODS OF BEHAVIORAL ASSESSMENT

The most prevalent form of psychological and educational assessment conducted in the schools today is testing. Behavioral assessment may also involve some form of testing, but its methods are varied. Because behavioral assessment focuses on the contribution of controlling environmental variables (i.e., antecedent stimuli and consequences) and emphases the precise measurement of behaviors, its methods often are direct.

A description of some of the more common methods of behavioral assessment follows. These include indirect and direct methods that can be employed to assess controlling variables and responses.

Indirect Methods

Indirect methods are defined as methods that involve retrospective reporting (i.e., after the fact) of events. Interview assessment and inventories are included in this class of methods.

Interview Assessment.   Behavioral interviewing is the most common method used in behavioral assessment (Haynes & Jenson, 1979). In a recent survey of assessment techniques used by school psychologists in schools, behavioral interviewing was reported as the most often employed behavioral assessment method

(Anderson, Cancelli, & Kratochwill, 1984). Although considered by many to be an important assessment technique (Ciminero, 1977; Ciminero & Drabman, 1977; Duley, Cancelli, Kratochwill, Bergan, & Meredith, 1983), the paucity of information available regarding the reliability and validity of the method suggests that it must be used cautiously, if not skeptically (Ciminero & Drabman, 1977). Employing parental interviews to collect data on a child's behavior was found to have questionable validity (Evans & Nelson, 1977). The types of questions asked in interview assessment affect the validity of the information reported (Hersen & Bellack, 1977).

One of the major difficulties impeding the study of the psychometric properties of interviewing is the lack of standardized scripts for posing questions (Kratochwill, 1982). Few standardized interviews are available for children, parents and teachers; interviews that are available lack psychometric evidence to support their use (Wells, 1981). One of the more comprehensive interview systems, the Behavioral Consultation Model, developed by Bergan and his associates, is discussed elsewhere in this volume (see Chapter 8, Behavioral Consultation).

The use of behavioral interviewing can be particularly effective in collecting data for making decisions "about the areas in which intervention is needed, the particular targets for further assessment, [and] some tentative targets for intervention, methods, and goals" (Kratochwill & Cancelli, 1983, p. 325). The interview may also be useful in collecting data to supplement other forms of traditional data employed in making diagnosis/classification decisions, a mainstay in educational decision-making. Finally, behavioral interviewing can be employed to evaluate outcomes of intervention programs. Although interviewing is a questionable technique for measuring actual behavior change (Forehand, Griest, & Wells, 1979), it can be effectively employed to socially validate behavior change; the perceptions of change gauged by the client or those responsible for the client's behavior, such as a child's parent or guardian (Wells, 1981).

Behavioral interviewing can be employed to collect data on controlling variables and responses. It can be used in collecting data directly from the individual whose behavior is in question or from those who have observed the behavior, such as parents or teachers. Because the data collected are retrospective in nature, the interview can be conducted at the convenience of both the assessor and informant.

Inventories.   The second indirect method employed in behavioral assessment is inventories. Inventories gained popularity as a result of their use in intrapersonal assessment, particularly by "trait theorists" who developed them as standardized paper- and pencil-assessment instruments in the 1950s (Bellack & Hersen, 1977). Best known as personality inventories, they usually involve self-reports of an individual's behaviors, thoughts, and feelings on items designed to tap underlying dynamic constructs.

Behavioral inventories employ self-reports and observer reports. In the behavioral literature behavioral inventories are commonly referred to as behavior checklists, rating scales, and questionnaires. A listing of inventories useful in behavioral assessment is reported in Walls, Werner, Bacon, and Zane (1977).

Behavioral self-report inventories are employed to assess potential target behaviors and controlling antecedent thoughts and feelings. Among the self-report inventories developed for school use are the Mooney Problem Checklist (Mooney & Gordon, 1950), the STS Youth Inventory (Remmers & Bauernfeind, 1968; Remmers & Shimberg, 1967), and the Preschool Behavior Questionnaire (Behar, 1977). Few inventories specifically assess environmental controlling variables. Usually, the behaviors sampled in most inventories, even when clearly defined, are not tied to specific situations. Therefore, they are more valuable for sampling different type behaviors than situations in which the behaviors occur. However, a few inventories, those designed from a procedure known as the behavior analytic method (Goldfried & Sprafkin, 1976), do sample behaviors specific to situations that are potentially problematic. The procedure is now being used to develop inventories of specific school situations that may be potentially problematic for youngsters.

In addition to self-report inventories, there are a variety of observer checklists and rating scales designed to be completed by a person who has had the opportunity to observe the individual whose behavior is in question. Observer inventories are used for the same purpose as self-report inventories and have the same limitation of not being situation specific. Items on the Revised Behavior Problem Checklist (RBPL) (Quay & Peterson, 1983) are typical of this type of inventory, ranging from the more behaviorally unambiguous (e.g., fights) to the more impressionistic (e.g., depressed, always sad). The need for follow-up assessment that is designed to detail specific behaviors and the situational context in which they occur is necessary when inventories are employed for behavioral intervention planning. Other examples of observer checklists and rating scales commonly employed in the schools are Burks' Behavior Rating Scales (Burks, 1977), the Walker Problem Behavior Identification Checklist (Walker, 1976), the Devereaux Child Behavior Rating Scales (Spivack, Haimes, & Spotts, 1967; Spivack & Spotts, 1968; Spivack & Swift, 1967), the Behavior Rating Profile (Brown & Hammil, 1978), the Conners Teacher's Rating Profile (Conners, 1973).

It has been suggested that in the design of inventories for behavioral assessment consideration be given to several factors critical to the assumptions governing behavioral assessment. For example, Bellack and Hersen (1977) have argued that self-report inventories for behavioral assessment should be constructed to (a) reduce the ambiguity of the wording by using explicitly defined terms so less interpretation of the item is left to the informant; (b) use nonquantitative statements or ask for quantitative reports that require low or zero frequency response; and (c) employ data from self-reports for idiographic purposes and avoid summarizing "typical" behavior through performance across items. Although these suggestions are well taken and provide some guidelines for the construction of behavioral self-reports, concerns for the reliability and validity of such measures cannot be addressed through care in test construction alone. As with traditional measures, it is important that the interpretation made with data from behavioral self-reports be validated for the purposes for which they are designed. Although the constructs measured are fundamentally different than those employed in traditional assessment, the fact remains that they are constructs, and the psychometric properties of measures of such constructs need to be established. In this area, behavioral assessment is woefully lacking and lags behind traditional assessment (Curran, 1978; Leitenberg, 1978).

Despite the paucity of psychometric evidence that bears on the reliability and validity of most current behavioral inventories, there are advantages to recommend their restricted use (Kratochwill, 1982). Several instruments are particularly important for use in the schools. First, inventories are economical in cost, time, and effort, especially when compared to direct assessment methods. Teachers can complete inventories at their leisure and in private. Second, inventories provide a structure for training a comprehensive picture of an individual's functioning in a variety of potentially problematic areas. A third and related advantage is that the use of inventories may identify problems missed through the use of other assessment methods. Fourth, data from inventories can be organized through the use of procedures, such as factor analysis, to aid in the diagnosis/classification process. For example, the RBPC offers validity evidence to support its use in aiding diagnosis and special education classification of emotionally disturbed children (Quay & Peterson, 1983). Fifth, as with interview assessment data, the inventories' data may be used to socially validate outcomes of intervention.

Direct Methods

Direct methods of behavioral assessment involve the measurement of responses and controlling variables at the time they occur. Even with the acceptability of indirect methods for certain purposes, direct methods remain the major components of behavioral assessment. Although indirect methods have their utility for description, diagnosis/classification, and prediction, direct methods boast more validity for the development of specific interventions. Direct methods can be classified to include naturalistic observation, analog assessment, and self-monitoring.

Naturalistic Observation.   The naturalistic or direct observational method involves the measurement of responses and controlling environmental variables in the settings where the responses naturally occur. It usually includes the precise definition of targeted behaviors, the measurement of these behaviors as they occur is the natural environment, the use of impartial observers trained to code behavior, and the use of a specific set of rules for recording behavior (Doke, 1976; Jones, Reid, & Patterson, 1975). In addition, direct observation is usually employed to record environmental variables, especially the behavior of others, at the time the targeted behavior is emitted. (See Haynes, 1978, for a detailed literature review of naturalistic observation in behavioral assessment).

Kratochwill, Alper, and Cancelli (1980) distinguish between observational procedures and observational instruments. Observational procedures involve the use of a set of rules for the development of an observational system to employ in assessment work. Observational instruments are generic in character and capable of being used across situations. However, although in demand, such instruments are scarce and underdeveloped (Anderson et al., 1983). The lack of attention paid to the development of these instruments has been, in part, attributed to the highly specific character of behavior assessment (Mash & Terdal, 1981).

The increase in understanding of naturalistic observation has raised important methodological issues that have made present day behavioral observation a complex assessment procedure. Several recommendations for the effective application of the method are summarized by Kratochwill and Cancelli (1983). First, individuals who engage in observation should be well trained. The training issue is particularly important when paraprofessionals are employed as observers. Second, interobserver agreement on the response measure should be obtained by using two or more observers. Third, ratings should be taken by the observers over a period of time to insure consistent levels of agreement. Fourth, the observers should be kept as naive as is practically possible about the purposes of the assessment. Fifth, observational codes should be constructed to rate a convenient number of behaviors at any one time. Sixth, definitions of target behaviors should be precise enough to ensure high interrater reliability. Seventh, where possible, observation should be unobtrusive. Eighth, behavioral measures should be obtained across settings when practically feasible to identify the generality of the behavior. This helps to define the extent of the problem and generality of behavior change subsequent to intervention. Ninth, the collection of normative data (e.g., data regarding the performance of a "typical" child) is helpful, especially in identifying the need for behavior change.

Although naturalistic observation legitimately remains the centerpiece of behavioral assessment, efforts need to be directed at making the procedure more versatile and cost efficient. Although the classroom remains an accessible environment for study, formats for easily conducting observations by personnel who are unfamiliar with observational systems need to be developed for the effective engineering of this highly valuable method in the schools.

Analog Assessment.   Analog assessment is a method of collecting behavioral data in an environment designed to simulate conditions found in the natural environment. Cone (1977, 1978) identifies two types of analog assessment, free behavior and role play. In the former, the analog environment is constructed and the individual performs in a free and natural way in that environment. For example, teachers can instruct a child in a simulated environment as they normally would in the classroom. Specific information on the instructional strategies employed by the teacher, such as the use of materials, modeling, rehearsal, feedback, and praise, can be recorded.

Role playing in an analog setting occurs when individuals are instructed to role play or perform as they would in a given situation. Role play analog assessment has been used most often in the assessment of social skills. Adapted for adult populations, such techniques have recently been extended for work with children. The Behavioral Assertiveness Test for Children (Bornstein, Bellack, & Hersen, 1977, 1980) and the Assertiveness Test for Boys (Reardon, Hersen, Bellack, & Foley, 1979) are examples of the instruments available for role playing use in analog settings.

There are several advantages to analog assessment (cf. Haynes, 1978; McFall, 1977a; Nay, 1977). Two of the major advantages are (a) the control that can be exercised over simulated environments is not available in the natural settings; and (b) the efficiency of measuring low frequency behavior quickly (lengthy observation may be necessary if observation was conducted in the natural environment). The major disadvantage of analog assessment is the inherent artificial nature of the assessment. Whenever a behavior is performed out of its natural setting, one runs the risk of having modified circumstances that could make the measurement of the response meaningless. Different demand characteristics may be operative and salient environmental variables present in the natural setting may be missing in the analog environment. Little evidence of the validity of analog methods is available (Kratochwill & Cancelli, 1983; Wells, 1981). The analog method is more easily adapted for school use than naturalistic observation, because it can be conducted at the convenience of the teacher or parent. It is particularly useful for measuring parent-child or teacher-child interactions. When other elements of the natural environment are not deemed critical (e.g., peer presence), it can be very useful in isolating specific behavioral episodes for study.

Self-Monitoring.   Self-monitoring is a method that uses clients to collect data about their own behavior. It is a direct method because the behavior and potential controlling events are recorded as they occur. There are many factors that should be considered before self-monitoring is employed, factors that relate to the accuracy and reactivity of the method.

McFall (1977) identifies 10 factors that may influence the accuracy of the data and eight factors that may be influential in determining whether the method is reactive. Factors such as how well the individual is trained to collect the data, the care in collecting the data, and how systematic the procedure is for collecting the data are included as potential threats to the accuracy of the data collected in self-monitoring.

Reactivity occurs when the measurement procedure is obtrusive to the extent that the behaviors are influenced by the method employed to assess them. In self-monitoring the potential reactivity of the method is high because the individual is being asked to record his/her own behavior. Introducing self-monitoring may influence the response itself. The potential interference of the method is so great that, in certain circumstances, self-monitoring has been shown to be an effective component of intervention (Thoresen & Mahoney, 1974).

The advantages of self-monitoring are very appealing. It is relatively cost-efficient compared to naturalistic observation, and the client's direct involvement may have motivation benefits for intervention. This may be a particularly relevant point for school assessment. Most often behavior change is requested by agents other than the child: nevertheless, self-monitoring may prove advantageous in developing a sense of self-determination in changing one's own behavior. This is considered by some to be an essential ingredient in affecting sustained and generalizable behavior change (Deci, 1975, 1980).

APPLICATIONS OF BEHAVIORAL ASSESSMENT IN THE SCHOOLS

The choice of which assessment procedures to employ in helping to make any decision is a complex one. To make an effective choice, a clear specification of the purpose for which the data are being collected must be delineated. In special education decision making, for example, are the data being collected to distinguish as accurately as possible between those who are handicapped and those who are not? Is the purpose to make decisions regarding the best educational program to provide for a child who is having difficulty in a regular education program? Or, are data being collected for both purposes? As a preliminary step in decision making, the answers to these questions are essential to the design of an assessment strategy. Each assessment procedure provides data that are more relevant to answering some questions than others. In psychological and educational assessment, the relevance of any particular procedure is usually defined in terms of validity.

Validity

The validity of assessment procedures is not inherent to the procedures, it lies in the interpretations made with the data collected from their use. Consequently, an assessment procedure may have validity for making some decisions but not for making other decisions. As emphasized by Cancelli and Duley (1985), there is no such thing as a valid assessment procedure, only procedures whose interpretations offer a degree of validity for its use in some circumstances but not in others. The key to the selection of any assessment strategy is to choose those procedures that are most valid for the decision one wants to make.

Some behavioral rating scales and checklists offer validity evidence to support their use in aiding diagnosis and educational classifications. The most common use of behavioral assessment technology has been as an aid to intervention or instructional planning. Selecting assessment devices for intervention planning is an important task in educational decision making. The ultimate goal of much of what is decided in schools with psychological and educational assessment data is for the purpose of determining how to affect academic and social behavior change in children. With such a mission, it is apparent that the use of behavioral assessment has an implicit value in the process.

A strong argument for the psychometric integrity of the direct methods of behavioral assessment is based on their high content validity and lack of dependence on recall. However, even with direct methods, utility can never be solely dependent on content. Evidence for use of direct methods must be derived from studies that report the validity of the use of the methods in accomplishing their purpose. This type of validity evidence is the strength of naturalistic observation.

Most naturalistic observation is conducted with the aid of general procedures rather than by the use of an "observation instrument." These procedures provide a structure for targeting behavior and analyzing environmental circumstances. They have been employed in scores of studies that have successfully modified the behaviors measured. This literature provides ample support for the procedures and evidence of the validity of their use for supporting intervention decisions. The literature on self-monitoring also offers such support, but it is not as voluminous. Analog assessment and indirect methods must be used cautiously. Their major strength is as a vehicle for generating hypotheses for further assessment.

ISSUES IN THE IMPLEMENTATION OF BEHAVIORAL ASSESSMENT TECHNOLOGY

Although there are many advantages for using behavioral assessment technology in schools, several highly visible factors can be offered as possible impediments to its adoption. One factor relates to the perceived value of behavioral assessment to school practice. There are a variety of perceptions among various school personnel about what behavioral assessment is, its value to school practice, and its relationship to existing assessment employed in educational decision making. A second factor involves the readiness of school personnel to adopt methods that are at variance to traditional school practice. The adoption of behavioral assessment technology would require modifications in existing systems that may be perceived difficult to implement. A third factor relates to the existing skills of school personnel responsible for conducting psychological and educational assessment. Behavioral assessment technology is advancing at a rapid pace, a pace that makes it difficult for practitioners to keep abreast of those advances that would aid in implementation. A fourth factor involves the readiness of the technology itself to address behaviors of major concern to the schools. Emphasis of behavioral assessment has been in the area of social-behavior disorders. Less attention has been paid to the behavioral assessment of academic skills, a major focus of school assessment (Kratochwill, 1982).

Are factors such as those described denying or slowing down the full implementation of behavioral assessment practices in the schools? Our evaluation of the long-term trends in school practice indicates that, although progress may be slow for full implementation, there are powerful forces that support its eventual use. Because these forces are not necessarily coordinated with one another they are unable to gather strength to obtain the fullest and quickest impact. They have appeared at different times and vary in the degree to which they influence educational subsystems, such as special education. Nevertheless, they all have their roots in a behavioral tradition, and together create considerable momentum for continued change.

In the past few decades, one of the most significant movements in education that has spawned several forces consistent with a behavioral approach is Competency-Based Education (CBE; Tyler, 1976). The growing influence of CBE and its by-products, such as mastery learning (Gagne, 1977; Hall & Jones, 1976) and minimal competency testing (Klein & Kosecoff, 1973; Popham 1971) reflects the schools' philosophical commitment to a behavioral approach to instruction and learning. By accepting the concepts that behaviors are stated before instruction begins and performance must be observed in order to be evaluated, the educational community, on the whole, has accepted some of the fundamental principles of behavioral psychology.

In addition, legal mandates reinforce the use of behavioral technology, especially in educating handicapped children. Public Law 94-142 mandates that an individualized education program (IEP) be developed for each handicapped student. Each IEP must contain the following elements:

> (a) a statement of the child's present level of educational performance; (b) a statement of annual goals, including short term instructional objectives; (c) a statement of the specific special education and related services to be provided to the child . . . ; (d) the projected dates for initiation of services and the anticipated duration of the services; and (e) appropriate objective criteria for determining, on at least an annual basis, whether the short term instructional objectives are being achieved.'' (U.S. Department of Health, Education, & Welfare 1977, *Federal Register,* August 23, 1977, 42491).

Annual Reports from the U.S. Department of Education to the Congress of the United States (U.S. Department of Education 1981, 1982) state widespread compliance with implementing the IEP; however, the quality of many programs appears dubious (Research Triangle Institute, 1980).

In short, regardless of the form, CBE, the minimal competency testing movement, or the implementation of the IEP, the basic principles of a behavioral approach to learning have begun to take hold. Now, the major task is to engineer effectively behavioral assessment technology, where appropriate, into the standard operating procedure of the schools. Because the basic tenets of the technology have been adopted by some, does not mean that all those who consider employing the technology are comfortable with it. Philosophical and technical issues must be dealt with for effective implementation of behavioral assessment technology.

A VICTORY Organizational Readiness Model

Maher and Illback (1982) have suggested the use of the A VICTORY model for conceptualizing how one would go about assessing the schools' organizational readiness for change. A VICTORY is an acronym composed of eight factors that influence how an organization adopts or adapts an innovation. A VICTORY has been applied in several cases. For example, Maher and Yoshida (1985) suggested its use as an initial step in determining what kinds of organizational resources (time, training, commitments) had to be used to implement more effectively the requirements that schools use multidisciplinary approaches in assessing handicapped children. Maher and Bennett (1984) proposed the A VICTORY method as a basis for instituting an evaluation system for special education. The issues concerning the implementation of behavioral assessment technology also appear to be excellent topics for A VICTORY analysis.

The eight A VICTORY factors and their specific applications to behavioral assessment technology are described as follows:

- Ability. The extent to which a school system is able to provide the necessary resources to support the introduction, training, and maintenance of behavioral assessment approaches (e.g., training consultants; staff release time to participate in training session; continued availability of consultants to assist in implementation; the time necessary to perform behavioral assessments).
- Values. The value placed by school personnel, administrators and staff, on using behavioral assessment technology.
- Idea. The meaning of behavioral assessment technology, and the credibility of using that approach in evaluating children.
- Circumstances. The stable features of the school system that could affect how a behavioral assessment technology might operate (e.g., supportive superintendent, director of psychology services, and special education; proportion of staff already using such technology; the competency level of teachers and others who might use the approach).

- Timing. The dynamic, unplanned features of the school system that could influence how behavioral assessment technology might be implemented (e.g., lawsuit that influences the school board to seek new approaches to evaluation; state law that provides developmental seed money for school districts to try new approaches to assessment.
- Obligation. The need felt by school personnel for instituting a new approach to assessment.
- Resistance. The reluctance of personnel to become actively involved in learning and implementing a behavioral assessment approach (e.g., reluctance to participate in the training; staff decisions to spend resources on other perceived service needs, such as traditional testing methods).
- Yield. The anticipated benefits that might accrue to specific students, to individual staff members, and to the school district as a whole, as a result of using a behavioral assessment approach.

Maher and Bennett (1984) have detailed the methodology for conducting an A VICTORY assessment of instituting a specific organizational change in a school district. Their text provides examples of questionnaires and interview procedures that can be used with staff, administrators, and other interested parties, such as parents and students.

Three Approaches for Creating Change

How should one plan the necessary changes in school policy and procedures to increase the likelihood that staff will have the resources to perform behavioral assessment and will feel Obligated and not Resistant to the employment of behavioral assessment technology? Yoshida (1984) presented three ways that school personnel can exert leadership in making changes in school policies and operating procedures. First, school administrators can be very directive. After reviewing data collected in an A VICTORY assessment, administrators can recommend and institute for the entire school system new evaluation procedures that must include extensive behavioral assessments. In addition, the administration could develop a monitoring system and state criteria for determining staff effectiveness in implementing such a system. However, such an approach does not recognize the professional status of school personnel (Yoshida, Maher, & Hawryluk, 1984). Stinchcombe (1965) notes that affected personnel must be convinced that the proposed changes improve the performance of tasks that are not easily done within existing operating procedures. If administrators fail to consult staff or allow them to develop procedures, they may alienate the staff and affect the implementation of behavioral assessment technology into the school system's evaluation procedures.

A second approach is a direct opposite of the approach presented. Primary responsibility for implementing behavior assessment techniques rests with building staff, rather than the administrators. Because the implementation of school policies occurs at the school building or individual staff member level, administrators are involved only to the extent of issuing general statements supporting the use of behavioral assessment techniques in their schools. School staff develops ways of coping that will account for local variation in the resources available for implementation (or in A VICTORY terms, Ability). Although this approach may be appealing and recognizes some of the dynamics of translating policy into practice (Weatherly & Lipsky, 1977), its major negative effect will be the loss of consistency in performing assessments. Standards of performance will not be clear to staff members and evaluation decisions may become arbitrary. Arbitrary evaluations may also cause variations in decision making that results in biases towards culturally different children. Arbitrariness was a major problem cited in *Larry P. v. Riles* (1971). It will be very difficult to monitor and evaluate the efficacy of the assessment process using this approach.

Yoshida (1984) proposed an approach that recognizes the predicament of the administrator's responsibility to secure consistency in implementation and the building staff's need to design a system that can be performed with the available resources. The planning, implementation, and monitoring of behavioral assessments becomes a joint project. First, administrators must clearly identify and define the conditions under which behavioral assessment techniques may be used. For example: Will these techniques be used for all children or limited to cases involving potential special education placement? Should certain staff members perform such assessments? How extensive should these assessments be? Some of the responses to these questions may be influenced by current state and local regulations.

Once these decisions have been made, administrators must publish them so that all personnel are apprised of what potentially can be done with this assessment approach. We have learned from the multidisciplinary team decision--making literature that this is a very important step. In a large sample of Connecticut administrators, support personnel, and teachers, Fenton, Yoshida, Maxwell, and Kaufman (1979) found that less than one half knew what they were supposed to do during the evaluation process. Yoshida (1984) raised the question: Could staff members be held accountable for their performance when they did not know the tasks to be performed? Presuming personnel understanding of any school procedure is a dangerous practice. Administrators must communicate with staff about what must be done and routinely check to determine if that level of understanding is maintained.

In addition to the publication of policy, central office administrators must present the amount of resources (for example, fulltime equivalents assigned to perform behavioral assessments in a school building, training dollars, clerical/office support) that the building staff can use in performing its functions. Within these limits responsibility should be given to individual school building units, namely the principal, teachers, and assigned support personnel, to determine the specific procedures for implementing behavioral assessment techniques. The school building unit must then develop an operational plan on which the affected staff members and the principal, or the designated supervisor, agree. The plan should detail (a) the procedures (for example, who will be assigned to do what tasks); (b) the content (the types of information to be collected); and (c) the standards of personnel performance. Once the plan is found acceptable to the building staff, central office administrators review it and if appropriate accept it.

This approach has several advantages. First, the organizational literature has often posited the principle that employee participation in decision-making increases their satisfaction with and commitment to implement the decisions that are made (for a selected review of the literature, see Yoshida, Fenton, Maxwell, & Kaufman, 1978). By involving staff members who must ultimately implement behavioral assessment technology, administrators can determine whether this technology has a chance to become part of the school district's practice. Administrators will be able to estimate the Values, Ideas, Circumstances, Timing, Obligation and Resistance components of the A VICTORY approach. Second, by allocating and telling school building staff the resources available to them, the school staff and administrators should get a clear understanding of the district's Ability to perform behavioral assessment. With some school staff, such as school psychologists, already having to perform many tasks (Carroll, Bretzing, & Harris, 1981; Meacham & Peckham, 1978; Yoshida, Maher, & Hawryluk, 1984), this review should indicate whether behavioral assessments can be performed with current staff commitments and training levels. Finally, the school district can determine the Yield, the anticipated benefits that might accrue to specific students, staff, and the district as a whole, as a result of investing in this technology.

Many trends are favorable to the widespread implementation of behavioral assessment technology. However, in order for the technology to have a fair chance of being implemented and evaluated on its merits, school district administrators and staff must assess, whether using A VICTORY or some other method, the extent to which they are prepared and committed to such a technology. Without such an evaluation, school districts may hold unrealistic expectations about the potential Yield of this technology. When the level of Yield is not met, the school district will likely eliminate its use inferring erroneously that the technology has little merit. Performing an analysis of the organizational readiness beforehand reduces the likelihood of the wrong interpretation occurring and more importantly, clearly shows school personnel the changes that will have to be made to give behavioral technology a fair chance of succeeding.

REFERENCES

Alberto, P. A., & Troutman, A. C. (1982). *Applied behavior analysis for teachers.* Columbus, OH: Charles E. Merill.
Anderson, T., Cancelli, A. A., & Kratochwill, T. R. (1984). Self-reported assessment practices of school psychologists. *Journal of School Psychology, 22,* 17–30.

Bandura, A. (1977). *Social learning theory*. Englewood Cliffs, N.J.: Prentice-Hall.

Bandura, A. (1982). Self-efficacy mechanism in human agency. *American Psychologist, 37*, 122–149.

Behar, L. B. (1977). The preschool behavior questionnaire. *Journal of Abnormal Child Psychology, 5*,265–275.

Bellack, A. S., & Hersen, M. (1977). Self-report inventories in behavioral assessment. In J. D. Cone & R. P. Hawkins (Eds.), *Behavioral assessment: New directions in clinical psychology* New York: Brunner/Mazel.

Bergan, J. R. (1980). The structural analysis of behavior: An alternative to the learning hierarchy model. *Review of Educational Research, 50*, 625–646.

Bergan, J. R. (1981). Path-referenced assessment in school psychology. In T. R. Kratochwill (Ed.), *Advances in school psychology* (pp. 255–280). Hillsdale, New Jersey: Lawrence Erlbaum Associates.

Bornstein, M. R., Bellack, A. S., & Hersen, M. (1977). Social-skills training for highly aggressive children: Treatment in an inpatient psychiatric setting. *Behavior Modification, 4*, 173–186.

Bornstein, M. R., Bellack, A. S., & Hersen, M. (1980). Social skills training for highly aggressive children. Treatment in an impatient psychiatric setting. *Behavior Modification, 4*, 173–186.

Brown, L. L., & Hammill, D. D. (1978). *Behavior rating profile: An ecological approach to behavioral assessment*. Austin, TX: Pro Ed.

Burks, H. F. (1977). *Burks' behavior rating scales: Preschool and kindergarten edition*. Los Angeles, CA: Western Psychological Services.

Cancelli, A. A., Bergan, J. R., & Jones, S. (1982). Psychometric and instructional validation approaches in hierarchical sequencing of learning tasks. *Journal of School Psychology, 20*, 232–241.

Cancelli, A. A., & Duley, S. R. (1985). Behavioral assessment in school psychology. In J. R. Bergan (Ed.); *Contemporary school psychology*. Columbus, OH: Charles E. Merrill.

Cancelli, A. A., & Kratochwill, T. R. (1981). Advances in criterion referenced assessment. In T. R. Kratochwill (Ed.), *Advances in school psychology* (pp. 217–244). Hillsdale, New Jersey: Lawrence Erlbaum Associates.

Ciminero, A. R., Calhoun, K. S., & Adams, H. E. (Eds.). (1977). *Handbook of behavioral assessment*. New York: Wiley.

Ciminero, A. R., & Drabman, R. S. (1977). Current developments in the behavioral assessment of children. In B. B. Laney & A. E. Kazdin (Eds.), *Advances in child clinical psychology* (Vol. 1). New York: Plenum Press.

Cone, J. D. (1977). The relevance of reliability and validity for behavioral assessment. *Behavior Therapy, 3*, 411–426.

Cone, J. D. (1978). The behavioral assessment grid (BAG): A conceptual framework and a taxonomy. *Behavior Therapy, 9*, 882–888.

Cone, J. D. (1981). Psychometric considerations. In M. Husen & H. S. Bellack (Eds.), *Behavioral assessment: A practical handbook* (2nd ed.). Elmsford, NY: Pergamon.

Cone, J. D., & Hawkins, R. P. (Eds.) (1977). *Behavioral assessment: New directions in clinical psychology*. New York: Brunner/Mazel.

Conners, C. (1973). Rating scales for use in drug studies in children. *Psychopharmacology Bulletin, 9*, 24–84.

Curran, J. P. (1978). Review of ''Annual review of behavior therapy: Theory and practice'' (4th ed.). *Behavior Modification, 2*, 135–137.

Deci, E. L. (1975). *Intrinsic motivation*. New York: Plenum.

Deci, E. L. (1980). *The psychology of self-determination*. Lexington, MA: D. C. Heath.

Doke, L. A. (1976). Assessment of children's behavioral deficits. In M. Hersen & A. S. Bellack (Eds.), *Behavioral assessment: A practical handbook*. Elmsford, NY: Pergamon.

Duley, S. M., Cancelli, A. A., Kratochwill, T. R., Bergan, J., & Meredith, K. E. (1983). Training and generalization of motivational analysis interview skills. *Behavioral Assessment, 5,* 281–288.

Evans, I. M., & Nelson, R. O. (1977). Assessment of child behavior problems. In A. R. Ciminero, K. W. Calhoun, & H. E. Adams (Eds.), *Handbook of behavior assessment.* New York: Wiley.

Fenton, K. S., Yoshida, R. K., Maxwell, J. P., & Kaufman, M. (1979). Recognition of team goals: An essential step toward rational decision-making. *Exceptional Children, 45,* 638–644.

Forehand, R., Griest, D. L., & Wells, K. C. (1979). Parent behavioral training: An analysis of the relationship among multiple outcome measures. *Journal of Abnormal Child Psychology, 7,* 229–242.

Gagne, R. M. (1977). *The conditions of learning* (3rd ed.). New York: Holt.

Goldfried, M. R., & Kent, R. M. (1972). Traditional versus behavioral personality assessment: A comparison of methodological and theoretical assumptions. *Psychological Bulletin, 77,* 409–420.

Goldfried, M. R., & Sprafkin, J. N. (1976). Behavioral personality assessment. In J. T. Spence, R. C. Carson, & J. W. Thibaut (Eds.), *Behavioral approaches to therapy.* Morristown, NJ: General Learning Press.

Goodenough, F. L. (1949). *Mental testing.* New York: Holt.

Goodwin, D. L. (1969). Consulting with the classroom teacher. In J. D. Krumboltz & C. E. Thoresen (Eds), *Behavioral counseling cases and techniques* (pp. 260–264). New York: Holt.

Hall, G. E., & Jones, H. L. (1976). *Competency-based education: A process for the improvement of education.* Englewood Cliffs, NJ: Prentice-Hall.

Haynes, S. N. (1978). *Principle of behavioral assessment.* New York: Gardner.

Haynes, S. N., & Jenson, B. J. (1979). The interview as a behavioral assessment instrument. *Behavioral Assessment, 1,* 97–106.

Hersen, M., & Bellack, A. S. (1977). Assessment of social skills. In A. R. Ciminero, K. S. Calhoun, & H. E. Adams (Eds.), *Handbook for behavioral assessment.* New York: Wiley.

Hersen, M., & Bellack, A. S. (Eds.). (1981). *Behavioral assessment.* New York: Pergamon.

Jones, R. R., Reid, J. B., & Patterson, M. R. (1974). *Naturalistic observations in clinical assessment* (Vol. 3). San Francisco: Jossey-Bass.

Klein, S. P., & Kosecoff, J. (1973). *Issues and procedures in the development of criterion referenced tests.* Princeton, NJ: ERIC Clearinghouse on Tests, Measurement, and Evaluation, Educational Testing Service.

Kratochwill, T. R. (1982). Advances in behavioral assessment. In C. R. Reynolds & T. B. Gutkin (Eds.), *The handbook of school psychology.* New York: Wiley.

Kratochwill, T. R., Alper, S., & Cancelli, A. A. (1980). Nondiscriminatory assessment in psychology and education. In L. Mann & D. A. Sabatino (Eds.), *Fourth review of special education.* New York: Grune & Stratton.

Kratochwill, T. R., & Cancelli, A. A. (1983). *Nonbiased assessment in psychology and education.* Tucson: University of Arizona, Center for Educational Evaluation and Measurement.

Larry P. v. Riles, Civil Action No. 71-2270 (N.D. Cal. 1971).

Leitenberg, H. (1978). Review of "Behavioral assessment: A practical handbook." *Behavior Modification, 2,* 137–139.

Maher, C. A., & Bennett, R. E. (1984). *Planning and evaluating special education services.* Englewood Cliffs, NJ: Prentice-Hall.

Maher, C. A., & Illback, R. J. (1982). Organizational school psychology: Issues and considerations. *Journal of School Psychology, 20,* 244–253.

Maher, C. A., & Yoshida, R. K. (1985). Multidisciplinary teams in the schools: Current status and future possibilities. In T. R. Kratochwill (Ed.), *Advances in school psychology* (pp. 13–44). Hillsdale, NJ: Lawrence Erlbaum Associates.

Mash, E., & Terdal, L. (Eds.). (1981). *Behavioral assessment of childhood disorders.* New York: Guilford Press.

McFall, R. M. (1977). Analogue methods in behavioral assessment: Issues and prospects. In J. D. Cone & R. P. Hawkins (Eds.), *Behavioral assessment: New directions in clinical psychology.* New York: Brunner/Mazel.

Meacham, M. L., & Peckham, P. D. (1978). School psychologists at three-quarter century: Congruence between training, practice, preferred role, and competency. *Journal of School Psychology, 16,* 195–206.

Mischel, W. (1968). *Personality and assessment.* New York: Wiley.

Mooney, R. L., & Gordon, L. V. (1950). *The Mooney problem checklists.* New York: Psychological Corporation.

Nay, W. R. (1977). Analogue measures. In A. R. Ciminero, K. S. Calhoun, & H. E. Adams (Eds.), *Handbook of behavioral assessment.* New York: Wiley.

Nelson, R. O., & Hayes, S. C. (1979). The nature of behavioral assessment: A commentary. *Journal of Applied Behavior Analysis, 12,* 491–500.

Nelson, R. O., & Hayes, S. C. (1981). Nature of behavioral assessment. In M. Herson & A. S. Bellack (Eds.), *Behavioral Assessment* (pp. 3–37). New York: Pergamon Press.

Popham, W. J. (Ed.). (1971). *Criterion-referenced measurement.* Englewood Cliffs, NJ: Educational Technology Publishers.

Popham, W. J., & Husek (1969). Implications of criterion-referenced measurement. *Journal of Educational Measurement, 6,* 1–9.

Quay, H. C., & Peterson, D. R. (1983). *Revised behavior problem checklist.* Coral Gables, FL: University of Miami.

Reardon, R. C., Hersen, M., Bellack, A. S., & Foley, J. M. (1979). Measuring social skill in grade school boys. *Journal of Behavioral Assessment, 1,* 87–105.

Remmers, H. H., & Bauerfeind, R. H. (1968). *STS youth inventory* (Grades 4–8). Bensenville, IL: Scholastic Testing Service.

Remmers, H. H., & Shimberg, B. (1967). *STS youth inventory* (Grades 7–12). Bensenville, IL: Scholastic Testing Service.

Research Triangle Institute. (1980). *A national survey of individualized education programs for handicapped children* (Vols. 1–5). (Department of Education Contract No. 300-77-0527). Research Triangle Park, NC: Author.

Resnick, L. B., Wang, M. C., & Kaplan, J. (1973). Task analysis in curriculum design: A hierarchically sequenced introductory mathematics curriculum. *Journal of Applied Behavioral Analysis, 6,* 679–710.

Spivack, G., Haimer, P. E., & Spotts, F. (1967). *Devereux adolescent behavior rating scale manual.* Devon, PA: The Devereux Foundation.

Spivack, G., & Spotts, J. (1966). *Devereux child behavior rating scale manual.* Devon, PA: The Devereux Foundation.

Spivack, G., & Swift, M. (1967). *Devereux elementary school behavior rating scale.* Devon, PA: The Devereux Foundation.

Stinchcombe, A. L. (1965). Social structure and organization. In J. G. March (Ed.), *Handbook of organizations.* Chicago, IL: Rand McNally.

Stolz, S. B., & Associates (1978). *Ethical issues in behavior modification.* San Francisco: Jossey-Bass.

Thoresen, C. E., & Mahoney, M. (1974). *Behavioral self-control.* New York: Holt, Rhinehart, & Winston.

Tyler, R. W. (1976). *Perspectives on American education: Reflections on the past—Challenges for the future.* Chicago, IL: Science Research Associates.

U.S. Department of Education (1981). *Third annual report to Congress on the implementation of Public Law 94-142: The Education for All Handicapped Children Act.* Washington, DC: Author.

U.S. Department of Education (1982). Fourth annual report to Congress on the implementation of Public Law 94-142: The Education for All Handicapped Children Act. Washington, DC: Author.

U.S. Department of Health, Education, and Welfare, Office of Education (1977). Education of handicapped children: Implementation of Part B of the Education of the Handicapped Act. *Federal Register,* August 23, 42474-42518.

Walker, H. M. (1976). *Walker behavior identification checklist.* Los Angeles: Western Psychological Services.

Walls, R. T., Werner, T. J., Bacon, A., & Zane, T. (1977). Behavior checklists. In J. D. Cone & R. P. Hawkins (Eds.), *Behavioral assessment: New directions in clinical psychology.* New York: Brunner/Mazel.

Weatherley, R., & Lipsky, M. 1977). Street-level bureaucrats and institutional innovation: Implementing special education reform. *Harvard Educational Review, 47,* 171–197.

Wells, K. C. (1981). Assessment of children in outpatient settings. In M. Hersen & A. S. Bellack (Eds.), *Behavioral assessment.* New York: Pergamon.

Yoshida, R. K. (1984). Planning for change in pupil evaluation. In C. A. Maher, R. Illback, & J. Zinns (Eds.), *Organizational psychology in the schools* (pp. 83–100). Springfield, IL: Charles C. Thomas.

Yoshida, R. K., Fenton, K. S., Maxwell, J. P., & Kaufman, M. J. (1978). Group decision-making in the planning team process: Myth or reality. *Journal of School Psychology, 16,* 237–244.

Yoshida, R. K., Maher, C. A., & Hawryluk, M. K. (1984). School psychological practice: Organizational barriers to professional attainment. *Professional Psychology, 15,* 571–578.

3 Basic Skills Education

Wayne C. Piersel

A national "Blue Ribbon" Committee recently completed an 18 month study of one of the nation's major institutions. Their findings were made public in a report entitled "A Nation At Risk." The committee's report was not referring to nuclear parity or the arm's race, nor was it referring to an economic or natural disaster about to befall the country; it was referring to the many problems identified in the nation's schools (National Commission of Excellence in Education, 1983). The report indicated that society had lost sight of the basic principles and purposes of education, and relinquished the high expectations and willingness to put forth the effort and discipline necessary to gain and maintain excellence in education.

Among the many comments made by the National Commission of Excellence in Education are statements concerning the lack of adequate teacher preparation in the content area to be taught (e.g., perspective science teachers lack study in science). The Commission noted the "over emphasis" on "methods courses" in teacher education and the limited time devoted to knowledge courses. The decline in amoung of time students in public schools spend on basic subjects, such as English, mathematics, science, and literature, was cited as a contributing factor to the nation's educational decline. The committee also observed that the amount of homework assigned to students had declined significantly in recent years.

The findings of the National Commission are similar in tone and implication to previous studies on education (Coleman, 1966; Jencks et al., 1972). Information from these and other studies strongly suggests that academic performance is highly related to parents' education, family's, social class, income level, and other factors outside the school more than to the efforts of school personnel.

These findings provide additional support for the assumption that schools do not educate students (Baer & Bushell, 1981). The assumed failure of the Nation's public schools to educate students has a much greater impact on children and youth from environments that have limited resources (Becker, 1977).

"A Nation At Risk" did not come directly to terms with a major issue in the education of children and youth. The report noted excessive reliance of school personnel on curriculum materials to educate students and strongly criticized the "methods" courses taken by prospective teachers in colleges of education; however, the issue of how to manage the learning process and structure the classroom learning environment was not addressed. Increased attention to the management of the learning process will enable teachers, parents, and others to educate children and youth more effectively in the subject areas society has deemed important for students to master. The process of how to teach students and how to arrange and manage the educational environment, not how to assign curriculum materials, may well embody the essence of education. Sidney Bijou (1970) noted that psychology and education could form an effective partnership in improving education. B. F. Skinner (1984) in his article "The Shame of American Education," also commented on the need to utilize students' and teachers' time more efficiently and to manage the educational process for each individual student.

This chapter is about the management of the learning process. Content of the traditional academic subjects are not examined; instead the chapter focuses on what psychology has to offer education. More specifically, the contributions of applied behavior analysis and behavior modification to the arrangement of learning environments are discussed. Consideration is given to how to teach what we want students to learn.

The importance of a well managed and orderly instructional environment is an essential prerequisite to student learning (Baer & Bushell, 1981). A necessary prerequisite to a well managed classroom is appropriate organization and management of the learning process. Assuming that the ultimate measure of teaching success is student attainment of requisite academic skills and capabilities, such as reading, arithmetic, and written communication, effective approaches need to be identified, developed, and utilized by school personnel. In this chapter, evidence within applied behavioral analysis and behavior modification literature that pertains to student acquisition of academic skills is reviewed and synthesized. Such evidence indicates that planning, goal setting, analysis of learning activities, and application of principles of learning can assist students in increasing their mastery of basic school subjects. In particular, the chapter focuses on the relevance of applied behavior analysis and behavior modification for teaching attending to task, reading (word recognition, oral reading, and reading comprehension), oral and written reversal errors, written communication (penmanship, spelling, and creative writing), and mathematics (primarily addition, subtraction, multiplication, and division). A synthesis of the research on arranging learning opportunities is offered and areas for school-based research and program development are noted.

ATTENTION AND ON-TASK BEHAVIOR

In the 1960s, initial research on approaches to modifications of classroom behavior centered on elimination of disruptive student behavior and development of work related skills or "on-task" behaviors (see also Chapter 4). Because attentive and on-task behavior was a necessary and prerequisite skill to effective learning, it was believed that attention and other on-task behaviors would have to be developed and directly improved before teaching could focus on academic skills. If a student was rarely in his or her seat, seldom interacted with the learning materials, or was frequently disruptive, there was little likelihood that much learning would occur for the individual student or for the class. Behavioral research in this area has indicated that improvement of on-task behavior and decreases in disruptive behavior seldom resulted in improved academic learning (Ferritor, Buckholdt, Hamblin, & Smith, 1972; Kazdin, 1982; Klein, 1979; Winett & Winkler, 1972). However, direct reinforcement (provisions of positive consequences directly for school work) of increased academic performance, such as for completion of written assigemnts, has repeatedly demonstrated a decrease in disruptive behavior and increases in on-task behavior (Aaron & Bostow, 1978; Broughton & Lahey, 1978). For example, Ayllon and Roberts (1974) provided tokens to a group of disruptive fifth graders for correct completion of reading assignments. The teacher conducted 15 minutes instructional reading sessions daily with five fifth grade boys described as discipline problems. During the 15 minute sessions, the students could earn points for written work correctly completed. The points could be utilized to gain access to additional recess, time in the game room, doing additional work sheets, watching movies, or to have a note commending their efforts sent to parents. The students were also permitted to use points to reduce detention time or to have their lowest reading grade removed. Prior to implementation of the point system, students were completing less than 50% of the assigned work and were disruptive and off-task 34% of the time. Following implementation of the point (token) system, disruption decreased to less than 10% and work completion increased over 77%. As the rate of work completion increased, the inattentive and disruptive behaviors declined. Direct reinforcement of work completion increased work completion and on-task behavior and decreased off-task behavior.

Direct Reinforcement

Although considerable research has examined the effects of reinforcement contingencies on on-task behavior or product measures of academic learning, few investigations have examined the differential effect of modifying only one of the two variables. Hay, Hay, and Nelson (1977) selected two groups of male students from five regular third and fourth grade classrooms. Each group was exposed to the two interventions (reinforcing on-task behavior or reinforcing work completion) in counterbalanced order. Academic contingencies followed by on-task contingencies were applied to one group; the other group experienced on-task contingencies followed by academic contingencies. The resulting data indicated that on-task reinforcement contingencies improved only on-task behavior; academic reinforcement contingencies improved both on-task and academic behavior. Marholin and Steinman (1977) examined the differential effects of on-task and academic reinforcement contingencies in a teacher's presence and absence. Reinforcement in the form of points and teacher praise was given to eight students in a special education class either for the number of arithmetic problems correctly worked and number attempted (academic contingency) or for being on-task (attending contingency). The points were traded for free time. Marholin and Steinman found that reinforcement of academic performance increased both on-task behavior and arithmetic work completion, on-task contingencies increased only on-task behavior. Disruptive behavior, which was measured separately from on-task behavior, also decreased during reinforcement of academic behavior.

Indirect Reinforcement

Another approach to managing attending and on-task behavior involves ignoring the off-task student and giving positive reinforcement to appropriate on-task behavior of another student. The indirect method has been advocated as being beneficial because it: (a) prevents teachers and peers from inadvertently reinforcing (attending to) misbehavior; (b) facilitates prompting other students on how to be reinforced; and (c) helps cue misbehaving and potentially misbehaving students on the appropriate behavior to engage in to receive reinforcement.

To investigate the effects of indirect reinforcement on the behavior of off-task students, Boyd, Keilbaugh, and Axelrod (1981) arranged for teachers to praise on-task students when target problem students (elementary students with learning or behavioral problems) were off-task. Results indicated that problem students did not improve when the on-task student was praised; for some students, off-task behavior actually deteriorated. In a second investigation the addition of points for model students' attending behavior did not add to the usefulness of indirect teacher praise. Students who were not the direct target of rewards for attending and on-task behavior did not improve on-task behavior. These results combined with results from investigations reported previously suggest that direct reinforcement of specific behaviors can produce the most rapid behavior change.

Self-Monitoring

Self-monitoring (also referred to as self-charting and self-observation) includes three elements: (a) the student is aware of the behavior to be self-monitored; (b) the student observes him/herself engaging in the targeted behavior; and (c) the student records the observed occurance of the behavior in some manner (e.g., on a prepared card, on a wrist counter, etc). An excellent example of the description and utilization of self-monitoring is provided by Hallahan, Lloyd, Kosiewicz, Kaufman, and Graves (1979), (see also Chapter 2, Behavioral Assessment, and Chapter 4, Affective and Social Education).

Self-monitoring procedures have been applied to the attending problems of students identified as having learning problems. For example, during small group instruction, Hallahan, Marshall, and Lloyd (1981) trained three learning disabled boys to self-monitor on-task behavior. Students were trained to use wrist counters, they were to advance the wrist counter when a tone was heard on a tape recorder if they were on-task. Then, at the sound of a tape recorder students were asked to note to themselves whether they were on-task without the use of a wrist counter. Results of this investigation indicated that self-monitoring procedures that used a recording device were more effective than wrist counters in increasing on-task behavior. Unfortunately, measures of academic behavior were not reported.

Hallahan, Lloyd, Kneedler, and Marshall (1982) were successful in increasing on-task behavior and arithmetic worksheet completion by the use of self-monitoring of on-task behavior. They compared teacher assessment versus student self-assessment (self-monitoring). Both teacher monitoring and student self-assessment of on-task behavior increased on-task and arithmetic worksheet completion. Teacher assessment consisted of looking at the student when the tape recorder sounded a tone and giving the student a thumbs up for on-task or a thumbs down for off-task behavior. The self-assessment procedures consisted of the student asking him/herself, "Was I paying attention?" and noting the answer on a prepared recording sheet at the sound of a tone emitted by a tape player. Both conditions improved academic work completion and on-task behavior.

Severe Off-Task Behavior

The behavioral literature is generally consistent in demonstrating that reinforcement of on-task behavior is insufficient to increase academic behavior, and that positive reinforcement of academic responding increases the acquisition of skills and facilitates on-task behavior. In the case of severe off-task or disruptive behaviors, contingent reinforcement of on-task behavior may be a necessary prerequisite condition. Sindelar, Honsaker, and Jenkins (1982) examined the token reinforcement of appropriate behavior (orally reading from the assigned story), the time reinforcement was scheduled to be delivered, and response cost (loss of points) for the distractible behavior of two elementary school girls. The two students were awarded one point for each one half page they orally read without looking away. Positive reinforcement reduced "look aways" from four per minute to approximately one per minute for the 7-year-old. For the 10-year-old student, it was necessary to add a response cost provision, taking away one point per "looking away," to successfully reduce "off-task" behavior. The number of words read per minute increased from an average of 20 to an average of 30. For the second grade student, differential reinforcement was sufficient for decreasing off-task behavior and increasing oral reading. The use of token rewards for attending and token fines for "look aways" was needed for the fifth grader, because token reinforcement alone was ineffective in increasing on-task and oral reading behavior.

Summary

The conclusion to be drawn from the literature examining on-task behavior is that reinforcement in the form of teacher praise or points for particular academic behaviors is the most effective approach to increasing both academic work behavior and on-task behavior. Students with very low skill levels and severe off-task and disruptive behavior may need specific reinforcement programs to deal with disruptive and off-task behaviors. Student self-monitoring is also a promising approach, especially when combined with positive reinforcement of on-task behavior.

READING

Behavioral research on reading has examined word recognition, oral reading, and reading comprehension. A behavioral perspective on reading has led to the exploration of systematic application of reinforcement contingencies to increase student correct responding and to decrease student incorrect responding (Ross, 1981).

Many behavioral and educational researchers have assumed that various reading proficiencies (e.g., word recognition, word analysis skills, oral reading, and reading comprehension) are highly correlated or interdependent. The assumption that various reading proficiencies are interdependent was investigated by Lahey, McNees, and Schnelle (1977). Their study indicated that oral reading speed, oral reading accuracy, and comprehension are not interdependent. Applying reinforcement contingencies to one of the three reading behaviors positively influenced only that behavior. They concluded that functional independence is very much present for those three reading behaviors. Reading behavior that received contingent reinforcement denoted a change in learning rate.

Word Recognition

Reinforcement.   A typical approach for instructing students who have an identified reading problem is to initiate a systematic reinforcement program that involves a point or token system and teacher praise (Dineen, Clark, & Risley, 1977; Lahey, 1977). Working with a group of normal elementary students, (students who had no reading deficiencies) Lahey and Drabman (1974) investigated the effect of feedback only and feedback plus tokens on the learning of new sight vocabulary. The children were taught lists of 30 words to criterion in 10 word-teaching sessions. The students in one group were given feedback on the correctness of their response to the printed words. The children in the other group received the same feedback plus tokens. Retention on all words was assessed following the third training session and, again, 2 days later. Results indicated that students in the feedback plus token group learned the 30 words in one half as many trials and correctly recalled twice as many words on the 2 day retention test.

Another example of an approach to reading using reinforcement is illustrated in an investigation undertaken by Willis (1974). Prior to the intervention, tutors provided three elementary school students with social praise for correct oral reading and helped them to correct errors. The intervention consisted of dispensing green tokens for each correctly read line and red tokens for each error made. At the end of the session each student recorded the number of red and green chips on a chart, which was posted in the classroom. The combination of feedback, public posting, and self-charting was superior to the baseline approach. Additional studies have been conducted demonstrating the effectiveness of systematic use of tokens or points to facilitate reading behavior (Dalton, Rubino, & Hislop, 1973; Ryback & Staats, 1970).

Behavioral Rehearsal.   Flash cards to drill basic sight vocabulary have been widely used and have been successful in improving student word recognition proficiency (Axelrod, 1982; Eaton & Haisch, 1974; Egner, Burdett, & Fox, 1972). Eaton and Haisch (1974) discovered that drill on words missed during oral reading was especially helpful. Egner et al. (1972) combined drill, oral reading, and interest (i.e., reinforcing value) of learning to read with the use of a game format, such as "Bingo" (Kirby, Holborn, & Bushby, 1981). In the Kirby et al. (1981) evaluation, use of "Bingo" increased word recognition by 30%. Ceprano (1981), from an extensive review of literature on teaching sight words concluded that teaching in isolation (flash cards) and in context (words embedded in text) are both needed; isolated word drill alone does not readily transfer or generalize to other situations or contexts.

To teach reading to a first grade student with no vocabulary or reading skills, Piersel (1979) used a combination of flash card drill, and reading target words embedded in sentences. The student who could recognize only 10 letters of the alphabet at the time of the intervention, went from zero word recognition to a sight vocabulary of 109 words in 3 months. The combination of flash drill followed by sentence reading using the words from the drill proved effective, the approaches were not successful when used independently. By the end of the 3 months the student was able to recognize all letters of the alphabet, no additional effort was made to teach them. In this investigation the words (i.e., dog, cat, mother, father, car, bed) chosen to teach the child were selected by the student, and were considered as having meaning for the student. The teacher added action words (e.g., go, run, walk) and adjectives to permit the construction of sentences.

Oral Reading

Feedback.   Six methods of providing feedback for oral reading errors were examined in a study by Jenkins and Larson (1979). The six feedback procedures utilized by the teacher during oral reading consisted of: (a) teacher supplying the word; (b) no correction given; (c) teacher supplying word and student repeating sentence saying word; (d) teacher supplying word plus end of page review of words not known; (e) teacher supplying word plus discussion of word's meaning; and (f) teacher supplying word plus drill on all words missed at end of oral reading session. Although all methods of correction were better than the no correction control group, the isolated word drill procedure for more identified words far exceeded the remaining five correction procedures.

Modeling.   The role of modeling has received surprisingly little attention on teaching of reading, despite the widespread use of modeling as an instructional procedure (Hansen & Eaton, 1978; see also Chapter 4, Affective and Social Education). Smith (1979) described two case studies involving an elementary school teacher reading an assignment aloud for the student. The teacher read at the correct oral reading rate immediately prior to the student engaging in oral reading. The student began reading the story where the teacher stopped and completed the story. In the first case, the teacher's modeling of reading prior to student reading was sufficient to increase the student's oral reading rate and decrease errors. In the second instance, prereading modeling by the teacher plus corrective feedback was necessary to increase oral reading rate and decrease errors. In the first case, the student's oral reading rate increased by 14%; with the addition of the correction procedure, the oral reading rate increased another 13%.

Positive Practice and Reinforcement.   Noting that most teachers attend to oral reading errors more often than correct reading and that less proficient readers make proportionally more oral reading errors, Singh, Singh, and Winston (1984) examined the effects of positive practice overcorrection and positive reinforcement on the oral reading of four moderately retarded girls. Positive practice over correction involved: (a) telling the student how to pronounce a word that was missed; (b) having the student point to words in the text and repeat it correctly five times; and (c) having the student reread the entire sentence. The positive practice plus reinforcement sessions included the positive practice procedure and reinforcers, such as candy, for correct reading. The results of these teaching procedures revealed that positive practice alone decreased oral reading errors and positive practice plus reinforcement had an even greater effect on decreasing oral reading errors.

Antecedent Control.   Most behavioral research on reading has focused on the management of consequences for academic performance. Singh and Singh (1984) focused on managing two antecedent conditions to improve the reading behavior of four retarded students attending a special school. The first instructional approach consisted of the teacher discussing the material to be orally read prior to reading. Students were also exposed to a similar previewing condition, the discussion focused on an unrelated text. The results were in support of previewing the text to be orally read.

Reading Comprehension

Lovitt (1981) and Ross (1981) have noted that a primary purpose of reading instruction is to teach students to understand the passages read; a primary goal of reading instruction is to teach comprehension of what has been read. The complex problem-solving process of gaining meaning from print must be brought under stimulus control, it must not be just an appropriate response to isolated stimulus words or phrases.

To teach reading comprehension, Lovitt (1981) designed a reading project that required elementary school students to relate facts about stories they had just read. Students were provided feedback, received a demonstration on how to recall factual information, and were provided with reinforceing consequences for correct responses. This intervention package increased student factual comprehension by 60% relative to student performance prior to the program. Other investigations of behavioral approaches to increasing reading comprehension skills (e.g., Hansen & Eaton, 1978) have successfully utilized previewing types of information needed to answer questions and corrective feedback. Students were instructed on the types of questions they would need to answer and were given an overview of the reading.

Goal Setting.   In goal setting students are involved in systematically determining what they will attempt to accomplish in a particular span of time. For example, a student may decide to complete 20 math problems a day, read 10 pages of text and answer five questions per day, or complete 10 pages of work book per week. The establishment of goals is frequently guided by teachers, parents, or others. The important consideration is that the student rather than the teacher sets the goals.

Expanding on results provided by Hopkins, Shuttes, and Garten (1971), Lovitt and Esveldt (1970), and Semb and Semb (1972) examined the effect of fixed page versus fixed time assignments on the reading behavior of nine elementary school children. The results were supportive of fixed page assignments rather than the fixed time allotments for completing assignments. LaForge, Pree, and Hersazi (1975) investigated the effects of setting minimum objectives on 19 sixth grade students classed as reading problems. The students worked in two teams to accomplish the objectives. The setting of minimum objects had a positive influence on reading behavior.

Self-Management.   Verbal self-instruction or self-talk typically involves teaching the student to: (a) ask self about the nature and scope of the task to be performed; (b) instruct self about what is to be done specifically to guide performance; (c) to provide self with feedback about adequacy of performance, and (d) to provide self with reinforcement or correct feedback (see also Chapter 4, Affective and Social Education). Self-monitoring discussed previously under On Task Behavior is a formalized aspect of the feedback process.

In an investigation of self-selected versus externally selected schedules of reinforcement, Billingsley (1977) found that each approach was effective for some elementary students. There were no clear cut results about the effectiveness of either of the two approaches. Progressively increasing the degree of self-management was found effective in a study by Lovitt (1973). Research by Pacquin (1978) supported the use of self-charting reading and arithmetic responses. The results reported in the study on self-charting by Piersel and Kratochwill (1979), also supported their use.

The use of self-instruction (self-talk) to enhance reading comprehension in a group of reading deficit seventh and eighth grade students was successfully employed by Meichenbaum and Asarnow (1979). The students demonstrated the necessary prerequisite skills for reading with comprehension. Using instructor modeling, students were shown how to break the reading comprehension task into smaller manageable units, organize the units, and develop self-instruction statements to rehearse when initiating a reading exercise; students were being taught to talk themselves through the reading process. The results indicated that the self-instruction group was significantly superior to the control group that continued to receive conventional instruction. Egeland (1974) demonstrated that self-instruction could also enhance the reading comprehension of elementary school students.

Summary

The behavioral research on the teaching of reading suggests that instruction be focused on particular reading skills. Discussing and previewing the material to be

read contributes to increased oral reading accuracy and to reduced oral reading errors. Correct practice of incorrectly identified words is more efficient than practicing both correctly and incorrectly read words. Having the teacher read the passage (modeling) to be read by students also enhances reading proficiency. Reading comprehension continues to receive the least amount of attention from behavioral and education researchers. However, the use of prereading planning, instructional modeling, and self-instruction statements may enhance reading comprehension skills. Behavioral research on reading has focused almost exclusively on analysis and manipulation of consequent events, ignoring the role of antecedent conditions. As with other academic subject areas, little attention has been paid to generalization of newly learned reading skills.

REVERSAL ERRORS

One of the most common problems observed among children with learning problems is a high percentage of errors in responding to alphabet letters (e.g., letters such as b, d, p, and q) (Deno & Chiang, 1979). Students frequently write q for p and b for d and vice versa. Also, such numbers as 2, 3, 6, 7, and 9 are routinely written backwards. Cohn and Stricker (1979) have noted that reversal errors are relatively common in young children and are a developmental phenomena, independent of academic skill level. Comparing reinforcement alone with reinforcement and stimulus fading (gradually removing alternative letters), Lahey and McNees (1975) found that a combination of approaches was more effective than reinforcement alone in eliminating errors in teaching letter names. For example, to teach a student to recognize the letter b, the teacher would pair b with d and gradually remove (fade) d during practice sessions. Hasazi and Hasazi (1972) were able to modify number reversals with elementary school children by manipulation of teacher attention. Using reinforcement for correct naming of letters, Deno and Chiang (1979) eliminated identification errors in five boys labeled as severely learning disabled. Tawney (1972) trained 29 four-year-olds to discriminate letters by reinforcing the attention to critical features of each letter to be copied. Sidman and Kirk (1974), using elementary school children in regular classes, demonstrated that reversals in letter naming and writing were reduced by repeated testing.

Using a combination of reinforcement and feedback with four boys classified as severely learning disabled, Lahey, Busemeyer, O'Hara, and Beggs (1977) successfully remediated handwriting reversals and increased legibility. In a study containing the use of prompts (tracing on a pencil outline of the letter prior to writing the letter), instructions (having students identify the letter), and token reinforcement, Williams and Fry (1976) rapidly eliminated letter reversals in an 11—year-old mildly retarded boy. In a series of investigations with young children Stromer (1975) demonstrated that praise and feedback, modeling only, and feedback and charting were successful in reducing or eliminating letter and digit reversals.

Summary

The reversal errors that students make in naming and writing letters and numbers are readily corrected using a combination of prompting, practice, corrective feedback, and positive reinforcement. Research by Cohn and Stricker (1979) using a sample of 400 first grade students questions the value of attempting to correct such problems. They noted that reversal errors occurred with increasing frequency in more competent students, however, naming and writing reversal errors were readily corrected.

WRITTEN COMMUNICATION

The pronouncement that the majority of Americans of all ages use only the simplest sentence structure and the most basic vocabulary was highlighted in a 1975 issue of *Newsweek* (Kerr & Lambert, 1982). In spite of this problem and even though a large body of educational research exists on teaching written communication skills, it was not until the early 1970s that a behavioral approach began to be employed.

Three aspects of children's written communication have been examined using behavioral programs and procedures. First, a small literature on the teaching of spelling has begun to evolve. Second, penmanship, both print and cursive, has received increased research and evaluation attention. Third, the most evasive aspect of written communication, creative writing, has been the focus of a limited number of investigations.

Spelling

A major difficulty in locating and synthesizing the spelling research literature is that in many investigations spelling performance has been a secondary research concern (Kerr & Lambert, 1982; Lovitt, 1975). Because spelling is easily quantified and measured it has been made a target response to examine the effects of various reinforcement procedures (Lovitt, Guppy, & Blattner, 1969). These procedures include effective teaching procedures, such as peer tutoring (Dineen, Clark, & Risley, 1977); treatment packages, such as "the Good Behavior Game" (Axelrod & Paluska, 1975), and self-control procedures (Piersel & Kratochwill, 1979). Several important behavioral approaches to spelling instruction can be identified, including reinforcement, practice, modeling, and imitation.

Reinforcement. A variety of reinforcing activities and events have been employed to increase spelling performance. In one approach (Axelrod, 1982), students who attained perfect spelling test scores were permitted to engage in a preferred activity (e.g., washing chalkboards, listening to records). The percent of fourth grade children having spelling difficulties who subsequently obtained perfect test scores increased from 24% to 64%. The setting of a 100% criterion was an obvious limitation of this early endeavor, reinforcement combined with gradually increasing goals would have been more appropriate. Lovitt et al. (1969) made use of free time to improve the spelling test behavior of 32 fourth grade students. In addition to providing contingent free time, the students were tested daily. When students achieved 100% on the weekly spelling assignment, they were not required to take spelling tests for the remainder of the week. The use of free time is confounded with a version of distributed practice (daily tests). Nevertheless, the number of perfect spelling test scores more than doubled under the daily practice and contingent free time intervention.

Few investigations have focused on the effect of reward systems designed for groups or entire classrooms. Benowitz and Busse (1976) compared material incentives (prizes) and social incentives (teacher praise and grades). The results of their study supported the use of material incentives. Students in seven fourth grade classrooms received material incentives, they learned an average of six new spelling words weekly. Students in the social incentive condition learned an average of three new words weekly. Prizes were earned on the basis of the number of additional words mastered by ·the students on the weekly post test administered on Friday (pretest given each Monday). The results of this study were consistent with the results of previous studies (Benowitz & Busse, 1970; Benowitz & Rosenfeld, 1973; Thompson & Gallaway, 1970) supporting the use of classroom reinforcement systems.

Practice. A study by Reith et al. (1974) demonstrated the importance of spreading practice of words to be spelled over time. Each day Reith and associates presented portions of the weekly spelling list, the words presented were tested the next day. On Friday, students received a spelling test on the entire spelling list. The results provide strong support for educational interventions that introduce portions of the assignment on a daily basis and require several periods of practice over time. Having parents tutor students at home also has improved in class spelling performance (Broden, Beasley, & Hall, 1978). Homework, such as practicing the correct spelling of words, can be viewed as a form of distributed practice.

Distributed positive practice was investigated by Foxx and Jones (1978) with a sample of elementary and junior high school students. There were three phases to the investigation. Phase one involved increased feedback to students by providing a spelling pretest midway through the week. Phase two consisted of students practicing the spelling words missed on Friday's test, on the following Monday. The third phase included a pretest on Wednesday, positive practice activities for missed words, spelling test on Friday, and follow up positive practice on Monday for any words missed on Friday. The "positive practice" procedure consisted of (a) copying the correct spelling; (b) copying the correct phonetic spelling; (c) identifying the part of speech; (d) writing a complete definition from the dictionary; and (e) writing five sentences using each word. The results support phase three as the most effective approach to improving spelling test performance. Thus, "positive practice," that involves distributing practice over time and varied instructional activities, is an effective instructional procedure.

Modeling and Imitation.   In one of the few studies of spelling performance to examine the effects of varying antecedent conditions, Kauffman, Hallahan, Haas, Brame, and Boren (1978) investigated the influence of "modeling only" and "modeling plus imitation" with two spelling problems. The "modeling only" condition included having a student repeat each misspelled word and copying the word in a variety of ways. Modeling plus imitation included the teacher copying the student's misspelled word just as the student had written it and modeling the correct spelling. In a second aspect of the investigation, another student was exposed to the "modeling only" and "modeling plus imitation" for learning phonics. Again, the "modeling plus imitation" proved to be superior in teaching academic material. The modeling plus imitation condition also contained elements of distributed practice.

Summary.   Behavioral research on spelling indicates that "correct practice makes perfect." The provision of reinforcing consequences for correct spelling enhances spelling practice and test performance. Research suggests that distributed practice is more effective than massed practice; however, precisely how the spaced practiced should be conducted is not known. Parents and peers may successfully tutor students with spelling problems; however, little attention has been devoted to procedures and techniques that would facilitate generalization of acquired spelling skills.

Handwriting

Handwriting, or penmanship, is an area of instruction that has been influenced by modern research (Cole, 1946; Lamb, 1971). Like spelling, handwriting appears to have minimally attracted the interest of behavioral researchers. Handwriting research can be classified into studies of reinforcement for accuracy and rate; and studies of visual feedback and corrective procedures (Kerr & Lambert, 1982).

A major difficulty in the teaching of handwriting has been the lack of a measurement procedure that is convenient and accurate in assessing the quality of a student's writing. Fortunately, Jones, Trap, and Cooper (1977) demonstrated that overlays (Helwig, Johns, Norman; & Cooper, 1976) could be used as a measurement procedure. The overlays consisted of clear, transparent plastic sheets with letters printed on lines that matched the lines on the writing paper used by students. After students had printed a letter, they could align the overlay on the paper and determine how closely the letter resembled the letter on the evaluative overlay. Jones et al. demonstrated that first grade students could be instructed to check their handwriting using plastic overlays. Scoring agreement between teacher and students was high, exceeding 90%.

Reinforcement. Timed copying (printing for first graders and cursive for second graders) was used to investigate the effects of reinforcement (contingent access to varying lengths of free time) on penmanship. Access to free time was superior to the nonreinforcement condition; both rate and accuracy were positively enhanced (Hopkins, Schutte, & Garten, 1971). Salzberg, Wheeler, Devar, and Hopkins (1971) examined the effects of free time on the printing behavior of six kindergarten students. In addition to reinforcement, they examined the effects of feedback. Results demonstrated that letters followed by reinforcement were written more accurately than letters that only received feedback. Rapport and Bostow (1976) investigated access to free time for a group of third grade students. Although, in addition to cursive writing, this study also included other written communication tasks, the results were in strong agreement with previous studies. It supported the use of contingent positive reinforcement, particularly, the robust reinforcing value of free time. Brigham, Finfrock, Breuing, and Bushell (1972) increased the accuracy of six kindergarten students' performance using token rewards. The tokens could be exchanged for desired activities or for cookies during snack time.

Feedback and Correction Procedures. Although provision of reinforcement is a component of feedback, the consequation strategy of providing evaluative feedback to improve the quality of handwriting also has received the attention of behavioral researchers (Stowitschek & Stowitschek, 1979; Trap, Milner-Davis, Joseph, & Copper, 1978). Trap et al. (1978) using the overlays developed by Helwig, Jones, Norman, and Cooper, (1976) evaluated several feedback conditions with 12 students. Using a multiple baseline across subjects design, they examined the effects of no feedback, feedback using overlays, and reinforcement. All interventions employing visual feedback that used the evaluative overlays proved to be superior to the no feedback (baseline) condition.

Severe perpetual motor problems (writing and copying) have been successfully remediated by corrective feedback and positive reinforcement (Lahey, Busemeyer, O'Hara, & Beggs, 1977). In two studies, Lahey et al. (1977) were able to modify the handwriting of four learning disabled elementary school boys. Using corrective feedback consisting of (a) orientation of letter on pages (e.g., the letter should slant this way); (b) correctness of sequencing (e.g., the letters of this word go in this order); and (c) legibility (e.g., accuracy of letter formation), all boys demonstrated improvement. An intervention package utilizing tracing, modeling, and letter naming successfully improved the print of a 6-year-old

(Fauke, Bennett, Bowers, & Sulzer-Azaroff, 1973). In addition, generalization of the improved handwriting to the classroom was noted.

Self-Management. As an intervention, self-instruction procedures have been found to be an effective means of dealing with a variety of educational problems, including handwriting (Kosiewicz, Hallahan, Lloyd, & Graves, 1982). The package of self-instruction and self-correction was effective in improving cursive writing of lists of words and paragraph copying in a 9-year-old boy. Self-instruction of handwriting strategy involved: (a) saying the word to be written aloud; (b) saying the first syllable of the word; (c) naming the letters of the syllable; (d) naming each letter of the syllable as it is written; (e) repeating steps a through d for each succeeding syllable. Self-correction consisted of the student circling errors made on the previous day's writing assignment.

The design of the Kosiewicz et al. study does not permit conclusions about the relative effectiveness of each component. Kosiewicz, Hallahan, and Lloyd (1981) compared teacher selected and student selected approaches to treatment of handwriting problems. The teacher selected approach included a review of a list of rules to facilitate accuracy of writing; the student selected treatment involved circling correctly formed letters and words (student corrected). Although both approaches were superior to baseline performance, the student selected feedback condition was slightly more potent than the teacher selected treatment. Clark, Boyd, and McRae (1975), using tokens and self-correction, were successful in improving cursive writing of six adolescents. Self-management procedures are useful in the instruction of handwriting skills.

Summary. Behavioral research on handwriting indicates that effective handwriting instruction involves demonstration, presence of models, immediate feedback, and positive reinforcement. Having students evaluate their own print and cursive efforts using clear plastic overlays has been effective. The practice of correct print and cursive motor behaviors facilitates learning.

Creative Writing

The most efficacious approaches for encouraging creative writing, without sacrificing essentials of good composition have been the subject of debate (Taylor & Hoedt, 1966).

Reinforcement. In an early study investigating creative writing, Taylor and Hoedt (1966) divided 105 fourth graders into two groups. The students in one group received teacher feedback in the form of praise, the teacher circled the best sections on each student's composition. In the other group students received no teacher praise but they did receive evaluative feedback on sections needing improvement. The number of comments on papers were the same across groups.

Results indicated that, although writing quality of both groups improved, the group receiving teacher praise and positive feedback described the writing experience more favorably and increased the amount of writing over the group receiving negative feedback. Reinforcement for use of specific parts of speech (Maloney & Hopkins, 1973) have been reported as effective in altering various aspects of creative writing for fourth, fifth, and sixth graders.

Feedback. Additional studies have demonstrated the value of immediate teacher feedback and of having students make performance comments about their own creative writing (Van Houton, 1980). Combinations of positive reinforcement and feedback on word usage (total number of words, number of different words, and number of new words) (Brigham, Graubard, & Stans, 1972), increased the writing of 13 fifth grade problem boys. The combination of timing, length of assignment completion, and feedback on creative writing assignments increased the response rate and the writing quality of second and fifth grade students (Van Houton, Morrison, Jarvis, & McDonald, 1974). Timing, feedback via self-scoring, and public posting of writing activities doubled the number of words written and increased the quality of stories for 10th and 11th graders (Van Houten & McKillop, 1977).

Self-Management. The effectiveness of self-management on objective writing responses and on the subjective quality of a student's story writing was examined by Ballard and Glynn (1975). Working with 51 normal third graders, Ballard and Glynn found that simply having the students check (self-assess) their writing and recording the results of self-assessment did not increase the number of describing words, number of sentences, number of different action words, or the subjective quality of the stories. Having students select writing responses they (the students) would reward themselves for did increase rates of responding on the writing objective selected. The subjective quality of the stories, determined by independent judges, also increased.

Information on "on-task" behavior was also gathered. Even though "on task" was not directly targeted for change, "on-task" behavior increased as story quality increased. Ballard and Glynn's study represents an excellent example of the application of self-management (self-instruction) procedures to academic learning. The study also indicates that reinforcement continues to play an essential role in correct academic performance. It is important to note that the writing component selected for reinforcement is the element that increased.

Summary. Several important conclusions can be drawn about behavioral approaches to creative writing. First, there are few acceptable standards for judging "good" creative writing. Second, aspects of writing, such as certain compositional items (i.e., nouns, action verbs, adjectives, adverbs, sentence beginnings) can be directly influenced by contingent reinforcement. Third, specific feedback to students does not inhibit creative expression. Fourth, specific instruction on the aspect of writing the student is to focus on is more effective than general instructions (e.g., be more creative). Fifth, there is some evidence that creative writing skills generalize over time and across situations (Campbell & Willis, 1979). Use of positive feedback is more facilitative and creates a more positive view of writing than negative feedback. Behavioral research indicates that demonstration and modeling, feedback on writing quality, reinforcement of specific aspects of writing, and self-evaluation are important components for enhancing creative writing.

MATHEMATICS

Behavioral research on mathematics is more extensive than research in other academic areas. In investigating student performance in mathematics, the unit of responding is easily identified and there are numerous alternative responses to measure. Moreover, clearly indentified skill hierarchies exist within this subject domain. The behavioral approaches that have been the focus of mathematics research include modeling, antecedents and strategy training, reinforcement and timing, homework, parent administered programs, and self-management. The mathematics skill areas that have been targets of evaluation include basic skills of addition, subtraction, multiplication, and division.

Modeling.

In a series of three investigations, Smith and Lovitt (1975) examined the effects of different aspects of modeling on students' mathematics performance. In study one a teacher showed (demonstration) the student how to work a set of arithmetic problems, the sample (model) was left for the student to use. Study two included teacher demonstration, modeling, and feedback. Study three consisted of demonstration, no permanent model, and no feedback. The results supported demonstration, model availability, and feedback (Study 2).

In another investigation, children with below average arithmetic achievement were exposed to modeling or didactic instruction, arithmetic performance was followed by praise (Schunk, 1981). Subsets of students were also praised for high effort (good scores) or critized for poor effort (low scores). Although praise for high effort was effective, the children exposed to modeling (how to solve division problems) were superior in overall performance.

Antecedents and Strategy Training

Self-instructions can be viewed as a set of problem-orienting and problem-solving statements that an individual emits. Self-instructional statements focus a student's attention on relevant aspects of the problem situations and guide the learner through a process to deal with the demands of the task (Meichenbaum & Goodman, 1971). Self-instruction training aids in utilizing problem-solving strategies.

In an early study (Lovitt & Curtiss, 1968), an 11-year-old boy's mathematic behavior was increased with the use of self-instruction. The student talked himself through the problem (rehearsal), before actually doing the assignment. More recent research (Cullinan, Epstein, & Lloyd, 1981; Lloyd, Saltzman, & Kaufman, 1981; Whitman & Johnston, 1983) has continued to expand strategy training and self-instruction. The effects of teaching students a mathematics preskill training and attack strategy training was assessed on the acquisition of multiplication and division skills. The investigation involved four elementary school boys who could not correctly answer the pretest problems (Lloyd, Saltzman, & Kaufman, 1981). The teaching of preskills, consisting of rote counting sequences of 5's, 7's, 10's, 3's, and 4's, was not sufficient for the students to acquire multiplication skills. When students were taught the strategies for using the skills, their mastery of multiplication increased. Strategy training consisted of teaching students to (a) identify the number to count by; (b) make hash marks; (c) count by the number identified for each hash mark; and (d) write the last number stated as the answer. An adult trainer modeled each strategy step by working a multiplication problem. The student was then instructed to work a multiplication problem saying each of the steps out loud. As the student worked through a series of problems, he gradually stopped saying the steps aloud. The study was repeated with division skills, similar results were achieved.

The efficiency of self-instructional programs has also been demonstrated with educable mentally handicapped (Whitman & Johnston, 1983). Nine mentally retarded elementary students were taught a self-instructional sequence for dealing with addition and subtraction problems. The training involved teaching the students to verbalize the instructions and perform the required motor responses. The self-instructional (self-talk) program increased performance accuracy from 27.4 to 82.4% for addition and subtraction. This study was an extension of an earlier study completed by Johnson, Whitman, and Johnson (1980). In the earlier study, three elementary learning disabled students were instructed individually; in the present study, students were successfully taught self-instructional procedures in groups of three, making the procedure much more efficient and desirable.

In a related study, the effects of self-instructions on mildly and moderately retarded elementary school student's arithmetic performance was investigated by Albion and Salzberg (1982). Four students were taught self-instruction statements, such as "Work closely and carefully," "Keep your eyes on the paper," and "Which is the biggest number?". The study also included self-evaluation and self-charting of responses. Although it is not possible to identify the component that uniquely contributed to increased performance, the package that included self-instructions was highly successful in increasing arithmetic performance for three of four students.

Reinforcement and Timing

The importance of setting time limits for completion of assignments and for utilization of reinforcement has been demonstrated repeatedly (Iwata & Bailey, 1979; Lovitt & Esveldt, 1982; Van Houton & Thompson, 1976). Key elements include explicit time limits, immediate feedback, and reinforcing consequences (i.e., freetime, points, etc.); these three elements are part of successful arithmetic performance programs. The key distinction between programs for students learning new skills and students elaborating on acquired skills has not been explored. Conceivably, the timing variable may be more critical on drill activities than during the initial acquisition of new material, but this remains an interesting research question.

Distributed Practice

Homework represents a form of distributed practice and parent involvement. Despite the importance and use of homework in schools, few studies have examined the contributions of homework to mathematics performance, and even fewer studies have examined the variables that enhance or inhibit the effects of homework. Harris and Sherman (1974) examined the effects of homework on classroom performance for arithmetic and the variables that contributed to effective homework. Their results indicated that homework plays a facilitating role if it is completed, if it is accurate, and if consequences are attached for homework and related classroom performance. Assigning homework without monitoring completion or linking it to classroom performance had little noticeable overall effects on academic progress. Homework's contribution to learning is consistent with the literature, demonstrating that distributed practice is more effective than massed practice. Homework is by its nature completed at a point in time outside the classroom; it represents an additional instance of practice.

The role of home-based consequences for mathematics performance has also been investigated (Atkeson & Forehand, 1979; Blechman, Kotanchik, & Taylor, 1981; see also Chapter 7). Working with a group of students from grades 2 to 5, who revealed a high degree of performance in consistency, Blechman et al. (1981) demonstrated that parent-administered reinforcement based on teacher communication reduced student performance variability and increased overall accuracy on computational work sheets. An untreated control group demonstrated no change. An interesting aspect of this study was training the families to develop and write behavioral contracts.

Self-Management

The self-selection of standards for receiving reinforcement has been examined in several studies (Dickerson & Creedon, 1981; Felixbrod & O'Leary, 1973; Lovitt & Curtiss, 1968). The results have been inconsistent, only Lovitt and Curtiss

(1969) obtained results that supported self-imposed standards. Dickerson and Creedon (1981), in a replication and extension of previous research on self-selection, compared self-selected standards and teacher-selected standards. They used a sample of 30 second and third graders (15 in each condition). Although both groups participated in calculation of daily earning and charting, the self-imposed standards group demonstrated a significantly greater number of correct writing and arithmetic responses.

Another important issue in facilitating mathematics performance is the individual who actually gathers and records the assessment information (Hallahan, Lloyd, Kneedler, & Marshall, 1982; see also Chapter 2). The issue of whether self-recording is a more potent treatment (reactive) than recording by an external individual has received little attention in the literature. Noting the importance of self-recording as an aspect of self-management, Hallahan et al. (1982) compared the effects of a 7-year-old learning disabled student's self-recording and teacher-assisted self-recording on-task behavior and completion of addition assignments. Results clearly demonstrated that self-recording and teacher-assisted self-recording produced increases in on-task behavior and smaller increases in number of arithmetic problems completed. Of particular interest was the continued high rate of on-task behavior and increasing mathematics work completion following termination of these procedures. The relative ease, minimal amount of teacher time, and potential generalization makes this approach very attractive. The literature on student charting of grades and scores in mathematics (Fink & Carnine, 1975; Lovitt, 1981; Paquin, 1978) provides additional support for involving students in the assessment and monitoring processes.

Summary

Behavioral research on the learning of basic mathematics skills is among the most definitive and systematic. The behavioral literature indicates that antecedents and strategy training, modeling, prompting, feedback, and reinforcement are central components to the teaching of new mathematics skills. Self-instruction (self-talk) has contributed to learning and continued use of problem solving strategies. In particular, the role of training cognitive strategies has been informative in developing a behavioral technology for mathematics instruction. The presence of well defined skill hierarchies and task analyzed curriculum has facilitated research in this area.

BEHAVIORALLY BASED INSTRUCTIONAL PROGRAMS

In most educational settings, behavioral techniques and procedures are utilized on a small scale; they are typically employed for one or a few academic subjects, utilized for a limited portion of the school day, and focus on a limited number of students. Behavioral instructional programs have been implemented on a larger scale with entire classrooms and with complete programs, such as Head Start and Follow Through (Becker, 1978). Instructional programs represent application of combinations of behavioral principles and procedures within a carefully developed, organized, and integrated educational intervention package. Instructional programs go beyond the narrowly defined procedures discussed earlier, they specify how to arrange and manage complete instructional environments for an entire school day. The following three programs illustrate the multifaceted behavioral procedures: Direct Instruction, Applied Behavioral Analysis, and Project Excell.

Direct Instruction

The Direct Instruction model is based on the work of Engelmann, Becker, Bereiter, and Carnine (e.g., Becker, 1977; Becker & Carnine, 1982; Becker & Engelmann, 1979; Bereiter & Engelmann, 1966; Engelmann & Carnine, 1982). The Direct Instruction model utilizes several of the behavioral principles described including: (a) direct, immediate, frequent reinforcement of student learning; (b) direct measurement of student progress; (c) highly structured and sequenced instruction; (d) teaching of strategies for approaching and solving problems; (e) rapid paced, teacher-directed, small group instruction; (f) carefully structured school days with time allocated according to teaching priorities; (g) clear specification of what teachers and students are to do and when they are to accomplish each activity; and (h) careful attention to skill acquisition and skill maintenance for each student. In Direct Instruction students are taught systems for operating on and solving educational problems. Critical attention is given to the selection of examples that may or may not be representative of the concept being taught.

The focus of the Direct Instruction model on strategy training has resulted in increased application of strategy training in mathematics instruction and reading comprehension. There is heavy reliance on teacher modeling, demonstration, guided practice, and subsequent repeated practice spaced over time. The students practice a strategy, such as adding two digit numbers that involve "carrying," with decreasing amounts of teacher guidance and decreasing reliance on overt statement of the problem solving rules. Direct Instruction was found to be the most effective of the nine model programs in the Follow Through Project, in bringing about student learning across academic skills areas (Becker, Engelmann, Carnine, & Rhine, 1981).

The effectiveness of the Direct Instruction model has not been confined to the Follow Through Program. The Direct Instruction model has been utilized successfully with learning disabled students (Lloyd, Cullinan, Heins, & Epstein, 1981) and mentally retarded students (Maggs & Morath, 1976). The Direct Instruction model has not been routinely employed with normal children. The

Direct Instruction model departs from other behaviorally based approaches, a special curriculum (DISTAR) was designed to be implemented in this educational program. The DISTAR curriculum programs for reading, mathematics, and language arts were designed to teach strategies for solving academic problems and to teach basic skills in each area.

Applied Behavioral Analysis

The Applied Behavioral Analysis model assumes that teaching is a technology and that student behavior follows the principles of learning. From an educational viewpoint the important principle is that behaviors that are followed by reinforcement are more likely to be repeated (learned). Emphasising the management of reinforcement, many Applied Behavioral Analysis Programs utilized token rewards for correct academic responses. The earned tokens were utilized by the students to gain access to desired activities (e.g., free time, listening to records) and items, such as games, toys, and other materials. Equally important, behaviors that are not followed by reinforcement are less likely to occur (be learned) in the future. Therefore, Applied Behavior Analysis model has placed emphasis on withholding positive reinforcement when students have emitted incorrect academic responses. The educational studies described by Haring, Lovitt, Eaton, and Hansen (1978) are representative of this Model.

The Applied Behavioral Analysis model has utilized small group instruction (six to eight students), immediate feedback, and positive reinforcement. A typical instruction activity involves a small group of six to eight students studying a skill area, such as addition. While students are working on their respective assignments, a teacher or teacher's aide moves from student to student checking each student's progress. Written work is monitored during the student performance activity and checked immediately following assignment completion. Students are allowed to ask questions about their responses to provide an indication of their understanding of the academic task, and token reinforcement is usually provided. Social praise is provided throughout the learning process.

Strong reliance on the use of tokens is a means to effect teacher and student behavior. Having teachers frequently dispense tokens helped to focus teacher attention on appropriate student behavior. In the model, teachers are viewed as managers of the learning process. Parents have also been considered teachers. Parents have been encouraged to become involved in educational programming and have received training in the management of consequences for correct and incorrect behavior. The involvement of parents sets the Applied Behavoral Analysis model apart from most other behaviorally and nonbehaviorally oriented educational programs.

Applied Behavioral Analysis programs utilize commercially available curriculum, they do not develop instructional materials to accompany the Behavioral Analysis instructional model. Teacher behavior is carefully monitored to ascertain appropriate implementation of the Applied Behavioral Analysis model. Instructional staff are monitored on administration of praise and token reinforcement, attention to on-task behavior, assessment and reinforcement of acacemic progress, and management of the practical aspects of token programs. Because the Applied Behavioral Analysis model views teaching as a management activity, teachers must focus on management of the delivery of consequences for student learning behaviors.

Project Excell

Project Excell is a demonstration project that combines elements of the Behavioral Analysis and Direct Instruction Models and utilizes task analysis technology (Lloyd, Epstein, & Cullinan, 1981). Project Excell has focused on teaching students identified as learning disabled, in contrast, Direct Instruction and Applied Behavior Analysis view the student population as culturally disadvantaged. Project Excell combines reliance on reinforcing consequences and careful teacher management behavior with precise curriculum management and the teaching of problem solving strategies. Lloyd et al. reports the results of an ongoing study that compares learning disabled elementary students who were taught with the Project Excell model with students who were taught in "comparison classrooms." The "comparison classrooms" continued to utilize the practices that were in place and did not make systematic use of Applied Behavioral Analysis and Direct Instruction procedures. Results indicated that students in the Project Excell classrooms demonstrated greater progress in all academic subjects than did students in the comparison classrooms.

Summary

The behavioral approaches described contain many similarities. Common elements include: (a) a direct focus on academic performance and competence; (b) opportunities for frequent responding or practice; (c) manipulation of antecedent conditions; (d) attention to sequencing of instructional material and content; and (e) active student participation. The most significant characteristic across the programmatic applications of behavioral principles is emphasis on careful sequencing of curriculum material to facilitate mastery, current content must be mastered before the next unit in the instructional sequence is introduced. There is continuous evaluation of student progress within the curriculum being taught. Commitment to continuous evaluation of student performance is a central part of behaviorally oriented programs in education (see also Chapter 10). Insistance on continuous monitoring of students performance permits teachers and administrators involved in the teaching experience to determine immediately whether procedures and materials are accomplishing the intended goal, and provides immediate feedback to students. As noted earlier having the student participate in the evaluation process can enhance individual learning.

Behavioral models view teaching as the means to plan, design, and execute plans for initiating change in student behavior. More specifically, teaching is developing and implementing plans to change student environment to produce changes in behavior. It is difficult for a teacher to make and execute plans when instructing typical learners; it is even more difficult to develop and implement plans for atypical learners. The use of programmatic applications of learning principles and knowledge of behavioral instructional materials permits teachers of atypical learners to individualize and monitor student progress more readily. Educational programs, such as Direct Instruction, Applied Behavioral Analysis, and Project Excell, provide teachers with the structure for managing the learning environment and for providing varying amounts of the content for instruction. Programmatic applications of behavioral principles provide the modeling, demonstration, guidance, and positive reinforcement necessary for effective teaching.

IMPLICATIONS FOR INSTRUCTION

Several implications are apparent from behavioral research on student acquisition of basic skills. These implications generally apply to all skill areas. The empirical investigations considered in this chapter suggest that to facilitate acquisition of basic skills the learning environment needs to include a number of events discussed later.

Skill Progression. Because, at one point in time, it is not feasible for students to master an entire lesson or content, educators have been aware of the need to organize and sequence instruction. Sequencing exposes a student to small, more manageable units. Careful attention must be given to the skill progression to be mastered. Studies on the acquisition of mathematics and reading skills suggest that learning of subordinate skills facilitates learning of higher order skills. Task analysis of various curriculum areas has facilitated careful focusing on the task to be taught. Some academic skills areas, such as written expression, do not require careful skill sequencing. Penmanship, spelling, and creative writing skills are somewhat independent. Although a student needs good penmanship and spelling skills to write creatively, the acquisition of penmanship and spelling skills does not enhance creative writing.

Clear Specification of What is to be Learned. The student must be aware of what is being taught. The literature supports the finding that what is taught is what is learned. Events that are the focus of management are learned concepts. A clear statement of what is to be learned facilitates reinforcing appropriate student learning behavior. Investigations on goal setting and self-instruction represent the most relevant examples of this requirement. Having students state what they are to learn also facilitates acquisition.

Planned, Immediate Delivery of Contingent Positive Reinforcement. The studies examined demonstrate that reinforced academic areas are the most rapidly acquired. It is important to articulate clearly what is to be learned and then to provide immediate feedback. When students are reinforced for being on task, they increase in on-task behavior; when students are rewarded for number of letters printed, they print more letters. However, accuracy or neatness does not improve and may deteriorate. When the focus of instruction is on accuracy and neatness, these are the skills that show change.

Frequent, Immediate Delivery of Feedback. Since practice assists students in learning and retaining responses, it is important that they practice correct responses. In such academic behaviors as the motor skill of printing letters, the lack of immediate feedback could permit a student to practice printing a letter incorrectly. Once a student has learned incorrectly how to print the letter "s", the student may have to unlearn that incorrect approach and still learn the correct response. Additionally, utilization of immediate feedback can serve to teach the student to monitor and correct his or her own behavior. Students can also be taught to evaluate their own work and provide their own feedback.

Demonstration, Permanent Models, and Guided Practice. During the initial phases of learning, the use of demonstrations (modeling), presence of examples, and guiding of the student's initial attempt to respond can be especially important. To the extent that the area of learning is new, the use of models and demonstrations is especially critical. Motor skills such as print and cursive handwriting are especially influenced by permanent models and by guided practice. Having the student trace over a model, copy a number below the model, and/or actually guiding the student's hand through the motor path represent ways to implement these important principles. The presence of models also provide a standard that students can utilize when they are attempting self-management. The students can check their own work against the model provided by the teacher. This is one major antecedent condition that teachers can manipulate that has a dramatic influence on student behavior.

Distributed Practice/Practice Over Time. When learning basic information or skills, the use of repeated practice over a period of time appears to facilitate initial learning and enhances retention. The field-based studies reviewed indicate that such academic skills as spelling words and learning basic vocabulary particularly benefit from distributed practice. Also, the practice of unlearned information is important. For example, daily testing on spelling words missed on the previous day's test or drilling on vocabulary missed during the previous session result in more rapid learning and longer retention than just practicing intensely prior to a test. The use of homework represents another method by which practice can be extended over time and increased in frequency.

Self-Monitoring of Performance. This is becoming increasingly recognized as an important aspect of academic skills instruction. Self-monitoring of academic behavior is a central element of self-instruction. An example of self-monitoring would be to have students check their letter printing using plastic overlays and then note on a progress sheet the correctness of their printed letters. The motivational properties of self-monitoring have also been noted. For example, as students observe and record their progress in mastering basic math facts, they are self rewarded by observing their progress and self reminded of how much they need to improve when performance is less than expected.

Direct Instruction. The old adage that what students are taught is what they will learn has received support from many investigations of students' learning. If students are to improve the neatness of print or the speed at which assignments are completed, it may be advantageous to make that the focus of instruction (and, incidently, the focus of reinforcement). If students are to learn to engage in self-instruction, what they are to do must be clearly stated, and self-instruction skills must be taught. Although related skills may also improve, it is not efficient to expect a student to develop comprehension skills during reading instruction if reading instruction focuses on correct oral reading.

Establishment of Time Limits for Assignment Completion. A clear statement of time limits is essential for drill and practice exercises. Time limits communicate to students that they have a fixed amount of time to accomplish a particular task. Without time limits, students are more likely to engage in other competing behaviors, and not complete the assigned task. Time limits are more critical for students who are having difficulties mastering content and who have not acquired self-instruction skills.

Self-Instruction/Self-Control. There are several components to self-management or self-instruction. The emerging research suggests that efficient students have developed strategies that assist them in dealing with the learning environment. The studies reviewed in this chapter have indicated that instructing students in the academic skill components of a task is not sufficient to bring about learning, students must be taught to talk themselves through activities (self-talk). Explicit reminders to students to self-talk is beneficial for academic actvities that have several components, such as reading comprehension, creative writing, or complex arithmetic problems.

Efficient and effective education of students required careful attention to the management of the learning process. The learning activity must be clearly identified and stated, and teachers must model, demonstrate, and guide as necessary. Specification of learning outcomes will facilitate the necessary reinforcement and feedback for relevant academic behaviors. Although self-instruction is an important aspect of learning, instruction in school has only infrequently included this in teaching. Teaching self-instruction must be combined with the teaching of basic skills. If practice is an essential requirement, opportunities for correct practice over time represents the optimal instructional combination for learning.

CONSIDERATIONS IN IMPLEMENTING BEHAVIORAL APPROACHES

Behavioral principles and technology have been successful in the laboratory and field settings. Therefore, they would readily and rapidly be adopted into educational practice. The assumption, widespread and rapid utilization of behavioral principles and procedures, was reinforced by awareness that results of successful demonstrations were being rapidly disseminated in a variety of professional outlets (i.e., professional journals, presentations at professional meetings, technical reports, indexing in various information services, such as ERIC, and inservice training programs in applied settings). There are, however, a number of considerations that influence and facilitate the implementation and effective utilization of any new area of knowledge, including behavioral modification procedures. Such factors as perceptions, situational and organizational fit, practicability, and degree of effort required to use the approach govern the implementation of behavioral approaches and other instructional management systems.

Challenge to Tradition

We cherish our traditions. Things that have been utilized and are ongoing are more likely to be continued. The fact that lemon juice could cure scurvy was discovered in 1601. More than 180 years passed before the British Navy began to employ citrus juice on a regualr basis, another 70 years passed before scurvy was eliminated in the Mercantile Marine. There was a time lag of 24 years between the advent of the cure and widespread implementation. Although we cannot state with any certainty why 264 years passed before citrus juice was made available on a widespread scale, we can comment on why psychological and educational principles and demonstrated effective applications have not received strong, general support.

The behavioral psychology literature, with its focus on frequent, immediate use of reinforcement for occurance of appropriate behavior, directly conflicts with the prevelant belief that people, especially students, are supposed to do certain things because they should do those things. Many of the more successful and better known applications of behavioral principles have stressed modifying student conduct, adding to the reluctance of many educators to explore behavioral applications. Even when professionals acknowledge the demonstrated effects of behavioral procedures, they continue to object to the ''technology'' aspect of the management approach and the demands imposed by the programmatic applications of behavioral principles. The perception exists that individual creativity is somehow inhibited. For many professionals, teaching is considered more an "art," not a "science." The idea of developing a technology or even a body of knowledge on how to manage the learning process represents a challenge to held beliefs.

The school organization, where student education takes place, needs to be considered carefully. The implementation of program applications of behavior management procedures on a large scale will directly impact on the entire system (Piersel & Gutkin, 1983). Budgets will need to be reexamined, and the recent purchase of a new curriculum may be seriously questioned, in view of the behavioral program being considered for use. System-wide commitment to an educational philosophy that conflicts with the behavioral principles being proposed for widespread application will tend to increase system resistance to a program such as Direct Instruction or Project Excell.

Behavioral modification and behavioral analysis are deceptively simple when initially encountered. Attempts by inexperienced and naive educators are likely to be ineffective for student learning. An incomplete understanding of modeling, demonstration, and token reinforcement by school professionals may result in a massive increase in work load without any consequent reinforcement to the involved teacher. Resources, such as knowledgeable consultants and educational opportunities, must be a planned part of the implementation of behavioral approaches to education (see also Chapter 8). In trying new procedures school personnel need the opportunity to make and correct mistakes without experiencing negative consequences. Teachers are seldom directly reinforced for classroom behavior that is the very source of implementation of effective instructional management procedures. Utilization of programmatic curriculum and structured classroom management approaches may create the perception that the teacher is not creative, or that the teacher must be undertrained. The reinforcement contingencies that are important for effecting student behavior may need to be restructured to encourage and maintain application of behavioral principles and programs.

Successful Implementation

Successful implementation of behavioral teaching practices requires consideration of the needs and philosophy of the system. Resources and skills available will directly impact on the type and extent of application of behavioral technology. The vocabulary of behavior modification and behavioral analysis is foreign to many educational personnel, parents, and students. Care must be taken to avoid such jargon to prevent the loss of important knowledge. The behavioral program must be feasible to the administrators and teachers involved in behavioral programming. Strategies and procedures that require increased effort, resources, or time will be viewed as less feasible.

If individual teacher flexibility can be maintained, behavioral approaches are more likely to be accepted in schools. Focusing on the use of positive consequences and the management of learning of new academic responses is important in marketing new approaches to the community. Although information from professional journals may be an important criterion for acceptability to behavioral researchers, it may not be important to others. It is important to demonstrate to parents, teachers, and administrators that behavioral approaches can bring about desired change. Targeting critical student behavior for a demonstration of a new program's importance may be essential for continued use. Efforts must be made to integrate behavioral approaches into existing programs. Many highly successful behavioral programs have been terminated when outside funding or support was no longer available. The failure to integrate behavioral procedures into the philosophy and structure of the classroom, school, and larger system leaves behavioral programs and techniques visible as separate entities; therefore, they are vulnerable. Teacher education programs need to change their curriculum content to provide prospective educators with the basic knowledge and philosophy regarding management of the learning process. Most importantly, the implementation of behavioral principles must be done within the context of effective management of the learning process. As behavioral principles continue to be applied in school settings, the dissemination of successful applications that focus on feasibility, acceptability, and effectiveness will be utilized and become increasingly important (see also Chapter 10).

REFERENCES

Aaron, B. A., & Bostow, D. E. (1978). Indirect facilitation of on-task behavior produced by contingent free-time academic productivity. *Journal of Applied Behavior Analysis, 11,* 197.

Albion, F. M., & Salzberg, C. L. (1982). The effects of self-instructions on the rate of correct addition problems with mentally retarded children. *Education and Treatment of Children, 5,* 121–131.

Atkeson, B. M., & Forehand, R. (1979). Home-based reinforcement programs designed to modify classroom behaviors: A review and methodological evaluation. *Psychological Bulletin, 86,* 1298–1308.

Axelrod, S. (1982). *Behavior modification for the classroom teacher* (2nd ed.). New York: McGraw-Hill.

Axelrod, S., & Paluska, T. (1975). A component analysis of the effects of a classroom game on spelling performance. In E. Ramp & G. Semb (Eds.), *Behavioral analysis: Areas of research and application* (pp. 277–282). New York: Prentice-Hall.

Ayllon, T., & Roberts, M. D. (1974). Eliminating discipline problems by strengthening academic performance. *Journal of Applied Behavior Analysis, 7,* 71–76.

Baer, D. M., & Bushell, D. (1981). The future of applied behavior analysis in the schools: Consider its past and ask a different question. *School Psychology Review, 10,* 259–270.

Ballard, K. D., & Glynn, T. (1975). Behavioral self-management in story writing with elementary school children. *Journal of Applied Behavior Analysis, 8,* 387–398.

Becker, W. C. (1977). Teacher reading and language to the disadvantaged: What we have learned from field research. *Harvard Educational Review, 47,* 518–543.

Becker, W. C. (1978). The national evaluation of Follow Through: Behavior therapy eased programs come out on top. *Education and Urban Society, 10,* 431–458.

Becker, W. C., & Carnine, D. W. (1982). Direct instruction: A behavioral theory model for comprehensive educational intervention with the disadvantaged. In S. W. Bijou & R. Ruiz (Eds.), *Behavior modification: Contributions to education* (pp. 145–211). Hillsdale, NJ: Lawrence Erlbaum Associates.

Becker, W. C., & Engelmann, S. (1979). Systems for basic instruction: Theory and application. In A. C. Catania & T. A. Brigham (Eds.), *Handbook of applied behavior analysis* (pp. 325–372). New York: Irvington.

Becker, W. C., Engelmann, S., Carnine, D. W., & Rhine, W. R. (1981). Direct instruction model. In W. R. Rhine (Ed.), *Making schools more effective: New directions from follow through* (pp. 96–118). New York: Academic Press.

Benowitz, M. L., & Busse, T. V. (1976). Material incentives and the learning of spelling in a typical school situation. *Journal of Educational Psychology, 61,* 24–26.

Benowitz, M. L., & Rosenfeld, J. G. (1973). Three types of incentives and the classroom learning of middle- and lower-class children. *Psychology in the Schools, 10,* 79–83.

Bereiter, C., & Engelmann, S. (1966). *Teaching disadvantaged children in the preschool.* Englewood Cliffs, NJ: Prentice-Hall.

Billingsley, F. F. (1977). The effects of self- and externally-imposed schedules of reinforcement on oral reading performance. *Journal of Learning Disabilities, 10,* 549–559.

Bijou, S. (1970). What psychology has to offer education—now. *Journal of Applied Behavior Analysis, 3,* 63–71.

Blechman, E. A., Kotanchik, W. L., & Taylor, C. J. (1981). Families and schools together: Early behavioral intervention with high risk children. *Behavior Therapy, 12,* 308–319.

Boyd, L. A., Keilbaugh, W. S., & Axelrod, S. (1981). The direct and indirect effects of positive reinforcement on on-task behavior. *Behavior Therapy, 12,* 80–92.

Brigham, T. H., Graubard, P. S., & Stans, A. (1972). Analysis of the effects of sequential reinforcement contingencies on aspects of composition. *Journal of Applied Behavior Analysis, 5,* 421–429.

Broden, M., Beasley, A., & Hall, R. V. (1978). In class spelling performance: Effects of home tutoring by a parent. *Behavior Modification, 2,* 511–530.

Brigham, T. A., Frinfrock, S. R., Breuing, M. K., & Bushell, D. (1972). The use of programmed materials in the analysis of academic contengencies. *Journal of Applied Behavior Analysis, 5,* 177–182.

Broughton, S. F., & Lahey, B. B. (1978). Direct and collateral effects of positive reinforcement response cost, and mixed contingencies for academic performance. *Journal of School Psychology, 16,* 126–136.

Campbell, J., & Willis, J. (1979). A behavioral program to teach writing in the regular classroom. *Education and Treatment of Children, 2,* 5–15.

Ceprano, M. A. (1981). A review of selected research on methods of teaching sight words. *The Reading Teacher, 34,* 314–321.

Clark, H. B., Boyd, S. B., McRae, J. W. (1975). A classroom program teaching disadvantaged youths to write bibliographic information. *Journal of Applied Behavior Analysis, 8,* 67–75.

Cohn, M., & Stricker, G. (1979). Reversal errors in strong, average, and weak letter names. *Journal of Learning Disabilities, 8,* 533–537.

Cole, L. (1946). *The elementary school subjects.* New York: Rinehart.

Coleman, J. S. (1966). Equality of educational opportunity. Washington, DC: U.S. Department of Health, Education, and Welfare, Office of Education.

Cullinan, D., & Lloyd, J. (1981). Strategy training: A structured approach to arithmetic instruction. *Exceptional Educational Quarterly, 3,* 41–49.

Cullinan, D., Epstein, M. H., & Lloyd, J. W. (1981). Strategy training: A structural approach to arithmetic instruction. *Exceptional Education Quarterly, 2,* 41–49.

Dalton, A. J., Rubino, C. A., & Hislop, M. W. (1973). Some effects of token rewards on school achievement of children with Down's syndrome. *Journal of Applied Behavior Analysis, 81,* 251–259.

Deno, S. L., & Chiang, B. (1979). An experimental analysis of the nature of reversals errors in children with severe learning disabilities. *Learning Disabilities Quarterly, 2,* 40–45.

Dickerson, E. A., & Creedon, C. F. (1981). Self-selection of standards by children: The relative effectiveness of pupil selected and teacher selected standards of performance. *Journal of Applied Behavior Analysis, 14,* 425–434.

Dineen, J. P., Clark, H. B., & Risley, T. R. (1977). Peer tutoring among elementary students: Educational benefits to tutor. *Journal of Applied Behavior Analysis, 10,* 231–238.

Eaton, M. D., & Haisch, L. (1974). *A comparison of the effects of new vs. error word drill on reading performance* (Working paper No. 23). Experimental Education Unit, Child Development and Mental Retardation Center, University of Washington.

Egeland, B. (1974). Training impulsive children in the use of more efficient scanning techniques. *Child Development, 45,* 165–171.

Egner, A. W., Burdett, C. S., & Fox, W. L. (1972). *Observing and measuring behavior.* Austin, TX: Austin Writers Group.

Engelmann, S., & Carnine, D. (1982). *Theory of instruction: Principles and applications.* New York: Irvington.

Fauke, J., Bennett, J., Bowers, M. A., & Sulzer-Azaroff, B. (1973). Improvement of handwriting and letter recognition skills: A behavior modification procedure. *Journal of Learning Disabilities, 6,* 296–300.

Ferritor, D. E., Buckholdt, D., Hamblin, R. L., & Smith, L. (1972). The noneffects of contingent reinforcement of attending behavior on work accomplished. *Journal of Applied Behavior Analysis, 5,* 7–17.

Fink, W. T., & Carnine, D. W. (1975). Control of arithmetic errors using information feedback and graphing. *Journal of Applied Behavior Analysis, 8,* 461.

Foxx, R. M., & Jones, J. R. (1978). A remediation program for increasing the spelling achievement of elementary and junior high school students. *Behavior Modification, 2,* 211–230.

Hallahan, D. P., Lloyd, J. W., Kneedler, R. D., & Marshall, K. J. (1982). A comparison of the effects of self versus teacher assessment of on-task behavior. *Behavior Therapy, 13,* 715–723.

Hallahan, D. P., Lloyd, J., Kosiewicz, M. M., Kaufman, J. M., & Graves, A. W. (1979). Self-monitoring of attention as a treatment for learning disabled boy's off-task behavior. *Learning Disabilities Quarterly, 2,* 24–32.

Hallahan, D. P., Marshall, K. J., & Lloyd, J. W. (1981). Self-recording during group instruction: Effects of attention to task. *Learning Disabilities Quarterly, 4,* 407–413.

Hansen, C. L., & Eaton, M. D. (1978). Reading. In N. G. Haring, T. C. Lovitt, M. D. Eaton, & C. L. Hansen (Eds.), *The fourth R: Research in the classroom* (pp. 41–92). Columbus, OH: Charles E. Merrill.

Haring, N. G., Lovitt, T. C., Eaton, M. P., & Hansen, C. (1978). *The fourth R: Research in the classroom.* Columbus, Ohio: Charles E. Merrill.

Harris, V. W., & Sherman, J. A. (1974). Homework assignments, consequences, and classroom performance in social studies and mathematics. *Journal of Applied Behavior Analysis, 7,* 505–519.

Hasazi, J. E., & Hasazi, S. E. (1972). Effects of teacher attention on digit reversal behavior in an elementary school child. *Journal of Applied Behavior Analysis, 5,* 157–162.

Hay, W. M., Hay, L. & Nelson, R. O. (1977). Direct and collateral changes in on-task and academic behavior resulting from on-task academic contingencies. *Behavior Therapy, 8,* 431–444.

Helwig, J. J., Jones, J. C., Norman, J. E., & Cooper, J. O. (1976). The measurement of manuscript letter strokes. *Journal of Applied Behavior Analysis, 9,* 231–236.

Hopkins, B. L., Schutte, R. C., & Garten, K. L. (1971). The effects of access to a playroom on the rate and quality of printing and writing of first and second grade students. *Journal of Applied Behavior Analysis, 4,* 77–88.

Iwata, B. A., & Bailey, J. S. (1974). Reward versus cost token systems: An analysis of the effects on students and teacher. *Journal of Applied Behavior Analysis, 7,* 567–582.

Jencks, C., Smith, M., Acland, H., Cohen, D., Gintis, H., Heyns, B. & Michelson, S. (1972). *Inequality: A reassessment of the effects of family and schooling in America.* New York: Basic Books.

Jenkins, J. R., & Larson, K. (1979). Evaluating error correction procedures for oral reading. *Journal of Special Education, 13,* 145–156.

Johnston, M. B., Whitman, T. L., & Johnston, M. B. (1980). Teaching addition and subtraction to mentally retarded children: A self instructional program. *Applied Research in Mental Retardation 1,* 141–160.

Jones, J. C., Trap, J., & Cooper, J. O. (1977). Students' self recording of manuscript letter strokes. *Journal of Applied Behavior Analysis, 10,* 509–514.

Kauffman, J. M., Hallahan, D. P., Haas, K., Brame, T., & Boren, R. (1978). Imitating children's errors to improve their spelling performance. *Journal of Learning Disabilities, 11,* 217–222.

Kazdin. A. E. (1982). Applying behavioral principles in the schools. In C. R. Reynolds & T. B. Gutkin (Eds.), *Handbook of school psychology* (pp. 501–529). New York: Wiley.

Kerr, M. M., & Lambert, D. L. (1982). Behavior modification of children's written language. In M. Hersen, R. M. Eisler, & P. M. Miller (Eds.), *Progress in behavior modification* (Vol. 13, pp. 79–108). New York: Academic Press.

Kirby, C. K., Holborn, S. W., & Bushby, H. T. (1981). Word game bingo: A behavioral treatment package for improving textual responding to sight words. *Journal of Applied Behavior Analysis, 14,* 317–326.

Klein, R. D. (1979). Modifying academic performance in the grade school. In M. Hersen, R. M. Eisler, & P. M. Miller (Eds.), *Progress in behavior modification* (Vol. 8, 293–321). New York: Academic Press.

Kosiewicz, M. M., Hallahan, D. P., & Lloyd, J. (1981). The effects of LD students' treatment choice on handwriting performance. *Learning Disabilities Quarterly, 4,* 281–286.

Kosiewicz, M. M., Hallahan, D. P., Lloyd, J., & Graves, A. W. (1982). Effects of self-instruction and self-correction procedures on handwriting performance. *Learning Disabilities Quarterly, 5,* 71–78.

LaForge, J. F., Pree, M. M., & Hasazi, S. E. (1975). The ease of minimal objectives as an on going monitoring system to evaluate student progress. In E. Ramp & G. Sembs (Eds.), *Behavioral analysis: Areas of research and application* (pp. 261–268). New York: Prentice-Hall.

Lahey, B. B., Busemeyer, M. K., O'Hara, C., & Beggs, V. E. (1977). Treatment of severe perceptual-motor disorders in children diagnosed as learning disabled. *Behavior Modification, 1,* 123–140.

Lahey, B. B., & Drabman, R. S. (1974). Facilitation of the acquisition and retention of sight word vocabulary through token reinforcement. *Journal of Applied Behavior Analysis, 7,* 307–312.

Lahey, B. B., & McNees, M. P. (1975). Letter-discrimination errors in kindergarten through third grade: Assessment and operant training. *Journal of Special Education, 9,* 191–199.

Lahey, B. B., McNees, M. P., & Schnelle, J. F. (1977). The functional independence of three reading behaviors: A behavior systems analysis. *Corrective and Social Psychiatry, 23,* 44–47.

Lamb, P. (1971). *Guiding children's language.* Dubuque, IA: W. C. Brown.

Lloyd, J., Cullinan, D., Herns, E. D., & Epstein, M. H. (1981). Direct instruction: Effects on oral and written language comprehension. *Learning Disability Quarterly, 3,* 71–76.

Lloyd, J., Epstein, M. H., & Cullinan, D. (1981). Direct teaching for learning disabilities. In J. Gottlieb & S. S. Strichart (Eds.), *Developmental theory and research in learning disabilities* (pp. 278–300). Baltimore: University Park Press.

Lloyd, J., Saltzman, N. J., & Kaufman, J. M. (1981). Predictable generalization in academic learning as a result of preskills and strategy training. *Learning Disabilities Quarterly, 4,* 203–216.

Lovitt, T. C. (1973). Self-management projects with children with behavioral disabilities. *Journal of Learning Disabilities, 6,* 138–150.

Lovitt, T. C. (1975). Applied behavior analysis and learning disabilities. *Journal of Learning Disabilities, 8,* 504–518.

Lovitt, T. C. (1981). Graphing academic performance of mildly handicapped children. In S. Bijou & R. Ruiz (Eds.), *Behavior modification: Contributions to education* (pp. 111–143). Hillsdale, NJ: Lawrence Erlbaum Associates.

Lovitt, T. C., & Curtiss, K. A. (1968). Effects of manipulating an antecedent event on mathematics response rate. *Journal of Applied Behavior Analysis, 1,* 329–333.

Lovitt, T. C., & Esveldt, K. A. (1970). The relative effects on math performance of single and multiple schedule: A case study. *Journal of Applied Behavior Analysis, 3,* 261–270.

Lovitt, T. C., Guppy, T. C., & Blattner, J. E. (1969). The use of a free-time contingency with fourth graders to increase spelling accuracy. *Behavior, Research and Therapy, 7,* 151–156.

Maggs, A., & Morath, P. (1976). Effects of direct verbal instruction on intellectual development of moderately retarded children: A 2-year study. *Journal of Special Education, 10,* 355–364.

Maloney, K. B., & Hopkins, B. L. (1973). The modification of sentence structure and its relationship to subjective judgment of creativity in writing. *Journal of Applied Behavior Analysis, 6,* 425–434.

Marholin, D. H., & Steinman, W. M. (1977). Stimulus control in the classroom as a function of the behavior reinforced. *Journal of Applied Behavior Analysis, 10,* 465–478.

Meichenbaum, D., & Asarnow, J. (1979). Cognitive-behavioral modification and meta cognitive development: Implications for the classroom. In P. C. Kendall & S. D. Hollon (Eds.), *Cognitive-behavioral interventions: Theory, research, and procedures* (pp. 11–26). New York: Academic Press.

Meichenbaum, D., & Goodman, J. (1971). Training impulsive children to talk to themselves: A means of developing self-control. *Journal of Abnormal Psychology, 77,* 115–126.

National Commission of Excellence in Education (1983). *A nation at risk: The imperative for educational reform.* Washington, DC: U.S. Department of Education.

Pacquin, M. J. (1978). The effects of pupil self graphing on academic performance. *Education and Treatment of Children, 1,* 5–16.

Piersel, W. C. (1979). *Sight word vs. passage approach to teaching a severely learning disabled child to read.* Unpublished manuscript, University of Nebraska, Lincoln.

Piersel, W. C., & Kratochwill, T. R. (1979). Self-observation and behavior change: Applications to academic and behavior problems through behavioral consultation. *Journal of School Psychology, 12,* 151–161.

Rapport, M. S., & Bostow, D. E. (1976). The effects of access to special activities on the performance in four categories of academic tasks with third-grade students. *Journal of Applied Behavior Analysis, 9,* 372.

Reith, H. J., Axelrod, S., Anderson, R., Hathaway, F., Wood, K., & Fitzgerald, C. (1974). Influence of distributed practice and daily testing on weekly spelling tests. *Journal of Educational Research, 68,* 73–77.

Rose, T. L., Koorland, M. A., & Epstein, M. H. (1982). A review of applied behavior analysis interventions with learning disabled children. *Education and Treatment of Children, 5,* 41–58.

Ross, A. O. (1981). *Child behavior therapy: Principles, procedures, and empirical basis.* New York: Wiley.

Ryback, D., & Staats, A. W. (1970). Parents as behavior therapy technicians in treating reading deficits (dyslexia). *Journal of Behavior Therapy and Experimental Psychiatry, 1,* 109–119.

Salzberg, B. H., Wheeler, A. A., Devar, L. T., & Hopkins, B. L. (1971). The effects of intermittent feedback and intermittent contingent access to play on printing of kindergarten children. *Journal of Applied Behavior Analysis, 4,* 163–171.

Schunk, D. H. (1981). Modeling and attributional effects on children's achievement: A self-efficacy analysis. *Journal of Educational Psychology, 73,* 93–105.

Sidman, M., & Kirk, B. (1974?). Letter reversals in naming, writing, and matching to sample. *Child Development, 45,* 616–625.

Sindelar, P. T., Honsaker, M. S., & Jenkins, J. R. (1982). Response costs and reinforcement contingencies of managing the behavior of distractable children in tutorial settings. *Learning Disabilities Quarterly, 5,* 3–13.

Singh, N. N., & Singh, J. S. (1984). Antecedent control of oral reading errors and self-corrections by mentally retarded children. *Journal of Applied Behavior Analysis, 17,* 111–119.

Singh, N. N., Singh, J. S., & Winton, A. S. (1984). Positive practice overcorrection of oral reading errors. *Behavior Modification, 8,* 23–37.

Skinner, B. F. (1984). The shame of American Education. *American Psychologist, 39,* 947–954.

Smith, D. D. (1979). The improvement of children's oral reading through the use of teacher modeling. *Journal of Learning Disabilities, 12,* 39–42.

Smith, D. D., & Lovitt, T. C. (1975). The use of modeling techniques to influence the acquisition of computational arithmetic skills in learning disabled children. In E. Ramp & G. Semb (Eds.), *Behavior analysis: Areas of research and application.* Englewood Cliffs, NJ: Prentice-Hall.

Stowitschek, C. E., & Stowitschek, J. J. (1979). Evaluating handwriting performance: The student helps the teacher. *Journal of Learning Disabilities, 12,* 203–206.

Stromer, R. (1975). Modifying number and letter reversals in elementary school children. *Journal of Applied Behavior Analysis, 8,* 211.

Tawney, J. W. (1972). Training letter discrimination in four-year-old children. *Journal of Applied Behavior Analysis, 5,* 455–465.

Taylor, W. F., & Hoedt, K. L. (1966). The effect of praise upon the quality and quantity of creative writing. *Journal of Educational Research, 60,* 80–83.

Thompson, E. W., & Galloway, C. G. (1970). Material reinforcement and success in spelling. *Elementary School Journal, 70,* 395–398.

Trap, J. J., Milner-Davis, P., Joseph, S., & Cooper, J. O. (1978). The effects of feedback and consequence on transitional cursive letter formation. *Journal of Applied Behavior Analysis, 14,* 381–394.

Van Houten, R. (1980). *Learning through feedback.* New York: Human Sciences Press.

Van Houten, R., & McKillop, C. (1977). An extension of the effects of the performance feedback system with secondary school students. *Psychology in the Schools, 14,* 480–484.

Van Houten, R., Morrison, E., Jarvis, R., & McDonald, M. (1974). The effects of explicit timing and feedback on compositional response rates in elementary school children. *Journal of Applied Behavior Analysis, 7,* 547–555.

Van Houton, R., & Thompson, C. (1976). The effects of explicit timing on math performance. *Journal of Applied Behavior Analysis, 9,* 227–230.

Whitman, T., & Johnston, M. B. (1983). Teaching addition and subtraction with regrouping to educable mentally retarded children: A group self-instructional training program. *Behavior Therapy, 14,* 127–143.

Williams, R. L., & Fry, B. L. (1976). The differential effects of tracing prompts and a training package in the remediation of letter reversals. In T. A. Brigham, R. Hawkins, J. W. Scott, & T. F. McLaughlin (Eds.), *Behavior analysis in education: Self-control and reading.* Dubuque, IA: Kendall/Hunt.

Willis, J. (1974). Effects of systematic feedback and self-charting on a remedial tutorial program in reading. *The Journal of Experimental Education, 42,* 83–85.

Winett, R. A., & Winkler, R. C. (1972). Current behavior modification in the classroom: Be still, be quiet, be docile. *Journal of Applied Behavior Analysis, 5,* 499–504.

4 Affective and Social Education

Susan G. Forman

The basic mission of the public schools is to prepare youth to function effectively in society. Traditionally, the primary objective of schools has been academic education; however, effective adult participation in society requires more than academic knowledge and technical competence. Understanding of and competence in affective and social responding are essential for functioning in a complex societal context. Emotional reactions provide the basis for behavioral patterns in all settings including those related to vocational, family, and leisure activities. The nature of society implies that a large percentage of any individual's time will be spent in social interactions. Affective and social education programs focus on the development of student awareness, understanding, and control of emotions or feelings, and on the development of student ability to interact appropriately and constructively with others in a social context. Affective and social education programs are appropriate and necessary if schools are to achieve their socialization mission.

In addition, affective and social functioning has been shown to have a major impact on school adjustment and academic achievement. A number of studies have demonstrated that emotional and social functioning is related to academic success and that training in these areas can have a positive effect on achievement levels (Cartledge & Milburn, 1978). Most teachers know that inappropriate and unconstructive emotional and social responses interfere with task completion and mastery of academic subject matter. Negative emotional reactions to specific academic tasks, the school environment, and situations outside of school can be detrimental to classroom performance. Inappropriate interpersonal behavior can also disrupt the learning process for the individual student and others who share the educational setting.

Affective and social education consists of training in a number of areas. Focus has been on decreasing inappropriate emotional and interpersonal responses and on increasing constructive emotional responses and social skills. Affective interventions in the schools have resulted in decreases in school-related fears, anxiety responses, or anger as goals. Some programs have been prevention-oriented, the goal being the general improvement of emotional health and emotional self-control. Social interventions have focused on decreasing aggression, disruption, social withdrawal, and immature behaviors (e.g., short attention span, passivity) and on increasing social skills that include interpersonal interaction skills (e.g., sharing, having a conversation) and task-related social skills (e.g., attending, verbal participation in academic classroom activities). Prevention oriented social skills programs have focused on general improvement in social problem-solving and interpersonal skills.

Affective and social education programs have been conducted with the entire public school population from preschool children through high school students. The range of students included ''normal'' nonproblem students, students with mild emotional and/or social problems attending regular classes, emotionally and/or behaviorally handicapped students in special education classes, and students with other types of handicapping conditions (e.g., learning disabilities, mental retardation) that have emotional and/or social components.

The content of and procedures used in affective and social education programs have been derived from psychological theories about the nature of human behavior and adjustment. Thus, approaches to affective and social education have been fairly diverse. Psychodynamic approches have been based on the concept that individuals have inner needs and drives that may clash with environmental presses and produce emotional distress and that insight concerning the nature of this conflict will lead to improved functioning. Humanistic approaches are based on the concept that disturbance occurs when the individual does not attain his/her potential and emphasize the importance of making the most of one's life. Psychosocial approaches are based on the idea that disturbance is a reaction to interpersonal conflict and attempt to enhance the individual's ability to communicate. The behavioral approach to affective and social education views inappropriate and unconstructive behavior as behavior that developed through the learning process and is amenable to change through new learning. The behavioral approach encompasses a variety of techniques that have been conceptualized in four sets of procedures: applied behavior analysis procedures, counterconditioning procedures, social-learning theory procedures, and cognitive-behavior modification procedures (Kazdin & Wilson, 1978). Use of these procedures to improve affective and social functioning of students within the school setting is described in the remainder of this chapter.

THE BEHAVIORAL APPROACH

Applied Behavior Analysis-Environmental Control

Applied behavior analysis has been defined as the application of interventions to alter behaviors of clinical and social importance (Baer, Wolf, & Risley, 1968). These interventions typically rely on techniques of operant conditioning and are the most widely used behavioral procedures in educational settings. A basic assumption of applied behavior analysis is that behavior is a function of its consequences. The procedures are based on the relationship between specific overt behaviors and environmental events. Applied behavior analysis programs are based on the idea that behavior can be modified by systematic manipulation of antecedents and consequences.

Reinforcement Techniques.   Positive reinforcement is a consequence that increases the probability that a specified behavior will occur in the future. Social, activity, primary, and token reinforcers have been used extensively in school settings to improve affective and social functioning by increasing deficit behaviors.

Social reinforcers consist of consequences, such as attention, praise, physical contact, and positive facial expressions. An example of the use of social reinforcers is reported by Allen, Hart, Buell, Harris, and Wolf (1964) in a case study of a child who did not interact with peers during play and demanded teacher attention. Interactions with other children were increased by giving the child teacher attention only in response to peer interactions. No attention was given if the child played by herself or attempted to interact with an adult. Marlowe, Madsen, Bowen, Reardon, and Logue (1978) also demonstrated the impact of teacher attention with low achieving, disruptive seventh grade students. Their study showed that teacher attention in the form of approval for acceptable social behavior and good academic performance was effective in reducing the students' unacceptable, off-task behavior.

Use of social reinforcement in an educational setting has a number of advantages. There is no economic cost, and parents and the general public are likely to approve of use of this procedure, it is fairly easy and quick to administer, and students do not tire of praise. However, there are limitations. Not all students respond positively to teacher approval or praise. Because of previous experiences some children and adolescents will not work for adult approval and may attempt to provoke reprimands in an effort to gain peer status. In addition, not all teachers are able to communicate genuine positive social reinforcement and may need training and assistance in this area. Praise statements should vary in content so that repetition is avoided and students do not become habituated to a given statement. Statements should specify the behaviors being praised (e.g., ''I really like the way you're sharing your crayons with Johnny.'') Such descriptive praise aids the student in identifying and responding to the reinforcement contingency and should be used even when other forms of reinforcement are administered.

Activity reinforcers have also been used to improve children's affective and social functioning. Use of activities is based on the Premack Principle (Premack, 1965), which states that a low probability behavior can be increased when its execution is followed by an opportunity to engage in a preferred behavior. For example, Long and Williams (1973) successfully used free time to alter disruptive classroom behavior. During free time students were allowed to talk to peers, play games, and read magazines if they cooperated and obeyed classroom rules.

Preferred activities that are readily available in educational settings include games, leisure reading materials, records, film strips, drawing and painting, running errands, and extra time at recess. The greatest advantage of using a reinforcement procedure in which the Premack Principle is employed is that potential reinforcers are always present. There are always some activities that students prefer to engage in. The teacher's main task is to make access to preferred activities contingent on performance of the target behavior. Because reinforcing activities can be varied, students do not usually tire of such systems. There are, however, some limitations of use of activity reinforcers in school settings that need to be considered before such a program is implemented. Because some activity reinforcers may disrupt ongoing classroom activities, they often cannot be used immediately. In addition, if students are engaging in reinforcing activities they may distract other students from their work. Adequate space needs to be provided for students to engage in reinforcing activities and the students need to be supervised. If personnel and space constraints are present it presents problems in use of some types of activity reinforcers.

Edible reinforcers have also been used in school settings. For example, Grieger (1970) increased appropriate classroom behavior and decreased physical and verbal aggression of an entire class. He used candy as a reward at the end of each class period during which specified disruptive behaviors were not demonstrated. There are some important issues that need to be considered when using edible reinforcers in schools. First, it is necessary to get parent permission. Some children may have health problems or food related allergies. Use of nonnutritious food may interfere with children's appetites and their diets may become unbalanced. Satiation, the reduction of the effectiveness of a reinforcer that occurs after it is used frequently, is also a problem, and repeated use of an edible reinforcer can become expensive.

When other types of reinforcers fail, many students will make an effort to earn tangible reinforcers, such as small toys, school supplies, or trinkets. Tangible reinforcers are often impractical to deliver immediately after the target behavior occurs; therefore, they are usually used within the context of a token reinforcement system. Tokens are tangible items that have no intrinsic value, but acquire value when they can be exchanged for an object or event that is reinforcing. A variety of items, such as chips, stars, play money, stamps, points, checkmarks, have been used as tokens. A reinforcement system based on tokens is called a token economy. In this type of program, tokens are used to reinforce desired behaviors immediately. The tokens can be accumulated and used later to purchase back-up reinforcers that may include a variety of objects. activities, or consumables.

Token economies have been widely implemented in both regular and special education classes. For example, Iwata and Bailey (1974) found that token systems were effective in controlling the inappropriate social behavior (off-task and rule violations) of mildly handicapped special education students. Token programs have also been used to increase cooperative play (Hart, Reynolds, Baer, Brawley, & Harris, 1968) and nonaggressive play (Horton, 1970). A token program implemented with junior high school students who had serious behavior problems, resulted in the reduction of the number of expulsions, suspensions, and grade failures. (Heaton & Safer, 1982; Safer, Heaton, & Parker, 1981). Durability of the behavior change also was demonstrated. Students who participated in the token program showed higher rates of entrance into high school, better school attendance, better classroom conduct, and lower rates of withdrawal from school relative to control subjects.

Use of token systems has a number of advantages. First, token systems tend to be more effective than other types of reinforcement programs. If a variety of back-up reinforcers are available, a token system can accommodate the preference of an entire classroom and satiation is not likely to be a problem. Tokens are fairly easy to administer and the number of tokens given can be adjusted to the difficulty of the target behavior. Despite these advantages, the development of a token program can be complex. The behavior modifier must be willing to develop a system in which specific numbers of tokens are administered for specified target behaviors and an exchange system for regulating back-up reinforcers. To work effectively, the token economy must be precisely planned and consistently administered.

In a recent review of research on use of the token economy, Kazdin (1982) emphasized the importance of training and monitoring staff to insure that token programs are carried out effectively. Kazdin also pointed out that reports have indicated that token economies deteriorate when supervision of program execution is withdrawn or is not present from the beginning of the program. Thompson, Brassell, Persons, Tucker, and Rollins (1974) reported on token economies that were implemented in elementary school classrooms and were initially successful in altering student classroom behavior. The experimental investigators had provided resources for supervision and data collection; however, after the initial implementation period these resources were withdrawn. When the investigators returned 1 year later for follow-up assessment, the programs had been discontinued and teacher and student behavior had returned to preprogram rates. This type of implementation procedure is fairly typical in educational settings. A consultant or research investigator may provide initial training and support for classroom implementation; however, after initial behavior change in the students the support is withdrawn. Kazdin (1982) also points out that when token economies are implemented in institutional settings, such as schools, limited budgets for back-up reinforcers and insufficient personnel to reward students as frequently as needed become problematic. Continued resources and support for the program implementor (usually the teacher) are needed to insure program integrity (i.e., that the program is carried out as intended) and program effectiveness.

Reinforcement techniques also have been used to reduce excess behaviors as a means of improving affective and social functioning. Three reinforcement procedures have focused on decreasing undesirable behaviors: differential reinforcement of low rates of responding (DRL), differential reinforcement of other behaviors (DRO), and reinforcement of alternative responses (ALT-R).

DRL is used when reduction, but not complete elimination, of the target behavior is desired. The individual is reinforced if he/she exhibits the target behavior at or below a specified frequency. If the target behavior is exhibited at a greater level than specified, the individual does not receive the reinforcement. Deitz and Repp (1973) used DRL to decrease the rate at which high school students engaged in social conversation instead of conversation about academic work during a discussion period. They also reported effective reduction of "talking out" behavior (talking, singing, humming without the teacher's permission) for trainable mentally retarded youngsters as a result of use of DRL. The children had a baseline of 32.7 "talk-outs" per minute. When the class made five or fewer talk-outs in 50 minutes, each member would receive two pieces of candy. Talking-out declined to an average of 3.13 instances per session.

A time-based DRL system allows for progressive reduction in inappropriate behavior. For example, in the Deitz and Repp (1973) study with high school students the procedure was implemented in four phases. During each phase fewer social discussions were allowed until the allowable number of discussions was zero during the final phase. A major disadvantage of a DRL system is that it focuses attention on the undesirable behavior and emissions of desirable behaviors may be overlooked.

DRO also is used to reduce undesirable behavior. This procedure involves reinforcing the individual for any behavior except the one to be suppressed. After a specified period of time, if the target behavior is not occurring or has not occurred, any other response is reinforced. For example, Repp and Deitz (1974) report two cases in which a DRO program was used to reduce aggressive behavior. In both cases, if the children did not display aggressive behavior during the specified time period, they were rewarded with stars that were exchangeable for tangible rewards. DRO reduces behavior rapidly; however, because any behavior other than the target behavior may be reinforced it is possible that the child will receive reinforcement for inappropriate behaviors. To prevent this, the teacher or therapist can specify that the child will not be reinforced for intervals during which highly undesirable behavior occurs, even if the target behavior has not been emitted.

ALT-R does not present this problem. ALT-R consists of strengthening a behavior that offers an incompatible alternative to the unwanted behavior. By increasing the frequency of a desirable incompatible behavior the frequency of the target behavior will decrease. Ayllon, Smith, and Rogers (1979) present an example of treatment of school phobia that relied, in part, on ALT-R. An assessment of the situation indicated that the school phobia was being maintained in part by positive consequences (e.g., extra contact with mother, fun at a neighbor's house) that resulted from avoiding school. The treatment involved providing positive reinforcement (e.g., favorite foods and activities) for school attendance. Kirby and Toler (1970) report a case study in which ALT-R was used to decrease the isolated behavior of a preschooler. He was reinforced after he passed out candy to his classmates and subsequently was found to spend a greater amount of time in social interactions.

Extinction and Punishment Techniques.   Extinction involves reducing behavior by withholding reinforcement for a behavior that has previously been reinforced. Extinction has been found to effectively reduce a variety of undesirable school behaviors, such as disruption, aggression, and anxiety-related behavior. For example, withholding reinforcing teacher attention has been shown to control aggressive interactions in a nursery school class (Brown & Elliott, 1965). School phobia also has been treated with extinction combined with reinforcement of appropriate behaviors. Hersen (1970) reported a case in which it was determined that school phobic behavior was being maintained in part by additional attention given the child. The attention was given by the child's mother coaxing him to go to school and by school personnel attending to crying and anxiety responses. Treatment included training the parent and school guidance counselors to ignore the child's crying and other school-related avoidant behavior and to verbally reinforce the child for appropriate coping behavior.

To utilize extinction effectively in school settings the behavior modifier needs to be aware of the manner in which individuals respond to extinction procedures. Extinction usually does not have an immediate effect. When the reinforcing consequences are removed, the inappropriate behavior will continue at first and may increase in rate and intensity. A brief period of aggression may also accompany extinction in the initial stage. For example, when the teacher begins to ignore the inappropriate behavior a student who is used to gaining teacher attention when he talks out in class, at first may talk out more frequently, or louder, or in exasperation poke the student next to him. However, continued ignoring will decrease the inappropriate behavior. Combining extinction with reinforcement of appropriate behavior will enhance the process.

The major task in designing an effective extinction program is identification of the consequences that have been reinforcing the undesirable behavior. Use of extinction in the form of ignoring misbehavior is frequently attempted in school settings. However, many of these attempts fail, because attention was never demonstrated to act as a reinforcer for the misbehavior. In a classroom, if teacher attention has not been demonstrated to act as a reinforcer for disruptive behavior, withholding attention for disruptive behavior does not constitute extinction. Thus, identification of the reinforcers are crucial. School behavior is controlled by a complex set of contingencies. The educator must be aware that in addition to teacher behavior, peers, parents, or others in the student's community may be providing social reinforcement for behavior that school personnel may wish to extinguish.

Punishment procedures, which involve use of aversive consequences to decrease behavior, also are used in school programs if the goal is improved social functioning. These procedures are usually used as one part of a comprehensive program that also includes positive reinforcement for appropriate constructive behaviors. Punishment procedures that have been used in school settings include negative teacher attention, response cost, time-out, and overcorrection.

In attempts to decrease inappropriate behavior in school settings the most frequently used procedure is negative teacher attention. This procedure consists of verbal reprimands, statements of disapproval, negative voice tone, gestures, and facial expression. Negative attention has been shown to be effective in suppressing inappropriate behavior when used along with other behavioral procedures. For example, Jones and Miller (1974) illustrated that negative teacher attention, which consisted of a brief verbalization, gestures, and facial expression indicating disapproval, and positive attention for appropriate behavior, decreased disruption in behavior disordered children. The manner in which reprimands are given may have an impact on their effectiveness in reducing behavior. O'Leary and Becker (1968) and O'Leary, Kaufman, Kass, and Drabman (1970) showed that quiet or soft reprimands are more effective than loud reprimands. Loud reprimands may draw reinforcing attention of classmates to the misbehaving student. Negative teacher attention alone, however, has not been shown consistently to be effective in improving classroom behavior; therefore, it should be used in conjunction with positive reinforcement for appropriate behavior.

Response cost, another behavior reduction procedure, involves withdrawal of specified amounts of a reinforcer contingent on performance of an undesirable behavior. Rapport, Murphy, and Bailey (1978) used response cost to decrease off-task behavior. Each time an incident of off-task behavior occurred the teacher removed 1 minute of a possible 30 minutes of free time allowed students. In school settings response cost frequently involves a loss of tokens. Iwata and Bailey (1974) used a response cost program to decrease disruptive behavior in an elementary school special education class. Students received tokens that could be traded for snacks and inexpensive toys. They lost tokens for violating class rules, such as getting out of seat, calling out, and disturbing peers. The program substantially increased appropriate social behavior and decreased disruptive behavior in the classroom.

Response cost programs can be implemented in two ways. Reinforcers can initially be provided noncontingently and then withdrawn for inappropriate behavior; alternatively, students can be required to earn the reinforcers. Token reinforcement combined with response cost is usually more effective than either procedure used alone. When combination token reinforcement/response cost programs are used, students must be allowed to build up a reverse of tokens and to have the opportunity to sample the back-up reinforcers.

Time-out is a procedure in which access to all sources of reinforcement are removed contingent on performance of an undesirable target behavior. During time-out, the child does not have access to positive reinforcers that are normally available in a classroom or school setting. Time-out can consist of removing the child totally from the situation or moving him/her to the periphery of the activity. Time-out has been very effective in altering disruptive social behaviors in school settings. For example, Lahey, McNees, and McNees (1973) report a case in which a classroom teacher modified the obscene vocalizations and facial twitches of a 10-year-old boy through use of time-out. Time-out consisted of removing the student to a time-out room for a minimum of 5 minutes, until he was quiet for 1 minute. The room was 4 ft × 10 ft, well lighted, stripped of all objects, and connected to the classroom. Drabman and Spitalnik (1973) used a time-out procedure in a classroom with three children who were residents of a children's psychiatric hospital. Out-of-seat disruption and aggressive behavior in the classroom were decreased substantially as a result of the intervention. When a student violated previously determined rules, the teacher told him that he must leave the classroom because of his misbehavior. A teaching assistant then escorted the child to a small room. After the child had spent 10 minutes in the room he could return to the classroom.

If time-out is to be used effectively, the behavior modifier must be certain that all sources of reinforcements are removed from time-out settings. Standing outside of the classroom has frequently been used by teachers in an attempt to implement time-out. However, in this situation many forms of reinforcement, such as talking to other youngsters and school staff that pass by, may be available. Time-out can effectively reduce behavior only if the student's environment changes from one in which reinforcement is available to one in which it is not. Time-out from an aversive situation, such as a class which a student intensely dislikes, will not decrease inappropriate behavior.

The duration of time-out should be relatively brief. Short time-outs (i.e., 2 minutes) have been shown to be effective; long time-outs do not necessarily increase the effectiveness of the procedure. Duration should be limited to 15 minutes. When isolation time-out is to be used, written parental permission should be obtained. The time-out room must be safe, comfortable, well ventilated and approximately 6 ft × 6 ft. Someone must monitor the child during time-out to ensure safety (Gelfand & Hartman, 1984).

Because time-out that involves isolation can result in lost learning time and opportunities, alternatives to isolation have been developed. These procedures let students remain in classroom surroundings. For example, the teacher may have the child wear a time-out ribbon to indicate that the child is receiving time-out (Foxx & Shapiro, 1978). Children also might be given brightly colored cards that can be removed to indicate time-out (Spitalnik & Drabman, 1976). Time-out can also occur at a desk that is removed from the other children in the classroom. Porterfield, Herbert-Jackson, and Risley (1976) developed a procedure called contingent observation. This procedure has been used as an alternative to isolation with preschool children. The teacher places disruptive children on the sidelines of the class and tells them how to act appropriately. They are told to stand aside and watch the other children behave appropriately. After less than a minute, they are asked if they are ready to rejoin the group and behave appropriately.

Overcorrection is a form of punishment used to modify behavior that is disruptive to the environment (Foxx & Azrin, 1972). There are two forms of overcorrection. The first, restitutional correction, requires the individual to correct the environmental effects of the misbehavior. The child is required to make amends for any damage and to overcorrect or improve the original environmental state. For example, a child who hits someone might be required to pat the injured area gently for 30 seconds and then to apologize ("I'm sorry") 10 times after each hitting incident (Ollendick & Matson, 1976). The second, positive practice overcorrection, consists of repeatedly practicing the appropriate behaviors. Azrin and Powers (1975) used positive practice overcorrection to decrease disruptive behaviors of elementary school boys in a summer school program. When misbehavior occurred, the student was required to state the correct classroom behavior, raise his hand and wait to be recognized by the teacher. This sequence was practiced for 5 minutes.

The main advantage of overcorrection is that it focuses on teaching constructive behaviors. However, some implementation issues may make it difficult to use overcorrection in the classroom. Close supervision is required to ensure that the student engages in the overcorrection activity. It may be difficult for the teacher to do this while managing the rest of the class. Also, the activity itself may be disruptive to ongoing class activities. However, it has been found that the overcorrection activity can be delayed until recess or free time and still be effective. The major task in designing an overcorrection procedure is to ensure that the overcorrection activity is relevant to the misbehavior. In the case of restitutional overcorrection, the student must experience the effort that would be required by others to undo the disruptive behavior. With positive practice overcorrection, relevant, appropriate behaviors that can be substituted for inappropriate behaviors must be identified.

Although a number of punishment techniques have been shown to be effective in altering social behaviors of students, potential problems exist when punishment is relied on heavily as a behavior change method. First, most punishment procedures train the student in what not to do and development of competence is not addressed. Undesirable side effects of punishment may include avoidance, escape, and aggressive responses. Because of these potential problems, punishment should be used sparingly. Punishment should be part of a large program based on positive reinforcement so that desirable behavior alternatives are promoted. When reduction of behavioral excesses is the goal, reinforcement procedures should be tried first, followed by the least instrusive, least severe forms of punishment (see also Chapter 11).

Generalization and Maintenance. A wide variety of reinforcement and punishment techniques have been shown to be effective in changing school-related affective and social behaviors of preschool through secondary school students in regular and special education classes. A large number of studies have shown that these procedures result in behavioral changes while the program is in effect. Major goals of behavioral programs are generalization and maintenance. Generalization refers to the transfer of training to settings and situations beyond those in which the program was conducted. Maintenance refers to program durability, or ensuring that the changes in behavior are maintained after the program is terminated (see also Chapter 10).

Behavioral programs in school settings have demonstrated that generalization and maintenance do not occur unless specific procedures are planned and programmed to address these issues. The design of programs that will ensure generalization and maintenance must be addressed by applied behavior analysis researchers and practitioners. A number of reviews that focus on current information concerning these issues are available (Goldstein, Lopez, & Greenleaf, 1979; Marholin & Siegel, 1978; Stokes & Baer, 1977). Although additional research that can be used in educational settings is needed, a number of techniques have been identified that can be used to enhance transfer of training and program durability.

If generalization of behavior across settings is expected, reinforcement and punishment procedures aimed at changing social and affective behaviors should be implemented in a variety of situations. This would include behavioral programming in academic classes, less structured school situations, such as recess or lunch, and in other social environments in which the child interacts, such as the home. In addition, to enhance generalization and maintenance the sources of reinforcement should be varied. This will involve enlisting the support of parents, peers, or other important persons in the student's environment and will require that these individuals receive some training in implementing contingencies of reinforcement. Group-based contingencies, peer-administered contingencies, and home-based contingencies are program designs that incorporate other individuals in the child's social environment into the contingency program.

Group-based contingencies involve providing reinforcement based on the performance of the group as a whole. For example, Switzer, Deal, and Bailey (1977) reduced stealing in second grade classrooms through use of a group contingency in which students could earn 10 extra minutes of free time if nothing was missing in the classroom. A classroom token economy, known as the good behavior game, was investigated by Barrish, Sanders, and Wolf (1969). In this study, a regular fourth grade class was divided into two teams. After reviewing class rules, the teacher explained that whenever she saw a student breaking a class rule the student's team would receive a mark. The team with the fewest marks (or both teams if neither had more than five marks) would receive privileges and free time at the end of the day. This procedure successfully decreased out-of-seat and talking-out behavior for the entire class. Group-based contingencies often result in peer social reinforcement for appropriate behavior so the group can earn the specified rewards.

Peer-administered contingencies are a more direct means of peer involvement, peers administer reinforcing and punishing consequences to the target student. For example, Strain, Shores, and Timm (1977) trained two boys in a preschool classroom to initiate and reinforce social interactions. The boys successfully increased the social interaction of other withdrawn children in the classroom.

Home-based contingencies usually involve a program in which the child earns rewards at school and receives the rewards at home (see also Chapter 7). For example, Vaal (1973) used a home-based contingency system to reduce the school phobia of a 13-year-old boy. If the boy came to school on time without tantrum behavior, attended all classes, and remained in school until dismissal, at home he was allowed to engage in various privileges and activities, such as going bowling and playing basketball. Home-based reinforcement programs provide a means for ensuring that school personnel and parents are aware of the target behaviors and are supporting efforts at behavior change.

When new behaviors are being developed, reinforcement should be provided immediately on a continuous basis. Generalization and maintenance may be enhanced by overlearning, a procedure in which learning is extended over more trials than necessary to produce initial changes in the individual's behavior. Thus, the behavior change agent must be careful not to terminate programs too quickly after an initial change in behavior. Once desired behaviors are learned, generalization and maintenance is likely to occur if the reinforcement schedule is gradually "thinned" so that reinforcement is provided on an intermittent and unpredictable basis.

During implementation of a contingency program, provision of feedback (i.e., information about performance) may enhance maintenance. Verbal information about the specific results of the student's performance combined with other reinforcers such as praise or tokens may increase program effectiveness. In addition, discriminative stimuli or cues that will also occur in the post-training environment should be provided. The objective is development of stimulus control that exists when there is a high probability that a particular response will occur in the presence of a particular antecedent stimulus. Stimulus control is developed through differential reinforcement that consists of reinforcing a given response in the presence of a particular stimulus. If verbal instructions are used to cue behavior, they can be faded so that posters, brief written rules, or brief verbal or nonverbal cues may be used to occasion the behavior in the post-training environment.

Finally, the type of reinforcement used should be gradually changed so that it approximates reinforcement found in the natural environment. If tangible reinforcers are required for initial behavior change to take place, the trainer should gradually move toward use of social reinforcement that is naturally available in most settings. This can be accomplished by pairing social reinforcement with whatever is reinforcing to the target child.

Behavioral Self-Control

Self-control is displayed when an individual changes behavior in the relative absence of external constraints. Self-regulation of behavior can be achieved by teaching an individual to: (a) specify and monitor a target behavior (see also Chapter 2 and Chapter 3); (b) identify the antecedents and consequences of the target behavior; and (c) initiate a plan that changes antecedents and consequences (Thoresen & Mahoney, 1974). The objective of self-control programs is to teach students to utilize behavioral principles in managing their own behavior. Workman (1982) enumerates three important benefits for educators that result from the use of behavioral self-control programs: (a) teachers will not always be present to provide reinforcement and/or feedback; (b) students need to learn to take responsibility for their own behavior; and (c) behavioral self-control may enhance generalization and maintenance of behavior change that results from external contingencies. Four major procedures have been used in behavioral self-control programs (Glynn, Thomas, & Shee, 1973): (a) self-assessment, the individual determines whether he/she has performed the target behavior; (b) self-recording, the individual records the frequency or duration of the target behavior; (c) self-determination of reinforcement, the individual determines the nature and amount of reinforcement to be received; and (d) self-administration of reinforcement, the individual dispenses his/her own reinforcement (this may or may not be self-determined).

Moletzsky (1974) reported two cases in which self-recording successfully reduced disruptive classroom behavior. The first involved a boy who raised his hand constantly, even when he could not respond correctly to the teacher's question. The self-recording procedure involved the use of a wrist counter to record the frequency of hand-raising when the child did not know the answers. In the second case, an 11-year-old girl used a wrist counter to record out-of-seat behavior. The disruptive behavior was drastically decreased.

Bolstad and Johnson (1972) found that a combination of self-recording and self-administration of token reinforcement was as effective as an external token reinforcement program in reducing talking-out, hitting, and out-of-seat behavior. After the baseline phase all subjects were placed on an external token program. Some of the students were taught to record their own disruptive behavior. They were given points contingent upon low rates of disruptive behavior and the accuracy of their recording as indicated by an observer's data. In the next phase, based on self-recording, students gave themselves points for low rates of disruptive behavior.

Kaufman and O'Leary (1972) compared the effectiveness of token reinforcement to a combination of self-assessment and self-determination of reinforcement in decreasing disruptive classroom behavior (out-of-seat, aggression, noise-making) in adolescents in a hospital school. Following an initial token condition, the students were taught to rate themselves according to the scale used by the teacher during the token condition. They were allowed to determine the number of tokens they would receive or lose depending on their self-ratings. The token condition and the behavioral self-control conditions were equally effective in reducing disruptive behavior.

In addition, it has been found that self-determined punishment is as effective as teacher-determined punishment in reducing disruptive behavior. Pease and Tyler (1979) found that students in a class for children with learning disabilities and/or behavior disorders could successfully decrease their disruptive behavior through use of self-administered time-out.

In a program that combined the four components of behavioral self-control, Glynn, Thomas, and Shee (1973) increased the rates of on-task behavior of second graders. The self-control procedure required that at the sound of a "beep" the children self-assess whether they were on task. The children partially self-determined the reinforcer (type and maximum amount were teacher determined) and were allowed to self-administer the reinforcement.

Behavioral self-control training occurs through a number of instructional strategies. These include verbal instructions, modeling the desired behavior, rehearsal, prompting to initiate self-regulatory behavior, feedback, and reinforcement (Gelfand & Hartman, 1984). Many behavioral self-control programs have been developed because of the need for generalization and maintenance after withdrawal of external contingency programs. Most of the effective self-control programs that have been investigated began with external contingency programs and used a matching and fading process. For example, Drabman, Spitalnik, and O'Leary (1973) used a procedure with 9- and 10-year-olds in special classes for children with academic and emotional problems. The procedure used gradually faded evaluation and reinforcement from the teacher to the student. First, the students were exposed to a teacher-imposed token economy. They were rewarded for good behavior and completion of academic tasks with points that could be exchanged for food and pennies. A matching procedure was then introduced; students earned bonus points for accurately matching the teacher's assessment of their behavior. The matching procedure was faded by requiring fewer and fewer students to match the teacher's assessment until self-evaluation determined how many points they received. In a review of use of behavioral self-control in the classroom, Roberts and Dick (1982) viewed self-control as existing along a continuum on which individual students require degrees of external environmental support to initiate and maintain self-controlling behaviors. They state that the classroom may range from a highly structured environment to one in which the students have responsibility for their behavior.

Although behavioral self-control procedures are effective in improving social behavior in the classroom, the number of studies that have evaluated these procedures has been relatively small. Additional investigation with particular attention to maintenance effects is warranted.

Counterconditioning Procedures

Counterconditioning procedures have been applied most often to decrease fears and anxiety. The development of these procedures was influenced by respondent conditioning principles. These principles state that certain behaviors are elicited automatically by a particular stimulus and that new behaviors can be learned through repeated pairings of a stimulus and a response. Conditioned emotional responses, such as anxiety, fears, and phobias, can be changed by teaching the individual a different emotional response to an aversive conditioned stimulus (e.g., an anxiety or fear provoking situation).

Desensitization.   Desensitization is a procedure based on the assumption that a fear response can be inhibited by substituting a response that is incompatible with fear, most frequently a relaxation response. The desensitization process is accomplished by exposing the individual to the feared situation in small gradual steps, through imagery or in real life (in vivo) as the child is engaging in a relaxation response. There are three phases to systematic desensitization: (a) relaxation training; (b) development of an anxiety hierarchy, and (c) exposure to the hierarchy through imagery or in vivo.

The most widely used techniques for teaching relaxation focus on teaching muscle relaxation. The first step in relaxation training is to have the individuual become comfortable. A soft chair in a quiet, softly lighted room will facilitate this process. Relaxation instructions usually include the following: (a) directions to tense and relax particular parts of the body ""Wrinkle your forehead. Point to where it feels particularly tense. Slowly relax your forehead and pay special attention to those areas that were particularly tense"); (b) directions to experience the feeling of relaxation ("Spend a few seconds noticing how it feels to have the muscles loosen, switch off and relax"). At first the child may have to be physically guided through some of the steps. Cautela and Groden (1978) recommended use of the following sequence of muscle groups: (a) forehead, (b) eyes, (c) nose, (d) smile (mouth), (e) tongue, (f) jaw, (g) puckering lips, (h) neck, (i) arms, (j) legs, (k) back, (l) chest, (m) stomach, and (n) below the waist.

When the child has gained proficiency at relaxation training, he/she should be encouraged to practice at home and during quiet periods at school. These practice sessions should occur at least twice a day for 10 to 15 minutes. In most cases, relaxation training lasts from three to four sessions.

Following the relaxation phase, an anxiety hierarchy is planned with the child for each fear or anxiety that has been identified and that the child wishes to change. Usually the child is asked to write or dictate descriptions of 10 situations related to the fear that produce increasing amounts of discomfort. The child is asked to rate the situations according to the degree of discomfort they produce by assigning a number that is a multiple of 10. The situation that is assigned the number 100 would be the most anxiety-provoking; the situation that is assigned the value 10 would be the least anxiety-provoking. Intermediary items are added to insure the availability of a slow, even gradation of anxiety-provoking situations (most hierarchies contain 20 items). At this point, a very relaxing scene that the child can easily imagine and that would be rated as a zero on the hierarchy should be identified (e.g., riding a bicycle, watching a TV program).

Desensitization sessions then begin. The child is asked to relax for 5 minutes and to indicate when he/she feels very relaxed by raising the right index finger. After the child signals, the scenes are presented, beginning with the zero level scene, and the child is asked to imagine each scene. The child is told to signal immediately if there is any tension. Each scene is followed by a relaxation period. The scene should be presented until the child has three consecutive successes (i.e., no discomfort experienced). If anxiety is experienced, the previous scene should be repeated.

Morris and Kratochwill (1983) describe six variations in the use of systematic desensitization. Group desensitization involves the same phases as individual systematic desensitization but the phases are adapted for group administration, usually five to eight children per group. In group desensitization the relaxation training and hierarchy construction are conducted in the group and the group rank orders the hierarchy items. The desensitization is geared to the slowest progressing child in the group. A second variation, in vivo desensitization, exposes the child to the items on the anxiety hierarchy in the real situation, rather than through the child's imagination. Instead of relaxation training, feelings of comfort, security, and trust that the child has developed for the therapist are used as the counterconditioning agent. In automated systematic desensitization, the child goes through the desensitization process by listening to a series of tape recorded scene presentations prepared by the therapist with the assistance of the child.

Thus, the treatment can be conducted at the child's own pace at home. Emotive imagery, used by Lazarus and Abramovitz (1962), involves use of anxiety inhibiting hero images that arouse feelings of adventure and pride, as the counterconditioning agent. Contact desensitization, developed by Ritter (1968), combines aspects of desensitization and modeling. The therapist demonstrates a particular step on a fear hierarchy, helps the child perform that step, and gradually removes prompts until the child can perform the step alone. The last type of desensitization, self-control desensitization, trains the child in use of relaxation as a coping skill so he/she can deal with fearful situations independent of the therapist.

Desensitization has been used to treat a variety of school-related fears including school phobias, anxieties related to social interaction, test anxiety, and academic-related anxiety. For example, Taylor (1972) used successfully systematic desensitization to treat a 15-year-old female who was school phobic and had withdrawn from social relations in school. For this treatment anxiety hierarchies involved three themes: riding in the school bus, being in school, and participating in class activities. A number of studies have reported successful use of systematic desensitization to decrease test anxiety. The treatment most often has been administered in groups instead of individually. One study (Barabasz, 1973) reports the use of teachers as therapists as opposed to psychologists or counselors, as is usually the case. Anxiety related to school work has also been successfully treated through use of systematic desensitization. Bauer (1968) reported that six sessions of systematic desensitization and tutoring improved grades and decreased self-reported anxiety in a seventh grade math-anxious boy. Muller and Madsen (1970) used group desensitization to treat seventh grade students with reading problems that appeared to be anxiety-related. General anxiety and self-reported reading anxiety were reduced in the desensitization condition and in a reading practice (placebo) condition. Similarly, Johnson, Tyler, Thompson, and Jones (1971) found that group systematic desensitization was as effective as a speech practice condition in reducing self-reported speech anxiety of middle school students.

A relatively small amount of controlled research has been conducted on the effectiveness of desensitization with children and the factors that contribute to its effectiveness; a relatively large number of uncontrolled case studies have been reported in the literature and a substantial amount of research has been done with adults (Hatzenbuehler & Schroeder, 1978). Nevertheless, desensitization has been reported to be the most frequently used behavior therapy procedure for reducing childrens' fears.

Morris and Kratochwill (1983) identify a number of factors that may contribute to the effectiveness of desensitization with children. First, age of the child is important, few studies have reported success with children under the age of 9. Imagery level is also an important factor, with this procedure the child must be able to produce vivid mental images. In addition, the child must be able to achieve a relaxed state. Methods other than desensitization should be considered if the therapist is unsuccessful at helping the child to become relaxed or to improve visual imagery.

Relaxation Training.   Recently, use of relaxation training alone has been investigated as a treatment procedure for affective and social problems related to school functioning. This approach has been examined in relation to classroom disruption, test anxiety, and anxiety-related to academic tasks. Relaxation training is useful because the physiological state of relaxation is incompatible with feelings of fear, anxiety, and anger; it is also incompatible with aggressive behavior. Relaxation has been taught in a number of ways. Progressive muscle relaxation, described previously, is used most often. In addition, cue-controlled relaxation, in which the individual is taught to become relaxed in response to a cue word, such as "relax" or "calm," often is used. Use of imagery, in which the child imagines happy, restful scenes, such as the beach or the forest, can be helpful. Finally, biofeedback equipment that provides auditory feedback about muscle tension occasionally has been used with children and adolescents. Relaxation training can be done in an individual or group setting, using live or taped instructions.

Braud (1978) suggested that overactive children who behave inappropriately may be overly tense and compared use of progressive relaxation to biofeedback-induced relaxation with hyperactive students. The children in the progressive relaxation group listened to relaxation tapes individually twice a week over a 6 week period with instruction and assistance in practicing relaxation. Both groups improved significantly on a number of behavioral measures. Investigating use of relaxation training to improve academic functioning, Schuchman (1977) compared progressive muscle relaxation to biofeedback-assisted relaxation and non-directive counseling. Schuchman found that all three groups of test anxious students declined in anxiety and increased in Scholastic Aptitude Test scores. Padawer (1977) used relaxation training with black, inner-city elementary school children designated as the poorest readers in their classes. Following a 2-week training program for the children and their teachers, relaxation exercises were added to the regular classroom curriculum for 2 months. Children who had received relaxation training achieved significantly higher on measures of reading skills.

In addition, classroom programs have incorporated relaxation training into self-control procedures used to improve classroom behavior. Robin, Schneider, and Dolnick (1976) reported successful use of the "Turtle Program" in improving classroom behavior of 4- and 5-year-olds. The Turtle Program consists of teaching children coping behaviors including (a) withdrawing into an imaginary shell when they feel threatened in a problem situation; (b) relaxing their muscles while "doing turtle"; and (c) using problem solving techniques in which the child thinks through alternative courses of action and their consequences.

The studies that have investigated the efficacy of relaxation training with children have a variety of methological problems. Thus, support for use of these procedures with school children is minimal. However, studies reported indicate that relaxation training is more likely to be effective when parents and/or teachers are involved in supporting the training program by providing practice time for sessions or providing additional training.

Social Learning Theory Approaches

Social learning theory (Bandura, 1977) assumes that behaviors are developed and maintained on the basis of three systems: (a) classical conditioning processes; (b) external reinforcement; and (c) cognitive mediational processes. The cognitive processes are most important and determine the influence of environmental events. Cognitive processes determine the environmental influences that are attended to, how they are perceived, and whether thay affect future behavior.

Social Modeling. Modeling is behavior change that results from the observation of another person. Social modeling procedures have been used to alter affective and social functioning in children. Behavioral targets include: increasing social interaction, increasing cooperation, improving conversational skills, increasing assertive behaviors, decreasing aggression, and decreasing school-related anxiety.

The basic elements of a social modeling program for the development of new social behaviors include: (a) instructions; (b) exposure to the model; (c) rehearsal; (d) performance feedback; and (e) practice (Cartledge & Milburn, 1980; Goldstein, Sprafkin, Gershaw, & Klein, 1980). Because social skills usually consist of a number of individual behaviors, the first task in developing a social modeling program is identification of specific subskills. For example, the subskills involved in initiating a social interaction consist of behaviors such as making eye contact, saying hello, giving your name, and smiling. It is suggested that the child to be helped to identify the components of the skill rather than being told what the components are.

The next step is exposure to the model. Goldstein, Sprafkin, and Gershaw (1976) point out that the behaviors to be imitated should be presented: (a) in a clear, detailed manner, (b) in order from least to most difficult behaviors; (c) with enough repetition to make overlearning possible; (d) with as little irrelevant detail as possible; and (e) with several different models. Characteristics of the model that enhance acquisition include: similarity in sex, age, race, and attitudes; prestige; competence; warmth and nurturance; and reward value (Perry & Furukawa, 1980). Live and symbolic models have been used effectively. Live modeling involves live demonstration of the behavior; symbolic modeling involves presentation of the model through film, videotape, or puppets.

Observed behavior will not necessarily be learned unless the child has the opportunity to practice or rehearse the behavior. Bandura (1977) has suggested that behavior can be rehearsed through covert responding (i.e., imagery), verbal responding (i.e., the child talks through the desired staps) and/or motor resonding (i.e., role-playing). Through role-playing the child is required to act out the response observed and subsequently discusses and evaluates the performance. Feedback can take the form of verbal feedback, tangible reinforcers, or self-evaluation. Once the child can demonstrate the new behavior, practice under other conditions with other people (outside the training setting) is necessary to ensure generalization. This is usually accomplished through a series of "homework assignments." For example, a child may be directed to practice initiating conversation on the playground during recess. The results are discussed in additional training sessions.

Goldstein, Sprafkin, Gershaw, and Klein (1980) report a number of studies that indicate that this type of social modeling program has been used successfully in school settings with conduct problem adolescents to improve self-control, assertiveness and negotiation skills. Goldstein's program, which is called Structured Learning, is an intervention designed to enhance prosocial, interpersonal, stress management, and planning skills. In a study examining use of modeling to increase social interaction in withdrawn preschoolers, O'Connor (1969) assigned nursery school children to a filmed modeling group and a neutral film control group. The modeling film showed increasing social interactions between children with positive consequences for those interactions. After viewing the film and returning to the classroom, the children in the modeling group had increased levels of social interaction, those in the control group did not. Modeling procedures have also been used with anxiety problems. Mann and Rosenthal (1969) examined the use of modeled desensitization and direct desensitization on seventh and eighth grade test-anxious students. Modeled desensitization involves observing a model being desensitized. Both types of treatment produced significantly better self-report scores and test performance than a no-treatment control condition.

Modeling procedures have been used effectively with a variety of affective and social behaviors. However, generalization and maintenance are major issues that require attention by researchers and practitioners.

Coaching. Coaching is a procedure that involves giving students direct verbal instructions in social skills. The coaching strategy typically involves three steps: (a) presentation of concepts, rules and standards for behavior; (b) behavior rehearsal with the coach or a peer partner; and (c) feedback from the coach on performance, with discussion and suggestions on future performance. Coaching provides a conceptual framework that can be used as a model for behavior and as a context in which the behavior can be modeled, shaped, and responded to (Oden, 1980).

Oden and Asher (1977) used coaching to train third and fourth grade students in social skills. The content of the instruction focused on participation, cooperation (e.g., taking turns, sharing), communication (e.g., talking and listening), and validating or supporting (e.g., giving attention or help). Coaching was effective in increasing the children's acceptance on a sociometric scale. Coaching also has been used to decrease aggressive behavior. Zahavi and Asher (1978) decreased the aggressive behavior of preschoolers using a coaching procedure that involved teaching three concepts: (a) aggression hurts another person and makes the person unhappy; (b) aggression does not solve problems; and (c) positive ways to solve conflicts are sharing, taking turns, and playing together. In this study, each child was coached on one occasion for 10 minutes.

Coaching is an intervention that appears to be especially amenable to implementation in the school setting. However, research on this procedure with social and affective school-related problems is relatively limited.

Programming for generalization and maintenance of behavior change in modeling and coaching programs may be accomplished if attention is given to some of the following principles (Goldstein et al., 1979; Marholin & Siegel, 1978; Stokes & Baer, 1977). Generalization has been shown to be facilitated by providing the learner with general mediating principles. Thus, training should include emphasis on general rules, strategies, or principles that can lead to successful performance. A variety of behavioral responses should be trained in a variety of situations. In addition, it has been found that training in a number of settings will enhance transfer. If training cannot take place in the setting in which the behavior is to occur, the training environment should be designed to approximate the natural environment as closely as possible. Finally, effects of modeling and coaching programs can be enhanced by training other significant individuals in the natural environment to reinforce desired affective and social behaviors.

Cognitive-Behavior Modification

Cognitive-behavioral procedures emphasize the importance of cognitive processes and private events as mediators of behavior change (Meichenbaum, 1977). A major assumption of cognitive-behavior modfication is that reactions to events are greatly influenced by individual's cognitions or thoughts. Therefore, the primary focus of this type of intervention is to change the person's thought patterns, beliefs, attitudes, and opinions. Four major types of cognitive-behavioral procedures have been used in school settings to help improve students' affective and social functioning: social problem-solving, self-instructional training, stress incoulation, and rational-emotive therapy.

Social Problem-Solving.   Social problem-solving training is based on the idea that an individual may have problems in interpersonal functioning because of deficits in systematic problem-solving skills. Components of the training include instruction in social problem identification, generation of alternative solutions, prediction of possible consequences of these solutions, and selection of appropriate behavioral responses. Spivack and Shure (1974) found that good problem-solvers tended to have better social adjustment than individuals with more limited problem-solving skills.

In the problem identification phase of the training the student is taught to recognize that a problem exists and to understand the nature of the problem and related environmental and emotional factors. This is frequently done by examining problem situations encountered by children in: (a) identifying feelings of being upset; (b) determining when the feeling started; (c) determining what happened; and (d) determining what the child wants to have happen. In the next step of the training the child is assisted in generating alternative responses to the situation and possible consequences for each of the alternatives. Subsequently, a decision-making step involves ordering the list of alternatives from most preferred to least preferred and identifying the exact way to carry out the most desirable alternative. The child may then role-play the solution and try the solution in real-life conditions. Finally, an evaluation is conducted with the child to review the effectiveness of the strategy and, if necessary, to develop alternative solutions.

In a number of studies Shure and Spivack (1978, 1979) have shown that as a result of social problem-solving training inner-city preschoolers learned alternative and consequential thinking skills and improved on teacher ratings of behavior. Similarly, Elardo and Caldwell (1979) and Weissberg et al. (1981) found improvements in behavior measured by teacher ratings for elementary school children following exposure to a social problem-solving curriculum.

Several large scale investigations in school settings have been conducted by examining use of social problem-solving curricula with preschoolers and elementary school children. It is clear that social problem-solving skills can be trained; however, the link between improved social problem-solving skills and improved social adjustment has not been firmly established (Olexa & Forman, 1984); future research should attend to this issue.

Self-Instructional Training. The goal of self-instructional training (Meichenbaum, 1977) is to teach the child to guide behavior through "internal dialogue." The internal dialogue is usually structured through four questions: (a) What is my problem? (b) How can I do it? or What is my plan? (c) Am I using my plan? and (d) How did I do? Thus, verbal self-instructions consist of problem definition, problem approach, focusing of attention, coping statements, and self-reinforcement.

Camp, Blom, Hebert, and VanDoorninck (1977) have reported that aggressive elementary school children improved in prosocial behavior after participating in the Think Aloud Program (Camp & Bash, 1978) that combines self-instructional training and social problem-solving. The first part of the program involves teaching the children to use verbal self-instruction through practice with cognitive tasks (e.g., coloring, mazes). Statements related to problem definition, alternative plans, coping with errors, monitoring the proposed plan, and evaluation are included. Subsequently, interpersonal problem situations consisting of conflicts with peers, teachers, parents, and siblings are introduced. During this segment of the program consequential thinking is addressed by teaching the students to identify emotions, physical and emotional causality, and possible alternatives and their consequences. Evaluative thinking and decision-making are addressed by teaching the child to consider the safety, fairness, effectiveness, and effect on others of potential solutions. Finally, the skills are rehearsed through role-play and verbal practice and are applied to real-life situations.

Roberts and Dick (1982) have enumerated a number of factors that influence the effectiveness of self-instruction as cues for responding. Although research designed to identify these factors has been limited, the following trends have emerged:

1. Overt self-instructions are more effective than silent self-instructions.
2. Self-verbalizations may be more effective cues than trainer produced verbalizations.
3. Self-instructions should address both specific content (i.e., what to do in situation X) and general problem-solving skills that can be employed across situations.
4. Self-instructions must label the motor behavior or the steps in the problem-solving process to facilitate a self-controlling response.
5. The content of the self-instruction should include features of the long-term consequences of the behavior.

Kendall (1977) enumerates a number of general factors that should be considered in developing self-instructional training programs for children. First, the cognitive capacity of the child should be sufficient to deal with the training. In addition, use of contingent rewards as part of the training program should be considered to increase the child's attention and effort. Instructions should be individualized for each child to be maximally effective. Finally, generalization can be enhanced by relating the focus of the training and the training setting to the type of behavior change that is desired and by using general, conceptual instructions as well as specific, concrete instructions.

Much of the research on self-instructional training has been conducted in laboratory settings and has involved relatively short-term training (Pressley, 1979). When researchers have examined effects on children's classroom behavior they failed to establish a link between changes on paper- and pencil-tasks or in analogue situations and changes in the child's functioning in the classroom. It is clear that students can learn to manipulate their cognitions, however, generalization effects remain to be demonstrated.

Stress Inoculation.   Stress inoculation, a variation of self-instructional training is a three step process during which the individual is taught to: (a) understand the nature of the problem (educational phase); (b) develop cognitive coping skills (rehearsal phase), and (c) apply the skills under stressful situations (application phase) (Meichenbaum, 1977). Through this type of training the individual learns to develop specific thinking skills that can be applied in stressful situations.

During the educational phase the antecedent events and the cognitive, physiological, and affective aspects of the stressful situation are examined. During the rehearsal phase a four step model for rehearsing coping cognitions is presented. It includes: (a) preparing for a stressor—using self-statements recognizing the nature of the situation ("Here comes Bill. He's mad at me."); (b) confronting and handling the stressor—using self-statements to increase self-confidence ("Keep cool. There's no need to get upset."); (c) coping with becoming upset— using self-statements to try to keep these feelings under control ("Take a deep breath. Relax"); and (d) reinforcing self-statements—evaluating one's performance ("I handled that one pretty well."). During the application phase role-playing and imagery are used and the child is given assignments to use the techniques outside of the training setting.

Moss and Finch (1979) have developed a stress inoculation program used to help children control anger. The program incorporates training in relaxation and verbal self-instructions. The self-instructions are modeled by the trainer and rehearsed by the child using the following sequence:

1. The therapist models the verbalizations, talking out loud as the child observes (cognitive modeling).
2. The child instructs himself out loud with assistance from the therapist (overt verbalizations with external guidance).
3. The child instructs himself out loud with no assistance (overt verbalizations self-guidance).
4. The therapist whispers the statements.
5. The child whispers the statements.
6. The therapist models use of covert (silent) verbalizations.
7. The child uses covert verbalizations.

Research focusing on stress inoculation techniques has been done almost exclusively with adult subjects with phobias, interpersonal anxiety, anger control problems, pain, and job-related stress. These procedures hold promise for treatment of child and adolescent problems and additional research should focus on this area.

Rational–Emotive Therapy.   The basic premise of Rational–Emotive Therapy (RET) is that maladaptive behaviors result largely from irrational beliefs (Ellis, 1977). The objective of RET is to help individuals identify their irrational thoughts and replace them with rational thoughts that will facilitate constructive, appropriate behavior. Through RET individuals are taught to identify, dispute, and give up their irrational beliefs, and to think in more rational, constructive ways using didactic instruction, discussion, and behavior rehearsal techniques. Ellis (1977) has identified a number of irrational beliefs that, he states, results in much of the emotional disturbance in our culture. These include:

1. The idea that it is a necessity to be loved or approved of by every significant other.
2. The idea that one should be thoroughly competent, adequate and achieve in all respects to be worthwhile.
3. The idea that certain people are bad and wicked and should be punished.
4. The idea that it is awful and catastrophic when things are not the way one would like them to be.
5. The idea that human unhappiness is externally caused and that people have no ability to control their disturbance.
6. The idea that if something is or may be dangerous or fearsome, one should be terribly concerned.
7. The idea that it is easier to avoid than to face certain life difficulties and self-responsibilities.
8. The idea that one should be dependent on others and needs someone stronger than oneself to rely on.
9. The idea that because something once strongly affected one's life it will indefinitely do so.
10. The idea that one should become upset over other people's problems and disturbances.
11. The idea that there is a perfect solution to every problem and that it is catastrophic if this solution is not found.

Warren, Deffenbacher, and Brading (1976) showed that RET could be used to decrease the test anxiety of fifth and sixth graders. In addition, Block (1978) used RET with 11th and 12th graders with behavior problems to decrease disruptive classroom behavior. The students in this study met their treatment group 5 days per week, 45 minutes per session for a full semester. They received course credit in the social sciences for their participation. RET has also been incorporated into preventive mental health orograms in which the students receiving the training have no specific difficulties. These studies have shown that children in elementary school can learn the principles of RET and can become more rational in their thinking (DiGuiseppe & Kassinove, 1976).

There is considerable evidence that RET is successful in treating anxiety, fear, and depression in adults; the studies that have been done with children are also encouraging. However, well-controlled studies in this area are scarce. Additional research needs to be done for the utility of this procedure with school children to be firmly established.

IMPLEMENTATION AND EVALUATION ISSUES

Although the effectiveness of behavioral procedures in improving affective and social functioning of children and adolescents is relatively well-documented, their use in schools has been limited. A major task for practitioners and researchers is the identification of organizational conditions in the educational setting that will facilitate incorporation of the behavioral approach into existing school programs.

Planning

The link between knowledge and action can be developed through a planning process. As illustrated earlier, behavioral procedures provide an effective technology for implementation of affective and social education goals. An effective program planning process is needed so that this technology can be adopted by school staff. One well-known planning model used in human service settings is the A VICTORY model (Davis & Salasin, 1975). A VICTORY is an acronym that stands for important factors to be considered in planning change:

A-Ability—What are your resources and capabilities? (e.g., Are the personnel and financial resources needed to implement a behavioral program available?).

V-Values—Does the innovation match your style and beliefs? (e.g., Do the basic assumptions of the behavioral approach match the school staff's and community's beliefs and values concerning child development and education?).

I-Information—How do you find out about things? (e.g., Do you have an established staff development program, consultation program, feedback procedure?).

C-Circumstances—What is your environment like? (e.g., How will other aspects of the school program and the community impact on a behavioral social and affective education program?).

T-Timing—Is this the time to try? (e.g., Are there other occurrances in the school system that will inhibit or enhance adoption of a behavioral program at this time?).

O-Obligation—Is there motivation to change? (e.g., Has there been sufficient involvement of school staff and parents in assessing needs, determining goals, and deciding on use of behavioral technology to meet those goals?).

R-Resistances—What problems can you expect? (e.g., Who on the staff is likely to resist using behavioral procedures and why?).

Y-Yield—What is the reward for changing? (e.g., Is there sufficient "pay-off" for the staff to use behavioral procedures?).

Once these factors have been considered, plans should be drawn to alleviate potential hindrances if the program is to be successfully adopted.

Comprehensive planning is necessary if behavioral affective and social education programs are to be effectively implemented in the school setting. Planning should include: (a) identification of activities needed to accomplish the objective; (b) a list of resources needed to accomplish each activity; (c) estimation of a time frame for each activity; (d) development of a work plan that identifies the sequence and interdependency of the activities; and (e) a means of obtaining feedback and replanning when problems develop (Cunningham, 1982). Organizational research suggests that the type of participation that occurs during the planning process will determine the level of participation that occurs during other phases of program implementation. Educational innovations that address goals that are important to those at all levels of the school organization, including teachers, administrators, parents, and students, are more successful than those that are initiated without this support. Participative, collaborative, problem-solving, and team approaches to planning for affective and social education programs will yield greater satisfaction among program participants and greater program success.

Training

The success of any educational program is largely dependent on the willingness and ability of school staff to carry out planned activities. Behavioral programs based on applied behavior analysis are usually implemented by teaching staff. Programs based on counterconditioning, social learning therapy, and cognitive-behavior modification have been implemented by psychological consultants or support personel, such as school psychologists or counselors; however, the importance of involving the teacher in implementation and support of these procedures has been receiving increasing recognition. Thus, the issue of teacher training in behavioral procedures is one that must be addressed if a behavioral approach to affective and social education is to be successfully implemented (see also Chapter 9).

A number of different procedures have been used to train teachers in behavioral techniques. As in all areas of teacher preparation didactic training has been used most often. However, this type of training has not resulted in changes in teacher classroom behavior, although paper- and pencil-knowledge of behavioral procedures may result. The most effective teacher training programs combine didactic training with other procedures, such as cueing, role-playing, modeling, feedback, and reinforcement (Allen & Forman, 1984). A comprehensive staff training program incorporating multimodal training methods, follow-up consultation, and support from all levels of the organization will be necessary if the school staff is to incorporate behavioral affective and social education programs into existing school operations (Forman, 1984).

Evaluation

Kazdin and Wilson (1978) identify three major areas that should be considered when evaluating behavior change programs: client-related criteria, efficiency and cost-related criteria, and consumer satisfaction. These can be used as a framework for developing an evaluation process for affective and social education programs (see also Chapter 10).

Client-related criteria include determination of whether the individual or group changed as a result of the program. This has usually been accomplished through use of traditional experimental and quasi-experimental research designs and statistical procedures. The importance of the change is also relevant. Importance or magnitude of change addresses the issue of whether the target student engages in normative behavior or acceptable behavior after the treatment. In addition, if a group program is being evaluated, the proportion of participants who improve is a relevant issue. Side effects also are important in evaluating intervention. Two types of intervention may seem equally effective in changing behavior; however, side effects may make one less desirable than the other. Finally, the breadth and durability of the change are issues that should be considered.

Efficiency and cost-related criteria include duration of treatment, efficiency of implementation, costs of professional expertise, and participant costs. In addition to information about student changes that may be produced, the amount of student and staff time, costs of materials, and consultant costs are important in evaluating the cost-effectiveness of a program. The "integrity" of a program (Yeaton & Sechrest, 1981) (i.e., the extent to which it can be implemented by school staff in the manner in which it was developed and validated) also is a relevant issue. Can teachers, paraprofessionals, support staff, and/or parents be adequately trained to implement the program correctly and will they be willing to do so?

In a school setting consumer-related criteria may include perceptions of teachers, students, and the community concerning the acceptability of the program. Goals, procedures, and underlying theoretical assumptions about the nature of human behavior and the education process may influence the willingness of students to participate in a given program and the degree of support teachers, parents, and community members are willing to offer. Consumer-related criteria are receiving increased emphasis. Many researchers and practitioners have realized that even if the experimental efficacy of a given procedure has been demonstrated, if the procedure is unacceptable to teachers, parents, or students it is not likely to be implemented, and will be of little benefit (Witt & Elliott, in press).

Wolf (1978) uses the term *social validity* to refer to the evaluation of treatment by consumers. It is suggested that three aspects of a treatment procedure be evaluated in an attempt to establish social validity: (a) the acceptability of the treatment goals; (b) the acceptability of the treatment procedures; and (c) the social importance of the outcomes of the treatment.

The social validity of behavioral interventions in school settings has been examined in studies that investigated the acceptability of behavioral procedures to the classroom teacher. It has been found that positive or reinforcing interventions are judged by teachers as more acceptable than negative or nonreinforcing interventions. Unless the target behavior is severe, interventions that are relatively easy to implement and require little time and few resources have been rated as more acceptable (Elliott, Witt, Peterson, & Galvin, 1984). There is also some evidence to indicate that teachers prefer interventions in which they are involved more than those that require involvement of another person (Algozzine, Ysseldyke, Christensen, & Thurlow, 1982).

The behavioral approach has greater validity in research support concerning client-related criteria than any other approach designed to improve affective and social functioning of children and adolescents. Although additional training of school staff will be required, the costs of professional expertise can be minimized by extensive involvement of teachers, paraprofessionals, students, and parents in program implementation. It is extremely important to provide adequate training, consultation, and materials for the program implementors if effective behavioral programs are to be implemented in school settings. In attempts to reduce costs, school administrators must be careful to provide program resources that allow for effective program implementation. Consumer satisfaction of students can be enhanced by contracting, which allows target students to participate in program formulation. Research on consumer satisfaction of teachers reveals positive points and areas for concern. On the positive side teachers and behavioral researchers agree on the importance of using positive or reinforcing interventions before using interventions with aversive components. Areas of concern include teachers' preferences for quicker, easier interventions that do not involve others. Although some of the interventions reviewed in this chapter require little time or effort and can be implemented without outside assistance (e.g., social reinforcement, verbal reprimands), a number of interventions are complex, time consuming, and require support for additional materials, personnel for data collection, and consultative services.

Behavioral researchers and educators must work to close the gap between the importance of maintaining the "integrity" of behavioral programs and the importance of consumer desires. Behavioral researchers and behavioral consultants can address this issue by determining the individual program components essential for program effectiveness. Educators must be cognizant of the fact that elimination of staff, material resources, or procedures, or reduction in time allocated for the intervention may reduce program effectiveness. Current research indicates that a behavioral approach to affective and social education can provide effective result oriented programs that can help schools attain their goals. Increases in the degree to which the knowledge derived from behavioral research is utilized in educational settings will depend on further identification of organizational conditions that hinder and facilitate program implementation.

REFERENCES

Algozzine, B., Ysseldyke, J. E., Christensen, S., & Thurlow, M. (1982). *Teachers' intervention choices for children exhibiting different behaviors in school.* Minneapolis: University of Minnesota, Institute for Research on Learning Disabilities.

Allen, C., & Forman, S. G. (1984). Efficacy of methods of training teachers in behavior modification. *School Psychology Review, 13,* 26–32.

Allen, K. E., Hart, B. M., Buell, J. S., Harris, F. R., & Wolf, M. M. (1964). Effects of social reinforcement on isolate behavior of a nursery school child. *Child Development, 35,* 511–518.

Ayllon, L., Smith, D., & Robers, M. (1979). Behavioral management of school phobia. *Journal of Behavior Therapy and Experimental Psychiatry, 1,* 135–138.

Azrin, N. H., & Powers, M. A. (1975). Eliminating classroom disturbances of emotionally disturbed children by positive practice procedures. *Behavior Therapy, 6,* 525–534.

Baer, D. M., Wolf, M. M., & Risley, L. R. (1968). Some current dimensions of applied behavior analysis. *Journal of Applied Behavior Analysis, 1,* 91–97.

Bandura, A. (1977). *A social learning theory.* Englewood Cliffs, NJ: Prentice-Hall.

Barabasz, A. (1973). Group desensitization of test anxiety in elementary schools. *Journal of Psychology, 83,* 295–301.

Barrish, H., Saunders, M., & Wolf, M. (1969). Good behavior game: Effects of individual contingencies for group consequences on disruptive behavior in a classroom. *Journal of Applied Behavior Analysis, 2,* 119–124.

Bauer, D. (1968). A case of desensitization and tutoring therapy. *Exceptional Children, 34,* 386–387.

Block, J. (1978). Effects of a rational-emotive mental health program on poorly achieving, disruptive high school students. *Journal of Counseling Psychology, 25,* 61–65.

Bolstad, O., & Johnson, S. (1972). Self-regulation in the modification of disruptive classroom behavior. *Journal of Applied Behavior Analysis, 5,* 443–454.

Braud, L. (1978). The effects of frontal EMG biofeedback and progressive relaxation upon hyperactivity and its behavioral concomitants. *Biofeedback and Self-Regulation, 3,* 69–89.

Brown, P., & Elliott, R. (1965). The control of aggression in a nursery school class. *Journal of Experimental Child Psychology, 2,* 102–107.

Camp, B. W., & Bash, M. A. (1978). *Think aloud: Group manual.* Denver, CO: University of Colorado Medical School.

Camp, B., Blom, G., Hebert, F., & VonDoorninck, J. (1977). "Think aloud": A program for developing self-control in young aggressive boys. *Journal of Abnormal Child Psychology, 5,* 157–169.

Cartledge, G., & Milburn, J. F. (1978). The case for teaching social skills in the classroom: A review. *Review of Educational Research, 1,* 133–156.

Cartledge, G., & Milburn, J. F. (1980). *Teaching social skills to children.* Elmsford, NY: Pergamon Press.

Cautela, J. R., & Groden, J. (1978). *Relaxation. A comprehensive manual for adults, children, and children with special needs.* Champaign, IL: Research Press.

Cunningham, W. G. (1982). *Systematic planning for educational change.* Palo Alto: Mayfield.

Davis, H. R., & Salasin, S. E. (1975). The utilization of evaluation. In E. L. Stroning & M. Guttentag (Eds.), *Handbook of evaluation research* (Vol. 1, pp. 621–666). Beverly Hills, CA: Sage.

Deitz, S. M., & Repp, A. C. (1973). Decreasing classroom misbehavior through the use of DRL schedules of reinforcement. *Journal of Applied Behavior Analysis, 6,* 457–463.

DiGuiseppe, R., & Kassinove, H. (1976). Affects of a rational-emotive school mental health program on children's emotional adjustment. *Journal of Community Psychology, 4,* 382–387.

Drabman, R. S., & Spitalnik, R. (1973). Training a retarded child as a behavioral teaching assistant. *Journal of Behavior Therapy and Experimental Psychiatry, 4,* 269–272.

Drabman, R. S., Spitalnik, R., & O'Leary, K. D. (1973). Teaching self-control to disruptive children. *Journal of Abnormal Psychology, 82,* 10–26.

Elardo, P., & Caldwell, B. (1979). The effects of an experimental social development program on children in the middle childhood period. *Psychology in the Schools, 16,* 93–100.

Elliott, S. N., Witt, J. C., Peterson, R., & Galvin, G. A. (1984). Acceptability of behavioral interventions and factors that influence teachers' decisions. *Journal of School Psychology, 22,* 353–360.

Ellis, A. (1977). The basic clinical theory of rational-emotive therapy. In A. Ellis & R. Grieger (Eds.), *Handbook of rational-emotive therapy* (pp. 3–34). New York: Springer.

Forman, S. G. (1984). Behavioral and cognitive-behavioral approaches to staff development. In C. A. Maher, R. J. Illback, & J. E. Zins (Eds.), *Organizational psychology in the schools: A sourcebook for professionals* (pp. 302–322). Springfield, IL: Charles C. Thomas.

Foxx, R. M., & Azrin, N. H. (1972). Restitution: A method of eliminating aggressive-disruptive behavior of retarded and brain-damaged patients. *Behavior Research and Therapy, 10,* 15–27.

Foxx, R. M., & Shapiro, S. T. (1978). The timeout ribbon: A nonexclusionary timeout procedure. *Journal of Applied Behavior Analysis, 11,* 125–136.

Gelfand, D. M., & Hartmann, D. P. (1984). *Child behavior analysis and therapy.* Elmsford: Pergamon Press.

Glynn, E., Thomas, J., & Shee, S. (1973). Behavioral self-control of on-task behavior in an elementary school classroom. *Journal of Applied Behavior Analysis, 6,* 105–113.

Goldstein, A. P., Lopez, M., & Greenleaf, D. O. (1979). Introduction. In A. P. Goldstein & F. H. Kanfer (Eds.), *Maximizing treatment gains: Transfer enhancement in psychotherapy* (pp. 1–22). New York: Academic Press.

Goldstein, A. P., Sprafkin, R. P., & Gershaw, N. J. (1976). *Skill training for community living: Applying structured learning therapy.* Elmsford: Pergammon Press.

Goldstein, A. P., Sprafkin, R. P., Gershaw, N. J., & Klein, P. (1980). *Skillstreaming the adolescent.* Champaign, IL: Research Press.

Grieger, R. (1970). Behavior modification with a total class: A case report. *Journal of School Psychology, 3,* 103–106.

Hart, B. M., Reynolds, N. J., Baer, D. M., Brawley, E. R., & Harris, F. R. (1968). Effect of contingent and noncontingent social reinforcement on the cooperative play of a preschool child. *Journal of Applied Behavior Analysis, 1,* 73–76.

Hatzenbuehler, L. C., & Schroeder, H. E. (1978). Desensitization procedures in the treatment of childhood disorders. *Psychological Bulletin, 85,* 831–844.

Heaton, R. C., & Safer, D. J. (1982). Secondary school outcome following a junior high school behavioral program. *Behavioral Therapy, 13,* 226–231.

Hersen, M. (1970). Behavior modification approach to a school phobia case. *Journal of Clinical Psychology, 26,* 128–132.

Horton, L. E. (1970). Generalization of aggressive behavior in adolescent delinquent boys. *Journal of Applied Behavior Analysis, 3,* 205–211.

Iwata, B. A., & Bailey, J. S. (1974). Reward versus cost token systems: An analysis of the effects on students and teachers. *Journal of Applied Behavior Analysis, 7,* 564–576.

Johnson, T., Tyler, V., Thompson, R., & Jones, E. (1971). Systematic desensitization and assertive training in the treatment of speech anxiety in middle school students. *Psychology in the Schools, 8,* 263–267.

Jones, F. H., & Miller, W. H. (1974). The effective use of negative attention for reducing group disruption in special elementary school classrooms. *Psychological Record, 24,* 435–448.

Kaufman, K., & O'Leary, K. (1972). Reward, cost, and self-evaluation procedures for disruptive adolescents in a psychiatric hospital school. *Journal of Applied Behavior Analysis, 5,* 293–309.

Kazdin, A. E. (1982). The token economy: A decade later. *Journal of Applied Behavior Analysis, 15,* 431–445.

Kazdin, A. E., & Wilson, G. T. (1978). *Evaluation of behavior therapy: Issues, evidence, and research strategies.* Cambridge, MA: Ballinger.

Kendall, P. C. (1977). On the efficacious use of verbal self-instructional procedures with children. *Cognitive Therapy and Research, 1,* 331–334.

Kirby, F. D., & Toler, H. C. (1970). Modification of a preschool isolate behavior: A case study. *Journal of Applied Behavior Analysis, 3,* 309–314.

Lahey, B. B., McNees, P. M., & McNees, M. C. (1973). Control of an obscene "verbal tic" through time-out in an elementary school classroom. *Journal of Applied Behavior Analysis, 6,* 101–104.

Lazarus, A. A., & Abramovitz, A. (1962). The use of emotive imagery in the treatment of children's phobias. *Journal of Mental Science, 108,* 191–195.

Long, J. D., & Williams, R. L. (1973). The comparative effectiveness of group and individual contingent free time with inner-city junior high school students. *Journal of Applied Behavior Analysis, 6,* 465–474.

Mann, J., & Rosenthal, Y. L. (1969). Vicarious and direct counterconditioning of test anxiety through individual and group desensitization. *Behavior Research and Therapy, 7,* 359–367.

Marholin, D., & Siegel, L. (1978). Beyond the law of effect. In D. Marholin (Ed.), *Child behavior therapy* (pp. 397–415). New York: Gardner Press.

Marlowe, R. H., Madsen, C. H., Bowen, C. E., Reardon, R. C., & Logue, P. E. (1978). Severe classroom behavior problems: Teachers or counselors. *Journal of Applied Behavior Analysis, 11,* 53–66.

Meichenbaum, D. (1977). *Cognitive-behavior modification: An integrative approach.* New York: Plenum Press.

Moletzky, B. (1974). Behavior recording as treatment: A brief note. *Behavior Therapy, 5,* 107–111.

Morris, R. J., & Kratochwill, T. R. (1983). *Treating children's fears and phobias: A behavioral approach.* New York: Pergamon Press.

Moss, J. H., & Finch, A. J. (1979). *A manual for stress inoculation for anger control in children.* Unpublished manuscript, Virginia Treatment Center for Children.

Muller, S., & Madsen, C. (1970). Group desensitization for anxious children with reading problems. *Psychology in the Schools, 7,* 184–189.

O'Connor, R. D. (1969). Modification of social withdrawal through symbolic modeling. *Journal of Applied Behavior Analysis, 2,* 15–22.

Oden, S. (1980). A child's social isolation: Origins, prevention, intervention. In G. Cartledge & J. F. Milburn (Eds.), *Teaching social skills to children* (pp. 179–202). Elmsford, NY: Pergamon Press.

Oden, S., & Asher, S. R. (1977). Coaching children in social skills for friendship making. *Child Development, 48,* 495–506.

O'Leary, K. D., & Becker, W. C. (1968). The effects of intensity of a teachers' reprimand on children's behavior. *Journal of School Psychology, 7,* 8–11.

O'Leary, K. D., Kaufman, K. F., Kass, R. E., & Drabman, R. S. (1970). The effects of loud and soft reprimands on the behaviors of disruptive students. *Exceptional Children, 37,* 145–155.

Olexa, D. F., & Forman, S. G. (1984). Effects of social problem-solving training on classroom behavior of urban disadvantaged students. *Journal of School Psychology, 22,* 165–175.

Ollendick, T. H., & Matson, J. (1976). An initial investigation into the parameters of overcorrection. *Psychological Reports, 9,* 1139–1142.

Padawer, D. D. (1977). Reading performance of relaxation trained children. *Dissertation Abstracts International, 38*(3-A), 1306.

Pease, G. A., & Tyler, V. O., Jr. (1979). Self-regulation of time-out duration in the modification of disruptive classroom behavior. *Psychology in the Schools, 16,* 101–105.

Perry, M. J., & Furukawa, M. J. (1980). Modeling methods. In F. H. Kanfer & A. P. Goldstein (Eds.), *Helping people change* (2nd ed., pp. 131–171). Elmsford: Pergamon Press.

Porterfield, J. K., Herbert-Jackson, E., & Risley, T. R. (1976). Contingent observation: An effective and acceptable procedure for reducing disruptive behavior of young children in a group setting. *Journal of Applied Behavior Analysis, 9,* 55–64.

Premack, D. (1965). Reinforcement theory. In D. Levine (Ed.), *Nebraska symposium on motivation* (pp. 123–180). Lincoln, NE: University of Nebraska Press.

Pressley, M. P. (1979). Increasing children's self-control through cognitive interventions. *Review of Educational Research, 49,* 319–370.

Rapport, M. D., Murphy, A., & Bailey, J. S. (1978). The effects of a response cost treatment tactic on hyperactive children. *Journal of School Psychology, 18,* 98–110.

Repp, A. C., & Deitz, S. M. (1974). Reducing aggressive and self-injurious behavior of institutionalized retarded children through reinforcement of other behaviors. *Journal of Applied Behavior Analysis, 7,* 313–325.

Ritter, B. (1968). The group desensitization of children's snake phobias using vicarious and contact desensitization procedures. *Behavior Research and Therapy, 6,* 1–6.

Roberts, R. N., & Dick, M. L. (1982). Self-control in the classroom: Theoretical and practical applications. In L. R. Kratochwill (Ed.), *Advances in school psychology* (Vol. 3, pp. 275–314). Hillsdale, NJ: Lawrence Erlbaum Associates.

Robin, A., Schneider, M., & Dolnick, M. (1976). The turtle technique: An extended case study of self-control in the classroom. *Psychology in the Schools, 13,* 449–453.

Safer, D. J., Heaton, R. C., & Parker, F. C. (1981). A behavioral program for disruptive junior high school students: Results and follow-up. *Journal of Abnormal Child Psychology, 9,* 483–494.

Schuchman, M. C. (1977). A comparison of three techniques for reducing Scholastic Aptitude Test anxiety. *Dissertation Abstracts International, 38*(4-A), 2010.

Shure, M., & Spivak, G. (1978). *Problem-solving techniques in childrearing.* San Francisco: Jossey-Bass.

Shure, M. B., & Spivack, G. (1979). Interpersonal cognitive problem-solving and primary prevention: Programming for preschool and kindergarten children. *Journal of Clinical Child Psychology, 2,* 80–94.

Spitalnick, R., & Drabman, R. (1976). A classroom timeout procedure for retarded children. *Journal of Behavior Therapy and Experimental Psychiatry, 7,* 17–21.

Spivack, G., & Shure, M. B. (1974). *Social adjustment of young children: A cognitive approach to solving real-life problems.* San Francisco: Jossey-Bass.

Stokes, L. F., & Baer, D. M. (1977). An implicit technology of generalization. *Journal of Applied Behavior Analysis, 10,* 349–367.

Strain, P. S., Shores, R. E., & Timm, M. A. (1977). Effects of peer social initiations on the behavior of withdrawn preschool children. *Journal of Applied Behavior Analysis, 10,* 389–298.

Switzer, E. B., Deal, T. E., & Bailey, J. S. (1977). The reduction of stealing in second graders using a group contingency. *Journal of Applied Behavior Analysis, 10,* 267–272.

Taylor, D. W. (1972). Treatment of excessive frequency of urination by desensitization. *Journal of Behavior Therapy and Experimental Psychiatry, 3,* 311–313.

Thompson, M., Brassell, W. R., Persons, S., Tucker, R., & Rollins, H. (1974). Contingency management in the schools: How often and how well does it work? *American Educational Research Journal, 11,* 19–28.

Thoresen, C., & Mahoney, M. (1974). *Behavioral self-control.* New York: Holt, Rinehart, and Winston.

Vaal, J. J. (1973). Applying contingency contracting to a school phobia: A case study. *Journal of Behavior Therapy and Experimental Psychiatry, 4,* 371–373.

Warren, R., Deffenbacher, J. L., & Brading, P. (1976). Rational-emotive therapy and the reduction of test anxiety in elementary school students. *Rational Living, 11,* 26–29.

Weissberg, R., Gesten, E., Carnrike, C., Toro, P., Rapkin, B., Davidson, E., & Cowen, E. (1981). Social problem-solving skills training: A competence-building intervention with second- to fourth-graders. *American Journal of Community Psychology, 9,* 411–423.

Witt, J. C., & Elliott, S. N. (in press). Acceptability of classroom management strategies. In T. R. Kratochwill (Ed.), *Advances in school psychology* (Vol. 5), Hillsdale, NJ: Lawrence Erlbaum Associates.

Wolf, M. M. (1978). Social validity: The case for subjective measurement or how applied behavior analysis is finding its heart. *Journal of Applied Behavior Analysis, 11,* 203–214.

Workman, E. (1982). *Teaching behavioral self-control to students.* Austin, TX: Pro-Ed.

Yeaton, W. H., & Sechrest, L. (1981). Critical dimensions in the choice and maintenance of successful treatments: Strength, integrity, and effectiveness. *Journal of Consulting and Clinical Psychology, 49,* 156–167.

Zahavi, S. L., & Asher, S. R. (1978). The effect of verbal instructions on preschool children's aggressive behavior. *Journal of School Psychology, 16,* 146–153.

5 Vocational Education

Robert J. Illback

A crisis of confidence in the nation's public education system has been developing over the past decade. Schools have been described as overcome by a rising tide of mediocrity (National Commission on Excellence in Education, 1983). Products of the educational system have been characterized as unprepared to take on changing occupational roles in the workforce, because of the rapid evolution of technological and societal change (Mikulecky, 1981). Appropriate vocational education is seen as a critical need for the 1980s and beyond.

This chapter addresses the need for responsive vocational education by presenting a behavioral approach to the delivery of vocational education services. Following a brief review of the history of vocational and career education, the nature and scope of current vocational education efforts are described. Subdomains of vocational education, including vocational education and training, career awareness and development, vocational assessment, vocational guidance, counseling, and psychological services, are delineated. Literature that details application of behavioral methods and procedures to enhance vocational education are reviewed, because the central premise of the chapter is that a behavioral approach can serve to improve current vocational education practices. A discussion of some specific implications of this perspective is included. Finally, organizational factors that may enhance or impede a behavioral approach to vocational education are discussed.

HISTORICAL PERSPECTIVE ON VOCATIONAL EDUCATION

Vocational education has a long and complex history in this country; current trends in vocational education can only be understood against this backdrop.

Cegelka (1981) has described the "waxing and waning" of vocationalism in relation to societal, political, and economic events. For example, in times of great economic distress vocational education takes on greater meaning and urgency. In contrast, a broader, career-oriented perspective is more likely to prevail in a healthy economy. An example of the influence of political events on vocationalism is the impact of a war (e.g., World War II) on vocational education funds for training of manpower. In sharp contrast is the emphasis on science education and related liberal arts fields triggered by the Sputnik launching.

Legislative initiatives have also influenced the growth and development of vocational education. Most writers cite the Smith-Hughes Act of 1917 as the first federal law specifically geared toward vocational education in secondary schools (Batsche, 1984). This act provided for the development of curricula and instructional programs to ensure adequate vocational preparation in schools. By the early 1960s, vocational education had become firmly entrenched in the educational curriculum. Vocational education received further impetus as a function of the Manpower Development and Training Act of 1962, which provided vocational and remedial training to disadvantaged children. School dropouts and the unemployed benefitted from the creation of the Job Corps under the Economic Opportunities Act, 1962. Also in 1962, landmark legislation, the Vocational Education Act, clearly established a federal role in vocational education. The 1968 amendments confirmed the comprehensive scope of vocational education and extended it to all children, including the handicapped and disadvantaged (Cegelka, 1981).

The "career education" movement was initiated by the Nixon administration in the early 1970s. This resulted in a reconceptualization of the purposes of education. Career education, broader in scope than vocational education, focused on career choice-making, general preparation for entry into the world of work, and planning for the acquisition of marketable skills as a life-span activity.

Vocational and career education take on new meanings in the current school context. Technological and informational advancements require that children and youth be more competent in basic skill development (e.g., reading, writing, arithmetic) and capable of literacy with a burgeoning set of new technologies. Students will prepare to pursue new career paths in professions that have yet to be defined. This will require a reconfiguration of vocational and career training programs that take into account the specific skill sequences (behaviors required to perform various jobs, and considers cognitive and social problem solving skills that relate to career choice, career development, and job performance. Vocational and career education will be of particular relevance to the handicapped and disadvantaged, who are in danger of being left behind as society undergoes its transformation into the information age (Rozeghi & Davis, 1979).

NATURE AND SCOPE OF VOCATIONAL EDUCATION

Education can claim productive employment as an overriding goal, because employability is facilitated by the development of basic skills (e.g., reading), reasoning abilities (e.g., higher order cognitive processes), personal independence, and social awareness and responsibility. However, vocational education, by its constituent elements, is distinct from other educational programs, it directly seeks to prepare the individual to enter the world of work.

The field of vocational education is highly diverse and complex. Programs vary in content and focus, from career awareness and exploration curricula that may pervade the entire school experience, to specific training programs in discrete content areas (e.g., welding, computer programming) at the secondary level. To present relevant concepts and issues, in this chapter, vocational education consists of four major elements: vocational education and training, career awareness and development, vocational assessment, and vocational guidance and counseling.

Vocational Education and Training

Vocational education and training is an activity that occurs at the secondary and postsecondary level. Often, it is geared toward vocational skill development in preparation for paid employment in a discrete job category. Therefore, the focus of education and training programs is on specific vocational behaviors that are requisites for successful job performance. For example, a heavily subscribed vocational school program has been auto mechanics, a secondary-level (11th and 12th grade) program of preparation that helps students to acquire skills, such as preventive maintenance, troubleshooting, basic engine repair, and body work. Through planned and integrated experience students also learn about working in auto repair facilities and develop applied academic and social skills.

Although vocational education and training programs are seen in various configurations and content areas, traditional vocational education occurs most often in vocational school buildings, and is geared to students with aspirations in the service and technical fields. Offerings may include cosmetology, auto mechanics, practical nursing, child care, hotel/motel services, television/communications, construction fields (electricity, welding, carpentry, plumbing), and business and office occupations.

As the economy moves from a manufacturing base to an information base (Naisbitt, 1982), much of traditional vocational education is questioned. Vocational education is currently in crisis, a crisis of purpose and direction that is heightened if vocational services to handicapped learners are considered. Various legislative initiatives (e.g., Rehabilitation Act of 1973; Education for All Handicapped Children Act of 1975, Title II-Vocational Education) have established the right of educationally handicapped children to vocational education services. However, a range of policy and practical issues prevent the full implementation of these services. In a survey of State Education Agency (SEA) personnel on vocational education, Greenan and Phelps (1982) point to problems in interagency coordination and planning, personnel preparation, assessment, individualized programming, and program evaluation (see also Miller, 1981, for a description of problems in programming for secondary-level handicapped adolescents).

Career Awareness and Development

As an educational innovation, "career education" is usually traced to 1971, when the U.S. Commissioner of Education, Sidney Marland, initiated the career education movement. Career education is a concept distinct from (but complementary to) vocational education and training. Career education is a K-12 endeavor that stresses awareness and understanding of the world of work and emphasizes attitudinal and prevocational readiness skills. More specifically, career education helps students to understand the relationship between education and career opportunity, perceive social and economic structures in society that may affect them, make informed and responsible decisions about their career path, and acquire marketable skills in preparation for job-seeking (Marland, 1974).

A broader definition of career education includes the totality of all productive experiences, vocational, recreational, and social. Goldhammer (1972) proposed that career education prepares individuals for their careers as producer of goods, renderer of services, family member, participant in social and political life, and a range of other roles. Goldhammer's proposal has had particular appeal for special educators concerned with addressing the totality of the child's needs, to insure success in later life (Cegelka, 1981).

The essential features of school-based career education are summarized by Swanson (1972). They include early experience with career information and decision-making, infusion of career information into all subject areas, the use of a systematic approach to the study of occupations, and the development of linkages to business, industry, and the community at large.

In practice, career education programs in schools have declined. During the 1970s, as a result of large-scale federal, state, and local initiatives, a large body of career education curricula was developed for all grade levels. Much of the career education curricula was not infused into school curricula, because of inadequate staff development, poor articulation of basic concepts and issues, "turf" issues, and other readiness considerations. Despite severe implementation problems, career education is an important concept that must be dealt with in public education. (See Cegelka, 1981, for a comprehensive treatment of career education with particular reference to implications for the educationally handicapped)p.)

Vocational Assessment

Vocational assessment is the aspect of vocational education that provides information to decision-makers (e.g., teachers, parents, students) about vocational needs, skills, aptitudes, attitudes, and behaviors. As in other domains of assessment (e.g., cognitive assessment), a vast technological literature, psychometric tests, and related instrumentation of every description, have developed over the past few decades. Traditional vocational assessment has been closely aligned with psychological testing, and relies heavily on intelligence, aptitude, and achievement measures (Neff, 1970). In addition, a large and complex literature exists, describing vocational interest and preference measures.

Recently, partly due to the inability of global measures to predict vocational behavior (Ditty & Reynolds, 1980), a range of behaviorally focused instruments and procedures have emerged. These include vocational behavior rating scales, work-sampling approaches, observational systems, and self-report measures, (described in more detail later in this chapter).

Special educators, in particular, have been involved with the behavioral reconfiguration of vocational assessment methods (Nadolsky, 1981). Societal changes and recent technological advances have made the handicapped (and certain other minority groups) more employable, creating a need for sensitive and relevant assessment methods. For example, Stodden and Ianacone (1981) reviewed the vocational assessment literature for the handicapped and proposed a comprehensive model for the assessment of special needs individuals. Model Component I assesses personal and occupational awareness, exploration, and understanding. Model Component II assesses client behaviors in work tasks or tests to determine functioning level in career and vocational domains, and provides for a complete local employment market analysis. In Model Component III, the assessment data are formatted and interpreted in relation to programmatic considerations. Thus, the overall approach integrates and utilizes a range of career and vocational information in assessment and decision-making (see Stoddard & Ianacone, 1981, for a complete explanation).

Vocational Guidance Counseling, and Psychological Services

Vocational guidance and counseling has developed as a specialty area within the counseling psychology and school counseling professions. As a specialty, vocational guidance and counseling draws heavily on extant assessment technology (e.g., vocational and career preference tests, ability and aptitude measures) and on methods of individual and group counseling that are characteristic of these fields.

Issues of career choice and decision-making, employment seeking, vocational adaptation, and career maturity serve as the focus for vocational guidance and counseling. Thus, a career/vocational counselor may assist a client (or group of clients) with decision-making by providing a range of information about certain occupational clusters and the prerequisites needed for entering these fields. In a school context the counselor may choose, for efficiency and problem prevention, to implement a building-wide career and vocation information program through the career education curricula. If a client has a need to clarify vocational and career goals and aptitudes, the counselor may administer an individually-tailored assessment, and help the client understand the implications of the results through counseling.

School psychology is a specialized profession, traditionally concerned with a more narrow target population (e.g., educationally handicapped students) than concerns guidance counselors. An emergent subspecialty within school psychology has been termed "vocational school psychology," an area that relates the provision of assessment- and intervention-oriented vocational services to secondary-level handicapped and disadvantaged students (Hohenshil, 1982). Because of their extensive psychometric expertise, school psychologists can be instrumental in conducting and integrating vocational assessments, enhancing the individualized education programs (IEP) of handicapped learners. In addition, school psychologists have skill in areas such as teacher consultation, implementation of behavior management programs, staff development, training, and curriculum development. Because many vocational teachers are oriented toward their particular vocational content area, and may not be fully aware of pedagogical or behavioral issues, a school psychological perspective can enhance vocational education by complementing pedagogic and counseling viewpoints.

Because of the need for trained vocational specialists and program implementers, vocational guidance, counseling, and vocational school psychology are likely to flourish. Most vocational schools employ a counselor to engage in these and similar activities (e.g., school orientation, program admission and pupil progress tracking, program development and evaluation). Most secondary-level school counselors are also oriented toward career and vocational considerations. Because of the needs of the pupils they serve secondary-level school psychologies are performing these functions (Hohenshil 1982). Some schools also use counselors to coordinate work–study and career internship programs. Finally, many elementary school counselors are engaged with children in career education and prevocational activities.

BEHAVIORAL APPROACHES TO VOCATIONAL EDUCATION

Vocational education derives from a vast and somewhat undistilled literature. Like other fields in psychology and education, a behavioral perspective is beginning to emerge in vocational education that holds the promise of substantially redirecting and reconfiguring the field. This section reviews the available behavioral literature for three major content areas: vocational behavior assessment, vocational behavior intervention, and vocational behavior counseling. For each area, implications for the practice of behavioral vocational education are discussed.

Vocational Behavior Assessment

Vocational behavior assessment is part of the broader assessment of adaptive behavior (Forness, Thornton, & Horton, 1981). The term *adaptive behavior* refers to academic and nonacademic skills needed to function in life situations. More specifically, adaptive behavior is related to a range of self-help (personal self-sufficiency), social (interactions with peers and the community), and vocational (work performance) capabilities that individuals must possess to function in society.

It is difficult for the vocational assessor to select critical vocational behaviors necessary and sufficient for successful work performance. There is a complex interaction between workers and job environments; behaviors that may be adaptive and adequate in one setting for a particular individual may be maladaptive for the same person in another context. Delineating critical vocational behaviors entails more than merely specifying requisite cognitive and motoric behavior sequences. Workplaces are complex psychological environments, heavily influenced by social and organizational forces; the successful worker will need to operate smoothly within these parameters. Social skills, such as appropriate initiating behavior, situational assertiveness, and clear verbal communication, are likely to play a strong role in determining the adequacy of job performance.

Assessment of Work-Related Behavior

A number of discrete methods for collecting data about work-related behaviors can be identified in the literature (Nadolsky, 1971; Neff, 1968). Methods range from traditional psychological assessment approaches to highly specific behavioral assessment approaches (see also Chapter 2). Psychological assessment methods focus on variables, such as global cognitive functioning (e.g., intelligence, achievement) and emotional/social adjustment, as predictors of work performance. Although these variables are relevant and have been found to correlate with work performance, they do not always yield information that vocational educators can use in planning interventions. In contrast, behavioral methods focus on discrete, situation-specific variables through work sampling, direct behavior observation, behavior ratings and checklists, and self-report.

One method does not capture the complexity of the full range of work-related behaviors; a multiple-method approach is recommended. The trend is toward task-specific behavioral assessment, because of the specificity and gener-alizability advantages of this perspective (Goldfried & Kent, 1972).

Work Sampling.   Work sampling has emerged as one of the most widely reported vocational assessment practices. A small number of work sampling systems have been validated and are commercially available, but the majority of work sample programs are locally developed and highly situation-specific. The lack of local validation procedures has created much controversy (Neff, 1968). The criticisms are similar to those being leveled at behavior therapists for not attending to psychometric considerations in assessment (Cone, 1981).

Probably the most widely known work sampling program is the Vocational Evaluation System (VES) marketed by Singer Career Systems (Gannaway, Becket, & Weiner, 1979). The VES is comprised of a large number of topically-arranged work stations that present the client with "hands-on" tasks to complete. Task-related behaviors are observed and product outcomes are measured, providing an estimate of the person's behavioral capacities and vocational aptitudes. A number of studies have domonstrated the essential reliability and validity of the VES (Gannaway & Sink, 1978; Gannaway & Sink, 1981; Gannaway, Sink, & Becket, 1980).

The VES and similar work sampling approaches are not without detractors. For example, Irvin, Gersten, Taylor, Close, and Bellamy (1981) have noted that work samples tend to measure the products of prior learning, and may discriminate against disadvantaged and handicapped populations. In addition they note that work samples tend to focus on macroscopic behaviors, instead of pinpointing specific behavioral sequences, only measure current performance levels, and cannot reflect the person's capacity for profiting from direct instruction.

The Trainee Performance Sample (Bellamy & Snyder, 1976) has been offered as an improvement to other work sampling methods. It uses shorter and more discrete behavioral tasks, focuses on process variables instead of outcomes (e.g., ability to profit from instruction), and provides a format for estimating the rate of acquisition of new behavioral skills (data of greater relevance to intervention planning). The Trainee Performance Sample is especially relevant to severely handicapped or disadvantaged populations; it is more content valid for these groups (Irvin, et al., 1981).

Matthews, Whang, and Fawcett (1980) have developed and validated an occupational skills assessment instrument, a variation on the work samples theme, that utilizes analog behavioral situations. Relying heavily on role-playing, the occupational skills assessment instrument requires participants to perform 13 different employment-related skills, such as getting a job lead, telephoning a potential employer, accepting criticism, and explaining a problem to a supervisor. The occupational skills are related to obtaining and retaining employment. A subsequent study (Matthews, Whang, & Fawcett, 1982) demonstrated that the occupational skills instrument discriminated learning disabled (LD) from non-LD high school students, expecially in nonsocial interaction areas. This suggests the need for incorporating explicit occupational skills training into the vocational education of mildly handicapped youngsters.

Direct Behavioral Observation.   The hallmark of behavioral assessment traditionally has been direct behavioral observation. Behavioral observation involves the precise specification of relevant behaviors and the use of a range of observation strategies (e.g., time sampling, frequency counting, intensity estimation) to measure behaviors within the context of a particular setting and over a specific time period. Direct behavioral observation yields reliable and valid data about an individual's current functioning under specified conditions. The approach also allows for analysis of behavioral maintenance factors through the examination of antecedent and consequent conditions. A final advantage of direct behavioral observation for the vocational assessor is that it provides a benchmark against which to measure posttraining progress (observational data tend to be more criterion-relevant than other methods).

In the field of vocational education there are very few observational studies and few observational schemes are available. Direct behavioral observation is perhaps the most underdeveloped area of vocational assessment; there are, however, innumerable behavior rating scales (discussed in the next section). A work situation observation system was developed by Todd, Bellamy, and Leiter (1976). The system is constructed to reflect the ongoing behavior of the individual worker and the activities of persons in the work environment with whom the worker interacts. The system records behavioral events as they occur (not retrospectively), uses trained observer-coders, and requires few inferences for the coding of events. The scale includes general descriptors (e.g., task description, time parameters), situational codes (e.g., Work Productive Setting, Work Waiting, Training, Unstructured), subject behaviors (e.g., task completion, attention, social indicators, behavioral competence), and peer behaviors (e.g., social stimuli origination, interaction with peers and adults, number of people in area). The authors advocate 15 second interval recording of the behavior categories established.

Leiter (1976) has adapted the procedures developed by Todd, et al. (1976) for use in group situations to assess the behavior of workers in a given production setting. The behavioral categories have been altered to encompass broad task- and target-related behaviors, and to include teacher (trainer) variables. The approach is designed to approximate more closely a vocational training situation; the technology can be used to assess the progress of trainees at the group level. The data can also contribute to the formative evaluation of vocational education and training programs.

Behavior Ratings and Checklists.   An alternative to direct behavioral observation is the assessment of behavior through the use of rating scales and checklists; respondents are asked to rate job performance along a number of dimensions. Ratings are often clustered or factored to obtain a relative profile across a number of domains. In contrast, behavior checklists require respondents to denote the presence or absence of a particular behavior, regardless of its relative strength, yielding an inventory of vocational behaviors.

Behavior ratings and checklists in the field of vocational education have proliferated, they are available for nearly any desired variable. Walls and Werner (1977), in reviewing the state of the art for vocational behavior checklists, were able to obtain more than 200 devices, which they reviewed, categorized, and evaluated. For the purposes of their review, they delineated eight subscales of instruments, including prevocational skills, job-seeking skills, interview skills, job-related skills, union-financial-security skills, work performance skills, on-the-job social skills, and specific job skills. Walls and Werner specifically described 39 widely used scales in terms of items per subclass, objectivity, setting, and prescriptive-descriptive nature. The authors stated the relative merits and limitations of available instruments and suggested guidelines for their use (see Walls, Werner, Bacon, & Zane, 1977, for an annotated bibliography of 157 vocational behavior checklists).

Behavior checklists can serve a valuable function in behavioral assessment. They allow for the efficient consideration of a broad range of variables and reflect perceptions of the frequency, intensity, and duration of behavior, which have important implications for intervention.

Self-report. Self-report measures are a form of behavioral assessment because clients are asked to make certain determinations about their own behavior. Used clinically, self-report measures often ask clients to observe themselves through the use of ratings or checklists. In another form of self-report, clients may be asked to self-monitor their behavior in natural settings, and gather data over time. Applied to the area of vocational education, self-report implies the estimation of vocationally relevant behaviors by clients, and the use of this information in predicting and facilitating job performance.

The fields of vocational and career education are replete with instruments that measure personal preferences, attitudes, beliefs, and knowledge (for reviews, see Buros' Mental Measurements Yearbook, 1972). However, few instruments are specifically behavioral in nature (some could be described as cognitive-behavioral, in a broad sense). Thus, behavioral self-report is underdeveloped for use in vocational behavior assessment.

Assessment of Social and Applied Academic Skills

One cluster of vocational behaviors critical to work performance criteria can be termed *social and applied academic skills* (Forness, Thornton, & Horton, 1981), capabilities that transcend work and leisure activities activities and are global in nature. They include social knowledge and awareness, the ability to follow directions, and "survival" reading.

More traditional vocational assessment has focused on standard cognitive measures as predictors. Quinones (1978) has found that achievement tests have greater predictive value than other components of the psychological battery. However, Schreiner (1978) has demonstrated that samples of work behaviors in situ were of greater value than global cognitive measures. This finding is consistent with a behavioral perspective. Related social skills, such as verbal behavior, manners, and assertiveness have also been found predictive when assessed in job environments (Cunningham & Presnall, 1978; Malgady, Barcher, Tawner, & Davis, 1979).

Therefore, consistent with behavioral thinking, social and applied academic skill assessment is most useful when a task analytic approach is utilized; skills that relate directly to job performance are assessed in behavioral contexts that closely approximate actual work settings. For example, instead of measuring global academic achievement on a standardized measure, an applied skills measure that incorporates work-related terminology and concepts might be included as part of a broader assessment task, such as reading a repair manual and following the directions it contains.

Forness, et al. (1981) have developed the Applied Assessment Instrument (AAI). The AAI is comprised of four skill clusters designed to measure the applied functioning of developmentally disabled adolescents. The first section focuses on reading, comprehension, and direction-following; it requires the student to read paragraphs from actual projects, interpret directions, and follow them. The second section looks at number skills, such as counting, numbering, measuring, and telling time, using work-related materials. The third cluster, social skills, involves judgments about the student's concentration, frustration level, responsiveness, independence, maintenance of tools, and cooperation. In the final section applied motor skill functioning is assessed through a variety of tasks. The authors provide evidence of the concurrent validity of these procedures with correlation from teacher ratings and global achievement measures, but stress the need for more content validation.

Irvin, Halpern, and Reynolds (1977) have developed and revised the Social and Prevocation Information Battery (SPIB), a series of knowledge tests for mildly retarded individuals. Subtests on this measure include Hygiene and Grooming, Functional Signs, Job Related Behavior, Home Management, Health Care, Job Search Skills, Budgeting, and Banking and Purchasing Habits. The total scale is comprised of 291 items, and can take up to 3 hours for administration. Validation research indicates adequate reliability for the scale and substantial relationships to applied performance within the skill domains.

Summary

Vocational behavior assessment is in its infancy, when compared to other areas of behavioral assessment. Most of the effort has centered around vocational behavior checklists and work sampling, less attention has been given to direct observation and self-report. Psychometric and conceptual limitations occur with all the reported approaches. A major problem in assessment relates to limited understanding of how specific cognitive and motoric behavioral sequences relate to various occupational clusters and task characteristics. This creates major problems in assessing content and criterion-related validity. The relationship between various career and vocational behaviors is also unclear, rendering the selection and domain-referencing of behavior complex and somewhat arbitrary.

Because of these and related difficulties, the vocational assessor is wise to assess variables that are definable and measurable and closely related to outcome criteria. Inferences that require the use of abstract concepts, such as intelligence and vocational aptitude, should be avoided in favor of more discrete behaviors. Also, it is appropriate to focus on situation-specific tasks and predict performance only over short periods of time, using a task-analytic approach. Finally, and most importantly, it behooves assessors to utilize multiple methods to gather behavioral data and to draw inferences.

Vocational Behavior Intervention

This section reviews behavioral literature that focuses on the development and improvement of career and vocational behaviors and problem solving skills (cognitive behaviors). Applied behavior analytic (operant) literature pertaining to vocational behavior intervention is delineated, cognitive behavioral intervention strategies are reviewed, and a summary and recommendation are provided.

Applied Behavior Analytic Interventions. Essential aspects of applied behavior analysis include the specification of discrete behaviors, recording and analysis of these behaviors, and the manipulation of antecedent and consequent conditions to modify or better manage these behaviors (see also Chapter 3 and Chapter 4). Literature related to the modification of vocational behavior may be arbitrarily divided into research on behavior specification and task analysis, research on stimulus (antecedent) factors related to vocational behavior change, and research on contingency (consequent) manipulation.

Categorizing behavior specification as an intervention implies that, when expected vocational behavior is clearly specified and communicated to the client, there is a greater probability that such behavior will emerge, develop, and be maintained. The specification of expected behavioral outcomes shapes and directs vocational programming, which in turn moderates the stimulus and reinforcement conditions that impinge on the client. Thus, behavior specification and task analysis set the parameters for any subsequent intervention strategy (Thomas, 1979).

The term *behavior specification* denotes the precise statement of observable and/or measurable behaviors that describe actions clients will engage in during or after training. A fundamental assumption of training programs is that interrelated sequences of vocational behaviors cam be specified and arranged along a continuum to allow for the measurement of progress toward goal attainment. A behavioral approach also assumes that various vocational behavior domains can be described, and that attention to these domains can insure comprehensive intervention efforts.

As an example, Krantz (1971) has developed a list of "critical vocational behaviors." These behaviors are "critical," because they are seen as predictive of eventual employment; they are "vocational" because they relate directly to adult occupations across a broad spectrum of job titles. Krantz delineates six general domains of vocational behavior: job-objective behaviors, job-getting behaviors, job-keeping behaviors, social living competencies, community living competencies, and general and personal living competencies. Each domain contains a more specific list of vocational behaviors that must be emitted at some level to insure successful functioning. The intervention program designed for a particular client (or group of clients) can be examined in the context of critical vocational behaviors, and decisions can be made about client status and program relevance.

Task analysis is a form of behavior specification in which component behaviors of specific vocational tasks are delineated, sequenced, and gradually trained. For example, Friedenberg and Martin (1977) used a task analytic approach to train two severely retarded students to perform label stapling on a plastic bag. Two forms of label stapling, one by hand and the other by machine, were compared. Content analysis was used to break the task into teachable units. Instruction utilized four levels: nonpunitive indication of error, verbal direction, modeling, and priming. In their analysis, the authors demonstrate how task analysis contributed to the effects of training and facilitated a more sophisticated interpretation of results. Other examples of skills-oriented vocational behavior specification can be found in Bellamy, Wilson, Adler, and Clark (1980), Cross and Pine (1979), and Lynch (1979).

Although behavioral research has traditionally focused on the effects of altering the contingencies of reinforcement, an emerging behavioral literature has drawn attention to the potency of stimulus features in learning situations (manipulation of antecedent conditions). Through enhanced discrimination of cues (discrimination learning), learners will be more likely to engage in and maintain desired vocational behaviors.

Much of the behavioral research on discrimination learning in vocational skill acquisition has involved the mentally retarded, because there is some evidence that this population experiences difficulty attending to the salient features of learning situations (Zeaman & House, 1963). Research has demonstrated that subjects must learn to attend to relevant dimensions in tasks and to approach the correct cue on that dimension. Therefore, experimental work has examined the training and transfer effects of shift manipulations across different categories of cues, cue redundancies, and overlearning (Gold, 1972). A number of consistent findings have emerged for the mentally retarded (see Zeaman & House [1963] for a more detailed review of these studies).

Training procedures that involve the manipulation of stimulus features hold great promise for the field of vocational education, particularly if used with handicapped and disadvantaged populations. One approach involves the teaching of easier discriminations between cues on a particular task dimension (e.g., deciding between two tools when presented with a simple assembly task), to facilitate more complex stimulus discrimination (e.g., deciding between a number of tools when presented with a complex assembly task). Another procedure involves adding and fading extra relevant, or redundant, dimensions the subject is already familiar with or prefers. This allows for more rapid acquisition of discriminations along the new dimension, which are then brought under stimulus control (Irvin & Bellamy, 1977).

In response to the relative inefficiency of the previous two approaches, which often involve large numbers of trials, Irvin and Bellamy (1977) developed a third discrimination learning approach. Fifty-one severely retarded individuals were taught to visually discriminate cues on a complex assembly task using a combination of the two procedures previously described. Highly preferred color dimensions and large cue differences accompanied task presentation on a bicycle axle assembly line that required the individual to make choices about materials. Gradually, the color dimensions were faded and the large cue differences were diminished. This combined approach was found more rapid and durable than individual discrimination procedures applied in isolation. Behavioral literature on the salient features of vocational tasks used with nonretarded populations is minimal; it is an area in need of much development.

Manipulation of the contingencies of reinforcement (consequent conditions) to modify specific vocational behaviors is a powerful technology available to vocational educators. A number of studies reported in the literature demonstrate the efficacy of this approach with a wide variety of problems and populations. For example, Jens and Shores (1969) demonstrated that performance feedback in the form of behavioral graphs as reinforcers can substantially improve the work behavior of mentally retarded adolescents. Similarly, Huddle (1967) and Noonan and Barry (1967) investigated the differential effects of incentives, such as monetary reward, on the vocational behavior of retarded persons. The effect of token reinforcement on the productivity of multiple handicapped clients in a sheltered workshop was shown by Zimmerman, Stuckey, Garlick, and Miller (1969).

Behavioral approaches have considerable relevance to vocational training with retarded and emotionally disturbed children. As noted by Brown, Bellamy, Perlmutter, Sackowitz, and Sontag (1972), these groups are at considerable risk in the workplace, because of inaccurate or incomplete work performance, insufficient production rate, inappropriate social behavior, inadequate work attendance, and unacceptable variability in performance over time. Through systematic environmental manipulations, the authors demonstrated that work quality (accuracy), work quantity (completion at acceptable rates), and work durability (consistently accurate completion at competitive rates) can be developed and maintained. Through verbal directions, modeling, and prompting, retarded adolescents were taught to assemble packs of index cards accurately. Following a baseline period and a phase in which monetary payment occurred weekly, contingent reinforcement was introduced. Initially, monetary reinforcement was provided after each work session for accurate work; then, only successively higher rates of accurate work were reinforced. When subjects reached the criterion level (competitive rate), payments were faded to a daily, and eventually a weekly, basis. The competitive rate was maintained over time. The design of this study can serve as the basis for a range of vocational behavior training programs.

Brown and Pearce (1970) used teacher praise and peer models, coupled with performance feedback, to train a group of trainable mentally handicapped youngsters to stuff envelopes in 20-minute work sessions. Following a baseline period, trainable students observed five emotionally disturbed peers being reinforced for appropriate behavior. After a return to baseline, the subjects were reinforced directly and were given performance feedback. This resulted in appropriate and durable behavior change.

In a unique study, Kiel and Barbee (1973) used behavioral technology to train economically disadvantaged trainees in job interview skills. The authors viewed these persons as more likely to exhibit problem behaviors in interview situations because of their low achievement orientation, low perceptions of opportunity, external locus of control, and underdeveloped interpersonal skills. Problem behaviors associated with these factors included limited verbal skills, apprehensiveness in interviews, a reluctance to self-disclose, and a tendency to engage in brief and superficial dialogue. In response, the authors delineated target behaviors, such as responding completely to an interviewer's questions, clarifying personal circumstances as they relate to job/task considerations, relating past work and educational experiences to the job, and initiating questions in relation to work tasks, company policies, and opportunities for advancement. Thirty trainees underwent pre and posttraining videotaped interviews. Deficiencies in pretraining interviews were identified and alternative behaviors were suggested and role-rehearsed. Independent judges found significant differences on the Job Interview Rating Scale, as compared with control groups.

Cognitive-Behavioral Interventions. Cognitive components are being incorporated into behavioral treatment strategies, in response to criticisms about generalization and maintenance of behavior change in traditional operant treatments. Behavioral self-control holds great promise for vocational education, but little attention has been devoted to this application in the behavioral literature (Wehman, Schutz, Bates, Renzaglia, & Karan, 1977). One notable exception is a study by Connis (1979). Connis investigated the effects of a self-recording procedure using sequentially organized picture cues on independent task changes on four mentally retarded individuals. The subjects were asked to self-record behavior about the beginning of new tasks without directions or instruction. Not only did behavior change in the direction of greater independence, but behavior changes were maintained over a 10-week period following removal of the training procedures.

A creative behavioral self-control experiment with three mentally retarded adults demonstrated the effectiveness of time management training (Sowers, Rusch, Connis, & Cummings, 1980). The subjects were given a card with a clock face representation and clock hands, and were instructed to complete required vocational behaviors prior to the time when the real clock matched the clock face. Independent time management responding ensued, independent of the ability to tell time. For two individuals, results were maintained when the procedure was withdrawn.

Summary

The vocational behavior intervention literature encompasses a significant number of citations, but it is narrowly focused; the literature relates to the handicapped or disadvantaged. Most of the studies involve training for tasks that are simple and/or rote in nature. Therefore, there is a need for behavioral research with normal populations and across a broader and more representative range of vocational tasks. Similarly, there is a need for evaluation research at the program level, in contrast to purely single-subject and across-groups research in highly controlled settings.

At the same time, there is much in the literature that can serve to orient vocational education efforts. Behavior specification and task analysis are fundamental and critical elements of any behavioral intervention. Vocational educators would do well to specify the behavioral sequences inherent in their instructional programs. Moreover, the technology of applied behavior analysis is useful in structuring vocational education programs. Similarly, cognitive strategies, such as behavioral self-control, have broad applicability across a range of vocational training efforts.

BEHAVIORAL VOCATIONAL COUNSELING

There is a paucity of behavioral literature in the area of career and vocational counseling; presumably, due to difficulties in observing and measuring behavior. Nonetheless, a handful of relevant articles were gleaned from a review of the behavioral and vocational literatures. These can be categorized into two groups, career exploration and choice-making, and problem-oriented behavioral counseling.

Career Exploration and Choice-Making

In one of the few well-controlled studies in career counseling, Mithaug and Hanawalt (1978) investigated prevocational task preferences of three severely retarded persons between the ages of 19 and 21. Each subject's preferences for six tasks—collating, stuffing, sorting, pulley assembly, flour-sifter assembly, and circuit-board stuffing—were assessed systematically. Random-pairing choices were presented every 2 days for a period of 34 days to establish least and most preferred task preferences, which were validated against moderately preferred tasks. Consistency of task preference was demonstrated.

In a follow-up study, Mithaug and Mar (1980) investigated the relation between prevocational preference and the work that followed that choice. Following selection of a task object, clients performed tasks previously selected as more or less preferred than the one indicated by the object. The authors found that work that follows object choices reinforced or punished subsequent selections, indicating that object choices were valid indicators of preferences for working different tasks, and that classes of vocational behavior responses affect other classes of vocational responses (Premack principle). The generalizability of the two studies is undetermined, but they serve as a model for behavioral research on career and task preference.

Motsch (1980) investigated the relationship between peer social modeling and career exploration behavior. Ninth grade girls (216) were randomly assigned to four treatment conditions and two control groups. Various combinations of videotaped career counseling sessions and presentation of career stimulus materials (e.g., Self-Directed Search, occupational handbooks) were implemented to determine whether peer modeling of information-seeking behavior differentially affects subject behavior. It was found that observation of a career counseling group, combined with positive reinforcement and overt practice, is most effective in stimulating information-seeking behavior.

In a group contingency management study on career exploration and development, Randolph (1974) compared the effects of lessons presented in a behavior management approach with more traditional teaching. He found significant differences in favor of the behavioral approach on dependent measures, such as the Vocational Development Inventory and the Career Development Achievement Test. However, methodological problems make these findings difficult to interpret.

Vocational Counseling

No controlled studies can be found in vocational counseling. However, with the advent of cognitive-behavioral interventions, some literature has emerged advocating the use of these approaches (see also Chapter 4, Affective Social Education). For example, Weinrach (1980) discussed the application of concepts of rational–emotive therapy on occupational mental health. Weinrach defined prevalent forms of occupational stress, such as anxiety related to advancement, job change, lack of training, and discriminatory practices. Through individual and group counseling, the author advocates the use of rational disputation to help workers diminish stress and increase productivity and job satisfaction.

In a related study, Gerler (1977, 1980) proposed a multimodal model for career counseling and career education. Critical elements of this approach include the impact of information-seeking behavior on decision-making, the effects of emotion on decision-making, the role of painful or pleasurable sensation on work performance, the influence of mental imagery on career development, the effects of logical thought on career decision-making, relationships between interpersonal behavior and job-seeking and maintenance, and physiological factors as they relate to productivity. Based on these concepts, Gerler attempts to organize a range of vocational counseling interventions that in combination may address the total career/vocational needs of a particular client.

Summary

The area of behavioral vocational counseling is very underdeveloped. The few studies that have been done are either too narrow or have too many methodological problems to be of much use. Because of the recent emergence of cognitive behavior therapy, and the attendant methodology for defining and measuring thinking behavior, vocational behavioral counseling is a ripe area for systematic research. Until a coherent literature does emerge, the behavioral practitioner must rely on clinical judgment and on principles and procedures extrapolated from other areas of knowledge.

PLANNING FOR ORGANIZATIONAL CHANGE IN VOCATIONAL EDUCATION

A reconfiguration of vocational education practices to include broad-based behavioral approaches has been advocated in this chapter. However, the fact that behavioral thinking holds great promise for improving vocational education is not sufficient to insure that necessary change will occur at the local level. Explicit planning for organizational change must transpire, by delineating the nature and scope of the required changes and by assessing the readiness of the organization for these changes.

In planning for organizational change in vocational education, a number of issues become apparent. Perhaps the most fundamental pertains to the basic curricular issue: What will be taught? Educators routinely grapple with the scope and sequence of the skills continuum that should guide instruction. In an area such as vocational education, which transcends other curricular offerings, the task of infusing a consistent and comprehensive behavioral skill sequence into an already complex structure is, at best, difficult. Nonetheless, without a scope and sequence framework that explicates the manner in which divergent, but interrelated skills (e.g., knowledge of career clusters, career exploration, choice--making, job-seeking, and applied academic and social skills) are to be taught K-12, the district's vocational program will be fragmented and ineffective.

Once the vocational education components have been specified and sequenced, the issue: How will the instructional program be delivered? remains. In a behavioral approach, there is strong emphasis on explicitness and systematic practice. For individuals and groups of students, this will require that teachers and administrators engage in activities, such as assessing needs, setting goals, writing behavioral objectives, delineating and implementing behavioral intervention plans, and evaluating student progress toward goal attainment. However, educators are often unsophisticated in the use of behavioral technology, and will require considerable training and assistance.

More subtle problems in adopting a broad-based vocational education approach also exist. For example, it is unlikely that any program change will be adopted unless there is a perceived need at the local level to develop and improve vocational education. Objective evidence may indicate that the vocational education offerings are ineffective, but unless people involved with the program recognize the need to reconfigure, durable and meaningful change is unlikely to occur. Therefore, an initial strategy might be to reach agreement with all involved parties about the current status of the program, prior to discussing reconfiguration.

Another subtle, but powerful, issue is "professional turf." To consider adopting a new approach, school professionals with a wide range of training and experience very often need to re-evaluate long-held beliefs, attitudes, values, and practices. For example, a vocational assessment specialist might need to reconsider the use of intelligence tests as part of a standard vocational battery; a school counselor might have to discontinue certain career education practices at the elementary level, due to undemonstrated empirical validity. Moreover, reconfiguration of the vocational education program might require certain professionals to relinguish some degree of control or influence within the organization. These factors can result in resistance to the changes being sought, but can be countered by demonstrating the positive effects that will accrue to students and staff.

Behavior modification and behavior therapy are frequently "roses by any other name" (Woolfolk, Woolfolk & Wilson, 1977). Many teachers and administrators tend to think of behavioral approaches in narrow and simplistic ways, and associate behavioral terminology with operant and mechanical interventions, devoid of thought or affect. In contrast, behavior therapists have outgrown the early emphasis on overt and measureable behavior. They routinely develop interventions with cognitive, affective, interpersonal, and behavioral foci, reflecting a more complex view of the world. Behavior therapy stereotypes in education will need to be overcome before a broad-based behavioral approach to vocational education can be adopted.

REFERENCES

Batsche, C. (1984). Providing vocational education for special needs populations. In C. A. Maher, R. J. Illback, & J. E. Zins (Eds.), *Organizational psychology in the schools: A handbook for professionals* (pp. 173–197). Springfield, IL: Charles C. Thomas.

Bellamy, G. T., & Snyder, S. (1976). The Trainee Performance Sample: Toward the prediction of habilitation costs for severely handicapped adults. *AAESPH Review, 1,* 17–36.

Bellamy, G. T., Wilson, D., Adler, E., & Clark, J. (1980). A strategy for programming vocational skills for severely handicapped youth. *Exceptional Education Quarterly, 1,* 11–18.

Brown, L., Bellamy, T., Perlmutter, L., Sackowitz, P., & Sontag, E. (1972). The development of quality, quantity, and durability in the work performance of retarded students in a public school prevocational workshop. *Training School Bulletin, 68,* 58–69.

Brown, L., & Pearce, E. (1970). Increasing the production rates of trainable retarded students in public school simulated workshop. *Education and Training of the Mentally Retarded, 5,* 15–22.

Buros, O. K. (1972). *The seventh mental measurements yearbook* (Vols. 1–2). Highland Park, NJ: Gryphon Press.

Cegelka, P. T. (1981). Career education. In J. M. Kauffman & D. P. Hallahan (Eds.), *Handbook of special education* (pp. 640–662). Englewood Cliffs, NJ: Prentice-Hall.

Cone, J. D. (1981). Psychometric considerations. In M. Hersen & H. S. Bellack (Eds.), *Behavioral assessment: A practical handbook* (2nd ed., pp. 38–70). New York: Pergamon.

Connis, R. T. (1979). The effects of sequential pictorial cues, self-recording, and praise on the job task sequencing of retarded adults. *Journal of Applied Behavior Analysis, 12,* 355–361.

Cross, J. E., & Pine, A. L. (1979). The application of experimental behavior analysis in vocational training for the severely handicapped. In G. T. Bellamy, G. O'Connor, & O. C. Karan (Eds.), *Vocational rehabilitation of severely handicapped persons* (pp. 73–88). Baltimore: University Park Press.

Cunningham, T., & Presnall, D. (1978). Relationship between dimensions of adaptive behavior and sheltered workshop productivity. *American Journal of Mental Deficiency, 82,* 386–393.

Ditty, J. A., & Reynolds, K. (1980). Traditional vocational evaluation: Help or hindrance. *Journal of Rehabilitation, 46*(4), 22–25.

Forness, S. R., Thornton, R. L., & Horton, A. A. (1981). Assessment of applied academic and social skills. *Education and Training of the Mentally Retarded, 16,* 104–109.

Friedenberg, P., & Martin, A. (1977). Prevocational training of the severely retarded using task analysis. *Mental Retardation, 15*(2), 16–20.

Gannaway, T., Becket, W., & Weiner, M. (1979). *VES evaluators manual.* Rochester, NY: Singer.

Gannaway, T. W., & Sink, J. M. (1978). The relationship between the Vocational Evaluation System by Singer and employment success in occupational groups. *Vocational Education and Work Adjustment Bulletin, 11*(2), 38–45.

Gannaway, T. W., & Sink, J. M. (1981). A summary of research relating to the use of an audiovisual instruction based work sample program with educable mentally retarded students. *Journal for Vocational Special Needs Education, 3*(3), 24–26.

Gannaway, T. W., Sink, J. M., & Beckett, W. C. (1980). A predictive validity study of a job sample program with handicapped and disadvantaged individuals. *Vocational Guidance Quarterly, 29,* 4–11.

Gerler, E. R., Jr. (1977). The "basic id" in career education. *Vocational Guidance Quarterly, 25,* 238–244.

Gerler, E. R., Jr. (1980). Mental imagery in multimodal career education. *Vocational Guidance Quarterly, 28*, 3U6–312.

Gold, M. W. (1972). Stimulus factors in skill training of the retarded on a complex task: Acquisition, transfer, and retention. *American Journal of Mental Deficiency, 76*, 517–526.

Goldfried, M. R., & Kent, R. N. (1972). Traditional versus behavioral assessment: A comparison of methodological and theoretical assumptions. *Psychological Bulletin, 77*, 409–420.

Goldhammer, K. A. (1972). A careers curriculum. In K. A. Goldhammer & R. Taylor (Eds.), *Career education: Perspectives and promise* (pp. 121–168). Columbus, OH: Charles E. Merrill.

Greenan, J. P., & Phelps, L. A. (1982). Delivering vocational education to handicapped learners. *Exceptional Children, 48*, 408–411.

Hohenshil, T. H. (1982). Roles for school psychology in vocational education programs for handicapped students. In T. H. Hohenshil & W. T. Anderson (Eds.), *School psychological services in secondary vocational education* (pp. 77–83). Virginia Technical University. Blacksburg, VA.

Huddle, D. D. (1967). Work performance of trainable adults influenced by competition, cooperation, and monetary reward. *American Journal of Mental Deficiency, 72*, 198–211.

Irvin, L. K., & Bellamy, G. T. (1977). Manipulation of stimulus features in vocational skill training of severely retarded individuals. *American Journal of Mental Deficiency, 81*, 486–491.

Irvin, L. K., Gersten, R., Taylor, V. E., Close, D. W., & Bellamy, G. T. (1981) Vocational skill assessment of severely mentally retarded adults. *American Journal of Mental Deficiency, 85*, 631–638.

Irvin, L., Halpern, A., & Reynolds, W. (1977). Assessing social and prevocational awareness in mildly and moderately retarded individuals. *American Journal of Mental Deficiency, 82*, 266–272.

Jens, K. G., & Shores, R. E. (1969). Behavioral graphs as reinforcers for work behavior of mentally retarded adolescents. *Education and Training of the Mentally Retarded, 4*, 21–26.

Kiel, E. C., & Barbee, J. R. (1973). Behavior modification and training the disadvantaged job interviewee. *Vocational Guidance Quarterly, 22*, 50–56.

Krantz, G. (1971). Critical vocational behaviors. *Journal of Rehabilitation, 37*(4), 14–16.

Leiter, M. (1976). Behavioral observations for work situations: Revision for group observation. In G. Bellamy (Ed.), *Habilitation of severely and profoundly retarded adults* (pp. 119–125). Eugene, OR: University of Oregon, Center on Human Development.

Lynch, K. P. (1979). Toward a skill-oriented prevocational program for trainable and severely mentally impaired students. In G. T. Bellamy, G. O'Connor, & O. C. Karan (Eds.), *Vocational rehabilitation of severely handicapped persons* (pp. 26–39). Baltimore: University Park Press.

Malgady, R., Barcher, P., Tawner, G., & Davis, J. (1979). Language factors in vocational evaluation of mentally retarded workers. *American Journal of Mental Deficiency, 83*, 432–438.

Marland, S. P. (1974). *Career education: A proposal for reform.* New York: McGraw-Hill.

Matthews, R. M., Whang, P. L., & Fawcett, S. B. (1980). Development and validation of an occupational skills assessment instrument. *Behavioral Assessment, 2*, 71–85.

Matthews, R. M., Whang, P. L., & Fawcett, S. B. (1982). Behavioral assessment of occupational skills of learning disabled adolescents. *Journal of Learning Disabilities, 15*, 38–41.

Mikulecky, L. (1981). The mismatch between school training and job literacy demands. *Vocational Guidance Quarterly, 30*, 174–180.

Miller, S. R. (1981). A crisis in appropriate education: The dearth of data on programs for secondary handicapped adolescents. *Journal of Special Education, 15*, 351–360.

Mithaug, D. E., & Hanawalt, D. A. (1978). The validation of procedures to assess prevocational preferences in retarded adults. *Journal of Applied Behavior Analysis, 11*, 153–162.

Mithaug, D. E., & Mar, D. K. (1980). The relation between choosing and working prevocational tasks in two severely retarded adults. *Journal of Applied Behavior Analysis, 13*, 177–182.

Motsch, P. (1980). Peer social modeling: A tool for assisting girls with career exploration. *Vocational Guidance Quarterly, 28*, 231–240.

Nadolsky, J. (1971). *Development of a model for vocational evaluation of the disadvantaged*. Auburn, AL: Auburn University.

Nadolsky, J. M. (1981). Vocational evaluation in the public schools: Implications for future practice. *Journal for Vocational Special Needs Education, 3*, 5–9.

Naisbitt, J. (1982). *Megatrends: Ten new directions for transforming our lives*. New York: Warner.

National Commission on Excellence in Education (1983). *A nation at risk: The imperative for educational reform*. Washington, DC: U.S. Government Printing Office.

Neff, W. S. (1968). *Work and human behavior*. New York: Atherton Press.

Neff, W. S. (1970). Vocational assessment—theory and models. *Journal of Rehabilitation, 36*(1), 27–29.

Noonan, J. R., & Barry, J. R. (1967). Differential effects of incentives among the retarded. *The Journal of Educational Research. 61*, 108–111.

Quinones, W. (1978). A test battery for assessing the vocational competency of moderately retarded persons. *Mental Retardation, 16*, 412–415.

Randolph, D. (1974). A behavior management approach vs. a traditional approach to career education. *Vocational Guidance Quarterly, 21*(4), 293–297.

Rozeghi, J. A., & Davis, S. (1979). Federal mandates for the handicapped: Vocational educational education, opportunity and employment. *Exceptional Children, 45*, 353–359.

Schreiner, J. (1978). Prediction of retarded adults' work performance through components of general ability. *American Journal of Mental Deficiency, 83*, 77–79.

Sowers, J., Rusch, F. R., Connis, R. T., & Cummings, L. E. (1980). Teaching mentally retarded adults to time manage in a vocational setting. *Journal of Applied Behavior Analysis, 13*, 119–128.

Stodden, R. A., & Ianacone, R. N. (1981). Career/vocational assessment of the special needs individual: A conceptual model. *Exceptional Children, 47*(8), 600–608.

Swanson, G. I. (1972). Career education. In K. Goldhammer & R. E. Taylor (Eds.), *Career education: Perspective and promise* (pp. 107–120). Columbus, OH: Charles E. Merrill.

Thomas, M. A. (1979). Put the focus on instructional skills: A conversation with Edward L. Meyen about mentally retarded students. *Education and Training of the Mentally Retarded, 14*, 112–119.

Todd, N., Bellamy, G. T., & Leiter, M. (1976). Behavioral observations for work situations: Coding definition manual. In G. T. Bellamy (Ed.), *Habilitation of the severely and profoundly retarded* (Vol. 1, pp. 109–118). Eugene, OR: University of Oregon.

Walls, R. T., & Werner, T. J. (1977). Vocational behavior checklists. *Mental Retardation, 15*(4), 30–35.

Walls, R. T., Werner, T. J., Bacon, A., & Zane, T. (1977). Behavior checklists. In R. P. Hawkins & J. D. Cone (Eds.), *Behavioral assessment: New directions in clinical psychology*. New York: Brunner-Mazel.

Wehman, P., Schutz, R., Bates, P., Renzaglia, A., & Karan, O. (1978). Self-management programes with mentally retarded workers: Implications for developing independent vocational behaviors. *British Journal of Social and Clinical Psychology, 17*, 555–564.

Weinrach, S. G. (1980). A rational-emotive approach to occupational mental health. *Vocational Guidance Quarterly, 28*, 208–218.

Woolfolk, A. E., Woolfolk, R. L., & Wilson, G. T. (1977). "A rose by any other name. . .": Labeling bias and attitudes toward behavior modification. *Journal of Consulting and Clinical Psychology, 45*, 184–191.

Zeaman, D., & House, B. J. (1963). The role of attention in retardate discrimination learning. In N. R. Ellis (Ed.), *Handbook of mental deficiency*. New York: McGraw-Hill.

Zimmerman, J., Stuckey, T. E., Garlick, B. J., & Miller, M. (1969). Effects of token reinforcement on productivity in multiple handicapped clients in a sheltered workshop. *Rehabilitation Literature, 30*, 34–41.

6 Health and Physical Education

Bruce A. McClenaghan
Dianne S. Ward

Health and well-being are qualities of life desired by everyone. Current lifestyles, however, reflect a growing problem in the personal health practices of individuals. Lifestyle choices are resulting in death and disease that could be prevented. Specific goals and objectives for improving health have been included in recent major health policy documents developed by the federal government (U.S. Department of Health, Education, and Welfare, 1979a). Exercise, as a positive health behavior, is specifically mentioned in the federal government's directives.

Recent awareness of the many problems resulting from personal choice has forced educators to look closely at the learning processes involved in health and physical education (Powell, Christenson, & Kreuter, 1984). The development of positive health habits does not occur from the transmission of factual knowledge alone. Affective development, including the establishment of appropriate health habits, has become a central component of educational programs (Pate, Blair, & McClenaghan, 1982, see also Chapter 4). The evaluation of behavioral technology has significantly impacted on the educator's ability to assist students in formulating appropriate life skills.

The organizational structure of health and physical education programs in schools, often presents problems in the design and implementation of meaningful instructional change. Health and physical education are structured differently depending on local and state regulations or conventions. In elementary schools, for example, the classroom teacher may be responsible for instruction in both subject areas, or, a specialist in physical education may be responsible for all instruction or for supplementing the routine instruction of the classroom teacher. Health and physical education in high schools may occur as two separate courses, physical education a required course of study and health an elective course of study, or they may exist as one comprehensive school subject.

The inconsistency in organizational design probably relates to the overlap that exists in the two content areas. Health education has as its objective the promotion of healthy lifestyles. This objective implies a wholistic or "wellness" approach to health. Physical education has a similar but more specific objective—to develop a physically active lifestyle (Powell et al., 1984). The promotion of healthy lifestyles requires knowledge and attitude change in alcohol, tobacco, and drug use, fitness and weight control information and practices, and skills for the development of lifetime physical activity.

The focus of this chapter is behavioral technology and its facilitation of health and physical education of children and youth in schools. Because health and physical education may be structured differently in different schools, this chapter addresses the major topical areas of the disciplines involved in wholistic health and physical development: motor skill acquisition; physical fitness development, including weight control; and substance abuse.

BEHAVIORAL TECHNIQUES IN THE ACQUISITION OF MOTOR SKILLS

Acquisition of appropriate motor skills is a primary objective associated with the concept of promoting lifelong participation in some form of physical activity; however, achieving this objective is no simple task. Students must be provided with opportunities to acquire an adequate level of motor skills to experience success in physical activity.

The development of sophisticated movement abilities is a complex phenomena that begins during the prenatal period and continues through adulthood. Developmental theories of the acquisition of motor skills have been described by numerous authors (McClenaghan & Gallahue, 1978; Wickstrom, 1977). A fundamental concept that appears to be universally accepted is that motor skills are acquired from simple actions and refined into highly coordinated and complex movements. Two primary factors play a significant role in the development and refinement of motor skills, the maturation and integrity of the neuromuscular systems and the quality and variety of the individual's experiences with motor skills.

Instructional methods differ significantly as the child progresses through each of the stages of motor skill development. Infants and young children require a diverse selection of activities to assist in learning to process sensory information and to integrate the appropriate motor response. As motor patterns begin to be established, older children must be assisted to refine the qualitative aspects of their performance. Failure to refine these patterns during the early childhood years may result in difficulty with more advanced aspects of motor performance.

The teacher or coach instructing the advanced skill learner must take into consideration the individual's level of performance. Sufficient time and emphasis should be directed toward the development of increasingly more advanced skills. Behavioral strategies may be employed to enhance skill acquisition at all levels of skill development.

During the preadolescent and adolescent years, skilled physical performance is a valued characteristic. Individuals who possess high levels of skill receive recognition and positive reinforcement for their successes; children with low skill levels often experience negative peer rejection because of their failures (Drowatzky, 1981). Children are also fearful of failing and disappointing significant adults who often possess limitless hopes and unrealistic expectations (Holt, 1970).

Motor behavior is affected by numerous factors and by information provided from within the learning environment. As previously discussed, motor behaviors are acquired and refined through experiences and maturation of various physiological systems. Teachers can utilize the principles of operant learning to reinforce skill acquisition in practice sessions within the physical education setting. Behavioral techniques commonly utilized in physical education include reinforcement and feedback provided during practice.

Reinforcement

Participation in motor skills can be an intrinsically rewarding activity; therefore, the physical educator, or teacher working in physical activity, should have an easy task motivating students to practice and refine motor skills. This generally is the case when dealing with children in the elementary grades; their desire to learn and be active is at times overwhelming. As highly motivated learners grow older, however, they may lose the desire to participate in physical activity. Although successful participation in physical activity can be a strong positive reinforcer, unsuccessful experiences can negatively influence the desire to participate. The introduction of competition into physical activity can provide a strong motivating effect for improved performance. The reinforcing effects of competition depends on the nature of the task and characteristics of the learner. Low or poorly skilled individuals frequently find that highly competitive environments may be punishing (Martens, 1975).

A significant factor that makes participation in physical activity change from a positive to a negative experience is the environment in which the experience occurs. Adults frequently change the nature of the activity and place increased emphasis on successful performance. It is the role of the teacher working with children in a motor skill setting to introduce competition into the learning environment when the students are developmentally ready. The intensity of competition must never be allowed to overshadow successful experiences for all students. Orlick (1978) noted that when the games people play become more important than the people playing the game, competition begins to have a destructive effect. No student should be allowed to be reinforced at the expense of another.

A teacher attempting to refine children's motor skills must provide students with an environment in which to practice and provide sufficient information so that learning takes place. A primary function of a teacher is to observe student behavior and identify errors or incorrect responses. However, teachers may resort to aversive or negative statements when attempting to alter improperly performed motor skills. This may result in less motivated students and little, if any, positive skill change. Designing a positive learning environment requires the teacher's conscious effort to assist children who are performing incorrectly; the teacher must also provide sufficient information to improve performance. Teachers often respond to incorrect performance with a negative statement. Alternative statements such as "That was a good try but this time try it stepping off this foot," tend to be more effective than feedback that is preceded by a negative statement.

Schmidt (1982) noted that, although reinforcement techniques tend to be less beneficial to improved motor skill performance than informational feedback, they do provide a valuable function. First, reinforcement seems to contribute to the student's desire to participate in and to select a particular activity. Individuals tend to want to perform the skills for which they have received positive reinforcement. A second aspect involves the use of reinforcement as a motivator for practice. Practice is a strong determinant of skill development and has a direct influence on the refinement of motor abilities.

Positive reinforcement has been found to be effective in enhancing motor tasks that emphasize the speed and rate at which they are performed. Fine motor tasks that require greater accuracy and control tend to be less influenced by reinforcement (Sage, 1983). The increased influence of reinforcement on motor skills requiring speed rather than accuracy may be related to several causes: (a) generally, tasks that are performed quickly tend to become boring and are less intrinsically motivating than motor tasks requiring accuracy; (b) speed tasks usually require little learning and, therefore, less concentration; and (c) frequently, the goal is not identified in motor tasks that rely on speed of performance instead of accuracy (Martens, Burwitz, & Newell, 1972).

Reinforcement techniques have been utilized with a variety of populations in an attempt to demonstrate their effectiveness in improving motor skill performance. Johnston, Kelly, Harris, and Wolf (1966) conducted a study to determine whether reinforcement could encourage a 3-year-old boy to engage in vigorous play on a piece of climbing equipment. It was suggested that increased activity on a single piece of playground equipment was an appropriate step toward the ultimate objective of developing a child's physical skills. A social reinforcement strategy was employed to modify the child's behavior toward the target objective. Results of this study supported the premise that principles of operant learning can be successfully utilized to increase a child's participation in a specific physical activity.

Haridman, Goety, Reuter, and LeBlanc (1975) utilized operant procedures to encourage motor development of a preschool child in a variety of tasks including: walking longitudinally through a garden, climbing stairs, sliding down a board, rolling on the ground, climbing a ladder, and walking on a balance board. Similarly, fine motor skills, such as writing, have been improved utilizing reinforcement techniques (Brigham, Finfrock, Breunig, & Bushell, 1972).

The use of operant techniques for the modification and refinement of motor behaviors was suggested by Foss (1966), who recommended utilizing reinforcement to develop motor control in cerebral-palsied children. Similar studies have been conducted utilizing behavior modification to enhance the motor skills of handicapped children. Horner (1971), for example, demonstrated that a spina bifida child could be assisted in learning to walk with crutches when reinforced with social and tangible rewards. O'Brian and Azrin (1970) utilized reinforcing stimulus to assist subjects exhibiting poor posture gain upper shoulder control. In this investigation, an electrical apparatus caused vibrotactile stimulation when the wearer slouched.

Several investigators have suggested the use of operant principles in the sport setting (McKenzie & Rushall, 1974; Rushall & Siedentop, 1972). Komaki and Barnett (1977) utilized a behavioral approach to coaching football. Nine- and 10-year-olds who played offensive backfield on a youth football team were the subjects of this investigation. Three frequently run offensive plays were broken down into a series of five behaviorally defined stages, permitting the development of checklists that would allow for the observational assessment of individual players during both practice and the game. Reinforcement was provided in the form of positive feedback and recognition of desired play execution. Performance gains averaging 20% occurred for each of the selected plays after the application of the intervention. The results of this investigation suggest that behavioral specification and positive reinforcement of desired play execution is a viable approach to the coaching of football.

McKenzie and Rushall (1974) utilized reinforcement contingencies to remedy poor attendance and work levels of adolescent swimmers. Swimmers became more involved in their practices because they recorded their own attendance and monitored their individual work rates. There was an increased amount of training during and following the experimental treatment, without an increase in training time.

Allison and Ayllon (1980) conducted a study investigating the effects of a behavioral coaching strategy on the acquisition of selected football, gymnastics, and tennis skills. The study employed a coaching method that combined systematic use of verbal instructions and feedback, positive and negative reinforcement, positive practice, and time out. The motor skills selected for investigation included blocking in football; backward walkovers, front hand springs, and reverse dips in gymnastics; and the forehand, backhand, and serve in tennis. A total of 23 male and female subjects ranging in age from 11 to 35 years were included in this investigation. Utilizing behavioral coaching, gains of up to 10 times the baseline performance were achieved in each sport.

Hitchman (1982) conducted a study to investigate the effects of extrinsic reinforcement, in the form of ribbons, for performance on soccer skills and on the intrinsic motivation of the participants. Results of this investigation did not support the premise that contingent rewards decrease intrinsic motivation of the performer. Subjects who received reinforcement for their performance had the highest level of intrinsic motivation for the skill task. It is important to note, however, that the effects of excessive extrinsic reinforcement may be developed over several years; a single, short-term study does not determine long-term influences. Any coach or physical educator can relate experiences where children performed solely for the extrinsic reward that accompanied winning. Emphasis on the extrinsic values of physical activity may negatively influence the primary objective, producing individuals who desire to participate in physical activity primarily for its own reward.

Although physical activity tends to be intrinsically rewarding, the teacher should utilize reinforcement to enhance the learning environment. Positive reinforcement has been found to be an effective technique for teaching motor skills involving speed. Verbal praise and tangible rewards should be utilized to reinforce appropriate motor responses as they occur.

Feedback

Motor skills are similar to other learned behaviors because they are refined through experience. Practice is the most important variable in the learning of a motor skill. The effectiveness of practice on influencing level of performance is often dependent on the type of information about the qualitative aspects of the performance that is provided to the learner.

Feedback is the information generated by a behavior that can be utilized by the student to modify subsequent behaviors. Although feedback is frequently provided by the teacher (extrinsic), the performer also gains valuable information from sensory receptors located throughout the body (intrinsic). In this chapter discussion centers on the use of extrinsic feedback in the school setting.

Extrinsic feedback is information provided to the student by the teacher about the quality of a performance. Extrinsic feedback is intended to augment intrinsic information obtained from various proprioceptive and sensory mechanisms. Holding (1965) and Singer (1980) have described characteristics that define types of feedback utilized in the refinement of motor skills. Types of feedback may be categorized on the nature and/or frequency of presentation. Numerous studies have been conducted to explore the effects of the type of feedback and the frequency and timing of application on the learning of motor skills.

Quality of feedback is related to the precision (accuracy) of feedback. Accuracy of information provided to the learner influences the effectiveness of the feedback. An early study conducted by Trowbridge and Cason (1932) explored the issue of accuracy when providing information intended to improve motor skills. Children who were blindfolded attempted to reproduce lines of various lengths. Performance improved as the precision of the information provided to the performer increased. Quantitative information resulted in the greatest skill improvement; no feedback or irrelevant information resulted in no skill improvement.

Smoll (1972) examined the effects of various types of feedback when he presented children with three types of informational feedback, quantitative feedback accurate to one hundredth of a second; quantitative feedback accurate to tenths of a second; and qualitative feedback following an attempt to roll a ball at a specific velocity. Results indicated that more precise feedback was significantly more effective than qualitative information. There was no difference between the two levels of quantitative feedback, suggesting the possibility of a maximum level of precision that can be utilized by the learner.

Newell and Kennedy (1978) studied children in grades 1, 3, and 9 on a positioning task where the precision of feedback was varied. The study supported the concept of optimal level of precision and noted that the subject's ability to utilize more precise information increases with age. Rogers (1974) suggested that for some learners feedback may become too precise and inhibit the learning of a motor skill. Byde and McClenaghan (1984) found that moderately mentally retarded children did not respond to types of feedback that represented different levels of precision. It was suggested that the information provided to these subjects may have been beyond their ability to process and utilize.

The kind of feedback provided the learner has a significant influence on the acquisition of motor skills. Learners benefit most from quantitative feedback that provides information on the direction and magnitude of their errors. The precision of this information also influences the learning of motor skills. Advanced skill learners tend to benefit from precise information about their performance; less skilled individuals cannot effectively utilize this information to improve skill performance.

Feedback about the quantitative aspects of a motor performance is a significant contribution to the acquisition and refinement of motor skills. (Bilodeau, Bilodeau, & Schumsky, 1959). The effectiveness of feedback, however, appears to be related to the frequency and timing of its application. Authors have distinguished between the absolute and relative frequency of providing feedback to a student. Absolute frequency relates to the total number of presentations provided the learner during a practice session; relative frequency refers to the percentage of trials during which feedback is provided (Schmidt, 1982).

An early study conducted by Bilodeau and Bilodeau (1958) assessed the effectiveness of feedback schedules on the learning of a knob rotation task. Four groups of subjects received feedback on every trial, every third trial, every fourth trial, and every tenth trial. Performance on the experimental task improved only after those trials in which feedback was provided. Therefore, absolute frequency appeared to be more important than the relative frequency of the presentation of feedback.

Schmidt (1982), in reviewing studies related to the frequency of feedback, indicated that although absolute frequency of feedback is an important facilitator to learning, a more practical approach may be to provide feedback interspersed with trials with no information. Schmidt suggested that when no guidance is provided, the learner will be forced to rely on intrinsic information that will assist in the transition from teacher-assisted practice to independent skill performance.

Timing of the application of feedback also influences its effect on learning. Two factors should be considered when discussing the temporal aspects of the application of feedback: (a) feedback delay interval (amount of time that passes after a trial before feedback is provided); and (b) postfeedback delay (amount of time that passes after feedback is provided until the next trial is attempted).

It has been suggested that sensory information (kinesthetic and proprioceptive) about a performance must be utilized immediately following a movement because the ability to remember this type of information is limited (Sperling, 1960). Effects of varying the feedback delay have been the subject of numerous investigations. Although common sense would support the concept that the longer the feedback delay the more difficult it would be for the learner to utilize the information effectively to modify performance, the premise is not supported in the literature. However, it should be noted, that most studies were conducted on slow positioning tasks. Some controversy exists as to whether similar results would be obtained with motor skills that are rapid in nature.

Several authors have indicated that there should be some delay in the presentation of feedback. The interval following presentation of feedback (postfeedback interval) is frequently utilized by the learner to process intrinsic and extrinsic information and to develop new strategies to modify performance. Gentile (1972) noted that providing feedback immediately following a performance may interfere with the individual's processing of intrinsic information provided by the skill, and suggests briefly delaying the presentation of extrinsic feedback.

The postfeedback interval is important for the successful utilization of extrinsic information. Schmidt (1982) noted that if the subject is actively processing feedback and changing the movement during this period, significantly shortening the interval should decrease the effectiveness of the information, because learners would not have sufficient opportunity to develop a new response.

Gallagher and Thomas (1980) found that children were particularly affected by shortening the postfeedback interval. Therefore, age and skill levels must be considered when attempting to provide students with appropriate feedback. Beginning learners benefit more from feedback that directs them towards the correct performance than from information that points out errors. Advanced performers tend to benefit from identification of performance errors to allow for continued refinement of the motor skill (Drowatzky, 1981).

The development of motor skills is dependent on the quality and variety of an individual's experiences. Behavioral techniques commonly utilized in the physical education setting include reinforcement and extrinsic feedback provided to the learner during practice.

Feedback about the qualitative aspects of a performance is another technique commonly utilized to teach motor skills. Accuracy of the feedback and the frequency and timing of its application are significant factors that contribute to its effectiveness in the physical education setting. By providing appropriate feedback and reinforcement, the instructor may increase participation in physical activity and direct the learner to refine the performance of motor skills.

BEHAVIORAL APPLICATIONS FOR DEVELOPING PHYSICAL FITNESS

Research studies have documented the role of physical activity in the promotion of good health. Vigorous exercise is known to reduce symptoms of anxiety and depression, alleviate tension, and promote feelings of well-being (Dishman, 1982). Moreover, chronic exercise has been shown to reduce certain coronary risk factors, such as obesity and hypertension (Brooks & Fahey, 1984).

Four factors have been identified as essential to health-fitness status: (a) cardiorespiratory integrity; (b) muscular strength and endurance; (d) low-back flexibility; and (d) appropriate body composition (Pate, Blair, & McClenaghan, 1982). Cardiorespiratory fitness is related to the amount of whole body activity the individual can sustain; muscular strength and endurance refer to the maximal force the muscle can contract repeatedly; low-back flexibility is the range of movement possible at the lower back region; body composition is the degree of fatness or the ratio of fat weight to total body weight; and weight control is a function of the attainment of appropriate body composition.

The development of health-related physical fitness is a component of the larger goal of lifetime participation. If children learn to value health-fitness, to acquire fitness skills, and to understand how fitness is developed, they will be better prepared to assume a lifestyle of active physical participation. Behavioral techniques have been found effective in two critical aspects of physical fitness development: adherence to exercise and weight control.

Adherence to Exercise

Although for most children participation in physical activity is self-motivating, the continued involvement in physical activity (e.g. exercise) drops off markedly in adulthood. It is estimated that less than 50% of Americans have regular physical activity habits (U.S. Department of Health, Education, and Welfare, 1979a). Children are reflecting their adult models and demonstrating less energy expenditure than children 2 decades ago (Shephard, 1983).

Adherence to exercise programs is influenced by the social context in which exercise is carried out. Few studies have investigated the school as a social support network for behavior change. Other social support sources, such as family, friends, and the work site, have been observed and found to be powerful mechanisms for assistance in behavior change. School programs could utilize approaches taken in the work site or community as potential positive influences, such as the work site program conducted with Bell Telephone employees— exercise groups were formed and attendance reinforced (Brownell & Stunkard, 1980b).

A number of promising results in exercise adherence have been found, results are based on behavioral investigations. A simple technique of posting a reminder sign produced a significant effect in stair walking (Brownell, Stunkard, & Albaum, 1980). Over 45,000 people were observed in a shopping mall, train station, and bus terminal. With stairs and escalators positioned side-by-side, less than 5% of the people used the stairs. When a sign depicting the heart being exercised when taking stairs was positioned at the base of the stairs/escalator area, stair use tripled. The effect continued 1 month after removal of the sign but disappeared after 3 months. The school could utilize a similar cuing strategy by posting appropriate reminders of the importance of exercise in lunch rooms, snack bars, and locker rooms.

A study conducted by Epstein, Wing, Koeske, Ossip, and Beck (1982) focused on adherence to exercise utilizing lifestyle change and programmed aerobic exercise approaches. Thirty-seven obese 8–12-year-old children were assessed in terms of amount of exercise and weight change over a 17 month period. The lifestyle program involved energy expenditure through a wide variety of daily games and activities. The programmed aerobic alternative required the child to perform an aerobic exercise daily. Children in both exercise conditions were provided with lists of activities with associated point values based on metabolic equivalents. The children were provided with minimal weekly point goals, points could be earned for each exercise completed. Subjects in the programmed aerobics exercise group were required to select an aerobic exercise from the list, and to do the exercise at a specified time each day. Lifestyle participants were encouraged to earn their exercise points in any way they wanted from a list of common childhood activities. The programs differed in number of exercises chosen, flexibility of scheduling, and intensity of exercise. In addition, half of the youngsters in each of the above conditions were prescribed a diet that was low in caloric intake, the other children were provided only with information about program nutrition.

The program lasted for 8 weeks, with follow-up through the 17th month. At the end of the treatment programs similar changes in children were found for each of the conditions. However, at follow-up, the lifestyle group lost additional weight and maintained their weight loss better than the programmed aerobic exercise group. The investigators concluded that lifestyle exercise programs provide the opportunity to make behavior changes that are more easily incorporated into a person's routine.

Studies consistently have shown that adherence to and outcome of treatment can be improved by utilizing reinforcement strategies (Presbie & Brown, 1977). Poor adherence to an exercise program is a predictable consequence of the lack of prompt rewards. Exercise has a number of immediate negative consequences, such as discomfort, soreness, awkwardness. The positive benefits, such as weight loss, improved health, and feeling better, are less immediate. More immediate awards must be designed if adherence is to improve (Brownell & Stunkard, 1980b).

Numerous examples of the application of behavioral strategies to maintain participation in exercise programs may be observed in the physical education setting. Monitoring and feedback are two fundamental behavioral procedures that have been used for exercise adherence. Students can monitor their own activity by keeping a detailed log noting date, time, and place. This provides a record of accomplishment and a criterion for reinforcement. Recording the benefits of physical activity can be motivating for students.

Cooper's aerobic training program (1970), one of the most successful exercise programs utilizes a self-monitoring system of rewarding points based on the intensity and duration of the activity. Tangible rewards may be supplemented for individuals needing additional extrinsic reinforcement. Kall and Fisher (1974) utilized Cooper's system of points to distribute monetary rewards for participation in an exercise program. It was demonstrated that token reinforcement, specifically monetary rewards, could be successfully utilized to increase compliance to an exercise program. Although this training program was used with adults, it is also useful for secondary school students.

Wysocki, Hall, Iwata, and Riordan (1979) used contracting points and monitoring as techniques to encourage college students to exercise. Subjects selected activities for which aerobic point values had been established (Cooper's system) and elected to earn a specific number of points per week. Under terms of the contracts, subjects deposited six items of personal value (books, clothing, money) with the experimenters, two of the items could be earned back weekly. One item was returned for fulfilling point earnings; the other was returned for recording observational data on another subject. Continued depositing of personal items assured a constant source of reinforcement. Contract contingencies produced increases in the number of aerobic points earned. It was found that students could effectively monitor the earning of points through exercise. The self-monitoring procedures described by Wysocki et al. have applicability to public school physical education programs.

Weight Control Efforts

Reported prevalence data on obesity among childhood populations vary depending on the criteria used to determine obesity. However, regardless of the assessment technique used, conservative estimates find 6 to 15 percent of children to be obese. Children do not outgrow weight problems (Woodall & Epstein, 1983); obese children almost always grow up to be obese adults (Charney, Goodman, McBride, Lyon, & Pratt, 1976).

Mayer has argued that physical inactivity is the major contribution to obesity (Mayer, 1968). Many researchers have concluded, through both systematic observation and extensive clinical experience, that the obese eat no more than their normal weight peers (Brownell & Stunkard, 1980a). The problem is thought to be one of inappropriate energy balance, normal food intake but lowered levels of energy expenditure.

Bullen, Reed, and Mayer (1964) observed obese and nonobese girls participating in organized physical activities at a summer camp. Through time-lapse photography, the authors concluded that obese girls were significantly less active than their nonoverweight peers. This research has been found to be somewhat circumspect when caloric expenditure is converted to calories per pound of body weight. Analyzed in this manner, the obese child appears to have a similar level of energy expenditure (Waxman & Stunkard, 1980). Although the exact role of physical activity in the etiology of obesity is not clear, its therapeutic value is unquestionable (Dishman, 1982).

The earliest behavioral treatment programs for obese children occurred in the clinical setting not in the school environment. Clinical efforts have provided much of the direction for school-based programming. The first documented behavioral program for treating obese children was conducted at the University of Pennsylvania (Rivirus, Drummond & Combrinck-Graham, 1976). Ten low socioeconomic status (SES) black children and their mothers met weekly and kept records of food intake and adherence to the program. Parents with training utilized models, rewards, and contracting. Weight loss averaged 6.2 pounds for the 10 week period. Similar findings have been demonstrated in other studies (Weiss, 1977; Wheeler & Hess, 1976; see also Chapter 7).

The school presents an excellent opportunity to provide assistance to the underfit/overweight child and to structure broad-based prevention efforts through a program of physical education. Approaches for prevention and treatment should focus on process (i.e., how to eat and exercise) not product (pounds lost). Behavioral programs are based on the assumption that lasting change comes about by changing habits to produce lasting weight loss. The potential advantages offered by the school setting are numerous. They include the opportunity to reach large numbers of children, the provision of continuing assistance, minimal cost, and the use of an educational rather than a medical approach (Brownell & Kaye, 1982).

In addition, school-based programs provide a viable means of utilizing the child's social network to provide support for weight loss. Sixty-three obese children, ages 5–12 years participated in a program that included social support from peers, teachers, and parents in conjunction with a multidimensional treatment approach utilizing behavior modification, nutrition education, and physical activity (Brownell & Kaye, 1982). The behavior modification segments of the program included instructions for recording food intake, limiting situations for eating, slowing the rate of eating, and improving attitudes. The program also included contracting and reinforcement of changes in eating and exercising. Peers, parents, and school personnel were informed of the target childrens' program and were instructed in methods of social support. At the completion of the ten week program, 60 of the 63 children had lost weight, the average weight loss was slightly below 10 pounds.

In another school-based study, Botvin, Cantlon, Carter, and Williams (1979) investigated use of a 10 week multicomponent program that included instruction in behavior modification and nutrition, as well as exercise sessions, with 119 overweight junior high school students. The behavioral components of the program involved weight monitoring, instructions and modeling in modification of eating patterns, altering the rate of eating, and stimulus control. Students who participated in this program had significantly greater losses in weight and triceps skinfold measures than students in a control condition.

A number of behavioral strategies such as self-monitoring, contingency management, and stimulus control may be useful in developing weight control programs. Behavioral treatment for obesity begins with self-monitoring (Brownell & Stunkard, 1980a; see also Chapter , Chapter 3, and Chapter 4). Children can be taught to record data on caloric intake, physical activity, and eating behaviors. Self-monitoring is a valuable tool, especially in the initial stages of a program. These activities increase awareness, the first stage in the development of values (Krathwohl, Bloom, & Masia, 1954). Increased awareness alone helps some children become more independent and responsible.

Contingency management also has been shown to be an effective technique for child weight control programs. Typically, contracts are developed with the child, which, when satisfied, result in rewards (privileges, prizes, toys or money) for the child (O'Leary & O'Leary, 1972). A study by Aragona, Cassady, and Drabman (1975) illustrates the effective use of reinforcement and contingency contracting with overweight girls and their parents. In two experimental groups a response cost program was used. Parents lost previously deposited sums of money for missing a weekly meeting, failing to fill out charts and graphs on their child, or if their child failed to meet her specified weekly weight loss goal. In one group, parents also received instruction on reinforming and changing their child's behavior, and daily and weekly reinforcers for weight loss were negotiated with the children. At the end of the 12 week treatment period, both experimental groups had lost significantly more weight than a control group, but the response cost plus child reinforcement group maintained more of the weight loss.

The control of stimuli that increase the probability of eating behavior is another important component in weight control programs. Students are encouraged to eat on a schedule, only in certain locations, and without associated activities (e.g., reading, watching TV). Other activities emphasized include slowing eating pace, drinking water between bites, using smaller utensils, and talking at meal times.

Children especially need encouragement to limit TV watching time. Television and passive games are thought to be instrumental in the lower levels of energy output that occurs in North American children (Shepherd, 1983; Ward, 1982). Behavioral techniques for reducing passive activities include self-monitoring, parent monitoring, rewarding limiting efforts, and contracting.

Attitude change may be particularly important with teenagers who adopt self-defeating postures. Cognitive-behavior modification procedures recognize the influential role of cognitive process and social interaction in behavior changes. Social problem solving, self-talk, and stress management approaches could be taken to aid youth in adopting an appropriate cognitive framework (Meichenbaum, 1977; see also Chapter 4).

The behavioral approach offers great promise in improving levels of fitness and assisting in weight control. The school can prove to be a valuable setting for helping children develop healthy behaviors. Brownell and Stunkard (1980a, 1980b) have summarized the role of the school and its social structure in encouraging adherence to exercise and assisting in weight control as the following:

1. Encourage a buddy system between peers.
2. Employ group exercise.
3. Reward program attendance for completion of specific activities.
4. Contract for frequency of physical activity.
5. Encourage self-monitoring.
6. Provide feedback on physical changes and criterion-based accomplishments.
7. Provide educational information on nutrition and exercise.
8. Graph individual and group progress.

The school has often avoided providing specific opportunities to help the underfit or overweight child not to feel different or embarrassed. Contrary to previous thinking, children may elect special programs or appreciate extra opportunities to work on problem areas. By utilizing appropriate behavior modification techniques, physical education can become an environment for success rather than an arena for failure. Physical education can provide opportunities for prevention and treatment of weight control problems. The instructional program can educate students about the principles of weight management and reinforce appropriate weight control behaviors (Ward & McClenaghan, 1980).

SUBSTANCE ABUSE: PREVENTION AND TREATMENT

The use and misuse of addictive substances continues to be a problem for today's youth. Regular alcohol and marijuana use, beginning in the preteen and early teen years (ages 10–15), is well documented. Smoking behavior has increased in the young, primarily increased smoking among teenage girls (U.S. Department of Health, Education, and Welfare, 1979b).

The development of effective behavioral intervention programs for substance use is supported by a number of educational and health-based researchers (Coates, Peterson, & Perry, 1982). Moreover, speculation exists as to the interrelationship between smoking and other forms of substance use and misuse. Because substance abuse is a complex societal problem, an appropriate focus for schools is prevention and intervention.

Preventing and Controlling Smoking Behavior

Early programs designed to prevent or alter smoking patterns in children and adolescents placed too much emphasis on the dangers of smoking instead of on the behavioral issues that are at the root of this serious health problem (Evans & Raines, 1982). School-aged children are aware of the dangers associated with smoking, because they receive this information regularly from family, school, community, and voluntary agencies. The knowledge and belief of this fear of smoking is inadequate to discourage children from beginning to smoke.

The adage of "the earlier, the better" in prevention of inappropriate health behaviors does not necessarily hold true in smoking research. Evans (1983) and colleagues at the University of Houston have pursued a comprehensive study of smoking among school-aged children. Findings from research with thousands of school children have shown that by the age of 12 children believe smoking cigarettes may be dangerous to their health. But by the teen years many of these children will have begun a smoking pattern. This knowledge suggests the need to develop strategies to resist the pressures to begin this risk-bound behavior.

What influences children to begin a smoking habit is not understood completely, but the role of peer pressure is clear. Children indicate that urgings from one's social group and the need to feel accepted are strong influences in the initiation of the addictive process. Although media influences have been somewhat controlled, the pervasive presentation of smoking as a pleasurable and sophisticated pastime may be influential in encouraging the smoking habit. Parents who are smokers are also influencers. The probability of a child becoming a smoker is high when one or both parents smoke; when an older sibling smokes the risk is significantly greater (Evans & Raines, 1982).

Programs aimed at prevention or cessation of smoking in children and adolescents may be enhanced by techniques other than by providing factual information based on a fear element. Smoking prevention programs that employ behavioral management techniques have value in affecting the initiation of the abusive behavior.

McAlister, Perry, and Maccoby (1979) developed a program for adolescents, based on environmental influence, personal expectations, and psychological factors, to train students to deal with the pressure to smoke. The important features of their intervention included the employment of peer leaders and the use of modeling and role-playing to facilitate learning of pressure-resistance skills. Verbal and cognitive responses that can be used to resist pressures, such as advertising and peer pressure, were demonstrated and rehearsed during the sessions. After training, the percentage of seventh graders who reported smoking was lower for the experimental school than for the control school.

A similar finding was reported by Botvin, Eng, and Williams (1980). They used a comprehensive social, psychological smoking prevention strategy called Life Skills Training. The emphasis of the 12 session program was on basic life skills related to problems of adolescents, including the issue of smoking. Specific skills were taught through the use of modeling and behavior rehearsal. Sessions focused on self-image, decision making, advertising techniques, coping with anxiety, communication skills, social skills, and assertiveness training. Students also participated in a self-improvement project that utilized behavioral self-management principles. Adolescents who participated in the program had a lower smoking onset rate and greater pretest–posttest changes on several knowledge and psychological measures than did control group students.

The Houston study, based on the social learning-modeling paradigm of Bandura (1977), utilized the strategy of "inoculation" against pressure to smoke (Evans, 1983). Students were exposed to smoking deterrent messages in films and supporting posters presented at different times during the year. The films featured adolescents, approximately the age of the subjects, presenting smoking information. Students role-played social situations enacting pressure to smoke. Results indicated that smoking onset rates in the treatment group was significantly lower than in control groups. Three-year followups have revealed significant differences between control and test groups in both "smoking less" and "still not smoking" categories.

Perry, Killen, Telch, Slinkard, and Danaher (1980) compared the efficacy of traditional smoking prevention techniques and a behaviorally based experimental treatment model. The behavioral program, conducted during four 45 minute sessions in the students' high school health classes, focused on the immediate physiological effects of cigarette smoking and social cues that influence smoking. Students received instruction in identification of "selling strategies"; were involved in modeling, discussion, and role-play of ways to resist peer pressure; and were introduced to several smoking cessation procedures including self-monitoring, relaxation, and goal setting. Control students participated in health classes that emphasized the harmful long-term physiological effects of smoking. Results indicated decreases in self-reported smoking and lower levels of carbon monoxide for the experimental group subjects.

Preventing Substance Use: Drugs and Alcohol

As with smoking prevention programs, the more promising strategies have employed techniques to resist social pressures related to the onset of substance use and to create peer influence against the abuse of alcohol and other drugs (McAlister, 1982). A longitudinal pilot study was conducted with 526 junior high students (McAlister, Perry, Killen, Slinkard, & Maccoby, 1980). In the experimental school, high school students selected as influential models led six classroom sessions of instruction during the first school year and two additional sessions in the second year. The objective of the sessions was to psychologically inoculate students against the pressure to begin tobacco, alcohol, or drug use. Students who received the special training began smoking at less than one half the rate of those who did not receive special training. Frequent drug and alcohol use was also less prevalent among the students who received this training.

Cognitive-behavioral intervention was employed as an experimental strategy with a group of high school students in an attempt to alter tobacco and marijuana use (Lotecka & MacWhinney, 1983). Intervention included instruction and practice in decision making, use of self-statements, and relaxation. In addition, social and physiological consequences of smoking and the use of alternative responses were discussed. Control group students received instruction in popular tips on how to quit smoking. Only subjects in the cognitive-behavioral treatment condition reported significant tobacco smoking reduction at 1 month and 3 month posttests. In addition, experimental subjects revised their ideal level of marijuana consumption downward.

Assertiveness was employed as a behavioral focus for a study on drug and alcohol abuse prevention conducted by Horan and Williams (1982). From a population of eighth graders, 72 ranked as least assertive on an assertiveness behavior test were randomly assigned to three conditions. The experimental condition consisted of ten general assertiveness (i.e., nondrug) training situations and five additional situations involving peer pressure to use drugs. Instruction, modeling, role-play, and feedback were used during the training. The placebo treatment involved discussion about assertiveness, peer pressure, and drug use. The third group received no treatment. Posttest measures found highly significant gains in the experimental subjects on behavioral and psychometric measure of assertiveness and decreased willingness to use alcohol and marijuana. Results of a 3 year follow-up showed students continuing to demonstrate higher levels of assertiveness and less actual drug use.

The school offers an appropriate and useful vehicle for the prevention of substance-related problems. Employing strong social pressures present in the school environment to encourage children and youth to *avoid* harmful chemical substances is a novel approach. A more common approach, yet increasingly more difficult, is to design intervention programs to treat problems caused by peer pressure to initiate addictive habits.

CONCLUSIONS

Progressive programs in health and physical education have renewed their commitment to the goal of total health. The development of health promotion or wellness programs imply the traditional definition of total health as freedom from disease, and health as the enhancement of the quality of existence. Health and physical education have accepted this orientation by designing school curricula that reflect this new direction.

A lifestyle orientation to education creates the need to develop effective skills for participation in a wide variety of sports and leisure activities, to acquire necessary habits for fitness and weight control, and to make appropriate decisions about the use and misuse of addictive substances. Behavior modification techniques in health and physical education have been found to be successful for the development of psychomotor skills and for the formation of health habit change. Reinforcement and feedback, peer modeling, cue reduction, and social inoculation to peer pressure are examples of behavioral strategies for teaching the cognitive knowledges and affective skills associated with behavior change. Behavior modifying techniques must be integrated with traditional education methods to create a model for comprehensive health and physical education programming that emphasizes long-term life change.

REFERENCES

Allison, M. G., & Ayllon, T. (1980). Behavioral coaching in the development of skills in football, gymnastics, and tennis. *Journal of Applied Behavior Analysis, 13,* 297–314.

Aragona, J., Cassady, J., & Drabman, R. S. (1975). Treating overweight children through parental training and contingency contracting. *Journal of Applied Behavior Analysis, 8,* 269–278.

Bandura, A. (1977). *Social learning theory.* Englewood Cliffs, N.J.: Prentice-Hall.

Bilodeau, E. A., & Bilodeau, I. M. (1958). Variable frequency of knowledge of results and the learning of a simple skill. *Journal of Experimental Psychology, 55,* 379–383.

Bilodeau, E. A., & Bilodeau, I. M., & Schumsky, D. A. (1959). Some effects of introducing and withdrawing knowledge of results early and late in practice. *Journal of Experimental Psychology, 58,* 142–144.

Botvin, G. J., Cantlon, A., Carter, M. S., & Williams, C. L. (1979). Reducing adolescent obesity through a school health program. *The Journal of Pediatrics, 95,* 1060–1062.

Botvin, G. J., Eng, A., & Williams, C. L. (1980). Preventing the onset of cigarette smoking through life skills training. *Preventive Medicine, 9,* 135–143.

Brigham, T. A., Finfrock, S. K., Breunig, M. K., and Bushell, D. H. (1972). The use of programmed materials in the analysis of academic contingencies. *Journal of Applied Behavior Analysis, 5,* 177–182.

Brooks, G. A., & Fahey, T. D. (1984). *Exercise physiology: Human bioenergetics and its application.* New York: Wiley.

Brownell, K., & Kaye, F. (1982). A school-based behavior modification, nutrition education, and physical activity program for obese children. *American Journal of Clinical Nutrition, 35,* 277–283.

Brownell, J., & Stunkard, A. (1980a). Behavioral treatment for obese children and adolescents. In A. Stunkard (Ed.), *Obesity* (pp. 415–437). Philadelphia: W. B. Saunders.

Brownell, K., & Stunkard, A. (1980b). Physical activity in the development and control of obesity. In A. Stunkard (Ed.), *Obesity* (pp. 300–324). Philadelphia: W. B. Saunders.

Brownell, K., Stunkard, A., & Albaum, J. (1980). Evaluation and modification of exercise patterns in the natural environment. *American Journal of Psychiatry, 137,* 1540–1545.

Bullen, B. A., Reed, R. B., & Mayer, J. (1964). Physical activity of obese and nonobese adolescent girls appraised by motion picture sampling. *American Journal of Clinical Nutrition, 14,* 211–223.

Byde, R., & McClenaghan, B. A. (1984). Effects of selected types of feedback on an anticipation timing task with moderately retarded children. *Adapted Physical Activity Quarterly, 1,* 141–146.

Charney, M., Goodman, H., McBride, M., Lyon, B., & Pratt, R. (1976). Childhood antecedents of adult obesity: Do chubby infants become obese adults? *New England Journal of Medicine, 295,* 6–9.

Coates, T. J., Peterson, A. C., & Perry. C. (1982). *Promoting adolescent health: A dialog in research and practice.* New York: Academic Press.

Cooper, K. (1970). *The new aerobics.* New York: Bantam Books.

Dishman, R. (1982). Compliance/adherence in health-related exercise. *Health Psychology, 1,* 237–267.

Drowatzky, J. N. (1981). *Motor learning: Principles and practices.* Minneapolis: Burgess.

Epstein, L., Wing, R., Koeske, R., Ossip, D., & Beck, S. (1982). A comparison of lifestyle change and programmed aerobic exercise on weight and fitness changes in obese children. *Behavior Therapy, 13,* 651–665.

Evans, R. I. (1983). Deterring smoking in adolescents: Evolution of a research program in applied social psychology. *International Review of Applied Psychology, 32,* 71–83.

Evans, R. I. Raines, B. (1982). Control and prevention of smoking in adolescents: A psychosocial perspective. In T. J. Coates, A. C. Peterson, & C. Perry (Eds.), *Promoting adolescent health* (pp. 101–136). New York: Academic Press.

Foss, B. M. (1966). Operant conditioning in the control of movements. *Developmental Medicine and Child Neurology, 8,* 339–340.

Gallagher, J. D., & Thomas, J. R. (1980). Effects of varying post-RR intervals upon children's motor performance. *Journal of Motor Behavior, 12,* 41–46.

Gentile, A. M. (1972). A working model of skill acquisition with application to teaching. *Quest, 17,* 3–23.

Haridman, S. A., Goety, E. M., Reuter, K. E. & LeBlanc, J. M. (1975). Prizes, contingent attention, and training: Effects on a child's motor behavior. *Journal of Applied Behavior Analysis, 4,* 183–189.

Hitchman, M. G. (1982). The effects of rewards, age, and level of performance on intrinsic motivation for a sport activity. Unpublished doctoral dissertation, University of Oregon.

Holding, D. H. (1965). *Principles of training.* Oxford: Pergamon Press.

Holt, J. (1970). *How children fail.* New York: Dell.

Horan, J. J., & Williams, J. M. (1982). Longitudinal study of assertion training as a drug abuse prevention strategy. *American Education Research Journal, 19,* 341–351.

Horner, R. D. (1971). Establishing use of crutches by a mentally retarded spina bifida child. *Journal of Applied Behavior Analysis, 4,* 183–189.

Johnston, M. R., Kelly, C. S., Harris, F. R., & Wolf, M. M. (1966). Application of reinforcement principles to development of motor skills of a young child. *Child Development, 37,* 379–387.

Kall, M. C., & Fisher, J. (1974). Self-modification of exercise behavior. *Journal of Behavior Therapy and Experimental Psychiatry, 5,* 213–214.

Komaki, J., & Barnett, F. T. (1977). A behavioral approach to coaching football: Improving the play execution of the offensive backfield on a youth football team. *Journal of Applied Behavior Analysis, 10,* 657–664.

Krathwahl, D., Bloom, B., Masia, B. (1956). *Taxonomy of educational objectives: Handbook II: Affective domain.* New York: David McKay.

Lotecka, L., & MacWhinney, M. (1983). Enhancing decision behavior in high school "smokers." *International Journal of the Addictions, 18,* 479–490.

Martens, R. (1975). *Social psychology and physical activity.* New York: Harper & Row.

Martens, R., Burwitz, L., & Newell, K. M. (1972). Money and praise: Do they improve motor learning and performance? *Research Quarterly, 43,* 429–446.

Mayer, J. (1968). *Overweight: Causes, cost, and control.* Englewood Cliffs, NJ: Prentice-Hall.

McAlister, A. L. (1982). Introduction and overview. In T. J. Coates, A. C. Peterson, & C. Perry (Eds.), *Promoting adolescent health* (pp. 167–71). New York: Academic Press.

McAlister, A. L., Perry, C., & Maccoby, N. (1979). Adolescent smoking: Onset and prevention. *Pediatrics, 63,* 650–658.

McAlister, A. L., Perry, C., Killen, B. A., Slinkard, M. A., & Maccoby, N. (1980). Pilot study of smoking, alcohol, and drug abuse prevention. *American Journal of Public Health, 70,* 719–721.

McClenaghan, B. A., & Gallahue, D. L. (1978). *Fundamental movement: A developmental and remedial approach.* Philadelphia: Saunders.

McKenzie, T. L., & Rushall, B. S. (1974). Effects of self-recording on attendance and performance in a competitive swimming training environment. *Journal of Applied Behavior Analysis, 7,* 199–206.

Newell, K. M., & Kennedy, J. A. (1978). Knowledge of results and children's motor learning. *Developmental Psychology, 14,* 531–536.

O'Brian, F., & Azrin, N. H. (1970). Behavioral engineering: Control of posture by informational feedback. *Journal of Applied Behavior Analysis, 3,* 235–240.

O'Leary, K. D., & O'Leary, S. G. (Eds.). (1972). *Classroom management: The successful use of behavior modification.* Elmsford, NY: Pergamon Press.

Orlick, T. (1978). *Winning through cooperation.* Washington, DC: Hawkins & Associates.

Pate, R., Blair, S., & McClenaghan, B. (1982). Current approaches to physical fitness. In T. R. Kratochwill (Ed.), *Advances in school psychology: Vol. 2.* Hillsdale, NJ: Lawrence Erlbaum Associates.

Perry, C., Killen, J., Telch, M., Slinkard, L. A., & Danaher, B. G. (1980). Modifying smoking behavior of teenagers: A school-based intervention. *American Journal of Public Health, 70,* 722–725.

Powell, K. E., Christenson, G. M., & Kreuter, M. W. (1984). Objective for the nation: Assessing the role physical education must play. *Journal of Physical Education, Recreation, and Dance, 55,* 18–20.

Presbie, R. J., & Brown, P. L. (1977). *Physical education: The behavior modification approach.* Washington, DC: National Education Association.

Rivirus, T. M., Drummond, T., & Combrinck-Graham, L. (1976). A group behavior treatment program for overweight children: The results of a pilot study. *Pediatric Adolescent Endocrinology, 1*, 212–218.

Rogers, C. A. (1974). Feedback precision and postfeedback interval duration. *Journal of Experimental Psychology, 102*, 604–608.

Rushall, B. S., & Siedentop, D. (1972). *The development and control of behavior in sport and physical education.* Philadelphia: Lea & Febiger.

Sage, G. H. (1983). *Introduction to motor behavior: A neuropsychological approach.* Reading, MA: Addison-Wesley.

Schmidt, R. A. (1982). *Motor control and learning: A behavioral emphasis.* Champaign, IL: Human Kinetics.

Shephard, R. J. (1983). Physical activity and the healthy mind. *Canadian Medical Association Journal, 128*, 525–530.

Singer, R. N. (1980). *Motor learning and human performance.* New York: MacMillan.

Smoll, F. L. (1972). Effects of precision of information feedback upon acquisition of a motor skill. *Research Quarterly, 43*, 489–493.

Sperling, G. (1960). The information available in brief visual presentations. *Psychological Monograph, 74.*

Trowbridge, M. H., & Cason, H. (1932). An experimental study of Thorndike's theory of learning. *Journal of General Psychology, 7*, 245–260.

U.S. Department of Health, Education, and Welfare. (1979a). *Healthy people: The Surgeon General's report on health promotion and disease prevention.* Washington, DC: Author.

U.S. Department of Health, Education and Welfare. (1979b). *Smoking and health: A report of the surgeon general.* Washington, DC: Author.

Ward, D. (1982). *Developing programs for weight management.* Proceedings of Physical Activity for Children Conference, Indiana University.

Ward, D. S., McClenaghan, B. A. (1980). Special programs for special people: Ideas for extending the physical education program. *The Physical Educator, 37*, 63–68.

Waxman, M., & Stunkard, A. J. (1980). Caloric intake and expenditure in obese boys. *Journal of Pediatrics, 96*, 187–193.

Weiss, A. R. (1977). A behavioral approach to the treatment of obesity. *Behavior Therapy, 8*, 720–726.

Wheeler, M. E., & Hess, K. W. (1976). Treatment of juvenile obesity by successive approximation control of eating. *Journal of Behavior Therapy in Experimental Psychology, 7*, 235–241.

Wickstrom, R. (1977). *Fundamental motor patterns.* Philadelphia: Lea & Febiger.

Woodall, K., & Epstein, L. (1983). The prevention of obesity. *Behavior Medicine Update, 5*, 15–21.

Wysocki, T., Hall, G., Iwata, B., & Riordan, M. (1979). Behavioral management of exercise: Contracting for aerobic points. *Journal of Applied Behavior Analysis, 12*, 55–64.

7

Parent Education

Frank M. Gresham
Kathleen L. Lemanek

The family is one of the most important and one of the most beleaguered institutions in society (Bergan & Duley, 1981; Bloom, Asher, & White, 1978; Guidubaldi, 1980). Rapid sociocultural changes, such as increased geographic mobility, declining birth rates, high divorce rates, and, in many cases, the economic necessity of two working parents, have threatened the viability of the family as a societal institution.

Sociocultural changes function in complex ways making parenting a difficult and often stressful task. Individuals learn parenting skills primarily through modeling of their own parents' behavior (Bandura, 1977). Historically, this was more or less successful because society remained fairly stable in comparison with today's rapidly changing, often disruptive conditions. Changes in the demands on parents often leave today's parents at a loss for the most appropriate and effective way of rearing children. Parenting skills learned by modeling one's own parents 25 years ago may not be appropriate in today's society, because of major changes in societal institutions, such as the school, the church, and government. Sociocultural changes and increased and novel demands that will likely be placed on children, as a result of rapid technological developments, may result in parents' increased anxiety concerning parenting behavior (Guidubaldi, 1980).

The purpose of this chapter is to present an in-depth review of behavioral approaches to parent education. The authors present a conceptual overview of the relationship between children's school and home behaviors, the influence of various social systems on school behavior, a brief historical review of behavioral parent training, and critical reviews of behavioral techniques used to change problem behaviors. Major considerations in implementing parent education programs in schools is discussed and suggestions for evaluating the effects of parent education programs in school settings are provided. Because of the major difficulties, many of which are school-related, parents encounter with their children, it is suggested that the school play a major role in parent education programs designed to teach parents how to deal with their child's problem behaviors.

The following section highlights the importance of school–home behavior interrelationships, the use of parent training by school consultants, and a social systems conceptualization of behavior (Rogers-Warren & Warren, 1977).

SCHOOL–HOME BEHAVIOR INTERRELATIONSHIPS

Events that occur in the home influence many behaviors that occur in the school setting and vice versa. It has been demonstrated that intervention programs function more effectively when parents understand, participate in, and support the efforts of professional consultants (Bergan & Duley, 1981; Berkowitz & Graziano, 1972; Moreland, Schwebel, Beck, & Wells, 1982; O'Dell, 1974; see also Chapter 8). Simpson and Poplin (1981) point out that historically, parents have been denied participation in the design and implementation of their child's educational or treatment program and in many cases have been perceived as being partially responsible for their child's problems in the school.

School personnel have become increasingly interested in training parents in behavioral techniques to provide a more comprehensive and effective approach to preventing and eliminating behavior problems (Bergan, 1977; Bergan & Duley, 1981). Problem behaviors evidenced in the school are a function of school-situational events and that is a complex function of a child's learning history shaped by the operation of other social systems. A general conceptualization of how social systems influence behavior is presented in the following section.

Social Systems Influence on School Behavior

Problem behaviors presented by children and youth in the school environment are virtually never an exclusive function of situational events existing in the school setting. As previously mentioned, children and youth bring to the school situation learning history reflected in patterns of behavior that have been modeled and selectively reinforced in a variety of other settings. Learning history influences the behavior of children and youth in schools.

Some behavioral researchers have advocated a systems approach to the conceptualization of behavior (Conger, 1981; Wahler, Berland, Coe & Leske, 1977; Williams, 1974). According to the systems approach, behavior can be viewed at different levels within and between various social systems, such as the family, school, and community (Bronfenbrenner, 1979). Wahler et al. (1977) state the behavioral system conceptualization as follows:

Behavior seems to be determined by subsystems that always form the components of other systems. At the first level is the covarying system of behaviors within a child's repetoire of responses (sometimes known as a response class). At the next level is the interacting behavior system of the child's primary group, such as the family. At the third level, the family subsystem serves as a component of the community system . . . each level is a subsystem that forms a component of other systems of increasing complexity. (p. 215)

This conceptualization of behavior suggests that behavior is a function of not only situational events, but also complex interdependent events that operate within and between social systems (i.e., school, home, community). A comprehensive view of parent education must take into account these interacting social systems as they operate in complex ways to produce problem behaviors in children. Although it may not be possible to change some important social system variables (e.g., socioeconomic status), such factors can and should be considered in designing behavioral interventions (e.g., reinforcer selection and parent training manuals).

One advantage of a behavioral systems approach is that it may prove beneficial in promoting generalization, the occurrence of behaviors in settings or situations other than the ones in which education or training took place (Kazdin, 1977; see also Chapter 10). Behavioral approaches to the treatment of childhood behavior problems have failed to demonstrate generalization across settings convincingly (O'Leary & Kent, 1973; Stokes & Baer, 1977; Wahler et al., 1977). Generalization across settings is particularly important in parent training by school professionals, because the major goal is to teach behaviors that will be reinforced cross-situationally (i.e., the home and the school). A behavioral system's conceptualization of parent education and training may assist school consultants in planning and programming for generalization across settings, because behavior is viewed as being a result of situational and interdependent social systems' events.

Gerald Patterson and his research group at Oregon Research Institute have demonstrated that their parent training program is effective in reducing the aggressive/disruptive behavior of children in the home. The book, *Living with Children* (Patterson & Guillion, 1976), is used as the basis for a parent education program in which parents learn how to define, observe, record, and consequate behavior.

The Patterson program has several steps that are important in training parents (reviewed by Henry, 1981). First, an intake interview is conducted with all family members, treatment is described in the general course of the interview. Checklists are completed by the parent; the child is interviewed separately to assess perceptions of the family and intellectual and academic deficits. Parent training is initiated after a six-session baseline; home observations are collected during these sessions. Parent training begins by having parents read *Living with*

Children (Patterson & Guillion, 1976) or *Families* (Patterson, 1975). Parents are quizzed on the principles in the books; they receive phone calls to prompt reading and understanding of the material.

After parents pass the quiz, they are taught how to define and record behavior. Typically, they have to define and record two appropriate and two inappropriate behaviors for an hour per day for 3 days. Training in the form of modeling, behavior rehearsal, feedback, and reinforcement are used to teach appropriate use of behavioral principles (e.g., reinforcement, contingency, contracting, timeout, etc.). The training program takes from 23 to 32 hours of professional time per family, and Patterson estimates significant improvement is found in 67% of the cases (Henry, 1981).

A similar parent training program has been developed by Forehand and his colleagues at the University of Georgia. Although the program is based on the same social learning principles, it differs from the Patterson program. According to Wells and Forehand (1981):

> First, the program is not limited to changing single, discrete behaviors but focuses on modifying general parent–child interaction. Second, training occurs in a controlled learning environment in which parent behaviors are directly shaped during vivo interactions with the child. Third, parents are required to demonstrate changes in *their own* as well as their child's behavior before treatment termination. Fourth, the Patterson program has focused on children in the 5- to 13-year-old range. (p. 536)

Forehand and his associates have provided convincing data of the program's effectiveness in decreasing maladaptive behavior of conduct disordered children. Specific studies documenting the efficacy of the Patterson and Forehand parent training programs, however, are not reviewed in this chapter because they are primarily clinic-based rather than school-based.

BEHAVIORAL APPROACHES TO PARENT EDUCATION

Historical Perspective

The rudiments of behavioral parent training programs can be traced to the early 1900s when the first applications of learning principles were successfully utilized. The classic study by Watson and Rayner (1920), in which an 11-month-old child was conditioned to fear a white rat, was the first demonstration of conditioned fear with children. This study, and others, provided a theoretical base for how fears could be conditioned by temporal associations to environmental stimuli.

Four years later, Jones (1924a, 1924b) provided one of the first behavioral interventions to ameliorate a fear in children. Jones (1924b) used behavioral techniques to eliminate a conditioned fear of a small animal (white rabbit) in a young child.

The Watson and Rayner (1920) and Jones (1924a, 1924b) studies were conducted in a laboratory/clinic setting that limited their generalizability to the home. One of the first demonstrations of the effectiveness of behavioral principles with children in the home was the research by Mowrer and Mowrer (1938). The Mowrers successfully treated a number of cases of childhood enuresis (bedwetting). They used a urine sensitive pad placed under the child's bedsheet, the pad set off an alarm when wet. The Mowrers original work had a 100% success rate in treating enuresis. With success rates in the 80–90% range, it remains the most effective behavioral treatment of the problem (Turner, 1973).

The seminal work by Mowrer and Mowrer (1938) not only demonstrated the effectiveness of learning principles in treating children's problem behaviors, but also stressed the importance of parental involvement in child treatment. The success of the procedure used by the Mowrers may have been due, in part, to the involvement of parents in the treatment program. Although research was successful, it was not adopted for a number of years, because of the Freudian influence on the child guidance movement (Ross, 1981). Behavior problems were viewed as psychological symptoms of an underlying pathological process (i.e., disease model) instead of as dysfunctional behaviors to be treated in their own right. Moreover, parental involvement in treatment of children was virtually unheard of, in the Freudian view, parents were seen as primarily responsible for their child's problems.

It was not until the 1960s that learning principles were used to treat childhood behavior problems in the home. The vast majority of early studies focused on eliminating disruptive behavior. Disruptive behavior includes bothersome behaviors such as aggressive behavior (fighting, kicking, spitting, etc.), temper tantrums, annoying behaviors (whining, yelling), noncompliance, stealing, and firesetting (Wells & Forehand, 1981). Studies from this era demonstrated the efficacy of various learning principles (e.g., timeout, response cost, token economy, contingency contracting, differential reinforcement, etc.) in ameliorating disruptive behaviors in children. A particularly germane point to the present chapter is that in these studies parents were the primary agents of change. This demonstrates that parents could learn and successfully apply learning principles to treat their own children.

The historical review provides a framework for viewing the evolution of learning principles in treating childhood behavior problems. This is paralleled by the gradual realization by researchers and practitioners that parents can be and often are critical to the success of behavioral interventions. The following sections provide a review of behavioral procedures utilized by parents and school personnel to remediate a variety of problem behavior areas.

REVIEW OF BEHAVIORAL APPROACHES FOR SPECIFIC
PROBLEM AREAS

Academic-Related Behaviors

One of the most frequent complaints made by teachers is that students often do not exhibit behaviors crucial for success on academic tasks (see also Chapter 3). These behaviors can be viewed as important prequisites to academic performance and success in the classroom, and can be conceptualized as members of the same response class. Typical behaviors that constitute this response class include: (a) attending behavior; (b) classwork completion; (c) homework completion; (d) being on time to class; (e) bringing required materials to class (e.g., paper, pencils, etc.); and (f) task accuracy. A number of studies have demonstrated that the involvement of parents in increasing the aforementioned behaviors is practical, efficient, and effective in educational settings.

Home-Based Reinforcement.   Programs that join parents and teachers in a cooperative effort to increase academic-related behaviors are particularly effective intervention (see Atkeson & Forehand, 1979 for a review). The general approach in a home-based reinforcement program is for the parent to dispense rewards consistently to the child based on the teacher's report of the child's behavior at school. The teacher's responsibilities in a home-based reinforcement program are to specify classroom rules or expected behaviors, determine whether the student has met behavioral expectancies, and provide a means for communicating the child's behavior to the parent.

How is communication to the parent achieved in a home-based reinforcement program? It most typically takes the form of a daily report card on which the desired behaviors are specified and rated. Reports are taken home to parents by the child on a daily basis. Daily report cards can be constructed for several subject areas throughout the day and can be completed by more than one teacher, if the child has multiple teachers (junior- and senior-high school students have several teachers).

Daily report cards have several advantages over classroom-based reinforcement procedures. First, teachers do not have to alter their teaching style significantly to implement a home-based reinforcement program, they only have to check or rate the student's behaviors at the end of the day. Second, parents often have access to a wider variety of privileges (e.g., television, videogames, movies, money, etc.) than teachers. Third, home-based reinforcement programs usually are more time and cost efficient for teachers, enhancing the likelihood that they will view the intervention as acceptable. Fourth, home-based reinforcement programs circumvent ethical complaints that teachers may voice concerning the fairness of giving rewards or special dispensation to only a few students in the classroom. Finally, home-based reinforcement programs can serve to establish a vital communication link between the school and home, a link that may be viewed as extremely positive, increasing future cooperative efforts.

Daily report cards have been used to increase academic-related behaviors of kindergarten-age children (Lahey et al., 1977), elementary-age students (Saudargas, Madsen, & Scott, 1977), and adolescents (Schumaker, Hovell, & Sherman, 1977a, 1977b). The aforementioned studies employed several modifications of the daily report card system, such as varying the frequency with which the report cards were sent home, providing an audiotaped message to parents by way of a call-in service to the school, and providing an instructional manual for guidance counselors for implementing a daily report card system.

Lahey et al. (1977) used a daily report card system (Brag Sheets) in two kindergarten classrooms to increase work completion, following instructions and resting. Teachers completed a "Brag Sheet" on each student, at the end of the day the child took the brag sheet home to parents. A letter to the parents, explaining the purpose of the daily report card and instructions to tell their children what a good job they were doing in school, accompanied the first brag sheet. Parents also were told not to punish children for poor reports. Table 7.1 shows an example of a daily report card or brag sheet similar to the one used in the Lahey et al. (1977) study. The results of this study showed that the daily report card was effective in increasing the academic-related behaviors of kindergarten students (e.g., work completion, following instructions, and resting). Lahey et al. (1977) have stated that the consultants had only one contact with the teachers and provided absolutely no specific training for parents. This suggests that merely providing feedback to parents about children's classroom behavior is an effective and efficient means of promoting academic-related behaviors. Moreover, Lahey et al. (1977), using a questionnaire, assessed parent attitudes toward the daily report card. Virtually all parents viewed the intervention as a means of improving school–home communication, improving their child's school performance, and improving their child's attitude toward school. The study indicates

TABLE 7.1
Example of Daily Report Card for Kindergartners

Name _____ Date _____ Day _____	
	YES
1. Your child followed directions well today.	_____
2. Your child rested well today during nap time.	_____
3. Your child completed all work today.	_____
4. Your child played well with others today.	_____
Signed _____	
Teacher	

that daily report cards are effective and time efficient and viewed as a positive intervention by parents.

Some investigators have studied the effects of weekly versus variable-time report cards on academic-related behaviors. Saudargas et al. (1977) used both fixed-time (weekly report cards taken home by all students on Fridays) and variable-time (daily report cards taken home by a randomly selected subset of students in the class) report cards to increase assignment completion and accuracy in third grade students. Specific academic tasks included reading, mathematics, science, social studies, and geography. If at least 85% accuracy was obtained in each of these academic areas assignments were considered complete. Under the fixed-time schedule, each student, on Friday, was given a report card that listed the quantity of work completed and provided for teacher comments about the ability of the week's work. No requirements were made to ensure that parents signed the reports or that students returned them.

The fixed-time schedule lasted for 1 week. On the following Monday students were told that the report card procedure would change. The new schedule, a variable-time schedule, involved sending home daily reports to randomly selected students, none of the students knew when they would receive a report card. Each day teachers randomly selected seven to nine students for home reports. The students were not told they were getting a home report until 30 minutes before the end of the school day. Therefore, students could not predict when they would receive a daily report card nor discern how many reports they might receive in any 1 week. This condition lasted for 2 weeks.

Results of the investigation showed that assignment completion rates under fixed-time conditions were 83.1% (Fixed-Time I) and 73.9% (Fixed-Time II). The variable-time condition produced much higher rates of assignment completion, rates increased to 92.8% (Variable-Time I) and 110.9% (Variable-Time II). Percentages greater than 100% represent the completion of extra voluntary assignments. This study suggests that a variable-time schedule leads to higher rates of assignment completion than a fixed-time schedule. Apparently, having students not being able to predict when a report card will be sent home leads to higher rates of work completion. It should be remembered, however, that this effect might only be observed after students have experienced a fixed-time schedule.

Neither the Lahey et al. (1977) nor the Saudargas et al. (1977) studies made any provisions for training parents to administer consequences in the home contingent on the daily report card. Therefore it must be assumed that in these studies the report cards served as a prompt for parents to praise their children for good reports, but this can not be empirically substantiated. A study by Schumaker et al. (1977a) differs from the previously described studies, provisions were made to teach parents how to praise and administer other rewards in the home.

In the Schumaker et al. (1977a) study, parental cooperation with the daily

TABLE 7.2
Example of Daily Report Card for Junior High School Students

Name _____		
Date _____	Day _____	
Teacher _____		
The Student . . .		
	YES	NO
Came to class on time		
Brought supplies		
Stayed in seat		
Paid attention		
Spoke courteously		
Points on today's classwork		
Grade in today's test		
Teacher's initials		

report card program was obtained by the school guidance counselor. After parental permission and cooperation were obtained, an experimenter went to each of the three target students' homes to set up a home-based contingency program. The program involved teaching parents how to praise adolescents for good reports and how to implement a point system (students earned points to be exchanged for privileges, such as TV time, snacks, staying up late).

Academic-related behaviors, such as coming to class on time, bringing supplies, staying in seat, following directions, and academic performance in specific subject areas, were the targets for change. Table 7.2 presents a daily report card similar to the one used in the Schumaker et al. (1977a) study. Table 7.3 shows an example of a teacher's criteria for point values in relation to the daily report card.

The Schumaker et al. (1977a) study demonstrated that daily report cards in conjunction with the home-based reward program improved adolescents' classwork performance, conduct, and semester grades. For example, the three target students in the program raised their grade point averages from 1.46 (D+) to 1.99 (C) in a single quarter.

In a second experiment, Schumaker et al. (1977b) demonstrated that guidance counselors could effectively implement the same program and achieve results comparable with the results achieved by researchers in the first experiment.

TABLE 7.3
Example of Teacher's Criteria for Classwork Points

When class discussions are held:
5 points-Student listens and contributes three times to discussion.
3 points-Student listens and contributes twice to discussion.
2 points-Student listens and contributes once to discussion.
1 points-Student pays attention and listens to discussion.
0 points-Student does not listen to discussion.

When Class assignments are given:
5 points-Student works all of class time on assignment.
3 points-Student works 75% of class time on assignment.
3 points-Student works 50% of class time on assignment.
1 points-Student works less than 50% of class time on assignment.
0 points-Student does not work on assignment.

When tests are given in class:
5 points-Scores 90% or better
4 points-Scores between 80–89%
2 points-Scores between 70–79%
1 points-Scores between 65–69%
0 points-Scores less than 65%

Guidance counselors read a manual that provided a step-by-step description of the daily report card program. The manual (Schumaker et al., 1977b) instructs how to describe the program to families, obtain informed consent, present the program to teachers, devise grading criteria, negotiate privileges with families, monitor student progress through frequent family contact, and graph results of behavior change.

Results of one guidance counselor's implementation of the program increased an eighth grade student's grade point average from 1.07 to 2.16 in one quarter. This suggests that the daily report card program is effective and practical in improving academic-related behaviors and conduct in adolescents. Moreover, Schumaker et al. (1977a, 1977b) suggest that this program could be adopted by schools with a minimum of expense.

Daily report cards, when used in conjunction with home-based reward programs, are effective, efficient, and economical in changing the academic-related behaviors of kindergarten, elementary, and junior-high school students. Teachers tend to view these programs as positive and minimally intrusive (Saudargas et al., 1977; Schumaker et al., 1977a, 1977b); parents are generally pleased with the program and the results achieved (Lahey et al., 1977).Daily report cards and home-based reward programs are relatively easy to implement and typically do not require extensive specialized training.

Several guidelines should be kept in mind when setting up a daily report card program. First, the card should specify one, two, or three behaviors of primary concern to the teacher and parents.[1] The description of behaviors must be unambiguous to the teacher and parents, and should not be overly vague or overly specific. Second, the teacher should mark "yes" for a behavior category if the child is doing well in the category *relative* to past performance ("He wasn't in his seat every minute, but for him, he had a pretty good day."). The teacher can raise the criteria if the child is behaving better and further improvement is needed. Third, although the child may have more than one teacher each day, it is best to limit the use of the Daily Report Card to the one or two teachers for whom the child's behavior is most inappropriate. Fourth, each member of the program is responsible for performing certain behaviors. The parent is responsible for giving the card to the child each day and for providing the appropriate consequences; the teacher is responsible for evaluating the child's behavior and signing the card at the end of the day; and the child is responsible for taking the card to school, asking the teacher to fill it out each day, and for bringing it home to parents. If the child does not bring home the signed report card, the consequence is the same as if the card contains all "no" marks. Finally, it is essential that parents deliver response consequences based on the following recommendations: (a) punishment should never be given as a consequence for bad cards because a maladaptive iatrongenic spiral may develop (i.e., use of punishment, increase in child's inappropriate behavior, increase in use of punishment, etc.); (b) positive consequences should be delivered without barbs ("Well, its about time you had a good day."), and with a brief compliment ("That's great!"); (c) positive consequences should be potent, easily delivered, and if the child gets consistently good report cards, should represent a net gain in "good" things (e.g., after-school snacks, money, TV-viewing time) and points that can be accumulated to earn a large prize, such as a baseball glove, a trip to Six Flags; (d) the cards should be "faded" out when behavior improves to appropriate levels (i.e., daily report card to weekly report card, after 2 or 3 weeks of acceptable behavior, to no report cards), if the child's behavior deteriorates at any time, he can be placed back on a weekly or daily system; (e) watch out for forgeries, especially with older children; and (f) other significant adults (e.g., school counselors, teachers, principals) can mediate the daily report card system if parents cannot carry out their role as mediator.

Disruptive Behaviors

In addition to academic-related behaviors, common referrals from parents and teachers concern behaviors that disrupt home or classroom management (see also Chapter 4); However, specific behaviors labeled as disruptive may vary some-

[1]These guidelines were developed by Dr. Benjamin B. Lahey of the Psychology Department, University of Georgia. The authors wish to express their appreciation to Dr. Lahey for permission to reproduce these guidelines.

what between parents and teachers. The following behaviors have typically been included within the general response class: aggressive behavior (fighting, kicking, spitting, etc.), temper tantrums, annoying behaviors (whining, yelling), noncompliance, talking without permission, getting out of one's seat, and excessive motor activity (i.e., "hyperactivity") (Wells & Forehand, 1981).

Currently, the model treatment of disruptive behaviors in children involves comprehensive parent training programs developed by Patterson (see Patterson, Reid, Jones, & Conger, 1975) and Forehand (see Forehand & Peed, 1979). In comparison with earlier attempts, these programs focus on changing parent–child interactions rather than targeting specific problematic child behaviors. For example, parents are observed and trained in the home to issue single, discrete commands and warnings of consequences if misbehavior occurs a second time. Results of numerous studies have attested to the effectiveness of these programs (e.g., Forehand & King, 1974; Paterson, 1974; Patterson, Cobb, & Ray, 1973; Patterson & Reid, 1973; Peed, Roberts, & Forehand, 1977). To illustrate, Peed et al. (1977) treated 12 mother–child pairs who reported such problem behaviors as disobedience, temper tantrums, and hyperactivity. A significant increase in compliance to commands was evidenced both in the clinic and at home by these children compared with a waiting list control group. Data also showed that the mothers gave fewer vague commands, provided more positive reinforcement for compliance, and attended to the child's prosocial behavior.

Whereas the previously mentioned programs emphasize modifying disruptive home behaviors, home-based contingency programs are used when such behaviors occur at school. Home-based programs follow the same format as programs used to improve academic-related behaviors (i.e., teacher–parent communication in the form of progress reports, rewards and sanctions received at home). Teacher–parent communications include disruptive and academic-related behaviors within one home-based contingency program (Atkeson & Forehand, 1979). Atkeson and Forehand's (1979) evaluation suggests that home-based contingency management programs are effective across a variety of settings (education classrooms), subjects (elementary to high school students), and disruptive behaviors (e.g., aggression, rule-following). Ayllon, Garber, and Pisor's (1975) work with a third grade class displaying disruptive behaviors and low academic achievement is a prototype of these programs. The home-based reward program was explained to the children's parents during a 2 hour meeting. Students earned points during 15 minute intervals when no disruptive behavior occurred and lost points when disruptive behavior took place. A "good behavior letter" was given to students who did not exceed two disruptions per interval throughout the day. Parents delivered rewards contingent on receipt of the letter. During the time the program was operating disruptive behavior decreased to 10% compared with 90% during baseline.

Similar home-based programs have achieved equal success with junior high and high school students who had academic and/or behavioral problems (e.g.,

Bailey, Wolf, & Phillips, 1970; Coleman, 1973; Heaton, Safer, Allen, Spinnato, & Prumo, 1976). A typical example of these home-based programs would be to use a daily report card to increase the number of classes attended by individual students. In such a program, the student's class attendance would be checked on a daily basis by each teacher. If the student met the criteria (e.g., five classes attended out of six), reinforcement would be delivered at home. Praise, allowance, later bed time, and TV privileges are examples of rewards dispensed in previous home-based programs; rewards would be lost if the student did not attend the required number of classes. Weekly criteria and rewards also may be incorporated to provide incentives for increased performance. For instance, the student would have to attend 28 classes to receive the family car keys on Friday night for 4 hours.

In contrast with previously described home-based programs that focused on disruptive behavior, a study by Ayllon, Layman, and Kandel (1975) implemented a school-based program to improve disruptive behavior and academic performance. They compared the effectiveness of medication and a drug-free behavioral intervention. Behavioral intervention involved a token economy system, three children labeled *hyperactive* and *learning disabled* could earn checkmarks for each correct academic response. Checkmarks could be exchanged for school supplies, candy, and picnics in the park.

Results showed that when medication was withdrawn and the token economy system made rewards contingent on specific academic achievements (in math, then in math and reading), the average of correct responses rose from a baseline level of 12% to 85%; hyperactive behavior concurrently decreased. The study demonstrates the successful remediation of disruptive behavior in the classroom by rewarding incompatible responses (i.e., correct academic performance).

Parent behavior training, token economies, and home-based contingency programs have been highly effective in modifying disruptive behaviors in children and adolescents. A variety of disruptive behaviors (e.g., aggressive behaviors, noncompliance, getting out of one's seat) have been treated in school and at home. Involving teachers and/or parents in all stages of program design and implementation partially determines treatment success or failure. Cooperation in applying procedures consistently and over time is essential for a successful outcome.

Fears and Phobias

Some childhood fears are common to various developmental stages, others are considered excessive and extend beyond a "normal" period of development (see also Chapter 4).

Contingency management programs emphasize direct parental and/or teacher participation during treatment implementation. They focus on decreasing the child's fears by rewarding approach behavior and ignoring fearful reactions

(Johnson & Melamed, 1977). Parents and/or teachers assist the therapist in gradually increasing the child's contact with the feared object or situation by delivering praise and privileges (e.g., extended TV or "free" time) within homebased contingency programs.

The use of these programs in treating school phobia has been extensively researched and evaluated. Including parents in the treatment program is particularly relevant because of the established association between a child's refusal to attend school and the home environment (i.e., fear of leaving the home and parents, reinforcing consequences for staying at home). Obtaining the cooperation of teachers and other school personnel is equally important, treatment is conducted directly in the school and they perform the role of program implementors. Most treatment programs have employed operant-conditioning procedures (e.g., Ayllon, Smith, & Rogers, 1970; Gresham & Nagle, 1981; Hersen, 1970; Kennedy, 1965), respondent-conditioning procedures (e.g., Lazarus, 1960; Miller, 1972; Tahmisian & McReynolds, 1971), or a combination of procedures (Lazarus, Davison, & Polefka, 1965).

School attendance has been the primary and perhaps only legitimate treatment goal of these programs (Ayllon et al., 1970). Kennedy (1965) developed a home-based program for Type I school phobia; the program focuses on reducing complicating factors (reinforcement for staying at home, missed academic instruction). According to Kennedy, Type I school phobia may be characterized by an acute onset of fearful behavior, the first episode for a child in the lower grades, Monday onset following an illness the previous week, expressed concern about death or the mother's physical health, good communication and cooperation between parents in household manageMent, easy understanding of the child's current behavior, and participation in treatment plans by the parents. The treatment procedure for Type I school phobia includes:

1. Good communication with school personnel and parents to promote rapid referral.
2. A de-emphasis of somatic complaints.
3. Forced school attendance by significant others.
4. A structured interview with the parents to provide information concerning procedures and their responsibilities.
5. A brief interview with the child, the transitory nature of the phobia is described in the interview.
6. A telephone follow-up to collect data on the child's progress (school attendance, school performance, etc.).

Kennedy (1965) reported a success rate of 100% following treatment using his "rapid treatment method," making it one of the most successful approaches in reducing children's fears.

Although Kennedy's rapid treatment method provides parents with information and suggestions for managing their school phobic child, it does not focus on assisting the teacher to deal with the child's aversive behavior (e.g., crying, whining, somatic complaints, etc.) emitted in the classroom setting. A study by Gresham and Nagle (1981) illustrates the use of similar procedures by school personnel to eliminate these behaviors in the school situation.

In Gresham and Nagle's (1981) study, a mild timeout procedure (i.e., the child is placed in a corner of the room and not completely removed) was used by the teacher contingent upon crying and whining. Reinforcement of other behaviors with praise, attention, and access to desired classroom activities (i.e., a differential reinforcement of other behavior, or DRO, procedure) was also provided. Finally, somatic complaints, complaints regarding school attendance, and access to the principal's office during the day were ignored or withdrawn by parents and school personnel. Results of the study showed total elimination of crying and whining during the first 5 days of treatment with maintenance of treatment effect's at a 2-week follow-up period. The Gresham and Nagle (1981) study demonstrates the effectiveness of involving teachers, parents, and administrators in interventions with difficult problems in school settings.

Home-based and/or school-based operant procedures (e.g., timeout, extinction, shaping, DRO) have been successful in treating children's fears/phobias (particularly school phobia). Training parents or teachers to implement operant-based procedures has produced outcomes comparable with therapist-administered programs.

Health-Related Behaviors

As mandated by Public Law 94-142, special services for children with physical handicaps (e.g., cerebral palsy, spinal bifida) and other health-related problems (e.g., asthma, diabetes, seizure disorders) are required in the school setting. Therefore, school administrators are responsible for developing and instituting specific programs (e.g., academic, speech, physical education) and modifying environmental constraints to raise the educational and social attainment of these children. Familiarity with and correct use of behavioral procedures related to management of health-related problems is essential to promote the child's functioning at school (see also Chapter 6).

The efficacy of learning principles in managing health-related behaviors of children have recently been established. In comparison with treatment of other problem behaviors (e.g., academic-related and disruptive behaviors), parental and/or teacher involvement have been limited in this area. Treatment of obesity and seizures usually have been parent- or teacher-administered. Few programs, however, have attempted to enlist the aid of both parents and teachers within a home- or school-based treatment. Because of the positive results obtained from daily report cards and home-based reward programs with academic-related and disruptive behaviors, a similar treatment strategy would be equally effective in treating health-related behaviors. Sulzer-Azaroff and Pollack (1982) have suggested several improvements, such as methods for training parents and teachers, techniques for promoting compliance, and home-based data collection procedures to increase the efficacy of previous treatment programs. A review of behavioral procedures that have been utilized by parents or teachers to manage such conditions as obesity, asthma, seizures and diabetes follows.

Modification of the antecedents and consequences of eating behaviors through stimulus control (e.g., eating in only one place and at certain times), reward contingencies, and response-cost procedures have produced successful outcomes in the treatment of childhood and adolescent obesity (Aragona, Cassady, & Drabman, 1975; Epstein, Masek, & Marshall, 1978; Lansky & Vance, 1983). To illustrate, Lansky and Vance (1983) employed a school-based weight program with junior high school students. In this study, a physical-education instructor trained the students in the following procedures:

1. Self-monitoring of food intake and exercise.
2. Utilization of a food-exchange plan emphasizing three meals per day.
3. Stimulus control of eating (e.g., to change serving and preparation habits).
4. Problem-solving inappropriate eating and exercise habits.
5. Scheduled aerobic activities.
6. Reinforcement for weight loss of one half pound (e.g., passes for bowling).

In addition, four meetings were held with parents to provide feedback about the student's program and to generate ways to model and/or reinforce new eating and exercise habits. Following a 12 week program students in the treatment group decreased in percentage overweight 5.71% compared with the control group who gained 2.41%. Parental participation was also significantly correlated with outcome; students with participating parents tended to decrease more in percentage overweight.

Improvements in the respiratory functioning of asthmatics and seizure activity in children have been found when respondent-conditioning procedures (e.g., systematic desensitization, relaxation, biofeedback) were used (Davis, Saunders, Creer & Chai, 1973; Miklich et al., 1977). Operant-conditioning procedures (e.g., differential reinforcement, positive reinforcement, interrupting contingencies) have successfully reduced the frequency and/or duration of asthmatic attacks and seizures (Neisworth & Moore, 1972; Zlutnick, Mayville, & Moffat, 1975). worked with five seizure disordered children using a DRO or an interruption procedure. The procedure consisted of requiring a parent, teacher, or another child to shout ''NO!'' loudly and sharply, grasp the child by the shoulders, and give a vigorous shake during the preseizure stage of the disorder. Results showed either a significant decrease or complete elimination of seizure activity for the majority of children.

Behavioral treatment of children with diabetes or asthma has also focused on enhancing compliance to their medical regime (medication, special diets, exercise, inhalation equipment). Self-monitoring procedures, goal setting, contingency contracting, and token economics have been employed in various combinations to increase compliance by parents and/or therapists (Carney, Schechter, & Davis, 1983; Eney & Goldstein, 1976; Epstein, Beck, Figueroa, Farkas, Kazdin, Daneman, & Becker, 1981). For example, Carney et al. (1983) taught parents to apply contingent praise and a point system to encourage home blood glucose monitoring in diabetic children. Treatment effectively increased monitoring levels to 85% with maintenance at a 4 month follow-up.

Previous research has reported a high prevalence of behavioral problems in children with chronic illnesses (Levy, 1979; Pless & Roghmann, 1971). These problems have included social isolation, dependence, depression, anxiety, aggression (e.g., fighting), truancy, and other school-related difficulties (e.g., classwork completion, task accuracy). Parent training programs, similar to those developed by Forehand and Peed (1979) and Patterson (1976), and home-based reward programs would be a feasible and effective treatment approach to remediate these problem behaviors.

Parent-Adolescent Conflict

Parent-adolescent conflicts develop in many families as teenagers attempt to establish independence (Robin, 1981). Conflicts have focused on completion of chores, curfew, choice of friends, and car, telephone, and dating privileges. Student-teacher conflicts involving classroom behaviors (e.g., following rules, classwork and homework completion) also occur during this period. The inability of families to resolve conflicts effectively has been conceptualized from a "family skill deficit" model (Robin 1980). In this model, family members use mutually coercive methods to get what they want (e.g., yelling, threatening punishment, sarcasm, criticizing). In general, family members evidence deficits in problem-solving (e.g., generating solutions that are agreeable to both parents and the adolescent) and communication skills (e.g., expressing opinions without criticizing others). Student-teacher conflicts may also be explained by a skills deficit model, with further attempts to reach a solution resulting in negative feelings and attitudes (e.g., dislike, anger) associated with the school setting and the student.

The most common treatment approaches used to ameliorate parent-adolescent conflicts and, to a lesser degree, student-adolescent conflicts have been contingency contracting and problem-solving communication training. Within each approach the adolescent actively participates in developing and implementing the treatment program with parent(s) or teacher(s). For instance, parent(s)

TABLE 7.4
Example of a Contingency Contract
to Increase Work Completion

Effective Dates:
　From _____   To _____

Lorie agrees to make her bed before leaving for school and to wash the dinner dishes immediately after eating, from Sunday to Friday. In addition, she agrees to clean her room to her own and her mother's satisfaction on Friday or Saturday. In exchange Lorie will receive $2.00 on the evening the chores have been completed.

Lorie agrees to complete her homework assignments between 5 P.M. and 7 P.M. from Sunday to Thursday. In exchange Lorie may spend the rest of the evening doing what she chooses (i.e., watching T.V., talking on the phone, reading) without criticism from other family members.

Bonuses and Sanctions

If Lorie completes her chores everyday throughout the week, she will earn an extra $3.00 on Saturday afternoon.

If she completes her homework assignments every-evening, her curfew will be extended one hour on Friday or Saturday.

If Lorie does not fulfill her responsibilities as stated in this contract, for two days during the week, she must either:

　　forfeit $2.00 of her earnings or
　　forfeit one hour from her curfew on both Friday and Saturday.

Monitoring

Lorie agrees to record her daily and weekly chore completion.
Lorie's parents agree to record the duration and completion of homework.

_____   _____
WITNESS   LORIE'S SIGNATURE

_____   _____
DATE   PARENT'S SIGNATURE

This contract will be reviewed within two weeks from the above date and revised, if necessary.

---

and the adolescent negotiate the components of a contingency contract, including the behaviors targeted for change by each person, privileges earned for engaging in these behaviors, and a system for monitoring behavior change. Table 7.4 provides an example of a contingency contract that could be used to increase chore and homework completion.

This type of home-based program differs from others (i.e., daily report card, point system) because the parents/teachers and the adolescent perform behaviors requested by others to receive desired privileges, this is referred to as the reciprocity principle (Stuart, 1971).

Studies by Stuart and associates exemplify the application of contingency contracting to parent-adolescent conflicts (Stuart & Tripodi, 1973; Stuart, Tripodi, Jayaratne, & Camburn, 1976). In the initial study (Stuart & Tripodi, 1973) the efficacy of a 15, 45, or 90 day time-limited program with families of pre-delinquents and delinquents was compared with families who declined treatment. Results showed that on measures obtained in the home, school, and community, the contracting families outperformed those in the control group.

In contrast with contingency contracting, where specific problem behaviors are targeted for change (e.g., violation of curfew), problem-solving communication training focuses on improving parent's and adolescent's ability to resolve conflicts. Several programs using this approach have been developed to remediate particular problem situations and skill deficit (Blechman, Olson, Schornagel, Halsdorf, & Turner, 1976; Kifer, Lewis, Green, & Phillips, 1974, Robin, 1980, 1981; Robin, Kent, O'Leary, Foster, & Prinz, 1977).

Representative of the research in this area is the program developed by Robin et al. (1977). The program, based on D'Zurilla and Goldfried's (1971) model of problem-solving, entails four components: (a) training parents and adolescents in the skills necessary to negotiate solutions to specific arguments; (b) teaching family members receptive and expressive communication skills; (c) changing faulty cognitions or attitudes; and (d) assigning homework to practice negotiation-communication skills at home. Table 7.5 provides a detailed description of each component.

Training usually takes place over 7 to 12, 1 hour sessions. During each session a conflict situation is problem solved according to the four steps shown in

TABLE 7.5
Treatment Components of Problem-Solving-Communication Skills Training
for Parent-Adolescent Conflicts

---

1. Problem-Solving
   a. define the problem concisely and without accusation;
   b. brainstorm alternative solutions;
   c. decide on a mutually satisfactory solution by generating positive and negative consequences, assigning solutions positive or negative ratings, adopting one or more solutions rated positively by everyone;
   d. specify the details for implementing the agreement.
2. Communication Training
   verification of meaning, passive listening, active listening, I-messages, appropriate eye contact, appropriate nonverbal posture are skills taught to eliminate accusations, interruptions, lectures, put-downs, overgeneralizations, commands, sarcastic expressions.
3. Cognitive restructuring of faulty beliefs that winterfered with conflict resolution
   a. "underlying" cognitive distortion made explicit;
   b. logical premises of the distortion challenged through direct feedback, exaggeration and humor;
   c. alternative, more flexible belief suggested;
   d. "experimentation" by family members to implement a solution with the more flexible belief and to determine its success.
4. Homework assignments
   a. implement solutions negotiated during sessions;
   b. discussion of other problems at home;
   c. use of problem-solving communication skills in daily conversation.

Table 7.5. Various communication skills are also targeted for change. The therapist models, instructs, prompts, rehearses, and provides feedback at each step to modify problems in the way parents and adolescents interact. Controlled-group outcome studies (Robin, 1981; Robin et al., 1977) have indicated the success of the program in improving problem-solving communication skills and negative feelings (e.g., anger) associated with specific conflicts.

A similar program to decrease the frequency and range of student–teacher conflicts has not yet been developed. Because of the length of the program and the efficiency and effectiveness of other home-base programs (e.g., point systems, contingency contracting), problem-solving communication training may be more applicable to parent–adolescent conflicts.

At present, a limited number of studies have systematically evaluated the efficacy of behavioral procedures to parent/teacher–adolescent conflicts. Results have been favorable in teaching parents and adolescents more adaptive communication and problem-solving skills. To improve current and future conflict situations, programs have been parent/teacher and/or adolescent-administered. However, frequent therapist contact during the initial phase of treatment is essential to remediate problems in the treatment plan and promote compliance. Future research should focus on increasing the applicability of self-management programs (i.e., contingency contracting) and problem-solving skills training to ameliorate classroom and home behavior problems. In this way, adolescents may learn to assume responsibility for behavior without constant parent/teacher supervision.

METHODOLOGICAL ISSUES IN PARENT EDUCATION RESEARCH

The foregoing review demonstrates that parents can be taught to deal effectively with a wide variety of problem behaviors if they are given exposure, training, and professional consultation in the application of behavioral principles. Although the vast majority of studies show positive outcomes for parent education, several methodological issues must be evaluated before a complete endorsement of the approach can be made. Three areas are critical to the methodological evaluation of parent training programs: (a) parent training methods, (b) use of multiple outcome measures, and (c) monitoring of parent behaviors. Each methodological issue with suggestions for future research and practice is briefly discussed in the following sections (see also Chapter 10).

Parent Training Methods

Most of the previously reviewed studies have used a variety of procedures to teach parents how to change their child's behavior. Specific parent training methods have included instructions, modeling, behavior rehearsal, feedback, readings, social reinforcement, and combinations of techniques.

Few, if any, studies utilize a single method to teach parents how to change their child's behavior, a combination of methods is used. Some combinations are associated with changes in child behavior; however, the method or method combination that is most effective with behaviors or problem areas; the training methods responsible for changes in parent or child behavior, and whether parents actually learn and correctly and consistently apply behavioral skills as a result of parent education is not known. Future research should address these issues to isolate the specific parent education methods that are most effective and lead to correct and consistent application by parents.

Multiple Outcome Measures

The previously reviewed literature shows that a wide range of measures have been used to evaluate the outcomes of parent education. Outcome measures can be classified into three major groupings: (a) parent-recorded frequency of child behavior in the home; (b) teacher-recorded frequency of child behavior in the classroom; and (3) parent or teacher questionnaires or checklists. Generally, recorded frequencies of classroom behaviors agree with teacher questionnaire or checklist data, although there is a loss of specificity with the latter. Similarly, many studies suggest that parents report improvements in home behaviors subsequent to changes in school behavior (Atkeson & Forehand, 1979).

School consultants should utilize multiple measures to evaluate the outcomes of parent education programs. Parent and teacher rating scales or checklists may reflect not only behavior changes, but also changes in perceptions of the child regardless of behavior change. Therefore, evaluation of parent education programs should assess changes in child behavior (e.g., on-task, disruptive behavior, etc.), output (e.g., work completion, accuracy, etc.), and teacher and parent perceptions of child behavior change.

The evaluation of consumer perceptions of behavior change programs has been termed *social validation* (Gresham, 1983; Kazdin, 1977; Wolf, 1978). Social validity refers to establishing the social significance of the goals of behavior change programs, the social acceptability of the procedures used to effect behavior change, and the social importance of the effects of behavior change programs. Having parents, teachers, and children evaluate parent education programs on these dimensions represents an important aspect of parent education programs in the schools. Table 7.6 presents a summary of outcome measures that should be used to evaluate and socially validate the effects of parent education programs in the schools.

Monitoring of Parent Behavior

An essential prerequisite for concluding that parent education is responsible for changes in child behavior is an objective evaluation of whether the program was implemented as planned. Alt the majority of parent education studies cited in this

TABLE 7.6
Outcome and Social Validation Measures
for Parent Education Programs

Outcome Measure	Importance
A. Parent Data	
1. Parent recorded rates of behavior in home	Evaluate effectiveness of program
2. Parent perceptions of behavior change	Social validation and program effectiveness
3. Parent evaluation of parent education program	Social validation
B. Teacher Data	
1. Teacher recorded rates of classroom behavior	Evaluate effectiveness of program
2. Changes in output	Evaluate effectiveness of program (Academic behaviors)
3. Teacher perceptions of behavior change	Social validation and program effectiveness
4. Teacher evaluation of parent education program	Social validation
C. Child Data	
1. Child recorded changes in own behavior (self-monitoring)	Effectiveness of program
2. Child perceptions of behavior change	Social validation and prograram effectiveness
3. Child perceptions of parent education program	Social validation

chapter have demonstrated positive behavior changes, it is not known if parents are implementing the behavior change procedures in the home as planned.

The only way to ensure that parents were correctly implementing the procedures would be to monitor parent behaviors in the home; however, this is impractical. Because of the time, expense, and potential ethical problems associated with monitoring parent behavior, the cost-benefit ratio is low. A reasonable alternative is to assume that the program and procedures are not being implemented properly by parents in the home if behavior changes in the child are not observed in school after a reasonable period of time. This should prompt school consultants either to revise certain aspects of the intervention plan or stress to parents the importance of consistently administering the procedures in the home environment.

PARENT EDUCATION IN SCHOOL ORGANIZATIONS

The foregoing review of parent education literature indicates that parents can be taught to ameliorate effectively a variety of problem behaviors exhibited by children in school settings. Problem behaviors include academic deficiencies, disruptive behavior, fears and phobias, health-related behaviors, and parent–adolescent conflicts. Although there are several methodological issues to be resolved, the bulk of the research points toward parent education as a viable intervention in school organizations. The next section delineates several points relevant to organizational characteristics of the school that influence design, implementation, and evaluation of parent education programs.

School Organizational Considerations: Formative Evaluation

Several factors have been associated with an organization's response to infernal change and innovation (Hauser, 1979). Davis and Salasin (1975) have identified eight factors that are important in considering the school organization's response to new programs, such as parent education. The eight factors are designated by the acronym A VICTORY and represent the following ideas: Ability, Values, Idea, Circumstances, Timing, Obligations, Resistance, and Yield.

Hauser (1979) states that the A VICTORY can be used for conducting systematic inquiry into several areas: (a) the school's response to new and innovative programs; (b) how these responses might be expected to affect the program if adopted; (c) the school's readiness to accept changes that would be imposed by the new program; and (d) the steps necessary to enhance the program's chances of survival in the school organization.

This model is not an evaluation model because the intent is to supplement not to replace other program evaluation models. The A VICTORY model can be used to assess the extent to which changes brought about by a new program (e.g., parent education) affect the school organization and how the school's response to these changes affect the program (Hauser, 1979).

Summative Evaluation of Parent Education: A Behavioral Model

The A VICTORY model, described by Hauser (1979), was depicted as a formative evaluation model in which school consultants could assess the school organization's receptivity to a parent education program, identity values and resistance to program implementation, and to conduct a cost-benefit analysis of program implementation. It is a formative evaluation that provides school consultants with the information necessary to modify the proposed program to make it more acceptable to the school organization or to make a decision to scrap the proposed program.

Although formative evaluation is necessary, it is not sufficient to evaluate the effects of a parent education program. There are a number of summative evaluation models; the one proposed by Kratochwill (1980) to evaluate individual education programs from a behavioral perspective is particularly relevant in evaluating the outcomes of parent education programs. In Kratochwill's (1980) evaluation model, various evaluations are made over phases or stages of the parent education process. In this model there are five conceptualized phases: (a) Problem Identification; (b) Problem Analysis; (c) Plan Implementation; (d) Plan Evaluation; (e) Generalization; and (f) Follow-up.

Problem identification in parent education would involve specification of the problem or problems to be solved through parent education (Bergan, 1977; Kratochwill, 1980). In parent education programs, school consultants would have to assess the specific problem behaviors of most concern to parents and teachers before designing a parent education program. One way to assess the problem behaviors that are of most concern is to have samples of parents and teachers rank order a number of problem behaviors; behaviors receiving the highest rankings assume top priority for parent education programs.

Problem analysis represents the phase of evaluation in which school consultants identify environmental variables that would lead to changing behaviors identified during problem identification. In other words, school consultants would identify with parents, teachers, and children the antecedent, sequential, and consequent conditions surrounding the occurrence of problem behaviors, and an intervention program would be designed to solve problem behaviors.

Plan implementation requires school consultants to ensure that the plan designed during problem analysis is being implemented properly. As stated previously, the way to ensure that parents were implementing procedures properly would be to monitor parent behavior in the home. It was also suggested that monitoring parent behavior in the home was time consuming, expensive, and therefore, not cost beneficial. Although some monitoring can take place (e.g., via telephone calls, postcards, as prompts, etc.), it would be more acceptable to assume that the plan was not being implemented properly if behavior changes are not observed after a reasonable period of time.

Plan evaluation is perhaps the most important phase of the process from a summative evaluation standpoint because school consultants assess the overall effectiveness of the plan. Multiple outcome measures should be utilized (see previous discussion) to evaluate the total effectiveness of the plan. Remember, one should use not only actual changes in child behavior, but also social validity data in the form of parent, teacher, and child perceptions.

Generalization refers to changes in relevant behavior under different, non-training conditions (Stokes, & Baer, 1977). Generalization can occur across settings, behaviors, and subjects. Setting generalization refers to changes in behavior in settings that are different from the setting in which intervention occurred. Thus, if a child is less disruptive in the classroom subsequent to an intervention in the home, setting generalization has taken place. Behavior generalization refers to changes in behaviors not targeted for intervention. For example, if one observed an increase in academic performance concurrent with or subsequent to an intervention for aggressive behavior, behavior generalization has taken place. Finally, subject generalization refers to behavior changes in a child who is not the focus of intervention. Therefore, if a sibling's behavior changes after a parent education program, subject generalization has occurred. School consultants should consider the evaluation of generalization an important aspect of summative evaluation for parent education programs.

Follow-up actually describes a fourth type of generalization: time generalization. Time generalization refers to the continuation of behavior change in a setting after the withdrawal of an intervention. In the present context, time generalization could be claimed if a child's academic performance continued to increase or maintained after the formal withdrawal of a parent education program. Conducting follow-ups of parent education programs is extremely important because they are objective data that the program produces lasting effects on children's behavior. Objective data, in conjunction with social validity data, can be used to gain the school organization's support for continuation and expansion of parent education programs.

REFERENCES

Aragona, J., Cassady, J., & Drabman, R. S. (1975). Treating overweight children through parental training and contingency contracting. *Journal of Applied Behavior Analysis, 8,* 269–278.

Atkeson, B. M., & Forehand, R. (1979). Home-based reinforcement programs designed to modify classroom behavior: A review and methodological evaluation. *Psychological Bulletin, 86,* 1298–1308.

Ayllon, T., Garber, S., & Pisor, K. (1975). The elimination of discipline problems through a combined school-home motivational system. *Behavior Therapy, 6,* 616–626.

Ayllon, T., Layman, D., & Kandel, H. J. (1975). A behavioral-educational alternative to drug control of hyperactive children. *Journal of Applied Behavior Analysis, 8,* 137–146.

Ayllon,, T., Smith, D., & Rogers, M. (1970). Behavioral management of school phobia. *Journal of Behavior Therapy and Experimental Psychiatry, 1,* 125–138.

Bailey, J. S., Wolf, M. M., & Phillips, E. L. (1970). Home-based reinforcement and the modification of pre-delinquents' classroom behavior. *Journal of Applied Behavior Analysis, 3,* 223–233.

Bandura, A. (1977). *Social learning theory.* Englewood Cliffs, NJ: Prentice-Hall.

Bergan, J. R. (1977). *Behavioral consultation.* Columbus, OH: Charles Merrill.

Bergan, J. R., & Duley, S. M. (1981). Behavioral consultation with families. In R. W. Henderson (Ed.), *Parent–child interaction: Theory, research,* and *prospects* (pp. 47–68). New York: Academic Press.

Berkowitz, B. P., & Graziano, A. M. (1972). Training parents as behavior therapists: A review. *Behaviour Research and Therapy, 10,* 297–317.

Blechman, E. A., Olson, D. H. L., Schornagel, C. Y., Halsdorf, M., & Turner, A. J. (1976). The family contract game: Technique and case study. *Journal of Consulting and Clinical Psychology, 44,* 449–455.

Bloom, B. L., Asher, S. J., & White, S. W. (1978). Marital disruption as a stressor: A review and analysis. *Psychological Bulletin, 85,* 867–894.

Bronfenbrenner, V. (1979). *The ecology of human development: Experiments by nature and design.* Boston: Harvard University Press.

Carney, R. M., Schechter, K., & Davis, T. (1983). Improving adherence to blood glucose testing in insulin-dependent diabetic children. *Behavior Therapy, 14,* 247–254.

Coleman, R. G. (1973). A procedure for fading from experimenter-school-based to parent-home-based control of classroom behavior. *Journal of School Psychology, 11,* 71–90.

Conger, R. (1981). The assessment of dysfunctional family systems. In B. B. Lahey & A. E. Kazdin (Eds.), *Advances in clinical child psychology* (Vol. 4, pp. 199–242). New York: Plenum Press.

Davis, H. R., & Salasin, S. E. (1975). The utilization of evaluation. In E. L. Struenig and M. Guttentag (Eds.), *Handbook of evaluation research* (Vol. 1, pp. 621–666). Beverly Hills, CA: Sage.

Davis, M. H., Saunders, D. R., Creer, T. L., & Chai, H. (1973). Relaxation training facilitated by biofeedback apparatus as a supplemental treatment of bronchial asthma. *Journal of Psychosomatic Research, 17,* 121–128.

D'Zurilla, T. J., & Goldfried, M. R. (1971). Problem solving and behavior modification. *Journal of Abnormal Psychology, 2,* 71–73.

Eney, R. D., & Goldstein, E. O. (1976). Compliance of chronic asthmatics with oral administration of theophyllin as measured by serum and salivary measures. *Pediatrics, 57,* 513–517.

Epstein, L. H., Beck, S., Figuero, J., Farkas, G., Kazdin, A., Daneman, D., & Becker, D. (1981). The effects of targeting improvement in urine glucose on metabolic control in children with insulin dependent diabetics. *Journal of Applied Behavior Analysis, 14,* 365–375.

Epstein, L. H., Masek, B. J., & Marshall, W. R. (1978). A nutritionally based school program for control of eating in obese children. *Behavior Therapy, 9,* 766–778.

Forehand, R., & King, H. E. (1974). Preschool children's noncompliance: Effects of short-term therapy. *Journal of Community Psychology, 2,* 42–44.

Forehand, R., & Peed, S. (1979). Training parents to modify noncompliant behavior of their children. In A. J. Finch, Jr., & P. C. Kendall (Eds.), *Treatment and research in child psychopathology.* New York: Spectrum.

Gresham, F. M. (1983). Social validity in the assessment of children's social skills: Establishing standards for social competency. *Journal of Psychoeducational Assessment, 1,* 299–307.

Gresham, F. M., & Nagle, R. J. (1981). Treating school phobia using behavioral consultation: A case study. *School Psychology Review, 10,* 104–106.

Guidubaldi, J. (1980). The status report extended: Further elaborations of the American family. *School Psychology Review, 9,* 374–379.

Hauser, C. (1979). Evaluating mainstream programs: Capitalizing on a victory. *Journal of Special Education, 13,* 107–129.

Heaton, R. C., Safer, D. J., Allen, R. P., Spinnato, N. C., & Prumo, F. M. (1976). A motivational environment for behaviorally deviant junior high school students. *Journal of Abnormal Child Psychology, 4,* 263–275.

Henry, S. (1981). Current dimensions of parent training. *School Psychology Review, 10,* 4–14.

Hersen, M. (1970). Behavior modification approach to a school phobia case. *Journal of Clinical Psychology, 26,* 128–132.

Johnson, S. B., & Melamed, B. G. (1977). The assessment and treatment of children's fears. In B. B. Lahey & A. E. Kazdin (Eds.), *Advances in child clinical psychology* (Vol. 2). New York: Plenum Press.

Jones, M. C. (1924a). A laboratory study of fear: The case of Peter. *Pedagogical Seminary, 31,* 308–315.

Jones, M. C. (1924b). The elimination of children's fears. *Journal of Experimental Psychology, 7,* 382–390.

Kazdin, A. E. (1977). Assessing the clinical or applied importance of behavior change through social validation. *Behavior Modification, 1,* 427–452.

Kennedy, W. A. (1965). School phobia: Rapid treatment of fifty cases. *Journal of Abnormal and Social Psychology, 70,* 285–289.

Kifer, R. E., Lewis, M. A., Green, D. R., & Phillips, E. L. (1974). Training predelinquent youths and their parents to negotiate conflict situations. *Journal of Applied Behavior Analysis, 7,* 357–364.

Kratochwill, T. R. (1980). Behavioral assessment of academic and social problems: Implications for the individual education plan. *School Psychology Review, 9,* 199–206.

Lahey, B. B., Gendrich, J. G., Gendrich, S. I., Schnelle, J. F., Gant, D. S., & McNees, M. P. (1977). An evaluation of daily report cards with minimal teacher and parent contacts as an efficient method of classroom intervention. *Behavior Modification, 1,* 381–394.

Lansky, D. & Vance, M. A. (1983). School-based intervention for adolescent obesity: Analysis of treatment, randomly selected control, and self-elected control subjects. *Journal of Consulting and Clinical Psychology, 51,* 147–148.

Lazarus, A. A. (1960). The elimination of children's phobias by deconditioning. In H. J. Eysenck (Ed.), *Behavior therapy and the neuroses.* New York: Pergamon Press.

Lazarus, A. A., Davison, G. C., & Polefka, D. A. (1965). Classical and operant factors in the treatment of school phobia. *Journal of Abnormal Psychology, 70,* 225–229.

Levy, N. B. (1979). The chronically ill patient. *Psychiatric Quarterly, 51,* 189–197.

Miklich, D. R., Renne, C., Creer, T., Alexander, A., Chai, H., Davis, M., Huffman, A., & Danker-Brown, P. (1977). The clinical utility of behavior therapy as an adjunctive treatment for asthma. *The Journal of Allergy and Clinical Immunology, 60,* 284–294.

Miller, P. M. (1972). The use of visual imagery and muscle relaxation in the counterconditioning of a phobic child: A case study. *Journal of Nervous and Mental Disease, 154,* 457–460.

Moreland, J. R., Schwebel, A. I., Beck, S., & Wells, R. (1982). Parents as therapists: A review of behavior therapy parent training literature—1975 to 1981. *Behavior Modification, 6,* 250–276.

Mowrer, O. H., & Mowrer, W. M. (1938). Enuresis: A method for its study and treatment. *American Journal of Orthopsychiatry, 8,* 436–459.

Neisworth, J. R., & Moore, F. (1972). Operant treatment of asthmatic responding with the parent as therapist. *Behavior Therapy, 3,* 95–99.

O'Dell, S. (1974). Training parents in behavior modification: A review. *Psychological Bulletin, 81,* 418–433.

O'Leary, K. D., & Kent, R. N. (1973). Behavior modification for social action: Research tactics and problems. In L. A. Hammerlynck, L. C. Handy, & E. J. Mash (Eds.), *Behavior change: Methodology, concepts, and practice.* Champaign, IL: Research Press.

Patterson, G. R. (1974). Interventions for boys with conduct problems: Multiple settings, treatments, and criteria. *Journal of Consulting and Clinical Psychology, 42,* 471–481.

Patterson, G. R. (1975). *Families: Applications of social learning to family life.* Champaign, IL: Research Press.

Patterson, G. R. (1976). The aggressive child: Victim and architect of a coercive system. In E. J. Mash, L. A. Hamerlynck, & L. C. Handy (Eds.), *Behavior modification and families.* New York: Brunner/Mazel.

Patterson, G. R., Cobb, J. A., & Ray, R. S. (1973). A social engineering technology for retraining aggressive boys. In H. E. Adams & P. Unikel (Eds.), *Issues and trends in behavior therapy.* Springfield, IL: Charles C. Thomas.

Patterson, G. R., & Guillion, M. G. (1976). *Living with children: New methods for parents and teachers.* Champaign, IL: Research Press.

Patterson, G. R., & Reid, J. B. (1973). Intervention for families of aggressive boys: A replication study. *Behavior Research and Therapy, 11,* 383–394.

Patterson, G. R., Reid, J. B., Jones, R. R., & Conger, R. E. (1975). *A social learning approach to family intervention: Families with aggressive children.* Eugene, OR: Castalia Press.

Peed, S., Roberts, M., & Forehand, R. (1977). Evaluation of the effectiveness of a standardized parent training program in altering the interaction of mothers and their noncompliant children. *Behavior Modification, 1,* 323–350.

Pless, I. B., & Roghmann, K. J. (1971). Chronic illness and its consequences: Observations based on three epidemiologic surveys. *The Journal of Pediatrics, 79,* 351–359.

Robin, A. L. (1980). Parent-adolescent conflict: A skill training approach. In D. P. Rathjen & J. P. Foreyt (Eds.), *Social competence: Interventions for children and adults.* Elmsford, NY: Pergamon Press.

Robin, A. L. (1981). A controlled evaluation of problem-solving communication training with parent-adolescent conflict. *Behavior Therapy, 12,* 593–609.

Robin, A. L., Kent, R., O'Leary, K. D., Foster, S., & Prinz, R. (1977). An approach to teaching parents and adolescents problem-solving communication skills: A preliminary report. *Behavior Therapy, 8,* 639–643.

Rogers-Warren, A., & Warren, S. F. (Eds.). (1977). *Ecological perspectives in behavior analysis.* Baltimore: University Park Press.

Ross, A. O. (1981). *Child behavior therapy: Principles, procedures, and empirical basis.* New York: Wiley.

Saudargas, R. W., Madsen, C. H., Jr., & Scott, J. W. (1977). Differential affects of fixed- and variable-time feedback on production rates of elementary school children. *Journal of Applied Behavior Analysis, 10,* 673–678.

Schumaker, J. B., Hovell, M. F., & Sherman, J. A. (1977a). An analysis of daily report cards and parent-managed privileges in the improvement of adolescents classroom performance. *Journal of Applied Behavior Analysis, 10,* 449–464.

Schumaker, J. B., Hovell, M. F., & Sherman, J. A. (1977b). *A home-based school achievement program.* Lawrence, KS: H & H Enterprizes.

Simpson, R., & Poplin, M. (1981). Parents as agents of change. *School Psychology Review, 10,* 15–25.

Stokes, T., & Baer, D. (1977). An implicit technology of generalization. *Journal of Applied Behavior Analysis, 10,* 349–367.

Stuart, R. B. (1971). Behavioral contracting within the families of delinquents. *Journal of Behavior Therapy and Experimental Psychiatry, 2,* 1–11.

Stuart, R. B., & Tripodi, T. (1973). Experimental evaluation of three time-constrained behavioral treatments for predelinquents and delinquents. In R. D. Rubin, J. P. Brady, & J. D. Henderson (Eds.), *Advances in behavior therapy.* (pp. 231–251). New York: Academic Press.

Stuart, S. B., Tripodi, T., Jayaratne, S., and Camburn, D. (1976). An experiment in social engineering in serving the families of predelinquents. *Journal of Abnormal Child Psychology, 4,* 243–261.

Sulzer-Azaroff, B., & Pollack, M. J. (1982). The modification of child behavior problems in the home. In A. S. Bellack, M. Hersen, & A. E. Kazdin (Eds.), *International handbook of behavior modification and therapy.* New York: Plenum Press.

Tahmisian, J. A., & McReynolds, W. (1971). Use of parents as behavioral engineers in the treatment of a school-phobic girl. *Journal of Counseling Psychology, 18,* 225–228.

Turner, R. K. (1973). Conditioning treatment of nocturnal enuresis. In I. Kalvin, R. C. MacKeith, & S. R. Meadow (Eds.), *Bladder control and enuresis.* New York: Lippincott.

Wahler, R. G., Berland, R. M., Coe, T. D., & Leske, G. (1977). Social systems analysis: Implementing an alternative behavioral model. In A. Rogers-Warren & S. F. Warren (Eds.), *Ecological perspectives in behavioral analysis.* Baltimore: University Park Press.

Watson, J. B., & Rayner, R. (1920). Conditioned emotional reactions. *Journal of Experimental Psychology, 3,* 1–14.

Wells, K. C., & Forehand, R. (1981). Childhood behavior problems in the home. In S. M. Turner,

K. S. Calhoun, & H. E. Adams (Eds.), *Handbook of clinical behavior therapy* (pp. 527–567). New York: Wiley.

Williams, E. P. (1974). Behavioral technology and behavioral ecology. *Journal of Applied Behavior Analysis, 7,* 151–165.

Wolf, M. M. (1978). Social validity: The case for subjective measurement or how applied behavior analysis is finding its' heart. *Journal of Applied Behavior Analysis, 11,* 203–214.

Zlutnick, S., Mayville, W. J., & Moffat, S. (1975). Modification of seizure disorders: The interruption of behavioral chains. *Journal of Applied Behavior Analysis, 8,* 1–12.

8 Behavioral Consultation

Jason K. Feld
John R. Bergan
Clement A. Stone

During the last 2 decades, traditional psychodiagnostic, clinical, and report writing roles of special service providers, such as school psychologists, counselors, and other educational practitioners, have progressed in the direction of what many writers in the field view as a more constructive and innovative role, that of consultant (Bergan, 1977; Bergan & Tombari, 1976; Conoley, 1981; Conoley & Conoley, 1982; Meyers, 1973). Consultation has been viewed as the new path for school professionals in the delivery of more effective services concerning the educational, affective, and social needs of children (Bergan, 1977; Bergan, Feld, & Schnaps, 1984; Mannino & Shore, 1975; Reschly, 1976). In fact, some studies have shown that school personnel often prefer consultation rather than diagnostic testing approaches as a means of providing services to their students (see, for example, Lambert, Sandoval, & Corder, 1975).

The increased emphasis on consultation in the schools has been accompanied by a proliferation of responsibilities for practitioners that, at times, have appeared insurmountable. As Reschly (1976) points out, the role of the school consultant has increasingly included such endeavors as conducting research, designing educational programs, improving mental health, testing and diagnosing, and evaluating programs and personnel. Moreover, those features that distinguish consultation from other school-based services have become highly diverse. This diversity includes variations in: (a) definition of consultation; (b) roles and interactions between consultant and consultee; (c) populations served; (d) organizational level at which consultation occurs; (e) consultation goals sought and techniques employed; (f) emphasis placed on various factors related to the problem solving process; (g) criteria for evaluating outcome; and (h) criteria for determining when consultation should terminate (see, Dworkin &

Dworkin, 1975; Meyers, 1973; Reschly, 1976). This diversity stems from the variety of theoretical orientations that have guided the development of consultation approaches. To some extent, each approach has been implemented in school settings.

Consultation approaches currently implemented in schools include: mental health (Caplan, 1970; Meyers, Parsons, & Martin, 1979); organizational (e.g., process, ecological) (Alderfer, 1977; Jason, Ferone, & Anderegg, 1979; Schein, 1969; Schmuck & Miles 1971); and behavioral (Bergan, 1977; Bergan & Tombari, 1975, 1976; D'Zurilla & Goldfried, 1971). Although each approach has been implemented within educational settings, consultation within a behavioral framework has consistently demonstrated positive effects in remediating a variety of academic and behavior problems (see Bergan, Byrnes, & Kratochwill, 1979; Bergan & Tombari, 1976; Conoley & Conoley, 1982; Jason & Ferone, 1978; Jason, Ferone, & Anderegg, 1979; Medway, 1979; Medway & Forman, 1980; Piersel & Kratochwill, 1979). The effectiveness of behavioral approaches to consultation stems largely from the types of principles and procedures inherent in their use. Keller (1981) views these principles and procedures as part of a problem solving process that is closely guided by research activities; he views research as change. Accordingly, behavioral approaches to school-based consultation are constantly progressing in an empirical, self-correcting manner, providing an effective tool for facilitating the delivery of educational and psychological services in the schools.

The first section of this chapter is comprised of four related topics concerning the current status of behavioral consultation. First, the current conceptualization of behavioral consultation is reviewed. Second, an overview of other approaches to consultation and how they differ from behavioral approaches is provided. Third the utility of behavioral consultation, its effectiveness relative to other approaches, is discussed. This comparison is important because a variety of consultation approaches have been advocated for remediating problems and fulfilling needs in similar content areas and with similar clients. Knowledge of the effectiveness of different consultation approaches can provide the school consultant with guidelines for determining the approach that should be implemented to provide particular services to children. This is followed by an examination of how behavioral approaches have been applied in schools and the issues related to their application. In the second section, future directions for consultation, with emphasis on linking the behavioral approach to data-based instructional management and classroom organizational routines to foster educational growth, are delineated.

CURRENT STATUS OF BEHAVIORAL CONSULTATION

Consultation means different things to different people. Consultation is currently used to refer to any function traditionally performed by a school consultant.

Reschly (1976), for example, points out that consultation has included direct and indirect school-based services, occurring at any or all levels in the school system hierarchy (i.e., classroom, school, administrative, district).

The most widely held view about the nature of consultation is that it is an indirect, collegial, and problem-solving effort between a specialist (consultant) and one or more persons (consultees) who are responsible for providing some type of psychological, educational, or organizational service to another (client) (Alpert, 1976; Bergan, 1977; Caplan, 1970; Lambert, 1974).

Consultation is a form of indirect service; the consultant attempts to assist the consultee (i.e., change agent) in affecting a change in some aspect of client behavior. This feature makes consultation a potentially powerful tool for meeting children's needs and enhancing their development. Moreover, indirect service markedly increases the number of children who can benefit from the services offered. There is a multiplier effect that enables one consultant to affect the development of many children (Bergan, 1977). For example, a consultant may collaborate with several teachers, each of whom provides educational or social experiences for many children. Because the service is indirect, the consultant may influence the lives of many more children than would be possible with direct contact with children.

Consultation generally involves a collegial relationship between the consultant and consultee(s) (Bergan, 1977; Lambert, 1974). The consultant and consultee function as equals in the consultation process. Each fulfills a separate function in the problem-solving process, and brings a different kind of expertise to the problem-solving task.

Consultation is a problem-solving effort. Problem solving involves application of specific principles and procedures in an attempt to alter an existing state of affairs in the direction of a desired state of affairs (Bergan, 1977; Piersel, in press). Problem solving in school-based consultation usually involves but is not limited to interactions between a practitioner, such as a school psychologist, education coordinator, or child development specialist, as consultant, a teacher as consultee, and a student as client.

Behavioral Approaches to Consultation

Behavioral consultation in the schools has rapidly increased in recent years (Bergan, 1977; Kratochwill & Bergan, 1978). As mentioned earlier, the expanded use of behavioral consultation stems largely from its effectiveness in addressing concerns of teachers and needs of students. Behavioral consultation may be viewed as a problem-solving endeavor that occurs within a behavioral framework. In the broadest sense, the goal of the consultant in this endeavor is to assist the consultee in introducing changes in the client's environment to meliorate the educational, behavioral, or social-emotional needs of the client. Behavioral consultation may also focus on the consultee, the consultant guides the consultee toward developing and implementing a new behavioral repertoire and cognitive awareness for promoting the psychoeducational development of children.

Theoretical Orientation of Behavioral Approaches. The theoretical assumption underlying efforts in behavioral problem solving activities is that understanding, describing, and changing behavior in a productive way begins with objective analysis of the interactions between behavior, the individual, and the environment. The environment is involved if it applies to intrapersonal factors, such as an individual's physiological or emotional status, and to events occurring outside the individual, such as the behavior of other people toward the individual. Individual-environment interactions are mutually and reciprically influential (Bandura, 1978). Because it is assumed that behaviors are learned and maintained through the interactive process, the process must be examined and understood to develop a plan of action to affect a productive change.

Procedures implemented to assess the dynamics of interaction may focus on the motoric, cognitive, physiological, and structural aspects of the interaction as they pertain to individual behavior. Recognition is given to individual differences as well as to differences in the way each individual interacts with the environment. Stressing the importance of individual differences provides a means of tailoring intervention and educational programs to meet individual needs.

Stressing the importance of the environment is also a hallmark of a behavioral approach to consultation. The causes of problematic behaviors or academic difficulties may be identified from several sources. One source may be the lack of intellectual ability as measured by various instruments designed to assess constructs, such as intelligence. A second source may be a form of physiological or neurological impairment. A third source may be a lack of prerequisite social or academic skills that are necessary for higher order social functioning and learning to occur. Fourth, there may be environmental conditions that are encouraging and maintaining inappropriate behavior repertoires and/or inhibiting social and academic development. For example, environmental conditions may not be organized to promote development, fulfill individual needs, and create situations to minimize the occurrence of problems. The last two sources, and to some extent the second, are areas in which behavioral consultation's focus on environmental factors may be effective. Identified environmental factors affecting individual behavior can be altered to promote development and forestall problems. Moreover, it is an area in which the consultee, usually a teacher, has the resources available to promote positive changes.

The consultant operating within a behavioral framework must be knowledgeable of the theoretical assumptions that describe and explain interactions between variables influencing behavior. The consultant must have an understanding of the principles, procedures, and intervention strategies designed to ensure success of the consultation effort. Intervention strategies utilized within a behavioral framework may include task analysis, timeout, shaping, chaining, reinforcement, and modeling (see also Chapter 2 and Chapter 3). It is beyond the scope and purpose of this chapter to delineate the variety of strategies that may be utilized for consultation within a behavioral framework. These strategies are well documented in the works of Keller (1981), O'Leary and O'Leary (1976), O'Leary and Wilson (1975), and Sulzer-Azaroff and Mayer (1977). The principles and procedures for consultation within a behavioral framework are discussed to distinguish it from other models of consultation.

Principles of Behavioral Approaches. There are several principles that are fundamental to behavioral approaches to school-based consultation. These principles provide the foundation for developing an accountable consultation process that maximizies the potential for successful outcomes. Moreover, when applied properly, they create a dynamic state of affairs in which consultation is constantly evolving to better meet the needs of children. There are five principles: (a) direct and objective assessment; (b) operationalization of target behaviors and variables that may affect change; (c) assessment in multiple settings; (d) quantification of data; and (e) empirically demonstrating behavior change and plan effectiveness in the evaluation of outcome.

Assessment, a vital precursor to designing an effective intervention strategy, is a direct and objective process (see Chapter 2). Directness and objectivity imply a focus on observable current environmental variables related to behavior. At the same time, they avoid subjective inferences about phenomena that cannot be directly measured. Objectivity in assessment is one way to ensure that information can be reliably recorded. Information can be used to determine if a need or problem exists. Moreover, objective data provide the consultant with reliable information that can be used to refine intervention procedures to maximize the probability of problem resolution.

Because behaviors are assumed to be learned and maintained through an interactive process, objectivity and directness must prevail during initial assessments, monitoring progress, and evaluating change. Consequently, the variables hypothesized to influence behavior and the target behavior(s) are defined and operationalized; therefore, they can be tested and evaluated empirically. Operationalizing helps to ensure reliable recording of information. Operationalizing target behaviors and the variables affecting change involves breaking them down into observable and measurable components (e.g., frequency of homework completions) that provide a level of specificity. Components are described in such a way that if, for example, several observers were asked to record occurrence of a particular behavior, their judgments would reflect an acceptable level of agreement about the presence or absence of that behavior.

Assessment occurs in multiple settings and is closely linked to intervention. Multiple assessment provides the first step in programming generalization and maintenance into an intervention program and provides a means to evaluate effectiveness of the intervention effort. Demonstrating generalization and maintenance in behavioral approaches to school-based consultation is a practical concern and an ethical responsibility. No change agent can be expected to consider using a behavioral technique if it cannot be demonstrated that its effects are not totally restricted to the situation and time in which intervention occurred. Moreover, because of the demands on the participants involved in behavioral consultation and the expertise involved in setting up interventions, the continued beneficial effects of an intervention program once it is terminated must be substantiated.

Quantification provides the means by which change can be evaluated empirically and through which consultants and consultees become accountable for the decisions they make about the children under their care (see also Chapter 10). Evaluating effectiveness of the consultation process is based on verifiable information. This data-based approach affords the opportunity for the consultant to make comparisons between baseline rates of behavior, changes during intervention, and postintervention status. It also provides the information needed to make gradual changes in an intervention program based on the progress of the individual client.

Procedures in Behavioral Approaches.   Maximizing the effects of the problem solving process requires attending to its principles and instituting a set of procedures that form a well-defined sequence of events between the consultant, consultee, and client. These procedures and behavioral intervention strategies form the behavioral approach to school-based consultation.

There is some variation on the emphasis placed on the various factors comprising the set of procedures that define the behavioral consultation approach (see, Bergan, 1977; D'Zurilla & Goldfried 1971; Goldstein, 1978; Kanfer & Grimm, 1977; Kanfer & Saslow, 1969; Randolph, 1972; Rogers-Warren & Warren, 1977). Bergan's (1977) model represents a general set of procedures typically found across all variations. Bergan's model is described to allow the reader to become familiar with the behavioral approach and how this approach differs from nonbehavioral approaches to consultation. The approach advocated by Bergan is a four-stage analytic problem solving sequence. It includes phases of problem identification, problem analysis, plan implementation, and plan evaluation. An outline of each phase follows.

Problem Identification.   The identification of a client's needs and/or problems is the first step in the consultation process. As the initial phase, it assumes special importance. Other phases of problem solving depend on what is done in the identification phase. If the identification phase goes well, the conditions necessary for effective problem solving will have been established (Bergan & Tombari, 1975, 1976). This aspect of problem solving has been supported in studies by Abidin (1977) and Tyler and Fine (1974). They demonstrated that the more thoroughly and intensive consultation is handled the greater the potential for promoting positive outcomes; if identification does not proceed in an appropriate fashion, the ability to go forward in problem solving may be seriously compromised (Bergan & Tombari, 1976; Tombari & Davis, 1979).

The identification phase begins with a problem identification interview. In the interview, the consultant guides the consultee toward: (a) specifying performance goals and objectives for the client; (b) selecting measures of client performance articulated to the goals of consultation; (c) establishing and implementing data collection procedures on client performance; (d) summarizing data in a form that can be easily interpreted by the consultee; and (e) defining the problem or need by establishing the discrepancy between current performance reflected in the data collected and the desired performance indicated in objectives. For example, a teacher may indicate plans to include activities for learning math skills, which include addition skills, during the course of the school year. The consultant would assist the teacher in identifying the addition skills important for the students to learn. The degree to which each student is capable of performing the addition skills identified as important is determined by collecting data from work samples and verbal responses to addition problems or tests. This information allows the teacher the opportunity to determine the degree to which each student can demonstrate accurate performance on tasks assessing specific skills. The identification phase is completed when it is determined that a discrepancy exists between the current and desired conditions.

Problem Analysis.   Once a problem or need has been identified, consultation proceeds to problem analysis. The purpose of problem analysis is to identify variables that might facilitate or inhibit the achievement of a problem solution and to develop plan strategies and specific tactics designed to promote attainment of established goals.

Plan strategies specify the kinds of psychological principles or general courses of action that might be applied in a behavioral intervention program or that can be used to achieve instructional goals and objectives (see also Chapter 3 and Chapter 4). The consultant has the responsibility to guide the consultee through this phase of consultation. For example, the consultant might suggest the use of reinforcement procedures to encourage on-task behaviors. Using the addition skills example, the consultant might ask the teacher to suggest ways to organize the sequence of learning tasks to meet the educational needs of individual students. The teacher may decide to begin instruction in addition with concrete objects, followed by paper and pencil tasks, and finally, word problems. Plan tactics refer to the specific materials, procedures, personnel, and conditions involved in implementing a strategy for behavior change or in developing instructional activities to promote learning.

To develop the most appropriate solution for the identified problem or need, the consultant and consultee may focus on external or internal conditions that could be sources of the problem or need. Conditions may include lack of motivation on the part of the client or lack of resources for providing an effective learning environment. They may also focus on the kinds of skills the client would need to achieve consultation goals (Bergan, 1977). Skills may include the identification of subordinate skills needed to learn more difficult skills. Procedures are also developed to monitor performance during implementation and to evaluate the effectiveness of the implemented plan. Monitoring procedures will usually involve the continued use of baseline data recording procedures.

Plan Implementation. The third phase in the consultation process is plan implementation. The consultation process is to a great measure dependent on effective plan implementation. The best plans may not achieve the desired results if they are not properly implemented. The role of the consultant during implementation is to maximize the likelihood that the plan used will produce the desired results.

During the plan implementation phase, consultation may focus on assisting the consultee to make the necessary preperations to carry out implementation. Preparations include assigning roles to various people for carrying out the implementation plan, organizing materials, and developing the required skills in individuals who will implement the plan. When the plan is put into operation, the consultant monitors implementation and data collection and assists the consultee in making sure that the plan is functioning in the proper manner. When the need arises, the consultant works with the consultee to revise the plan to make it function in the desired fashion.

Problem Evaluation. The final phase of the problem solving process is problem evaluation. Two questions are addressed in this phase of consultation. One involves the extent to which the goals of consultation have been achieved; the other deals with the effectiveness of plans put into operation to achieve those goals (see also Chapter 10).

If the goals of consultation have been achieved, consultation may terminate and a decision may be made to continue monitoring the target behavior. In addition, the consultee may decide to implement the plan for another related problem or need. If the goals of consultation have not been achieved, consultation usually moves back to the problem analysis phase to revise the original plan or construct a new plan. Consultation may also recycle to problem identification to determine if there are other needs or problems that require attention prior to addressing the intial concern identified by the consultee. For example, a teacher may identify a child's inability to perform addition when first asked to identify concerns about math skills. The child may not improve on addition skills because he/she has not yet been able to learn some counting skills. Recycling to problem identification may identify this need (Bergan, Feld, & Schnaps, 1984).

When the goals of consultation have been achieved, the consultant and consultee evaluate the effectiveness of the plans implemented to achieve goals. Although the client may have reached the desired goal, one cannot conclude that the plan was responsible unless an appropriate evaluation design was implemented. An evaluation design specifies when observations of client behavior will take place and when plan implementation will occur in relation to client observations. If the appropriate controls are incorporated into the evaluation design, the design affords a means for reviewing each step in the consultation process and for empirically determining changes in client behavior associated with each component of the intervention plan. Single subject, time series designs have been found to be the most useful designs for evaluating plan effectiveness in behavioral consultation. These designs are described in detail by Bergan (1977), Glass, Wilson and Gottman (1975), Hersen and Barlow (1976), Kazdin (1978), Kratochwill (1977) and, Kratochwill and Bergan (1978).

Alternatives to the Behavioral Approach

As mentioned earlier, there are a variety of available alternatives to behavioral approaches to school based consultation. These approaches are nonbehavioral because their theoretical orientations, principles, procedures, and intervention strategies differ from those that specify a behavioral approach. Moreover, they differ in goals of consultation, roles of consultant and consultee, types of clients preferred, and criteria for evaluating effectiveness of the consultation process. Each alternative approach is discussed in terms of the way it departs from behavioral approaches to consultation.

Mental health consultation, like behavioral approaches to consultation, is viewed as a problem-solving effort. In implementing this approach, the consultant attempts to assist the consultee in maximizing the social-emotional development of clients under the consultee's care (Meyers, 1981). The theoretical base of mental health consultation is personality theory that focuses on an intrapsychic model of behavior change. Caplan (1970) developed categorization of mental health that consists of four parts: client centered, program centered, administrative consultee centered, and consultee centered administrative consultation. Consultee centered consultation, which has received the most attention in the research literature, focuses on improving the consultee's functioning rather than helping a specific client. In consultee centered consultation, the target for change is the consultee; the consultant helps the consultee to reflect feelings, enhance objectivity and skills in working with clients, gain insight into normal and abnormal emotional development, and enhance sense of self-worth.

The major principle underlying mental health consultation is that efforts to change consultee behavior must focus on underlying feelings and/or conflicts. The degree to which this aspect of mental health consultation is followed, determines the success of the consultation effort. Unlike the behavioral approach, in which consultee functions as a change agent, the consultant's role is that of change agent, providing direct rather than indirect service. The outcomes of the consultation process are evaluated through self-reports and informal consultant observations of behavior.

The mental health approach has been useful; it provides a framework for providing services to teachers and students. Moreover, this approach has provided some of the groundwork for examining environmental factors that may influence consultation outcomes (Conoley & Conoley, 1982; Meyers, 1981). Its emphasis on interpersonal variables (e.g., feelings, conflict) provides information that may be valuable in identifying and ameliorating problems that could stifle the consultation process.

Another widely used approach is organizational consultation. There are several varieties of organizational consultation including ecological consultation (Jason, Ferone, & Anderegg, 1979) and process consultation (Schein, 1969; Schmuck, Runkel, Saturen, Martell, & Derr, 1972). These approaches are directed toward improving organizational climates so change can evolve and solutions to problems can be achieved. These approaches view the organizational system or subsystem as the client. Within the context of the schools, the consultation goal is to modify the interactions between individuals and subgroups in the school and between the school and the surrounding community to facilitate pupil learning and pupil mental health (Alpert, 1977). Ecological consultation, involves developing interventions based on an understanding of the interactions between individual personality characteristics and the structure and functioning of organizational environments. The consultant's responsibilities are directed toward developing and implementing strategies that will provide the organization with the means to tolerate tensions and conflicts and increase its ability to adapt to change. Process consultation focuses on motivating an organization or system to utilize its own resources to improve its structure and functioning.

The intervention techniques used with these forms of consultation are focused on group processes. The role of the consultant is to facilitate the group's motivation and ability to identify, analyze, and solve problems by utilizing internal resources. This is done through group training techniques that include sensitivity training, reflection, feedback, role playing, and brainstorming. Self-report and structured observational techniques are used to evaluate outcomes. These approaches to consultation have been effective in promoting positive changes in interpersonal relations, communications, and group decision making effectivness in the schools (Blumberg, May, & Perry, 1974; Saturen, 1976; Schmuck, 1971; Schmuck & Miles, 1971).

There are no inherent guarantees for success in any one approach to consultation. The utility of any school-based consultation service is determined by the costs and benefits to the client, potential strengths and limitations, type of goals stressed, and most importantly empirical evidence of effectiveness. The decision to use one form of consultation over an available alternative must be based on a thorough knowledge of these factors and how they relate to each approach. Moreover, the usefulness of school-based consultation within a behavioral framework and the usefulness of other approaches is determined by factors that include (a) relative effectiveness of different approaches for specific clients and content (Bergan, Byrnes, & Kratochwill, 1979; Jason, Ferone, & Anderegg, 1979; Medway & Forman, 1980); (b) experience and skills of the consultant and consultee (Abidin, 1977; Bergan, 1977; Sandoval, Lambert, & Davis, 1977); (c) availability of resources and the types of constraints affecting the consultation process (Bergan, 1977; Bergan & Neumann, 1980); (d) perceptions of the consultee (Mann, 1973; Weissenberger, Fine, & Poggio, 1982); and (e) level of precision, quality, and appropriateness related to implementation (Abidin, 1977; Cossairt, Hall, & Hopkins, 1973; Tyler & Fine, 1974; Woolfolk, Woolfolk, & Wilson, 1977). For an in depth review of the effectiveness and limitations of the various consultation models applied in school settings the reader is referred to Conoley (1981) and Conoley and Conoley (1982).

The following section delineates the relative effectiveness of behavioral and nonbehavioral approaches to consultation, in remediating problems and addressing needs in similar content areas and for similar clients. This is followed by a discussion of issues relevant to the use of behavioral approaches to consultation as they relate to the four factors identified earlier.

Behavioral Versus Nonbehavioral Approaches

Medway (1979) reviewed 29 studies on the effectiveness of school consultation published between 1972 and 1977. In these studies, behavioral consultation produced positive effects on attitudes and/or behaviors of consultees and their clients more often than did mental health consultation.

In a study designed to examine psychologists' and teachers' perceptions of the relative effectiveness of mental health and behavioral approaches with behavior and academic problems, Medway and Forman (1980) found that teachers generally perceived a behavioral approach as more effective. In this study, a series of consultant-teacher dialogues during problem identification were presented using videotapes. In one set of tapes the consultant utilized a mental health approach; in the other set of tapes a behavioral approach was used. Three different problems were presented. The first problem was that of a student with acting out behaviors, talking and calling out inappropriately. The second problem involved a child who refused to stay in her seat, did not complete work, and was physically aggressive. The third problem concerned two boys who had difficulties in class in reading and math.

Findings from this study indicate that during problem identification teachers generally perceive a behavioral approach as more effective than a mental health approach; psychologists view mental health consultation more favorably. The teachers also favored the behavioral approach because of its helpfulness, usefulness of information, increased understanding of the children and classroom behaviors, remediation probability, and likelihood for future use and recommendation to other teachers. Moreover, teachers expressed positive attitudes about the behavioral consultant's directive and supervisory role, focus on environmental variables, and recommendations on data collection procedures. Teachers felt that the behavioral consultant's specificity, directiveness, questioning, and the use of behavioral principles was very helpful. They also felt that the consultant directed them to objectively examine their behavior and take a more active role in the eventual formulation of a remedial plan.

The relative effectiveness of behavioral and process approaches on consultation outcome and on attitudes of consultees was systematically studied by Jason and Ferone (1978). In this study, the authors provided consultation to two third grade teachers; each teacher identified four children having behavior problems. Over a 2 month period each consultant worked with a teacher, providing either process or behavioral consultation. Behavioral techniques included discussions of behavior modification principles, feedback on contingent praise, and individual behavioral interventions. Process techniques included the consultant's use of clarifying, supportive, and reflective statements to help the consultee better understand classroom problems and enhance the ability to work with problem children.

Results of the study indicated that only behavioral consultation was effective in reducing levels of children's inappropriate behavior. The teacher receiving behavioral consultation reported that she felt more control with her class and used behavioral principles more following consultation; the teacher receiving process consultation reported feeling better about her teaching ability and more comfortable handling problem children. The authors suggest, however, that because of several methodological problems the results should be interpreted with caution. First, only a small number of target children were used, and they were not initially matched on relevant characteristics. Second, the use of different consultants to implement the different approaches made it difficult to determine if outcome effects were due to the different experimental conditions or to the relationships established between consultants and consultees.

In a more controlled study, Jason, Ferone, and Anderegg (1979) evaluated the differential effectiveness of ecological, behavioral, and process consultation approaches for 6- to 9-year-old children identified as being disruptive in the classroom. Behavioral consultants identified types of disruptive behavior manifested by each child and discussed general behavior modification principles. This was followed by implementation of a series of behavioral strategies to remediate the problems. Techniques included daily positive and negative letters sent home to the parents resulting in parental praise or parental reprimand. Group contingencies and token exchange strategies were also implemented. The ecological consultants gathered information from teachers about present versus desired classroom environments. Ecological interventions included changing the structure of the class from a traditional format to one involving small groups, rearranging group composition according to student ability, and seating students so that none of the groups had more than one problem child. Weekly meetings held with the teacher consisted of discussions about the difficulties and benefits arising from implementing different class arrangements. The process consultants assumed a nondirective role with the teachers and used clarifying, supportive, and reflective responses to help the teachers resolve classroom problems. Teachers feelings, frustrations, and disappointments about the children were accepted as genuine, and consultants helped teachers work through these concerns. Consultation sessions focused on fostering more positive interactions with children, a deeper understanding of their problems, and eliciting more spontaneity and involvement in target children.

Generally, children participating in behavioral interventions evidenced significant reductions in both problem behaviors and teachers ratings of problem behaviors; these children achieved the largest improvements in grades. However, there were significant decreases in reading achievement based on pre- and postscores on the Wide Range Achievement Test. Teachers perceived the behavioral program as positive and helpful. Children in the process group made significant gains in reading and math achievement. However, there were significant increases in observed problem behaviors and teacher disapproval behaviors following these behaviors. Few significant changes were noted for children in ecological or control classes. In the ecological condition problem behaviors remained the same, children's grades tended to increase, and slightly higher scores were obtained on the achievement tests. After several forms of ecological interventions had failed, teachers had more negative reactions, rating the overall programs as neutral or unsatisfactory.

Applications and Issues

There is sufficient evidence to suggest that behavioral consultation is effective in improving the academic, social, and affective components of student behaviors in the classroom (Bergan, Byrnes, & Kratochwill, 1979; Canter & Paulson, 1974, Colligan, Colligan, & Dilliard, 1977; Farber & Mayer, 1972; Hops, 1971; Kosier, 1970; Piersel & Kratochwill, 1979). However, the continued use of behavioral approaches in school-based consultation, to a great extent, is dependent, on its ability to address the substantive issues surrounding its use and in refining the procedures guiding its application.

Experience and Skills of Consultants and Consultees. Success in the problem identification phase of consultation is particularly important because at this point success is predictive of problem solution (Bergan & Tombari, 1975; Curtis & Watson, 1980). Curtis and Watson's (1980) study, for example, examined the relationship between a consultee's skills in specifying an educational problem, followed by identifying the variables that might facilitate problem solution and the skill level of the consultant. The results indicated that classroom teachers who worked with high skilled consultants improved significantly more in identifying problems and variables than teachers who had worked with the low skilled consultants or who were in the control group. Working with high skilled consultants increased the quantity and quality of information about a child. That is, teachers working with high skilled consultants spent more time describing a child and based a greater portion of their descriptions on factual data than on speculations. Moreover, these teachers improved on such skills as stating the desired outcome and conditions under which outcome should occur, specifying current level of performance, specifying the problem behavior, describing procedures for measuring behavior, specifying incidence of behavior, and establishing priorities for solving problem behaviors. Abidin (1977) compared the reported similarities and differences between the steps engaged in by master's and doctoral level school psychologists as they conducted behavioral consultations with teachers. The major differences in the two groups involved the higher frequency with which doctoral students engaged in baseline and intervention observations. Abidin discussed these and other components of the behavioral consultation approach as critical in ensuring the likelihood of successful outcomes.

Lambert, Sandoval, and Yandell (1975) have suggested that it is essential to the development of consultation skills that the consultant learn how to be a consultee. An effective consultant is one who is aware of the different kinds of learning facing a consultee. Moreover, sensitivity to a consultee's affective concerns and basic listening skills have been considered important to behavioral consultation (Abidin, 1971, Fine, 1970; Grieger, Mordock, & Breyer, 1970). The consultee must understand what it means to be a consultant and what the consultation process is all about. Sandoval, Lambert, and Davis (1977) have advocated that, first, the consultee must learn how consultant-consultee interactions are different from other forms of interactions with mental health professionals. Second, the consultee must learn to describe problem situations so the consultant can understand and respond to needs. Third, the consultee must understand the consultant's role and the kinds of information and expertise that can be brought to the problem solving effort. Fourth, the consultee must learn how to maximize the tools of the consultation process and become aware of the kinds of help to expect from the consultant. Finally, the consultee must learn about him/herself, focusing on interactions in work settings and how these interactions relate to professional goals.

Resources and Constraints.   It is crucial to the consultation process that the consultant attend to the strengths, limitations, motivations, and skills of the consultee and client and to the various factors in the environment that may have an impact on the development and implementation of interventions (Bergan,

1977; Bergan & Neumann, 1980; Meyer, Liddell, & Lyons, 1977). Teacher knowledge about behavioral principles and strategies, for example, is typically viewed as critically important for successful behavioral consultation in the schools. Teachers who have at their disposal a variety of behavioral techniques, and who can implement them effectively are in a better position to facilitate the agreed upon intervention plan. Knowledge of behavioral techniques and their appropriate use may be considered resources. This is especially the case for interventions based on operant conditioning principles in which consultee reinforcement effectiveness is critical for successful outcomes (Grieger, Mordock, & Breyer, 1970; O'Leary & Drabman, 1971).

The ability of the consultant to elicit and develop resources is also viewed as critical for successful outcomes. The importance of consultant behaviors in helping the consultee to identify resources during development of intervention plans has been demonstrated by Bergan and Neumann (1980). Their study investigated the effects of consultant verbalizations and consultee verbalizations reflecting resources that might be used in plan implementation. Results of the study indicate that a consultant's use of plan-tactic elicitors (see, Bergan, 1977) has a positive affect on the occurrence of resource responses by the consultee. Resources were defined in the study as plan-tactic specification emitters verbalized by the consultee ("I think my saying 'you're doing very well' or 'that's good' will be one kind of reward") in response to a plan-tactic elicitor verbalized by the consultant. The odds of a plan-tactic elicitor producing a resource response instead of a response classified as a constraint or in the "other" category was more than 5 to 1 in this study. In contrast, the odds of any other type of consultant verbalization producing a resource as opposed to a response in the "other" category was substantially less than 1. Moreover, the odds of a plan-tactic elicitor producing a resource as opposed to a response in the "other" category was 14 times higher than the odds that a plan-tactic emitter (i.e., the consultant presenting resource information rather than calling for a response from the consultee) producing a resource opposed to a response in the "other" category. Bergan and Neumann suggest that focusing attention on constraints, such as all of the things a consultee can not do or is not willing to do, could have a negative impact on consultation. They conclude that the use of the plan-tactic elicitor to focus on resources may reduce the necessity for establishing constraints and can produce beneficial outcomes by directing the focus of consultation on the positive contributions of the consultee.

Perceptions of the Consultee.   The perceptions that a consultee has about the personal and professional characteristics of the consultant may affect both the consultee's willingness to participate in consultation and the overall effectiveness of the consultation process. Mann (1973), for example, found that likable consultants are viewed as more effective. In this study teachers who gave positive ratings to consultation and individual consultants cited such behaviors as perceived listening ability, having pleasant things to say about attempts made to resolve problems, appearing empathic and offering alternative means of dealing with problems. Moreover, Schowengerdt, Fine, and Poggio (1976) found collaborative facilitating consultants to be rated most highly by their consultees. Examining the basis for teacher satisfaction with consultation, Schowengerdt, Fine, and Poggio investigated teacher perceptions and reactions to age, years of experience, academic degrees, theoretical orientation, amount of time spent in consultation, teaching experience, and interpersonal facilitativeness. The psychologists interpersonal facilitativeness (i.e., empathy, openness, positive regard, congruence) was the primary factor contributing to teacher satisfaction.

Additional research by Weissenburger, Fine, and Poggio (1982) attempted to identify the relationship between consultant/teacher characteristics and consultative outcomes. Five variables considered to relate to and predict consultation success were examined. These included teacher dogmatism, teacher existential life position (see Berne, 1962), consultant facilitativeness as perceived by the teacher, years of teaching experience, and number of consultation experiences engaged in by the teacher during the year. Results indicated that a teacher's perception of a consultant's facilitative characteristic correlated most strongly with teacher-reported satisfaction, the teacher feeling better able to handle future problems, and the belief that the identified problem would be resolved. Consultant facilitativeness was also the factor that best predicted these three criteria of consultation success.

Precision, Quality, and Appropriateness.   The precision with which a consultation process is implemented, the quality of the process, and its appropriateness in addressing the identified needs of the client and the consultee are vital to the success of consultation.

In a study by Bergan, Byrnes, and Kratochwill (1979), behavioral consultation and medical model consultation were implemented with 60 first and second grade teachers. Medical model consultation focused on such factors as a child's I.Q. and its relation to achievement and past events assumed to influence current behavior. Following consultation, teachers participating in the study were asked to instruct a hypothetical child who was having difficulty learning to add. The hypothetical child was identified as educably mentally handicapped. An experimenter without knowledge of the predicted outcomes enacted the hypothetical child's behavior. In one form of behavioral consultation, the consultant cued the teacher to various antecedent and consequent conditions that might affect learning and prompted the teacher to specify the kinds of capabilities that the child would need to perform academic tasks targeted for instruction. In the second form consultation was augmented with task analysis procedures to indicate the kinds of prerequisite skills that the student had to acquire prior to mastering the tasks presented in instruction. The task analysis report indicated that the student had failed five different counting tasks and an addition task. The counting tasks were taken from a hierarchy constructed by Resnick, Wang, and Kaplan (1973) and validated by Wang (1973). The tasks showed that the specified counting hierarchy was prerequisite to the addition task targeted for instruction. Medical model consultation involved face- to face-interaction that focused on temporally remote environmental conditions accompanied by a psychological report specifying that the child achieved an IQ score that placed him in the educable mentally handicapped range. A control group was included to provide a standard against which to compare two approaches.

The behavioral consultation accompanied by a task analysis was the most effective procedure in fostering the development of addition skills. This occurred because the task analysis report told the teachers explicitly that the student needed to learn to count before he could learn to add. The behavioral condition, unaccompanied by a task analysis, was significantly more effective in providing more positive outcomes than the medical model condition and demonstrated significant superiority over the control group. These results suggest that, in a situation in which a child lacks prerequisite skills, verbally prompting a teacher to focus on environmental conditions and to consider prerequisite capabilities can be helpful. However, the fact that only 60% of the teachers in this condition were successful in teaching the child suggests that when behavioral consultation is used without providing specific information about prerequisite skills, significant numbers of teachers may fail to consider prerequisite skills that could facilitate learning. Only 20% of the teachers in the medical model group were able to teach the child successfully, and only 33% in the control group were effective in instructing the child. Teachers in the two behavioral conditions employed significantly less aversive control procedures than teachers in the control condition. Teachers participating in the two behavioral consultation conditions used aversive control techniques significantly less often than did teachers in the control condition. Teachers in the task analysis condition used aversive control procedures significantly less than those in the medical model condition.

Other studies have indicated that appropriate implementation of the procedures involved in behavioral approaches to consultation have significant positive effect outcomes. For example, Bergan and Tombari's (1975, 1976) research suggests that a consultant's ability to elicit a problem identification from the consultee is crucial for successful problem resolution. Moreover, their research shows that consultant characteristics, such as efficiency in responding to referrals, flexibility in applying psychological principles, and the ability to elicit information and action from the consultee, contribute to successful problem identification, enhancing the potential for successful problem resolution (Bergan & Tombari, 1976). Cossairt, Hall, and Hopkins (1973) demonstrated the effectiveness of a consultant's use of instructions, feedback, and social praise on teacher behavior for delivering praise to students. Other studies have demonstrated that consultant praise and frequent feedback to teachers have effectively increased the appropriate use of behavioral interventions (e.g., Cooper, Thomp son, & Baer, 1970).

A study by Woolfolk, Woolfolk, and Wilson (1977) suggests that the language used to describe behavioral interventions during consultation can inhibit or facilitate successful intervention. In their study, consultees received a set of classroom intervention procedures filled with behavioral terminology. Another group received a description of the same procedures in more descriptive, layman's terms. Teachers rated the latter description as more appealing and more likely to be successful. Time, extensive support, and troubleshooting throughout an intervention were also found to be beneficial to the success of behavioral consultation. The importance of these factors in the consultant-consultee interaction has been discussed by Abidin (1977) and Grieger, Mordock, and Breyer (1970).

Behavioral approaches to school-based consultation have provided effective tools to meet the increasing needs and concerns of students and school personnel in contemporary society. The methodology that has been used to define, assess, and design intervention programs during consultative problem solving has centered on a problem-centered approach, the focus is on problems that are of immediate concern to the consultee, and a developmental approach, the focus is on the achievement of long-range goals for children (Bergan, 1977). In the problem centered approach the interventions that are prescribed are specific to the immediate problem and situation (Bergan, 1977; McFall, 1982). In the developmental approach, consultation has been used to help teachers apply psychological principles in the design and implementation of educational programs to promote development.

One limitation of behavioral approaches is the worthiness or appropriateness of the changes produced (see also Chapter 11). Most of the literature on behavioral consultation does not include the requirement that the consultant carefully consider whether the problem identified by the teacher and the desired change in the child's behavior is a healthy, appropriate, or realistic change. Some researchers in the field have begun to focus on this issue in the academic area (e.g., Bergan, Byrnes, & Kratochwill, 1979; Bergan, Stone, & Feld, 1984).

A second limitation of behavioral approaches to school-based consultation is that they have focused on a relatively narrow range of child and teacher behaviors (Reschly, 1976), and have been practiced as a remedial intervention (Gallessich & Davis, 1981). Behavioral consultants have most often been called on the scene when a problem already exists and have focused their efforts on behavior problems.

Consequently, although immensely valuable in resolving individual child problems, behavioral approaches to consultation have not been widely used to be readily incorporable into the organizational routines of schools and/or widely utilized by teachers in facilitating the teaching–learning process. The sometimes idiosyncratic emphasis of behavioral approaches tends to discourage its use in addressing the broader range of instructional management needs of teachers and schools.

These limitations are addressed in the next section. An innovative system for incorporating consultation within a behavioral framework into classroom organizational routines to help guide instruction and promote development is discussed.

FUTURE DIRECTIONS: BEHAVIORAL CONSULTATION IN INSTRUCTIONAL MANAGEMENT

Consultation has been useful in rendering psychological services in educational settings in large measure because it affords a way to broaden the impact of services. A consultant in the schools can serve many consultees (teachers) each of whom provide direct services to students. Up to the present, the principal focus on behavioral consultation has been on serving individual students. A natural extention of such consultation technology would be to expand services to all students. This kind of expansion would markedly broaden the impact of consultation services. For example, effective learning requires effective instructional management. School administrators are often regarded as being most directly involved in management activities, however, teachers may also be thought of as instructional managers (Berliner, 1983). The heart of management is decision making, and teachers are constantly engaged in decision-making activities (Salmon-Cox, 1980).

The effectiveness of instructional management is necessarily limited by the assessment information used by the teacher in making instructional decisions. The teacher who has an in-depth knowledge of children's skills is in a better position to guide instruction and forestall future problems than one who does not possess this kind of information. Consequently, decisions regarding the instructional needs of students should include a consideration of objective data on children's learning and achievements.

What is required then, is a data-based assessment system that is perceived by teachers as providing useful information on student's skills so that decision making can occur. Moreover, a set of procedures is required which relate assessment information to the instructional decision-making process. Consultation may be used as an effective means for bringing assessment information to bear on instructional decision making (Bergan, 1977). In the remainder of this chapter one approach to extending consultation services of a behavioral nature is described. The approach is designed to aid in the management of instruction for all students in an educational organization, and for refining the consultation process in meeting the educational needs of individual students.

An Instructional Management Example from Head Start

The Center for Educational Evaluation and Measurement in the College of Education at the University of Arizona has completed a project for the Head Start organization. The project illustrates the use of assessment in instructional management and the role that procedures used in behavioral consultation may play in relating assessment to instructional decision making (Bergan, Anderson, Feld, Henderson, Johnson, Lane, Mott, Parra, Robinson, Schnaps, Stone, & Swarner, 1984). The project called for construction of developmental measures for use in instructional management in Head Start. Behavioral consultation technology was used to apply the measures in instructional management. The measures project eventuated in the production of the *Head Start Measures Battery,* which is composed of six scales (Language, Math, Nature & Science, Perception, Reading, and Social Development) designed to assess children's cognitive and social competencies.

These measures are based on a path-referenced approach to assessment (Bergan, 1980; Bergan, Stone, & Feld, 1985), child performance is referenced to position in empirically validated developmental sequences. Path referencing is particularly useful for instructional management because the information provided by a path-referenced assessment tool indicates what the child has accomplished and what new learning challenges lie ahead. Information about a student's current status is tied to possible future achievements and to past accomplishments. This tie relates instructional decisions to what the child has accomplished and to the direction to be taken by the consultant and consultee to promote further growth.

Planning Guides and Behavioral Consultation. A major obstacle to the conduct of behavioral consultation approaches to instructional management is that consultation goals and objectives have to be established for all students. The time required to accomplish this would be excessive if traditional consultation interviewing techniques were used. Planning guides were developed for the Head Start project to facilitate the specification of instructional goals and objectives for children, in a way that imposes minimum time requirements and constraints on consultants and consultees.

The guides were constructed to relate directly to the *Head Start Measures Battery.* Teaching and planning information obtained from planning guides can be used with assessment information obtained from path-referenced instruments to guide the consultation process. The guides are record keeping devices that can be used in problem identification or needs assessment. They enable teachers to detail content plans for an entire school year in each of the six areas for which the measures were developed. Information is used, during the identification of learning needs, to determine whether there is an incongruence between the child's developmental level, the teaching level, and the planning level for instruction. The guides are also used in problem analysis, planning, and evaluation.

Following the path-referenced approach, the format of the guides organizes the content of instruction in two ways. In the first, specific capabilities are nested within successively broader categories of competence. For instance, in the area of math, counting aloud to 10 is nested within the larger category of counting or numeration skills; numeration skills are placed in the category of working with numbers. The strategy of relating specific competencies to more general skill categories affords a way to relate content reflecting broad long-range instructional goals and plans to content representing specific instructional objectives and concrete lesson-planning activities. This helps to ensure that lesson plans will be directed toward specific performance objectives and an overall long-term goal.

The second type of organization used in the planning guides is developmental. The planning process (i.e., problem analysis) of behavioral consultation may be enhanced by considering the developmental sequencing of skills. The categories of competence identified in the planning guides are associated with validated learning sequences. Each skill designated by the categories in the guides can be described by its position in one or more developmental progressions. For example, a skill such as counting forward to 10 is identified as being subordinate to a counting skill, such as counting backward.

The developmental sequences in the planning guides correspond to sequences identified through path-referenced technology in the *Head Start Measures Battery*. Behavioral consultation using the planning guides and the measures provides a basis for planning instructional sequences congruent with children's development. Information on children's development affords the basis for placing children in an instructional learning sequence and for identifying their specific learning needs during consultation.

To provide the behavioral consultant with a mechanism for interpreting and using information obtained through path-referenced assessment tools, several profiles were developed for use in consultation with teachers. Two of these profiles, the *Individual Developmental Profile* and the *Class Developmental Profile,* are described to familiarize the reader with the nature of path-referenced assessment and how it may be incorporated into behavioral consultation.

Individual Developmental Profile.   A description of the organization of the Individual Developmental Profile follows.

The sample profile in Fig. 8.1 shows that groups of skills are placed in different categories. The skills are grouped into categories for each of the scales on the *Head Start Measures Battery* (HSMB). For example, some of the categories on the Language Scale include "Story Meaning," "Conversation," "Directions" and so on.

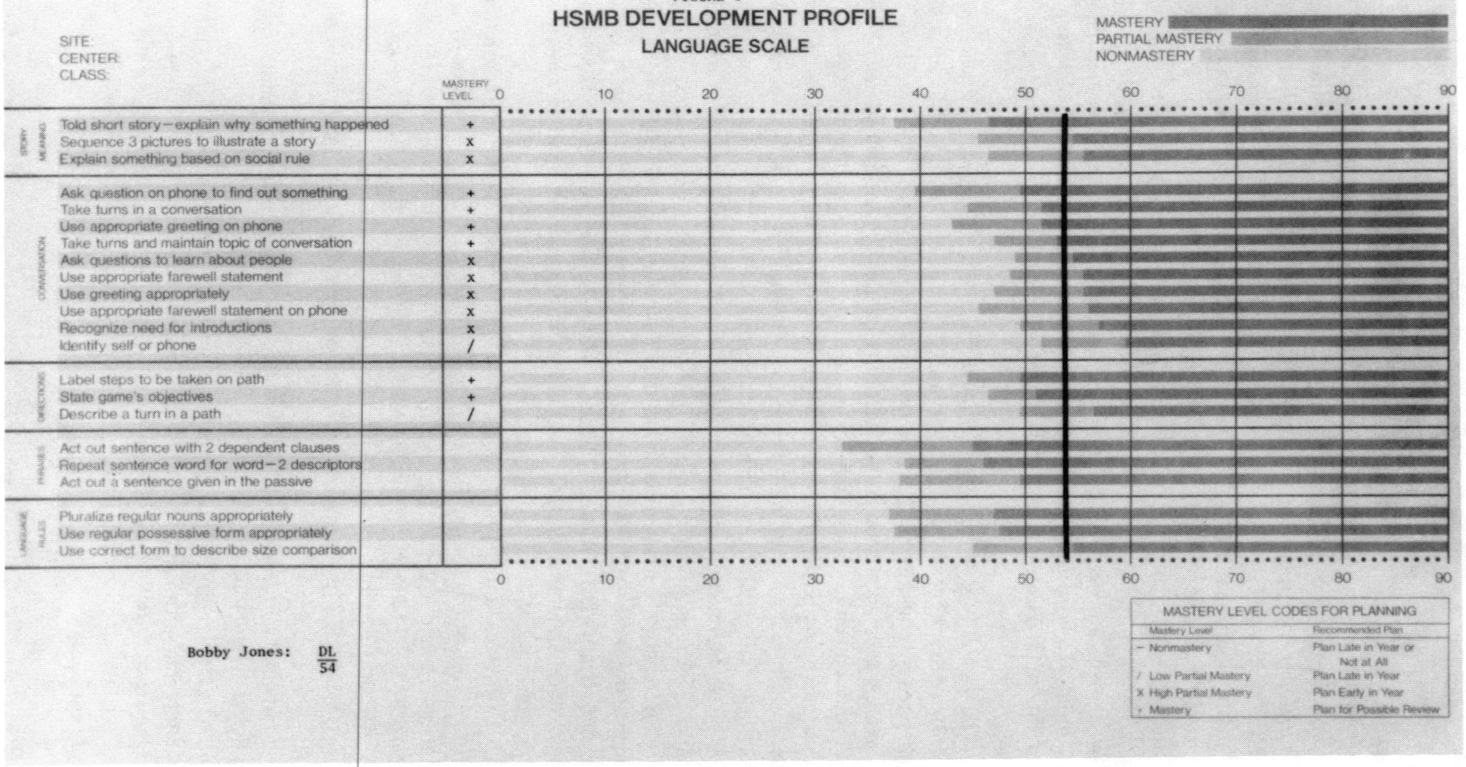

204

FIGURE 1

HSMB DEVELOPMENT PROFILE
LANGUAGE SCALE

MASTERY
PARTIAL MASTERY
NONMASTERY

MASTERY
LEVEL   0   10   20   30   40   50   60   70   80   90

Category	Item	Mastery Level
MEANING	Told short story—explain why something happened	x
	Sequence 3 pictures to illustrate a story	x
	Explain something based on social rule	
STORY		
	Ask question on phone to find out something	+
CONVERSATION	Take turns in a conversation	+
	Use appropriate greeting on phone	+
	Take turns and maintain topic of conversation	+
	Ask questions to learn about people	x
	Use appropriate farewell statement	x
	Use greeting appropriately	x
	Use appropriate farewell statement on phone	x
	Recognize need for introductions	x
	Identify self or phone	/
DIRECTIONS	Label steps to be taken on path	+
	State game's objectives	+
	Describe a turn in a path	/
PHRASES	Act out sentence with 2 dependent clauses	
	Repeat sentence word for word—2 descriptors	
	Act out a sentence given in the passive	
LANGUAGE	Pluralize regular nouns appropriately	
	Use regular possessive form appropriately	
	Use correct form to describe size comparison	

SITE:
CENTER:
CLASS:

Bobby Jones: DL
              54

MASTERY LEVEL CODES FOR PLANNING

Mastery Level		Recommended Plan
– Nonmastery		Plan Late in Year or Not at All
/ Low Partial Mastery		Plan Late in Year
x High Partial Mastery		Plan Early in Year
• Mastery		Plan for Possible Review

Each skill within a category is arranged according to level of difficulty; the first skill listed in each category is the easiest, the last skill is the most difficult. For example, within the category "Conversation," "asking a question on the phone to find out something" is the easiest skill; "recognizing the need for introductions" is one of the more difficult skills.

Notice that numbers are listed at the top and bottom of the profile. These numbers, called *Path Scores,* give the child's Developmental Level (DL) by indicating the child's position in a developmental sequence.

Path-referenced instruments provide information about a child's developmental level by means of path scores and path profiles. Path scores and path profiles can be used in consultation to identify needs, plan instructional content, and to evaluate the extent to which the goals of instructional management have been achieved. A path score represents the child's position in a developmental path, describes overall level of performance in each content area being assessed with path-referenced devices, and generates a profile of the level of competence (i.e., the level of mastery for specific skills determined by the percent of times a child accurately performs a set of tasks that represent a skill). The profile provides the consultee with an indication of the types of learning activities that should be challenging for the child, at the current level of development, and of the activities still too difficult for the child to perform.

Path scores provide information that can be used in consultation to plan the skills and activities that will benefit the child and encourage growth and progress. This information makes it possible to link the content of instruction to a child's current developmental level, and to sequence instructional activities to reflect progress in development. In addition, path scores provide the information needed to avoid redundancy of instruction in skills that have been mastered.

Path scores are not intended to dictate the level of instruction in a rigid fashion; they are designed to provide the consultee with information about developmental level that can be combined with information gained from other behavioral assessment strategies (e.g., direct observation or work samples). This information is used to arrive at an appropriate level of classroom planning and instruction that will provide opportunities to learn new skills. For example, the teacher may decide to provide instruction at the child's current developmental level, or slightly above to challenge the child. In some instances, to provide the child with immediate success, it may be advisable to focus on skills below the current level of functioning. When a child is having difficulty mastering a skill, path score information can be used to identify the unlearned subordinate skills that may be affecting mastery of the skill in question. Instruction can then be directed toward the mastery of the subordinate skills.

Path scores indicating developmental level (DL) range in value from approximately *0* to *90*. A child's DL indicates whether the child is a master, partial master, or nonmaster of each skill in a developmental sequence. The three levels of mastery have been defined in the following manner.

A child is considered a master of a skill if he/she can be expected to correctly perform between 75% and 100% of the tasks that measure the skill. For example, in a classroom a child may have the opportunity to perform a skill, such as counting objects up to nine, in many different situations. In counting objects, a child can count seven blocks, nine napkins, or five children. The child would be considered a master of the skill if the skill was accurately performed 8 out of 10 times (i.e., 80% of the time).

A child is considered a low partial master of a skill if he/she can be expected to perform the skill accurately 26% to 49% of the time and a high partial master if performing falls within the 50% to 74% range. For example, if a child is asked to perform the counting skill identified earlier and performs it accurately on tasks representing the skill 5 out of 10 times (i.e., 50 percent of the time), the child would be considered a high partial master.

A child is considered a nonmaster of a specific skills if he/she can be expected to perform the skill accurately less than 25% of the time. For example, if a child is asked to perform the counting skill identified earlier, and performs it accurately on 2 out of 10 tasks (e.g., 20% of the time), the child would be considered a nonmaster of the skill.

A child's DL is used in problem identification to determine the level of mastery for a particular skill. For example, using Figure 8.1, a child with a DL of *54* falls in the *mastery level* for the following skills:

STORY MEANING
Told a short story-explain why something happened

CONVERSATION
Ask a question on the phone to find out something
Use appropriate greeting on the phone
Take turns in a conversation
Take turns and maintain topic of conversation

DIRECTIONS
Label steps to be taken on a path
State games' objectives

The same DL score results in *high partial mastery* for the following skills:

STORY MEANING
Sequence 3 pictures to illustrate a story
Explain something based on social rule

CONVERSATION
Use appropriate farewell statement on phone
Ask questions to learn about people
Use appropriate farewell statement

Use greeting appropriately
Recognize need for introductions

DIRECTIONS
Describe a turn in a path

The same DL score results in *low partial mastery* for the following skills:

STORY MEANING
None

CONVERSATION
Identify self on phone

DIRECTIONS
None

The same DL score results in *nonmastery* for the following skills:

STORY MEANING
None

CONVERSATION
None

DIRECTIONS
None

Level of mastery is indicated by a "range," not by a particular point on the profile. For example, a child would be in the nonmastery range for the skill "asking a question on the phone to find out somesomething" if the path score was between *0* and *39*, ability to perform the skill accurately less than 25% of the time. A child would be in the a partial mastery range for the skill if the path score was between *0* and less than *50*, ability to perform the skill accurately between 26% and 74% of the time. A child would be in the mastery range for the skill if the path score was between *50* and *90*, ability to perform the skill accurately between 75% and 100% of the time.

The "range" indicates varying degrees of nonmastery, partial mastery, and mastery, and can be used during problem identification and problem analysis to maximize the precision and quality of a plan designed to promote learning of academic skills. For example, a child with a path score of *52* on the Language Scale is a master of "asking a question on the phone to find out something" and may be able to perform this skill accurately 75% of the time; a child with a path score of *65* may have mastered this skill to a greater degree, and may be able to perform the skill accurately 90% of the time. Although both children are in the mastery range for the skill in question, the second child is likely to have a deeper understanding of the skill. The first child may be viewed as having just become a master of the skill. During problem analysis the consultant and consultee may decide that additional learning opportunities for practice should be provided to increase the degree of mastery. For the second child the teacher may decide to present a skill other than the one the child understands. Next, look at the bottom of the profile. The child's name appears with information on Teaching Level (TL), and Developmental Level (DL).

Teaching Level (TL) information is obtained from the Planning Guide. Teaching Level is provided by teachers, it is based on the types of learning experiences that have actually been provided to the child. Teaching is defined as any activity designed to help children learn. The principal function of teaching information about the determination of goals and objectives during consultation is to better understand why teachers develop certain plans. For example, a teacher may not plan to offer instruction in an important content area because the material has already been taught.

As stated earlier, the path score indicates Developmental Level (DL). Path score and DL information are based on a child's performance on a path-referenced assessment tool. The DL indicates a child's position on a developmental path made up of skills arranged according to difficulty. Using the DL, consultant and consultee can determine the types of learning experiences that would be challenging for the child at the current level of development. In addition, the teacher can determine the types of learning experiences that may be too difficult or too easy for the child to master. Information about what has been learned provides the consultant with an additional basis for understanding teacher plans. For instance, if a teacher believes the class has already mastered a particular set of skills, it would be understandable if the teacher did not plan to offer further instruction in those skills, or skills far above the assumed developmental levels of the children.

Teaching Level (TL) information is provided when the teacher fills out the Planning Guide during problem identification and as teaching plans are revised during the year. TL is based on types of skills that are presented to children during the course of the school year. The types of activities to be presented to a child during problem analysis depends on what has been presented or taught in the past, and to a great extent, on the DL of the child. The teacher who has information about a child's DL is in a better position to organize the learning environment and plan learning opportunities for children than the teacher who does not have this information. When teaching is based on what a child already knows and on what a child is developmentally ready to learn, the potential for progress is greatly increased. Information on teaching provides the foundation for the specification of goals and objectives during the identification of learning needs, in instructional analysis and planning, and in evaluation. In gathering information on teaching goals, the consultant must make clear that what is desired is a specification of skills to be taught linked to the expectation that learning will ensue.

Path-referenced assessment instruments, such as the *Head Start Measures Battery*, and recording devices, such as planning guides, provide the tools by which behavioral consultation may achieve the goals of instructional management. Path-referenced instruments afford a means for placing teaching level, planning level and developmental level on the same number scale. Consequently, the consultant and consultee are in a position to make a direct and accurate comparison between what is being taught, what is planned, and what a child is ready to learn.

There are several types of comparisons that can be made between teaching, developmental, and planning levels to provide learning opportunities and enhance progress. Following these comparisons, several directions can be taken during problem analysis and plan implementation to provide learning opportunities for children:

1. The teacher can present new learning opportunities by presenting new skills that would provide an adequate challenge to the child.

2. The teacher can provide opportunities for the child to practice and apply skills that have already been learned to allow the child to "gain a deeper knowledge about those skills.

3. The teacher can provide opportunities for the child to develop confidence in his/her abilities by presenting tasks the child has already mastered and can perform well. Once a child's confidence is enhanced, the teacher may move on to more challenging tasks.

As a general guideline, teacher planning for the school year may initially include those skills that, based on the DL of the child, can be performed accurately between 26% and 75% of the time. The teacher may want to choose skills within this range that would provide a moderate challenge for the child and reserve skills that would provide a more difficult challenge for the child for later in the program year; the skills that may provide a moderate or more difficult challenge to the child are identified on the Individual Developmental Profile. The skills that may provide a moderate challenge to the child are indicated by a "X" (high partial mastery). These are the skills that the child has a good chance of performing accurately between 50% and 74% of the time. Those skills that provide a more difficult challenge are indicated by a "/" (low partial mastery). These are the skills that a child has a good chance of performing accurately between 26% to 49% of the time. A teacher may wish to present a good portion of the moderately challenging skills (X) to the child before presenting the more difficult skills (/).

It is important to keep in mind that the Individual Developmental Profile is only one source of information that can be used to determine the learning opportunities that should be presented to the child. In deciding what skills to include in the learning environment, the teacher is encouraged to select criteria that he/she feels most comfortable with. It is up to the teacher to decide what is to be taught; the decision should be based on the child's performance on path-referenced assessment tools, and on the teacher's knowledge of the child's capabilities, past experience, and characteristics.

The skills that the child may be able to perform accurately 75% of the time or more are identified on the profile by an "+" (Mastery). These are the skills the teacher may want to consider as already learned. The teacher may want to provide additional opportunities for the child to practice and apply these skills, to expand the child's experiences in the use of these skills and to provide for a deeper understanding of the skills. In addition, a child's self-confidence may be enhanced because there is a high probability of success on skills within the mastery range. The extent to which a teacher decides to concentrate on these skills should be based on knowledge of the child and expertise in the learning environment as it relates to the child.

The skills that the child would be able to get correct 25% of the time or less are identified on the profile by a "−" (Nonmastery). These are skills that the child is unlikely to understand. The child would probably have difficulty in learning these skills if they were presented before the skills identified by "X" and "/."

As mentioned earlier, TL is based on the information provided by the teacher when completing the Planning Guide. TL includes information on the learning experiences that have been provided in the past and what is currently being provided to the child. Teaching Level should be approximately the same as Developmental Level. The teacher can be expected to be very accurate in making teaching consistent with DL because DL information will be available, enabling the teacher to carry out the procedures specified. However, there may be some instances where TL and DL do not agree. If during or at the end of the program year the teacher notices that TL is higher than DL, large numbers of skills are being taught that a child is probably not learning. This may mean that the skills are too difficult for the child or that the way the learning environment is organized is not effective in helping the child to learn those skills. The teacher and consultant need to return to the problem analysis phase of consultation and revise teaching plans to approximate more closely the child's DL. When TL is much lower than DL, the child is not being challenged sufficiently. This also suggests the need to return to problem analysis, examine the goals that have been set for the child, and to revise goals to make them more consistent with the child's DL. For example, without DL information the teacher could underestimate the learning capabilities of a particular child. In this situation, the Individual Developmental Profile would be highly useful in providing accurate information about a child's DL. This information would increase the teacher's accuracy in planning learning experiences to meet the child's learning capabilities.

Consider an Individual Developmental Profile sample for the Reading Scale in Fig. 8.2.

FIGURE 2

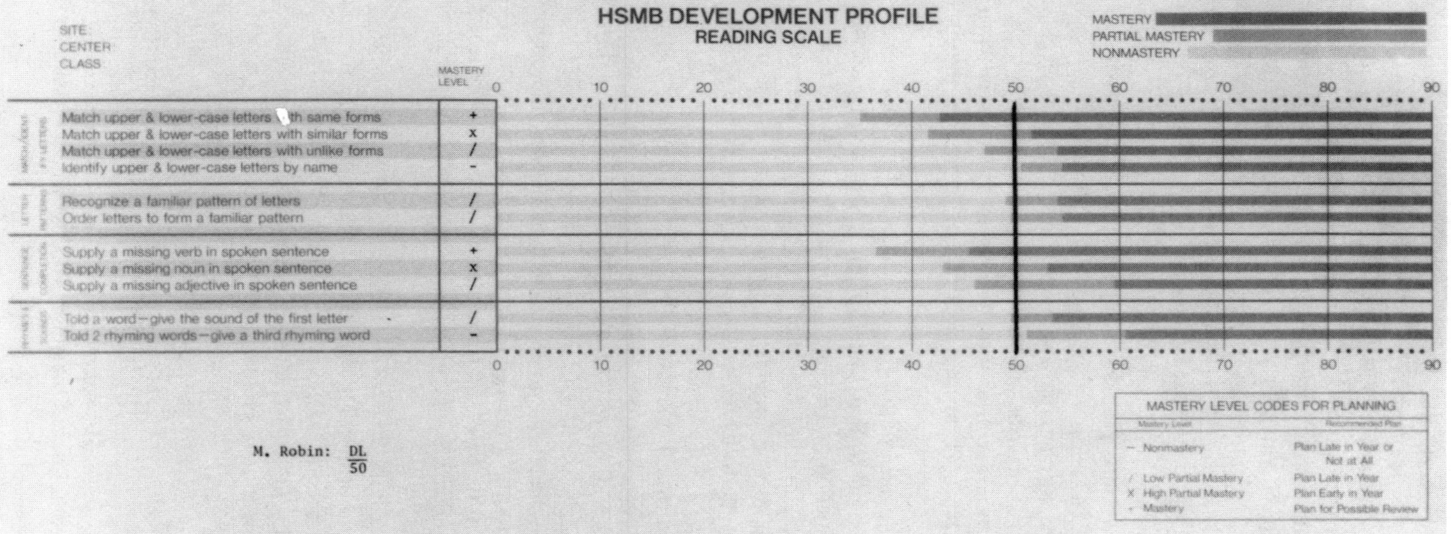
HSMB DEVELOPMENT PROFILE
READING SCALE
MASTERY
PARTIAL MASTERY
NONMASTERY
SITE:
CENTER
CLASS
MASTERY LEVEL
Match upper & lower-case letters with same forms +
Match upper & lower-case letters with similar forms x
Match upper & lower-case letters with unlike forms /
Identify upper & lower-case letters by name -
Recognize a familiar pattern of letters /
Order letters to form a familiar pattern /
Supply a missing verb in spoken sentence +
Supply a missing noun in spoken sentence x
Supply a missing adjective in spoken sentence /
Told a word—give the sound of the first letter /
Told 2 rhyming words—give a third rhyming word -
0 10 20 30 40 50 60 70 80 90
MASTERY LEVEL CODES FOR PLANNING
— Nonmastery Plan Late in Year or Not at All
/ Low Partial Mastery Plan Late in Year
X High Partial Mastery Plan Early in Year
+ Mastery Plan for Possible Review

M. Robin: $\frac{DL}{50}$

The child on the profile is M. Robin. The path score for this child is *50*. Look at the codes assigned to each of the individual skills based on the score.

Using this information the teacher can begin to plan learning opportunities for the child. The teacher may first want to consider planning learning activities that incorporate skills identified by X (high partial mastery) and slowly phase in skills identified by / (low partial mastery). Skills identified by a + (mastery) may be included in the learning environment to provide the child with the opportunity to practice, apply, and refine these skills. Inclusion of these skills in the learning environment will also provide the opportunity to experience success and build self-confidence in the area of reading. Skills identified by − (nonmastery) may not be included in planning activities; the teacher may decide to wait before including them as activities in the learning environment.

Knowledge of DL will help the teacher to be on target when using planning guides to develop a TL to meet a child's individual learning needs.

Class Developmental Profile.   The Class Developmental Profile contains information similar to that found on the Individual Developmental Profile; it provides information on DL, and TL for every child in the class on one form. It also provides the average scores for DL, and TL for the entire class. The Class Developmental Profile provides information that is useful during behavioral consultation in the following ways:

1. Gives an overall picture of the class and helps the teacher to determine where the class is in relation to overall teaching level.
2. Provides a quick way for the teacher to identify children who may need individualization.
3. Can help the teacher to determine whether it is appropriate to form different learning groups in the class based on children's DL's.
4. Can help the teacher to arrange the class environment so children with lower DL's can learn from children with higher DL's by observing and working with them.

The sample profile in Fig. 8.3 shows that each child has a score for DL, and TL. Notice that there is a letter in parenthesis to the left of each child's name. Consider, for example, two children, L. Jones and R. Hernandez. On the profile, information about these children appears as follows:

	DL	TL
L. Jones	45	50
R. Hernandez	50	55

The consultant and consultee can use this information to get a general idea of the developmental level of the class. This information can help teachers to make decisions on each of the four points listed earlier.

FIGURE 3

HSMB DEVELOPMENT PROFILE
MATH SCALE

SITE:
CENTER:
CLASS:

MASTERY
PARTIAL MASTERY
NONMASTERY

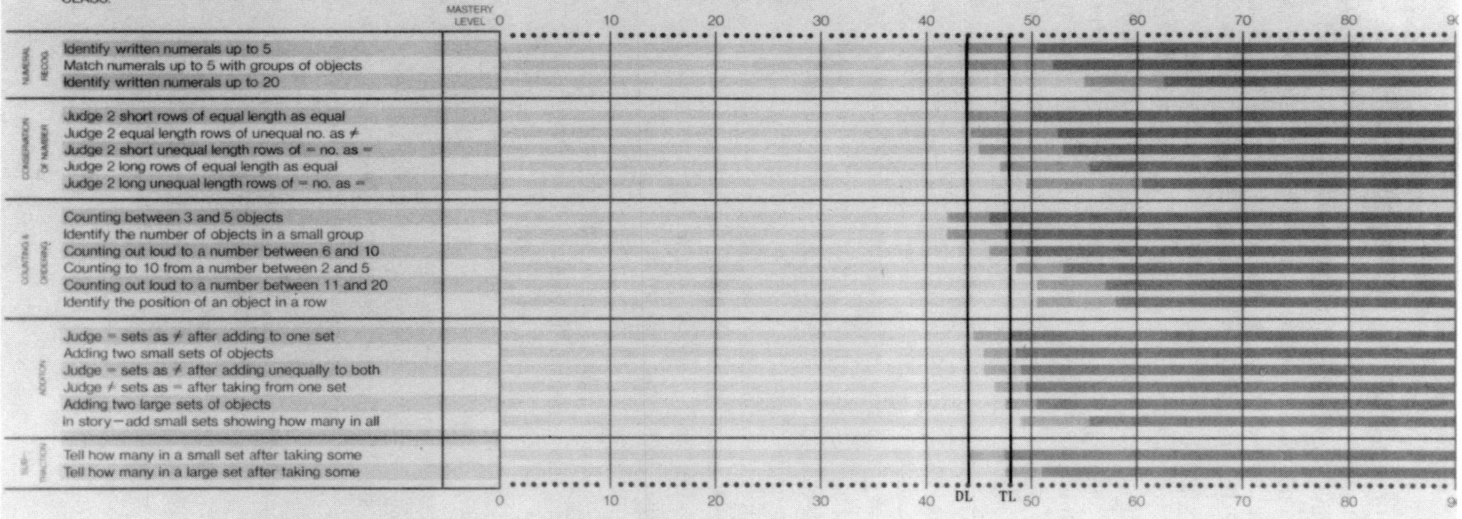

MASTERY LEVEL 0   0   10   20   30   40   50   60   70   80   90

NUMERAL RECOG.
Identify written numerals up to 5
Match numerals up to 5 with groups of objects
Identify written numerals up to 20

CONSERVATION OF NUMBER
Judge 2 short rows of equal length as equal
Judge 2 equal length rows of unequal no. as ≠
Judge 2 short unequal length rows of = no. as =
Judge 2 long rows of equal length as equal
Judge 2 long unequal length rows of = no. as =

COUNTING I
Counting between 3 and 5 objects
Identify the number of objects in a small group
Counting out loud to a number between 6 and 10
Counting to 10 from a number between 2 and 5
Counting out loud to a number between 11 and 20
Identify the position of an object in a row

ADDITION
Judge = sets as ≠ after adding to one set
Adding two small sets of objects
Judge = sets as ≠ after adding unequally to both
Judge ≠ sets as = after taking from one set
Adding two large sets of objects
In story—add small sets showing how many in all

SUB-TRACTION
Tell how many in a small set after taking some
Tell how many in a large set after taking some

	DL	TL
L. Jones	45	50
R. Hernandez	50	55
S. Krauss	42	47
B. Walker	51	54
R. Rasch	44	49
L. Burke	39	42
T. Dole	37	40

Class DL = 44
Class TL = 48

MASTERY LEVEL CODES FOR PLANNING

Mastery Level	Recommended Plan
— Nonmastery	Plan Late in Year or Not at All
/ Low Partial Mastery	Plan Late in Year
X High Partial Mastery	Plan Early in Year
▪ Mastery	Plan for Possible Review

The broad picture that this profile provides indicates a wide range of DL's for this particular class. In some cases there may be a need for individualization. The teacher may want to find out why some children have relatively low DL's; these children may have special needs. The teacher may feel that additional assessment procedures need to be carried out to determine why these children are in the nonmastery range for all of the skills on the scale. Children with relatively low DL's would be good candidates for individualization. In addition, the teacher may want to consider forming a small work group with these children and may also consider including children with somewhat higher DL's in the group to provide the less able children with an opportunity to learn by observing and working with other children in activity groups. There are several options from which the teacher can select. The determination as to what to do, should, in all cases, take into consideration the teacher's goals, knowledge of these children, and past experience in working with children.

At the other extreme there may be children that are well above the rest of the class. These children may be considered as having mastered most of the skills on the Math Scale and may also be candidates for individualization. The teacher may want to provide learning experiences in more advanced math skills, and may consider including these children in activity groups with children with somewhat lower DL's to provide the latter group with the opportunity to learn from working with and modeling after them. Again, the final determination as to how the teacher will organize the classroom environment should be based on the teacher's knowledge of the children, past experiences, and the goals set for the class.

The teacher may also decide not to form activity groups, and instead, individualize learning experiences for all the children in the class. The Individual Developmental Profiles would provide a guide for identifying the skills to be included in the learning environment for each child.

Finally, the profile provides an overall picture of the teacher's TL for the entire class and the DL for the class as a whole. The TL and DL provided on the profile help the teacher to determine if he/she is being responsive to the needs of the children. This information offers a starting point from which the teacher can refine the teaching process to better meet the needs of the children. If DL is well above or well below the DL for the class, it suggests the need to consider individualization of learning opportunities and perhaps a reorganization of the learning environment.

The Class Developmental Profile provides the consultant and consultee with an overall picture of the class and can serve as a guide for the teacher in deciding how to organize the classroom and meet the needs of all children. The major advantage in using this profile in behavioral consultation is that it provides the teacher with a picture of the children in the class. It is a starting point from which consultation procedures can be directed toward providing a learning environment that ensures children will benefit from the learning experiences provided.

CONCLUSION

Consultation is an area in which school professionals, particularly school psychologists, have been engaged for some time, in terms of applied research and practice. Several forms of consultation have been described in this chapter, they have been discussed in terms of their utility and limitations in providing educational and psychological services to children. A major issue emphasized in this chapter concerns the effectiveness of behavioral and other forms of consultation in addressing the needs of consultees and clients. The information provided indicates that maximizing the effectiveness of behavioral consultation efforts in the schools requires that the consultant go beyond simply implementing a particular approach. Research has demonstrated that the consultant who is knowledgeable of the factors that play a role in limiting or enhancing successful outcomes in consultation is in a better position to affect a positive change in consultee and client behavior than one who does not have this information.

Consultants may be thought of as advisors who possess special expertise that may be applied in problem solving. A major role of the behavioral consultant is to provide consultees with advice or information that can be used in decision making. The effective consultant is one who attends to factors related to the goal of producing successful outcomes. In behavioral consultation, the application of principles, procedures, and strategies is enhanced by attending to factors that influence the outcome of the consultation process. These factors have been described and include such variables as the experience and skills of the consultant and consultee, the consultee's knowledge of behavioral techniques, the availability of resources for implementing behavioral plans, the perceptions that the consultee brings to the consultation process, and the rigorousness with which the consultation process is carried out. Moreover, the appropriateness and effectiveness of any one approach to consultation is linked to the goals and objectives of the consultee, the clients served, and the content addressed. These and other factors discussed should be given careful consideration by the consultant prior to and during the implementation of behavioral consultation.

Although each approach to consultation discussed in this chapter has provided useful tools for the remediation of educational and psychological problems, consultation within a behavioral framework linked to instructional management, has an excellent potential for enhancing the goals of the teaching-learning process.

Incorporating the new path-referenced technology into behavioral approaches to consultation reflects an approach to the teaching-learning process that differs from existing practice in a number of significant ways. First, the techniques presented provide a direct link between instructional decision making and data on educational progress. Second, they make use of a consultation approach that relates the management of instruction to a problem solving perspective. Third, the techniques call for decision making activities that are more systematic and focus on a broader range of activities taking place in the schools. Fourth, they afford a way for consultation to serve a greater number of children over a broader period of time. The fundamental consequence of linking consultation to instructional management in this way ought to be an increase in the available information about thinking, learning, and teaching. The result to be hoped for is not only an increase in student knowledge, but also an increased understanding of the nature of learning and teaching between educators and their students.

REFERENCES

Abidin, R. R. (1971). What's wrong with behavior modification? *Journal of School Psychology, 9*, 38–42.

Abidin, R. R. (1977). Operant behavioral consultations as conducted by masters and doctoral level psychologists in Virginia. *Journal of School Psychology, 15*, 225–229.

Alderfer, C. P. (1977). Organizational development. *Annual Review of Psychology, 28*, 197–223.

Alpert, J. L. (1976). Conceptual bases of mental health consultation in the schools. *Professional Psychology, 7*, 619–626.

Alpert, J. L. (1977). Some guidelines for school consultants. *Journal of School Psychology, 15*, 308–319.

Bandura, A. (1978). Self esteem in reciprocal determinism. *American Psychologist, 33*, 344–358.

Bergan, J. R. (1977). *Behavioral consultation.* Columbus,OH: Charles E. Merrill.

Bergan, J. R. (1980). The structural analysis of behavior: An alternative to the learning hierarchy model. *Review of Educational Research, 50*, 225–246.

Bergan, J. R., Anderson, D., Feld, J. K., Henderson, R., Johnson, D. M., Lane, S., Mott, S., Parra, E., Robinson, L., Schnaps, A., Stone, C. A., & Swarner, J. C. (1984, February). *Head Start Measures Project: Final report* (Contract No. HHS-105-81-C-008). Washington, DC: Department of Health & Human Services.

Bergan, J. R., Byrnes, I. M., & Kratochwill, T. R. (1979). Effects of behavioral and medical model consultation on teacher expectancies and instruction of a hypothetical child. *Journal of School Psychology, 17*, 307–316.

Bergan, J. R., Feld, J. K., & Schnaps, A. (1984, March). *Consultation for instructional management* (Contract No. HHS-105-81-C-008). Washington, DC: Department of Health & Human Services.

Bergan, J. R., & Neumann, A. J. (1980). The identification of resources and constraints influencing plan design in consultation. *Journal of School Psychology, 18*, 317–323.

Bergan, J. R., Stone, C. A., & Feld, J. K. (1984). Rule replacement in the development of basic number skills. *Journal of Educational Psychology, 76*, 289–299.

Bergan, J. R., Stone, C. A., & Feld, J. K. (1985). Path-referenced assessment of individual differences. In C. R. Reynolds & V. L. Wilson (Eds.), *Methodological and statistical advances in the study of individual differences.* New York: Plenum Press.

Bergan, J. R., & Tombari, M. L. (1975). The analyses of verbal interactions occurring during consultation. *Journal of School Psychology, 14*, 3–14.

Bergan, J. R., & Tombari, M. L. (1976). Consultant skill and efficiency and the implementation of outcomes of consultation. *Journal of School Psychology, 14*, 3–13.

Berliner, D. C. (1983, September). The executive functions of teaching. *Instruction, 93*, 28–40.

Berne, E. (1962). Classification of positions. *Transactional Analysis Bulletin, 1*, 23.

Blumberg, A., May, J., & Perry, R. (1974). An inner city school that changed, and continued to change. *Education and Urban Society, 6*, 222–238.

Canter, L., & Paulson, T. A. (1974). A college credit model of in-school consultation: A functional behavioral training program. *Community Mental Health Journal, 10,* 268–275.

Caplan, G. (1970). *The theory and practice of mental health consultation.* New York: Basic Books.

Colligan, R. W., Colligan, R. C., & Dilliard, M. K. (1977). Contingency management in the classroom treatment of long-term elective mutism: A case report. *Journal of Applied Behavioral Analysis, 15,* 9–17.

Conoley, J. D. (Ed.). (1981). *Consultation in schools: Theory, research, procedures.* New York: Academic Press.

Conoley, J. C., & Conoley, C. W. (1982). The effects of two conditions of client-centered consultation on student teacher problem descriptions and remedial plans. *Journal of School Psychology, 20,* 323–328.

Cooper, M. L., Thompson, C. L., & Baer, D. M. (1970). The experimental modification of teacher attending behavior. *Journal of Applied Behavior Analysis, 3,* 153–157.

Cossairt, A. H., Hall, R. V., & Hopkins, B. L. (1973). The effects of experimenter instructions, feedback, and praise on student attending behavior. *Journal of Applied Behavioral Analysis, 6,* 89–100.

Curtis, M. J., & Watson, K. L. (1980). Changes in consultee problem clarification skills following consultation. *Journal of School Psychology, 18,* 210–221.

Dworkin, A. L., & Dworkin, E. P. (1975). A conceptual overview of selected consultation models. *American Journal of Community Psychology, 3,* 151–159.

D'Zurilla, T. J., & Goldfried, M. R. (1971). Problem solving and behavior modification. *Journal of Abnormal Psychology, 78,* 107–126.

Farber, H., & Mayer, R. G. (1972). Behavioral consultation in a barrio high school. *Personnel and Guidance Journal, 51,* 273–279.

Fine, M. J. (1970). Some qualifying notes on the development and implementation of behavior modification programs. *Journal of School Psychology, 8,* 301–305.

Gallessich, J., & Davis, J. (1981). Consultation: Prospects and retrospects. In J. C. Conoley (Ed.), *Consultation in schools: Theory, research, procedures* (pp. 295–302). New York: Academic Press.

Glass, G. V., Wilson, V. L., & Gottman, J. M. (1975). *Design and analysis of time-series experiments.* Boulder, CO: Colorado Associate University Press.

Goldstein, A. P. (Ed.). (1978). *Prescriptions for child mental health and education.* Elmsford, NY: Pergamon Press.

Grieger, R. M., Mordock, J. B., & Breyer, N. (1970). General guidelines for conducting behavior modification programs in public school settings. *Journal of School Psychology, 8,* 259–266.

Hersen, M., & Barlow, D. H. (1976). *Single case experimental designs: Strategies for studying behavior change.* Elmsford NY: Pergamon press.

Hops, H. (1971). The school psychologist as a behavioral management consultant in a special class setting. *Journal of School Psychology, 9,* 473–493.

Jason, A. L., & Ferone, L. (1978). Behavioral versus process consultation intervention in school settings. *American Journal of Community Psychology, 6,* 531–543.

Jason, A. L., Ferone, L., & Anderegg, T. (1979). Evaluating ecological, behavioral, and process consultation interventions. *Journal of School Psychology, 17,* 103–115.

Kanfer, F. H., & Grimm, L. G. (1977). Behavioral analysis: Selecting target behaviors in the interview. *Behavior Modification, 1,* 7–28.

Kanfer, F. H., & Saslow, G. (1969). Behavioral diagnosis. In C. M. Franks (Ed.), *Behavior therapy: Appraisal and status.* New York: McGraw-Hill.

Kazdin, A. E. (1978). Methodology in applied behavior analysis. In A. C. Catania & T. A. Brigham (Eds.), *Handbook of applied behavior analysis: Social and instructional processes.* New York: Irvington.

Keller, H. R. (1981). Behavioral consultation. In J. C. Conoley (Ed.), *Consultation in schools: Theory, research, procedures.* New York: Academic Press.

Kosier, K. P. (1970). Effects on task oriented behavior of teacher in-service, charted and videotaped feedback, and individual consultation. *Dissertation Abstracts,* 31-11-A, 5850.

Kratochwill, T. R. (1977). N=1: An alternative research strategy for school psychologists. *Journal of School Psychology, 15,* 239–249.

Kratochwill, T. R., & Bergan, J. R. (1978). Evaluating programs in applied settings through behavioral consultation. *Journal of School Psychology, 16,* 375–386.

Lambert, N. M. (1974). A school-based consultation model. *Professional Psychology, 5,* 267–276.

Lambert, N. M., Sandoval, J., & Corder, R. (1975). Teacher perceptions of school-based consultants. *Professional Psychology, 6,* 204–216.

Lambert, N. M., Sandoval, J., & Yandell, W. C. (1975). Preparation of school psychologists for school-based consultation: A training activity and a service to community schools. *Journal of School Psychology, 13,* 68–75.

Mann, P. (1973). Student consultants: Evaluation by consultees. *American Journal of Community Psychology, 1,* 182–193.

Mannino, F. V., & Shore, M. F. (1975). The effects of consultation: A review of empirical studies. *American Journal of Community Psychology, 3,* 1–4.

McFall, R. M. (1982). A review and reformulation of the concept of social skills. *Behavior Assessment, 4,* 1–33.

Medway, F. J. (1979). How effective is school consultation? A review of recent research. *Journal of School Psychology, 17,* 275–282.

Medway, F. J., & Forman, S. G. (1980). Psychologists' and teachers' reactions to mental health and behavioral school consultation. *Journal of School Psychology, 18,* 338–348.

Meyer, V., Liddell, A., & Lyons, M. (1977). Behavioral interviews. In A. R. Ciminaro, K. S. Calhoun, & H. E. Adams (Eds.), *Handbook of behavioral assessment* (pp. 117–152). New York: Wiley.

Meyers, J. A. (1973). A consultation model for school psychological services. *Journal of School Psychology, 11,* 5–15.

Meyers, J. (19B1). Mental health consultation. In J. C. Conoley (Ed.), *Consultation in schools: Theory, research, procedures* (pp. 35–58). New York: Academic Press.

Meyers, J., Parsons, R. D., & Martin (1979). *Mental health consultation in the schools.* San Francisco: Jossey-Bass.

O'Leary, K. D., & Drabman, R. (1971). Token reinforcement programs in the classroom: A review. *Psychological Bulletin, 75,* 379–398.

O'Leary, K. D., & O'Leary, S. G. (Eds.). (1976). *Classroom management: The successful use of behavior modification* (rev. ed.). Elmsford, NY: Pergamon Press.

O'Leary, K. D., & Wilson, G. T. (1975). *Behavior therapy: Application and outcome.* Englewood Cliffs, NJ: Prentice-Hall.

Piersel, W. C. (1985). Behavioral consultation: An approach to problem solving in educational settings. In J. R. Bergan (Ed.), *School psychology in contemporary society:* An introduction (pp. 252–273). Columbus, OH: Charles E. Merrill.

Piersel, W. C., & Kratochwill, T. R. (1979). Self-observation and behavior change: Applications to academic and adjustment problems through behavioral consultation. *Journal of School Psychology, 17,* 151–160.

Randolph, D. L. (1972). Behavioral consultation as a means of improving the quality of a counseling program. *School Counselor, 20,* 30–35.

Reschly, D. J. (1976). School psychology consultation: "Frenzied, faddish, or fundamental." *Journal of School Psychology, 14,* 105–113.

Resnick, L. B., Wang, M. C., & Kaplan, J. (1973). Task analysis in curriculum design: A hierarchically sequenced introductory mathematics curriculum. *Journal of Applied Behavior Analysis, 6,* 679–710.

Rogers-Warren, A., & Warren, S. F. (Eds.). (1977). *Ecological perspectives in behavior analysis.* Baltimore: University Park Press.

Salmon-Cox, L. (1980). *Teachers and tests: What's really happening.* Paper presented at the annual meeting of the American Educational Research Association, Boston, MA.

Sandoval, J., Lambert, N. M., & Davis, J. M. (1977). Consultation from the consultees perspective. *Journal of School Psychology, 15,* 334–342.

Saturen, S. L. (1976). O.D. in Adams County School District No. 50. *Education and Urban Society, 8,* 196–212.

Schein, E. H. (1969). *Process consultation.* Reading, MA: Addison-Wesley.

Schmuck, R. A. (1971). Improving classroom group processes. In R. A. Schmuck & M. B. Miles (Eds.), *Organization development in schools.* Palo Alto, CA: National Press Books.

Schmuck, R. A., & Miles, M. (1971). *Organization development in schools.* Palo Alto, CA: National Press Books.

Schmuck, R. A., Runkel, P. J., Saturen, S. L., Martell, R. T., & Derr, C. B. (1972). *Handbook of organization development in schools.* OR: National.

Schowengerdt, R. V., Fine, J. J., & Poggio, J. P. (1976). An examination of some bases of teacher satisfaction with school psychological services. *Psychology in the Schools, 13,* 264–275.

Sulzer-Azaroff, B., & Mayer, G. R. (1977). *Applying behavioral analysis principles with children and youth.* New York: Holt, Rinehart, & Winston.

Tombari, M. L., & Davis, R. A. (1979). Behavioral consultation. In G. D. Phye & D. J. Reschly (Eds.), *School psychology: Perspectives and issues* (pp. 49–67). New York: Academic Press.

Tyler, M. M., & Fine, M. J. (1974). The effects of limited and intensive school psychologist-teacher consultation. *Journal of School Psychology, 12,* 8–16.

Wang, M. C. (1973). Psychometric studies in the validation of an early learning curriculum. *Child Development, 44,* 54–60.

Weissenberger, J. W., Fine, M. J., & Poggio, J. P. (1982). The relationship of selected consultant/teacher characteristics to consultation outcomes. *Journal of School Psychology, 20,* 263–270.

Woolfolk, A. E., Woolfolk, R. L., & Wilson, G. T. (1977). A rose by any other name . . . : Labeling bias and attitudes toward behavior modification. *Journal of Consulting and Clinical Psychology, 45,* 184–191.

9 Human Resource Development

Charles A. Maher
Susan A. Cook
Louis J. Kruger

Without human resources, organizations, including schools, are merely abstractions (Hersey & Blanchard, 1982). A school's human resources, particularly its administrators, teachers, and related specialists, are essential to effective organizational functioning. When school professionals are involved in ongoing competency development, the likelihood that quality educational services and programs will be provided and that effective schools will result is increased. (Mackenzie, 1983). The development of human resources is not an easy matter. It may very well be the most challenging endeavor for American education during the remainder of this century (Maher, Illback, & Zins, 1984).

In most schools, a range of professionals are involved in human resource development (HRD). For example, a school superintendant is involved in HRD when educating new administrators about their roles and responsibilities; a curriculum supervisor is performing a human resource development function by training teachers to employ a new reading program; a school principal or director of special services who encourages staff members to redesign working arrangements is too, involved in HRD; a special services provider, such as a school psychologist, engages in human resources development by assisting teachers to better manage classroom behavior; and the classroom teacher is a HRD specialist who assists children and youth to acquire valued knowledge, attitudes, and skills.

To some educators and special services providers, HRD development may be an obvious and important aspect of school organization. What may not be apparent to school professionals is how HRD in the school context can be meaningfully conceptualized and what technology can be effectively employed to develop exemplary levels of behavior and performance of school personnel.

221

In this chapter, human resource development in schools is considered from a behavioral perspective, reflected in five areas of discourse. First, need for and nature of HRD in schools is considered. Second, areas of human resource development that can benefit from a behavioral approach are delineated. Third, strategies and methods for developing a school's human resources are described. Fourth, application of behavioral technology, including a selective review of promising interventions, to HRD is discussed. Finally, guidelines for facilitating implementation of HRD into school organizational routines is presented. This chapter focuses on human resource development of administrators, teachers, and special services providers, such as school psychologists and counselors.

OVERVIEW OF HUMAN RESOURCE DEVELOPMENT IN SCHOOLS

Need for HRD in Schools

The task of developing a school's human resources, although most important in American schools, is also critical to other countries' educational institutions. Recent national commission reports, such as "The Nation at Risk" (National Commission on Excellence in Education, 1983) and the Carnegie Report (Boyer, 1983), have expressed concern about educational excellence in the United States, including quality of on-the-job performance of teachers and administrators. Moreover, recent investigations conducted under the jurisdiction of the United Nations Educational, Scientific, and Cultural Organization (UNESCO) indicate the importance of developing human resources to facilitate educational program implementation in countries throughout the world (Schwebel, 1983). Faced with concern over quality education and the reality that funding to hire highly trained professionals is no longer readily available, educational leaders are being called on not only to retain and develop existing personnel, but to reconceptualize who constitutes a school's human resources (Sarason, 1982). The limited view that only professional educators can increase the quality of service in the schools is being broadened and reformulated to include consideration of other viable and available human resources. Sarason (1982) notes that alternative and under-utilized individuals can serve a valuable function in the schools. The traditional and narrow conceptualization of professional and paraprofessional school staff as comprised of administrators, pupil personnel workers, teachers, and aides precludes consideration of college students, parents, grandparents, community volunteers, and even students, as potential members of the school work force.

A Behavioral Perspective on HRD

A behavioral perspective on HRD in schools advanced in this chapter is a broad-based one: Administrators, teachers, and special services providers collaborate to effect behavior and performance improvement of themselves and others. Such a perspective places a premium on identifying and empirically describing areas of professional competence in need of development, and stresses staff collaboration in selecting the most important competence development areas (Harshbarger & Maley, 1974). The perspective also encourages staff involvement in design, implementation, and evaluation of HRD interventions (Maher, 1984; Tuttle, 1983). In addition, a broad-based behavioral viewpoint facilitates recognition that staff behavior and performance influence and are influenced by school organizational factors, such as programs, policies, and procedures (Riley & Frederiksen, 1984). The idea that the workplace and worker have a reciprocal influence on each other, is a far cry from earlier views on the relationship between worker and workplace. Previously, the worker, the human resource to be developed, was seen solely as an "operant" that could be influenced to perform effectively by "top-down" approaches, such as policy and job specification, without involvement in decision making. This view is not supported in this chapter, or in contemporary management practice.

As a technology, a behavioral perspective provides a way to intervene to effect behavior and performance improvement of administrators, staff, and others. HRD in schools focuses on particular role-related behaviors of personnel, for example, the school psychologist's role of assessing the psychoeducational needs of a child. Such role-related behaviors, however, are not viewed as ends in and of themselves but in relation to the performance of the worker. For example, the school psychologist's gathering of appropriate child assessment information is viewed as a means to design a quality program for the child.

Behavioral technology may facilitate human resources development in school by means of several sequential, interrelated HRD activities. These activities can be seen within the "PRICE framework". PRICE is an acronym for the following activities:

- *P*inpointing human resource development needs and problems of school administrators, teachers and specialists that are involved in on-the-job behavior and performance improvement.
- *R*ecording current levels of on job behavior and performance of target individuals and groups in observable, measurable, reliable ways.
- *I*ntervening to develop and improve behavior and performance, especially by actively involving school personnel in the process.
- *C*onsequating desired levels of behavior and performance, to develop, improve, or maintain educational service productivity.
- *E*valuating behavior and performance improvement interventions.

The PRICE framework, in relation to HRD in schools, is detailed in a subsequent section of this chapter. In the next section, attention centers on areas where human resource development efforts may be targeted.

AREAS OF HUMAN RESOURCE DEVELOPMENT IN
SCHOOLS

Several areas of human resource development can be targeted for behavioral interventions: technical, interpersonal, professional competencies, and job satisfaction. Enhancement of the functioning of school personnel in these areas can be intrinsically valuable to an individual and may facilitate quality service delivery to pupils.

Technical Competencies

Three types of technical competencies are identified: (a) knowledge or information necessary to perform job roles; (b) knowledge and application of specific instructional or behavioral strategies to enhance learning of pupils or personnel; and (c) application of generic job related skills of problem-solving, communicating, and leading.

A job role can be defined as a set of organizational expectations about on the job behavior (Rizzo, House, & Lirtzman, 1970). As Sampson (1971) notes, clear role expectations facilitate coordinated activity between individuals and groups. Lack of clarity about job role has been associated with dysfunctional consequences for the individual and organization (Rizzo, House, & Lirtzman, 1970). Job role research, reviewed by Van Sell, Brief, and Schuler (1981), has indicated that role ambiguity is related to lower productivity and job dissatisfaction; clarification of job roles can result in positive performance outcomes. For example, clarification of teachers' roles on multidisciplinary teams increased their previously low participation in team meetings (Trailor, 1982).

Knowledge and application of specific instructional or behavioral strategies is also germane to attainment of school organizational goals. Technical competencies allow education to be divided into specialized units, such as elementary and secondary schools, that improve public education's capability to meet the learning needs of a diverse society (Sergiovanni & Starratt, 1983). Various job roles demand different types of technical knowledge and competencies. For example, it is assumed that the classroom teacher has expertise in instruction and curriculum development. Nonprofessionals, such as instructional aides, can also be valuable human resources to schools. Nonprofessionals can develop instructional or technical competencies, more limited in scope than a professional educator.

Another area of technical competence that can be developed through behavioral interventions are proficiencies of a generic nature applicable to most job roles within the school organization. One example of a generic job role proficiency is problem-solving. All school personnel are confronted with job related problems. Thus, personnel may benefit from a systematic approach to solving problems. Numerous conceptualizations of the problem-solving process exist (Parnes, Noller, & Biondi, 1977), consultation, a specific version of the process, (Bergan, 1977) is discussed later in this chapter.

Communication, another generic job role proficiency, is exemplified in written or oral modes. Communication can occur within the school organization, between individuals occupying similar roles (e.g., teacher to teacher) or between individuals occupying different roles (e.g., principal to student), and with individuals outside the school (e.g., parent-teacher conferences). Beall's (1981) literature review of the relationship between teaching and communication suggests that a teacher's ability to communicate to students is an important factor of instructional effectiveness.

Leadership, being able to influence others in desired ways, is another job role proficiency that can be targeted for development. Leadership skills of students can be developed, and these students can become prosocial role models for peers (Madden & Slavin, 1983). Leadership can also occur between individuals in different roles. For instance, a supervisor can exhibit leadership by influencing employees to perform in exemplary ways. After examining the implementation of a number of federally funded educational programs, Berman and McLaughlin (1978) concluded that the school principal's leadership (i.e., how program responsibilities were communicated to staff) was critical to the successful and continued implementation of these programs. As has been reported in the effective schools literature, the school principal's leadership proficiency has been documented as an important contributing factor to high achieving schools (Mackenzie, 1983.)

Interpersonal Competencies

Teaching is often described as a lonely profession. Movement toward team-building, group decision making, peer evaluation, and peer coaching can lessen isolation and increase active teacher involvement and interaction. However, according to Neale, Bailey, and Ross (1981): "As long as there is interaction there will be conflict" (p. 174). Schools, like other organizations, are often faced with conflict situations, as might be expected when diverse groups of personnel and pupils, and diverse goals and interests interact daily. Interpersonal competencies, such as conflict intervention and resolution skills, decision making and problem solving skills, and assertiveness skills are becoming increasingly important to maintenance of productive working relationships. In successful Japanese firms, a complex appraisal system is employed to facilitate improved team performance. These firms pay as much attention to enhancing cooperative interactions among personnel as they do to bottom line productivity (Hatvany & Pucik, 1981), attributes considered significant to the smooth operation of the company.

Professional Competencies

A third area of focus concerns aspects of professionalism. An individual need not be a highly educated professional to approach job duties and activities with professionalism, (i.e., with a measure of responsibility or accountability) that conforms to role expectations. Fulfilling job related obligations reliably and punctually contribute to professionalism. Competency is facilitated by clearly defined roles, performance expectations, and job parameters. Time management or improving utilization of time techniques may serve to expedite performance of duties and, therefore, contribute to professionalism.

Job Satisfaction

The three domains mentioned earlier reflect behavioral competencies, relevant to a discussion of human resource development in schools and appropriate for intervention. Job satisfaction is not a competency; however, because elements of an organizational and individual nature that contribute to job satisfaction may affect performance or demonstration of competencies, job satisfaction is an area of focus for HRD in schools. According to Sarason (1982):

> Constant giving in the context of constant vigilance required by the presence of many children is a demanding, draining, taxing affair that cannot be easily sustained. Even where it is sustained on a high level, it still does not always prevent guilt feelings because the teacher cannot give all that he or she feels children need. To sustain the giving at a high level required that the teacher experience getting. The sources for getting are surprisingly infrequent and indirect. One can get from children, but this is rarely direct. One can get from colleagues and administrators, but this is even more infrequent. One can get from oneself in the sense that one feels one is learning and changing and that this will continue, but this crucial source of getting is often not strong enough to make for a better balance between giving and getting. (p. 200)

In 1980, the National Education Association conducted a survey poll that revealed that 35% of all public school teachers were dissatisfied with their jobs (National Education Association, 1980). A number of hypotheses on the cause of job dissatisfaction and low morale have been offered. One theory encompasses the familiar concept of "burnout." According to Sarason (1981), burnout involves negative changes in behavior and attitude as a consequence of "a demanding, frustrating, and unrewarding work experience." (p. 203). Rugus and Martin (1979), have reviewed literature on school culture. They suggest particular aspects of the school culture related to teacher dissatisfaction and low morale. These aspects include: (a) emotional, psychological, and physical demands of teaching; (b) uncertainty predicated on the lack of validated technical procedures; and (c) relative isolation from colleagues. Different frames of reference held by teachers and administrators are also a possible cause of dissatisfaction and low morale. Gorton (1976), having examined research studies on morale and satisfaction, developed a set of recommendations for school administrators. Recommendations include: (a) obtain input and feedback, on issues perceived to be of concern, from staff on a regular basis; (b) attempt to increase teacher satisfaction gained from classroom teaching; (c) mediate interpersonal problems; (d) employ positive interaction skills with staff; and (e) provide for meaningful involvement of teachers in decision making. Ferren (1980) and Ricken (1980) emphasize the need for principals to take an active role in assisting staff to cope with stress and burnout issues.

Dunn and Dunn (1977) suggest that teacher satisfaction is most often derived from responsibility and personal achievement, recognition for achievement, opportunities to continue to learn and grow professionally and the opportunity to advance. Thus, issues of an organizational and individual nature are related to job satisfaction and appropriate for HRD interventions employing behavioral technology.

APPROACHES TO HUMAN RESOURCE DEVELOPMENT IN SCHOOLS

Five approaches for developing human resources in schools within a behavioral perspective can be identified: (a) supervision; (b) consultation; (c) organizational development; (d) inservice training; and (e) job design. The approaches are not always clearly distinguishable. For example, a consultant, supervisor, or inservice trainer could use a coaching strategy to develop a teacher's skills to communicate to parents. Moreover, at times, these approaches could be used primarily for purposes other than human resource development. For example, consultation, could be pupil-centered and not focus on consultee skill and knowledge development. Furthermore, each approach could be implemented with behavioral or nonbehavioral interventions. However, the emphasis in this chapter is on aspects of the approaches consistent with a broad-based behavioral perspective and primarily directed toward developing on the job behavior and performance of administrators, teachers, and special services providers.

Supervision

A need exists for development of effective interventions within supervisory relationships. Blumberg's (1980) review of the research in this area suggests that teachers perceive supervision to be of little value and, as generally practiced in the schools, not collaborative.

Different supervision models have been proposed for different role responsibilities; clinical supervision for instruction (Sullivan, 1980) and a systems model for school psychological services (Curtis & Yager, 1981). Based on their understanding of behavioral psychology literature, Kratochwill, Bergan, and Mace (1981) have proposed guidelines for behavioral models of supervision. They proposed that empirical assessment of the supervisee's performance should result from the repeated collection of data under various conditions. The assessment, as much as possible, should be based on overt supervisee behavior. They recommended standard setting for determining mastery level of skills. Emphasis is placed on the supervisor's utilization of empirical procedures to develop a supervisee's conceptual and practical skills. Similarly, the supervisor should encourage the supervisee to use empirically based procedures to carry out job responsibilities. Finally, Kratochwill et al. stress the importance of operationally defining supervisee skills targeted for development.

Consultation

Gutkin and Curtis (1982), in their review of school-based consultation, note that school personnel view consultation as one of the most important services that school psychologists can provide (see also Chapter 8). Gutkin and Curtis embrace Medway's (1979) definition of consultation as a process of "collaborative problem-solving between a mental health specialist (the consultant) and one or more persons (the consultees) who are responsible for providing some form of psychological assistance to another (the client)" (p. 276). Caplan (1970) has developed a typology of consultation based on the different purposes consultation can serve. The consultee-centered case consultation closely approximates consultation for the purpose of developing job relevant resources of personnel. Consultation differs from supervision because consultation is typically voluntarily engaged in by the participants (Caplan, 1970). In contrast, supervision is either legally mandated and/or mandated by organizational policy (Sergiovanni & Starratt, 1983).

After reviewing the research on school consultation, Medway (1979) concluded that studies of behavioral consultation interventions reported more consistent positive outcomes than nonbehavioral consultation interventions. Bergan (1977) has developed the most detailed framework for engaging in behavioral consultation. However, his framework of behavioral school consultation is primarily concerned with resolving pupil problems and not with developing human resources (Bergan, 1977). Nonetheless, for HRD purposes, the problem-solving stages in Bergan's framework are relevant to behavioral consultation.

The first stage in Bergan's framework, problem identification, involves specifying the problems to be addressed. A problem is defined as a discrepancy between observed and desired behavior. Problem analysis, the second stage, entails identifying problem maintaining variables and designing an intervention plan. During plan implementation, the third stage, the consultee implements the plan developed during the previous stage. The fourth stage, problem evaluation, involves evaluating goal attainment and plan effectiveness.

Organizational Development

A third major approach to human resource development in the schools is organizational development (Schmuck, 1982; see also Chapter 8). Although it may encompass consultation, the focus of organizational development is to help the school organization engage in self-study and improvement. School personnel are actively involved in the assessment and change of their organization. Organizational development in the schools takes into account the unique features of the school organization through social processes.

Organizational development differs from other approaches to human resource development because it emphasizes changing organizational processes instead of the structure of the organization. The assumption is that if changes are made in how organizational members relate to each other, human resources will be utilized more effectively. Schmuck (1982) has delineated three potential target areas for organizational change: interpersonal or communication skills, subsystem norms and roles, and school capacity for problem-solving.

Jerrell and Jerrell (1981) have reviewed the studies of organizational change efforts in the schools. They assert that "well-planned" projects tend to facilitate communication between staff, improve the school's problem-solving strategies, and increase staff involvement in decision making; positive related effects have been noted in the classrooms of these schools. Nonetheless, organizational development in the schools is a relatively understudied planned change approach, conclusions about its effectiveness are considered tentative.

Inservice Training

The general focus of in service staff development, "on-the-job" training, has been the refinement or fine-tuning of existing skills, or the mastery of new ones. The ultimate goal has been to positively impact on student performance (Joyce & Showers, 1980). Techniques employed to impart knowledge have included visits to other schools, performance evaluations, conventions, professional journals, short or "one-shot" workshops, and courses at local colleges (Wagstaff & McCullough, 1973). In the early 1970s, teacher service centers began to emerge. In 1973–74, Schmieder and Yarger (1974) estimated that 4,500 teacher center programs were operating. Diverse in nature, the emphasis was on teachers sharing ideas with colleagues (Neale, Bailey, & Ross, 1981). In a study of 37 federally funded centers (Mertens & Yarger, 1981), a typical project recorded 330 instances per month of voluntary participation by teachers in programs that support professional needs.

Unfortunately, Wood and Thompson (1980) have reported state and national studies that suggest the majority of educators, teachers and administrators alike, are dissatisfied with staff development and in-service programs. Just as Wagstaff and McCullough reported in 1973, Wood and Thompson (1980) report, "inservice training, as it is now constituted, is the slum of American education. It is disadvantaged, poverty-stricken, neglected, and has little effect" (p. 374). As interpreted by Wood and Thompson, a major shortcoming is that workshops and courses devote energy to information dissemination instead of to facilitating appropriate practice or implementation of new information. The continued use of inadequate in-service training programs may be due, in part, to the paucity of outcome information relative to evaluating the extent to which teachers transfer learning from the in-service program to the classroom.

According to Wood and Thompson (1980), educators' dissatisfaction with current staff development programs encompasses complaints, such as poor planning and organization, inadequate needs assessments, program activities unrelated to day-to-day problems of participants, unspecified objectives, and lack of follow-up. It is worthwhile to note that despite their unhappiness with the current "state of the art", educators at all educational levels see staff development as a critical component to the improvement of education.

Having reviewed 97 research studies on in-service teacher education, Lawrence (1974) concluded that in-service programs would be more likely to accomplish their goals if they did the following: (a) individualized programming; (b) provided an active, rather than a passive, role for teachers; (c) integrated demonstrations; (d) included supervised practice and feedback; (e) offered opportunities for teachers to aid one another; (f) were complementary with a school's general effort to improve staff development (as opposed to isolated workshops); and (g) allowed teachers the opportunity to select relevant goals and activities.

Joyce and Showers (1980) reviewed 200 studies that explored the impact of various in-service training methods. They concluded that the most effective training programs would likely incorporate five steps: (a) presentation of theory and/or new skill; (b) demonstration or modeling of targeted skills; (c) response practice in a classroom or simulated setting; (d) structured and open-ended feedback; and (e) coaching in the application and transfer of new skills into the classroom.

Beyond addressing the introduction of new skills and teaching methods, staff development programs are beginning to incorporate workshops and short courses in areas relevant to the maintenance of high quality teaching and/or job satisfaction. These areas have included such topics as time management, stress management, and conflict management. Schools lag behind the business sector in providing employees with more individualized assistance with problems likely to reduce productivity and impede professionalism. Many companies, large and small, have developed employee assistance programs (EAPs), which originated some 40 years ago, to combat the problems of alcoholism. Many programs have now expanded to address such problems as depression, anxiety, life crises, divorce, marital problems, and addictions, problems that can result in deteriorating job performance. In addition to treatment of existing problems, the concept of "mental wellness" programming has emerged (Curran & Kiefhaber, 1980). In mental wellness, early identification of problems is emphasized, employees are provided with education programs to increase awareness of how personal problems can affect job performance.

In an era when stress and burnout are significant issues in schools, the educative and therapeutic EAP concept may be useful to consider within a broadened conceptualization of in-service staff development.

Job Design

Job design focuses on characteristics of and relationships between work tasks and how to set conditions so the tasks may be performed in an exemplary manner (Gilbert, 1978). Job design involves altering aspects of tasks and revising work environments (Beer. 1980). This HRD approach is based on the assumption that workers will be more satisfied with their jobs and perform at higher levels if they perceive their work as important, interesting, and varied. Designing jobs to enhance on-the-job behavior, performance, and satisfaction can be guided by several principles (Beer, 1980). These principles include; (a) structuring tasks that relate to one another and to the whole; (b) combining tasks; (c) increasing variety of tasks to be performed; and (d) developing improved communication channels among workers.

Educational work tasks, however, have often been viewed by school administrators and staff as inflexible (Boyer, 1983). For example, classroom teachers have considered themselves contained by norms for behavior and performance established in the school building and by curricular mandates (Goodland, 1984). Possibly, because of perceived limitations on the flexibility of their work, little empirical research has been done on the effects of job design interventions in the school setting. Job design research that has been conducted in the educational arena suggests several possible interventions. These include: (a) varying teacher work tasks through rotational assignments (Neale, Bailey, & Ross, 1981); (b) utilizing multidisciplinary work teams (Maher & Yoshida, in press); and (c) implementing teacher support teams and quality circle approaches with school staff (Maher, in press; Maher & Kruger, 1984).

USING BEHAVIORAL TECHNOLOGY TO DEVELOP HUMAN RESOURCES IN SCHOOLS

Behavioral technology in schools can be used with one or more approaches to human resource development: supervision, consultation, organizational development, in-service training, and job design. As discussed previously, the acronym PRICE serves to identify five activities of a problem-solving process that can guide implementation of HRD behavioral interventions. Interventions are targeted at developing technical, interpersonal, and professional competencies and job satisfaction. In general, public education has lagged behind business and industry in the utilization of HRD behavioral interventions, either because of perceived systemic constraints, or because of the nature of the field itself (i.e., productivity or performance standards often have not been measured by direct impact on student performance).

Pinpointing

The first activity of the problem-solving process involves pinpointing human resource development problems in observable and measurable ways. Maher and Bennett (1984) outline several steps in the process of pinpointing these problems. They recommend that multidisciplinary teams (MDT) be involved in the process (i.e., individuals from various disciplines, such as teachers, counselors, and principals).

Two criteria can be used to identify the human resource development problems to be clarified. Problems should be judged to be important relative to delivering services to students and problems should be amenable to the intervention effort. Two feasible methods of identifying problems are group discussion and use of survey instruments. Once identified, problems can be prioritized and selected for intervention. Again, two criteria can be used to guide prioritization and selection of problems for intervention: the perceived importance of the problem, and the extent to which the problem is clearly related to human resources (see Maher & Bennett, 1984, for a detailed description of such procedures). After problems have been prioritized and selected according to these guidelines, the personnel who are to be the recipients of human resource interventions can be identified. Staff needs for human resource development should be delineated for educational services and programs of concern. Delineation facilitates identification of competencies deemed instrumental for personnel to possess to implement the services and programs in question.

Maher and Bennett (1984) suggest at least three methods that can be used to help identify competencies: (a) the literature germane to the job role can be reviewed; (b) relevant staff can be interviewed or observed performing duties; and (c) brainstorming can be employed. The outcome of the *P*inpointing activity of PRICE is a list of competencies seen as instrumental to the delivery of educational services or programs.

Recording

Maher and Bennett (1984) also have proposed guidelines for recording the staff's existing competency levels. After a list of competencies has been generated, methods need to be selected to record or measure the extent to which staff posseses those competencies. Methods can be used to assess a staff's perceptions of their competencies and to measure their competencies directly.

Questionnaires and interviews are two common methods of collecting data on staff's perceptions of their competencies. Although surveying staff's perceptions may provide important planning information, the perceived need approach has limitations; surveys may be inconsistent with data gathered from more direct measures of competencies. For example, survey results may indicate that school psychologists do not perceive deficiencies in their report writing skills. However, systematic evaluation of reports written by psychologists, according to agreed standards, may suggest many deficiencies. When data generated from more direct measures of competency, such as observation, permanent product review, or performance tests, conflict with data gathered from a perceived-need survey, additional clarification of the human resource development problem is warranted. Due, in part, to the possibility of perceived-need survey data being inconsistent with more direct measures of competencies, it is desirable to collect both types of data. Furthermore, Maher and Bennett (1984) suggest the best candidates for HRD interventions may be those whose competency needs have been identified through both a perceived-need survey and more direct measures.

Following the selection of assessment methods, data collection instruments should be selected or constructed. Construction of data collection instruments, such as a questionnaire, requires considerable expertise. Schools should consult with persons knowledgeable about instrument construction when such assistance is needed (see Cronbach, 1980, for a more extensive discussion of instrument construction).

If the staff group to be assessed is large, sampling can be an efficient means of measuring competencies. Representative staff sampling can be less costly in time for both data collectors and those being assessed. If practical constraints dictate that not all human resource needs identified can be addressed, needs can be prioritized in order of importance. Maher and Bennett (1984) recommend that priority for intervention be given to needs that are related to a significant educational service delivery problem and are likely to be responsive to interventions.

Intervening to Change Behavior and Performance

A wide variety of behavioral interventions are available to address the myriad of problems found in any organization. Several of those with documented or potential applicability to HRD in schools are briefly discussed. These include: modeling, performance feedback, team building, behavioral self-management, decision making/problem-solving, and programmed instruction. (It is important to note that interventions may also be employed as part of supervision, consultation, organizational development, and in-service training approaches).

Modeling. Based on social learning theory (Bandura, 1977), behavior modeling has increased in popularity as an intervention for interpersonal and psychomotor skill development of employees (Meyer & Rarch, 1983). Modeling consists of sequential and interrelated strategies that include: (a) exposure to a modeled display of the target behaviors; (b) behavioral rehearsal; (c) social reinforcement; and (d) transfer/generalization of the newly learned skills to the work setting.

Exposure to a modeled display of the targeted behavior may occur through the use of live models or symbolic models (films, videotapes, etc.). Research has indicated that identification with the model and the behaviors engaged by the model, will enhance the skill development of the trainee. For example, in a study reported by Porras and Anderson (1981), supervisory personnel who engaged in a management program to develop more effective interaction skills with subordinate personnel were shown videotapes of a fellow supervisor effectively employing the targeted skills. The videotapes were filmed in plants run by the trainees company, this served to facilitate generalization from the training session to the work world of the employees.

Practice of new skills, also known as behavioral rehearsal, usually follows exposure to the model. This step is essential to acquisition of new skills. Staff development programs that omit this step often impart knowledge and theories, but lose efficacy because the trainees have not had the opportunity to rehearse the skill and to add it to their behavioral repetoires. Role-playing and simulations of actual problem situations that the trainee may encounter are coupled with feedback and coaching provided by the trainer for the execution of the targeted behavior. Practice is continued until the trainee has successfully acquired the skill. This procedure facilitates stable behavior changes and increases the probability of transfer to the work setting. Social reinforcement is provided by fellow trainees during behavior rehearsal and in response to trainees' attempts to utilize the new skill in the actual work settings. Skill generalization is promoted as trainees problem solve ways to apply newly acquired skills to new and unique problem situations.

In a study reported by Porras et al. (1982), a modeling procedure was employed to develop supervisory behaviors related to interpersonal skills in a large wood products corporation. Not only was the modeling program successful in the development and utilization of problem solving behaviors, the data further suggested an increase in productivity and improved labor relations.

Using a variation of behavioral modeling, Jones, Fermour, and Carples (1977) explored the pyramid model of training with elementary school teachers. Pyramid training attempts to increase the cost effectiveness of teacher training programs by teaching a limited number of teachers new skills (developing an in-house "expertise hierarchy"), and then having each teacher train several other teachers. In two inner city schools, a modeling/coaching procedure was employed to teach three elementary school teachers to implement a classroom management skill package. These three teachers, with supportive guidance, trained three other teachers. Results suggested that the three original teachers were able to train colleagues to a high level of proficiency in classroom management skills.

Wood and Thompson (1980) reported on a successful program conducted by the Long Beach Unified Schools District in California. In a program designed to improve teaching techniques in reading and mathematics, staff were provided training in four areas: (a) teaching math and/or reading objectives; (b) diagnostic and prescriptive instructional competencies; (c) clinical supervision; (d) and follow-up maintenance and skill "fine-tuning." For each component, the same programmatic sequence was followed: introduction and modeling of a skill by workshop facilitators, practice of the skill with small groups of students, provision of feedback by other observing participants, and analysis of the lesson. After 8 years and 1,000 teacher participants, the program has demonstrated its worth as measured by impact on student achievement.

Meyer and Rarch (1983) report a study using behavioral modeling with sales representatives to increase sales. Results indicated improved sales, and when the training group was compared with a control group that did not receive the modeling procedure, the unexpected benefit of reduced employee turnover.

Performance Feedback. According to Frederiksen (1982): "feedback intervention strategies, designed to provide information to individuals or groups about the quantity or quality of their performance, have been impressively effective producing organizational change" (p. 282). In the business sector, as compared with the educational community, the provision of performance feedback is made easier by the objective criteria of performance against which workers performance may be compared (e.g., number of objects assembled per day). Objective criteria against which to evaluate employee performance is essential to the success of the procedure.

Feedback systems feature numerous elements that make them attractive to an organization. Frederiksen (1982) notes that performance feedback interventions are cost efficient, simple to implement, often decrease reliance on punishment or disciplinary procedures, and are feasible for organizations limited in ability to provide rewards or monetary incentives to influence behavior. Performance feedback interventions frequently yield results that extend beyond improved job performance. For example, Sims and Szilagyi (1975) reported increased job satisfaction and improved productivity, following input based on objective job performance. These findings suggest a positive reciprocal relationship between employee satisfaction and job performance.

Mechanisms for the delivery of performance feedback generally fall into four categories: oral, written, mechanical, and self-recorded. Oral feedback is considered to be the most common form of delivery. Written feedback can be provided in a variety of formats, written evaluations, personal communications, and newsletters. Tape printouts and videotapes are subsumed under the mechanical feedback category. Self-recording, or self-monitoring, has potential advantages that include active participation of the employee and suitability to settings with minimal regulated supervision (Frederiksen, 1982). Komaki, Blood, and Holder (1980) used self-monitoring techniques to increase work-related social skills of fast food restaurant staff.

Performance feedback interventions, as effective as they seem to be, are not appropriate for all organizational problems. To help evaluate their suitability Frederiksen (1982) offers the following guidelines:

1. Determine if individuals with the organization possess the requisite skills for adequate job performance.

2. If workers do not possess the necessary skills for adequate job performance, implement appropriate training programs, personnel actions, etc.

3. If lack of skills or knowledge was not a component of performance problems, assess reasons for unacceptable performance. Identify the relative contributions of worker behavior and other factors (e.g., structural characteristics of the task) to the low performance level.

4. Determine the performance standards operating within an organization and their clarity. If performance standards are ambiguous or unreasonable, set new standards upon which an organizational consensus can be reached.

5. After performance standards are established, reassess the need for a performance feedback intervention. (p. 287)

Team-Building.   Team-building refers to a category of interventions that target the functional work groups of organizations (Beer, 1976). Team-building attempts to facilitate coordinated action between members of the same group or organization (Abelson & Woodman, 1983). Maher and Hawryluk (1983) have suggested that school-based teams may be an underutilized service delivery resource; Yoshida (1983) has questioned the efficacy of child study teams; and others (e.g., Weick, 1976), have claimed that the subsystems of educational organizations are ''loosely coupled'' and difficult to coordinate. Therefore, a need for team-building in the schools is indicated.

Beer (1976) has identified four frameworks of team-building: (a) role clarification; (b) goal-setting; (c) interpersonal; and (d) the managerial grid. Major aspects of the role clarification, goal-setting, and interpersonal frameworks have been implemented in the schools (Woodman & Sherwood, 1980). Often, elements from different frameworks are combined in team-building interventions. Although a variety of team-building activities have been identified in the literature, the typical sequence of activity phases are problem recognition, data collection, assessment, planning, implementation, and evaluation (Dyer, 1977; Woodman & Sherwood, 1980).

Of the 10 school related team-building studies reviewed for this chapter, 8 reported overall favorable outcomes. One study of team-building in elementary schools (Schmuck, Murray, Smith, Schwartz, & Runkel, 1975) and a study of team-building with a consortium of theology schools (Brown, Aram, & Boeh mer, 1974) failed to indicate overall positive outcomes. However, a study of team-building with school administrators (Coelho, 1975), 2 junior high school studies (Bigelow, 1971; Schmuck, Runkel, & Langmeyer, 1969), a high school study (Fosmire, Keutzer, & Diller, 1971), and 4 studies of multidisciplinary teams (Maher, 1980, 1981b, 1982; Trailor, 1982) reported positive results.

Only one of these studies could be classified as primarily role clarification in its orientation (Trailor, 1982). In the role-clarification study training was provided for teachers in their roles on child study teams. The training resulted in increased teacher participation during team meetings.

Four studies could be considered variants of the goals-setting version of team-building (Brown, Aram, & Baehner, 1974; Maher, 1980, 1981, 1982). The outcomes of the Brown, Aram, and Baehner (1974) study were mixed. No improvement in goals consensus was found and perceptions of coordination problems increased rather than decreased. On a positive note, both the accuracy and amount of information shared increased. All three Maher studies (1980, 1981b, 1982) indicated positive results. For example, Maher (1980) trained child study teams in an explicit problem-solving system. The training decreased response time to pupil referrals for specific services, and increased the number of individualized education programs planned and evaluated by the teams.

Two studies combined elements of the goal-setting and interpersonal frameworks for team-building; both studies reported favorable outcomes (Bigelow, 1971; Formire, Keutzer, & Diller, 1971). Bigelow (1971), for example, reported that team-building activities were associated with the development of improved school climate and teacher transfer of skills into the junior high school's class rooms.

Three studies involved elements of three team-building frameworks: goal-setting, interpersonal, and role clarification (Coelho, 1975; Schmuck, Murray, Smith, Schwartz, & Runkel, 1975). Of the three studies, only Schmuck et al. (1975) failed to find favorable outcomes. In the Schmuck et al. study, investigators speculated that the relative lack of positive outcomes for the experimental schools compared with control schools might, in part, have been a function of the control schools incidentially receiving organizational development assistance from other consultants.

Team-building in the schools for the purpose of human resource development, although underresearched, is a promising area. The goal-setting framework and elements from this framework have been studied more often than other team-building frameworks and, for the most part, the results support its efficacy.

Behavioral Self-Management.   Behavioral self-management programs actively engage individuals in assessment, monitoring, and modification of some aspect of their behavior that is judged desirable for change. Before any behavior change procedures are instituted, activities are employed to help clarify the problem. These activities are designed to accomplish the following: (a) specify the problem in behavioral terms; (b) identify the intensity, frequency, and/or duration of the problem; and (c) identify antecedents or consequences that serve to trigger or maintain the problem. The first step in clarifying a problem of self-management involves translating the problem into behavioral terms (pinpointing a problem behavior so that it is observable or measurable). Once a problem behavior has been targeted and operationalized, it is possible to select a method of measurement. The most familiar methods for self-monitoring a behavior include measuring frequency of occurrence and/or duration of occurrence (Frederiksen, 1982). A third form of behavioral measurement involves judgments of intensity. Problematic on-the-job feelings or emotions, such as anxiety, tension, or anger, can be recorded on rating scales or checklists. One checklist used is the Subjective Units of Discomfort Scale. Self-monitoring of frequency and/or duration can be completed through the use of watches or wrist counters. A frequency count would be appropriate to measure how may cigarettes an individual smokes a day; a watch would be appropriate to measure the amount of time one spends on the telephone with co-workers. If an individual wished to measure how often over the course of a week he/she was late for appointments and by how long, a combination of frequency count (how many times late) and duration count (how many minutes late) could be employed.

Self-monitoring what happens before and after a behavior occurs (i.e., behavioral antecedents and consequence) can provide information about the stimuli that trigger a particular behavior and what consequences encourage or discourage a behavior (Watson & Tharp, 1981). Keeping a log or diary of behavioral antecedents, targeted behavior, and behavioral consequences may help to select appropriate intervention strategies.

Stress management is another area in which behavioral procedures can be helpful. Events in the environment that cause an individual to respond maladaptively with physical, psychological, or behavioral symptoms can be construed as stressors. For any stress management program to succeed, an individual must become aware of stress responses and environmental events that may precipitate these responses (Miller & Pfohl, 1982). Monitoring events, mediating thoughts that precede stress responses (antecedents), resultant emotional reactions, or bodily sensations can facilitate awareness of stress responses.

When stressors and individual stress responses have been carefully defined, a number of cognitive-behavioral interventions can be considered. Interventions include cognitive restructuring techniques, rational–emotive strategies, stress innoculation, problem-solving, and techniques to induce physical relaxation responses (Miller & Pfohl, 19G2). For treatment of teacher stress and anxiety, Walton (1981) has proposed that biofeedback be used alone or in conjunction with relaxation training and systematic desensitization. Schloss, Sedlak, Wiggins, and Ramsey (1983) reported a 3 month stress reduction program that employed relaxation training and systematic desensitization with teachers of residentially placed, behavior disordered adolescents. Forman (1982) incorporated stress inoculation techniques into a stress management program to decrease stress and anxiety in 12 urban secondary school teachers. Sanders and Glynn (1981) successfully used self-management strategies, self-monitoring, goal selection, and planning skills, as an adjunctive strategy to facilitate maintenance and generalization of management skills used with preschool, behavior disordered children.

According to Sylvester (1983): "The school is generally considered to be a major source of stress in the lives of both students and staff" (p. 3). Among the many sources of stress identified by school administrators in a study by Koff, Laffey, Olson, and Cichon (1980), insufficient time for carrying out responsibilities emerged as an important source of stress. It is likely that most other school personnel would echo this lament. Napoleon Bonaparte's notable quotation, "You can ask me for anything you like, except time," rings as true today as in the past. Using self-management techniques to address time management problems, Dunn and Dunn (1977) advocated the use of self-administered time analysis logs. A daily time log requiring self-monitoring of activities at half-hour intervals, in addition to a time analysis log, may help an individual to reorder priorities. According to Dunn and Dunn, duties/activities can be characterized as high, medium, or low priority by an individual. One might immediately schedule high prioriety activities, delegate medium ones, and delegate or discard low ones.

As with all instances of behavioral self-management, selection and implementation of interventions are accompanied by self-reinforcement procedures and are followed by evaluation of effectiveness. Maher (1981a) reported a pilot study that succeeded in increasing the percentage of time devoted by school psychologists to behavioral counseling, and individualized education program planning and evaluation. The time management program employed a behavioral problem-solving approach that consisted of five steps: (a) orientation to time management; (b) time management problem analysis; (c) plan development; and (d) implementation; and (e) plan evaluation.

Another successful use of behavioral self-management was demonstrated by Burgio, Whitman, and Reid (1983). They taught staff at an institution to increase the frequency of their interactions with severely retarded residents. Strategies employed included teaching staff to self-monitor and graph, set standards, self-evaluate, and self-reinforce.

Along with stress and time management, school personnel, like members of any organization, are frequently faced with conflict situations. In these situations self-management strategies can be applied to facilitate problem resolution. Negben (1978) defines conflict as any interaction in which two or more parties perceive that they have incompatible goals. Maher (1981a) suggests that in work situations conflict can be either interpersonal or intrapersonal, related to role conflict or role ambiguity. Role overload conflict, poor administrative communication patterns, policy changes in the school, structural factors, or conflict-promoting interactions can also cause conflict. Negben (1978) offers four categories of conflict management techniques: (a) avoidance techniques; (b) use of force; (c) use of a third party; and (d) rational approaches. Rational approaches to interpersonal conflict resolution include strategies of problem-solving or constructive confrontation, compromise or bargaining, and persuasion. Maher (1981a) has also suggested the recognition and replacement of irrational ideas with more rational ones, and that the elimination of dichotomous reasoning and over-generalization can serve to diminish conflict.

Problem-Solving/Decision Making.   Much attention has been given to effective problem-solving and decision making strategies, because they contribute to efficient functioning of organizational systems (MacCrimmon & Taylor, 1976). Decision making is frequently subsumed under the umbrella category problem-solving, because it generally involves selection of a solution from a set of alternative choices. Problem-solving encompasses identification and assessment of a problem, generation and consideration of alternative solution choices, selection of alternative implementation, evaluation and reinforcement. To identify and assess a problem effectively, an individual must be cognizant of the current state of affairs (e.g., of job performance), the desired state of affairs, and the significance or impact of the gap that exists between the two states (MacCrimmon & Taylor, 1976).

Eight steps to collaborative problem-solving have been identified by Blake and Mouton (1961): (a) definition of the problem; (b) review of the problem; (c) generation of alternatives; (d) debate of alternatives; (e) search for solutions; (f) exploring solutions; (g) weighing alternative solutions; and (h) selection of the most appropriate solution.

Porras and Anderson (1981) reported on the development of a successful organizational program for supervisors in a large wood products firm. The program was designed to improve interpersonal behaviors and interactions with subordinates, and to address, among other things, decreased productivity. A problem-solving approach based on principles of social learning theory was employed, it encompassed phases of problem identification, problem-solving, and follow-up.

Inservice Training.   In their review of methods of training teachers in behavior modification, Allen and Forman (1984) identified six procedures; formal didactic instruction, cueing, modeling, role playing, performance feedback and positive social reinforcement. These procedures had been investigated in relation to training teachers in behavior modification.

Their review suggests that formal didactic instruction, alone, may not be an effective in-service training procedure; didactic instruction can be most effective when coupled with one of the other five procedures. Cueing may be defined as in vivo prompts intended to facilitate appropriate teacher responses. According to Allen and Forman, cueing has yielded ambiguous results. Modeling is teacher observation of a trainer demonstrating appropriate responses. In the studies reviewed, modeling was often used in conjunction with the role-playing of appropriate responses. Allen and Forman concluded that a moderate amount of evidence supported the efficacy of role-playing in combination with modeling. Of the six training procedures, performance feedback on teacher responses had the most empirical support. Feedback that occurred more frequently than once-a-day in a training package with didactic presentations was particularly effective in training teachers. Finally, Allen and Forman noted that although outcome data on the effects of positive social reinforcement (e.g., praise) was promising, only two studies had investigated the procedure as a means to train teachers in child behavior modification. Because of the relatively small number of studies reviewed and the methodological problems inherent in some of the studies, Allen and Forman's conclusions should be considered tentative.

Although the concept of in-service training or personnel development in the schools is often narrowly construed as the vehicle through which teachers improve teaching, the utility and value is much broader. In the area of special education, Maher and Bennett (1984) suggest three critical issues that make personnel development essential to the provision of good service. These include: (a) the need to keep people abreast of ever advancing knowlede in the field; (b) the need to reduce employee stress and burnout; and (c) the need to identify and provide for training needs of personnel, mandated by law.

Training provided to multidisciplinary teams is one area of personnel development that has received attention in the last several years. Groups of individuals are involved as teams in a critical process related to the education of exceptional children, the development of the Individualized Education Program (IEP). Several researchers have pointed to the increased efficiency and desirability of active participation by all team members in the decision-making process (the whole is greater than its parts). In response, Anderlini (1983) described an in-service or personnel development program designed to effect such participation. The program is presented to small groups of teams, and involves three components: team dynamics, communication, and problem-solving/decision-making. Through the team dynamics component, participants are provided with a better understanding of skills and concepts related to team building. To improve communication skills, the communication component focuses on improving participants' skills in actively listening and clearly sending messages. The object of the third component (problem-solving/decision making) is to improve participants' ability to employ a problem-solving sequence, the S-T-P Problem Solving procedure (Schmuck et al., 1977). Within the components of the program, group leaders employ a variety of training techniques that include presentation/lectures, simulations/role plays, and skill practice. The program has been implemented in several western states. It incorporates most of the elements of sound personnel development programs, discussed previously, and illustrates the utility of these programs with multi-disciplinary teams in schools.

Programmed Instruction. Based on the work of B. F. Skinner and S. L. Pressey, programmed instruction (PI) is an intervention designed to teach systematically new content/information in a self-paced fashion. PI is a method in which instructional segments or steps are carefully designed, later material is based on acquisition of earlier material. Two major variations of PI have been employed: linear programs and branching techniques (Hinrichs, 1976). Linear programs progress sequentially through material to be acquired; branching techniques employ subroutines to which a learner is directed when he/she has difficulty mastering particular content. Instruction in the PI format employs behavioral learning techniques, such as successive approximation, shaping, feedback of results, and reinforcement of correct responses. Hinrichs (1976) assets that those who support the use of carefully engineered PI favor it for the following reasons:

1. It involves the trainee by requiring active responses.

2. It is individualized and self-paced rather than under the authoritarian control of a trainer.

3. Knowledge of results can provide immediate reinforcement for correct responses in a nonthreatening (private) manner.

4. Challenge and interest can be built into the training sequence by branching techniques and humorous or unexpected responses within the program format.

5. When necessary updating and revision of the program can be done, based upon data and experience acquired through use.

6. Perhaps most important, writing the program requires careful organization and prestudy of the content of what is to be included, optimum sequencing of the content, and testing—a process which should supercede all training program designs, but which seldom does. (p. 850)

"Adjunctive autoinstruction" PI is not limited to books; it includes such formats as tape, slide, video, and computer-based instruction (Frederiksen, 1982). Despite such diversity, PI is limited to training and development in areas where objectives are easily operationalized and content is systematically organized. McCormick (1979) reports a study that successfully incorporated programmed instruction into an in-service program designed to teach teachers effective instructional practices that incorporate principles of learning. Having utilized filmed lectures and programmed instructional booklets, resulting posttest data indicated that teachers' knowledge of instructional skills and their ability to apply the new skills was significantly increased.

Consequating Desired Behavior and Performance

Applied behavior analysis is the application of a variety of techniques toward the attainment of the goal of modifying behavior. The concept of behavior modification originated with the work of B. F. Skinner (1953) and the development of principles of learning theory. Because a prime assumption of behavior management is that behavior is a function of its consequences, behaviorists have focused their energies on the law of effect: If behavior is followed by a positive consequence, the probability that particular behavior wll reoccur increases. A corollary to the law of effect is that behavior, followed by aversive procedures or consequences, is likely to decrease. Since its introduction, behavior modification has been used successfully with a wide variety of disabled populations (e.g., retarded individuals, autistic or behavior disordered children, psychiatric hospital patients, etc., O'Brien & Dickinson, 1982). More recently, principles and procedures of behavior modification have been applied to such diverse problems as smoking, obesity, littering, and energy conservation. During the last 15 years, industrial and other organization settings have begun to incorporate behavior principles into the management of problems, such as employee productivity, safety infractions, low work attendance, and tardiness.

The most frequently used consequences to effect behavior change include reinforcement and aversive procedures (punishment and extinction). Social reinforcement (i.e., compliments, praise, solicitation of advise from peers, etc.) is worthwhile, particularly for highly educated professionals, such as educators (Frederikson, 1982).

Other positive reinforcers include consumables (e.g., coffee breaks, wine and cheese parties), tangibles (e.g., plaques of commendation, desk space, prizes), visual and auditory stimulation (e.g., music, professional journals, popular guest speakers, asthetically appealing work environment), tokens (e.g., movie and theater tickets, vacation time, stock, money), and intrinsically related reinforcers (e.g., desired special assignments, paid time off, use of school, company recreation or other facilities for personal needs). However, Spuck (1974) and Lortie (1975) suggest that extrinsic reinforcers or incentives, such as salary increases for teaching, are limited in explication.

Luthans, Paul, and Baker (1981) compared changes in 82 retail store clerks performance behavior under two conditions. The control group of 41 clerks was informed of the performance standards work would be measured against. The experimental group of 41 workers was provided with a contingent reinforcement package that included paid time off, opportunity for a paid vactaion, and equivalent cash. Performance of the experimental group was significantly improved; the control group's performance remained the same. Miller (1977) was able to increase sales representatives performance dramatically in a chemical company when he changed bonus delivery from a yearly to monthly schedule.

Miller and Swick (1976) identified a number of rewards or incentives that would increase the probability that teachers would provide more effective instruction. These included: acknowledgment of efforts for self-improvement, compensation to support self-improvement efforts, rewards for accomplishments, and community acknowlegment of teacher efforts. McDonald (1979) studied extrinsic reward structure in the classroom. He reported that transmitting knowledge to students was the primary source of satisfaction reported by teachers.

Aversive or punishing consequences, particulary those of criticism (pay docking, and fines) also serve to reduce the probability that a targeted behavior will occur, but the research literature suggests that the change will likely be temporary in nature. Despite the above caveat, in industry control by sanctions continues to be the technique most frequently employed. Some examples of aversive procedures include: (a) time-out, which on the basis of engaging in an undesirable behavior, for example, operating a machine above safety standards, will result in a period of time in which the individual is deprived of the opportunity to gain positive reinforcement; and (b) response cost, which, as a result of engaging in an undesirable behavior, involves having the individual give back or lose something rewarding.

Most researchers agree that positive reinforcement, or the provision of desired rewards or incentives, is preferred over aversive procedures, particularly with adults.

Evaluating Changes in Behavior and Performance

Evaluating changes in behavior or performance for the purpose of staff or school improvement implies that data generated from the evaluation should be useful to plan future staff development. Therefore, the data must inform decision makers about the extent of change in the targeted behavior and of the extent to which the intervention was implemented as planned (see Maher & Bennett, 1984, for a more detailed discussion of implementation evaluation; see also Chapter 10.)

The approaches used to evaluate change in behavior or performance should, in part, be a function of the school's planning information needs relative to human resources development. Four different types of evaluation questions that correspond to four different types of information needs are discussed. These questions concern goal attainment, cause-effect, related effects, and consumer reaction.

One question concerns the extent to which the goals of the intervention were attained. Assessing goal attainment requires precisely defined objectives for each goal. Maher and Bennett (1984) have identified several methods for evaluating goal attainment of personnel development, including questionnaire, interview, reviewing work samples, ratings by peers and supervisors, and tests of knowledge.

A cause-effect question is concerned with whether the intervention was responsible for the observed changes in behavior or performance. This question can be asked when decision makers are concerned that factors other than the intervention may be responsible for the observed change. Approaches to cause-effect evaluation focus on minimizing the probability that nonintervention factors caused the change. Cook and Campbell (1979) provide an extensive discussion of the merits of various approaches used to evaluate cause-effect in field settings (see also Chapter 10).

The related effects question addresses the concern that the intervention may have effects other than the intended ones. Related effects can be judged to be positive or negative. A number of evaluation approaches, similar in design to cause-effect approaches, can be used to assess related effects (see Maher & Bennett, 1984 for one recommended approach).

Finally, consumer reaction to the intervention can be evaluated. Consumers are the recipients of the intervention and other individuals indirectly impacted by the intervention. Pupils, for example, might be consumers who are indirectly impacted by human resource interventions with teachers. The consumer reaction evaluation is one of the most common types of evaluations conducted with personnel development interventions (Maher & Bennett, 1984). Consumer reaction information might indicate ways in which intervention can be improved. Satisfaction with the intervention and perceptions of goal attainment are two commonly assessed consumer reaction variables. Questionnaire and interview are two survey methods typically employed in consumer reaction evaluations.

FACILITATING THE IMPLEMENTATION OF HRD IN SCHOOLS

A behavioral perspective on human resources development (HRD) in schools can facilitate the overall task of developing a school's human resources, including the design, implementation, and evaluation of HRD programs. Implementing HRD in schools is a fairly complex endeavor. Therefore, without recognition of the need to engage in a systematic way to implement HRD in schools, or without attention to organization factors that may inhibit implementation efforts, behavioral approaches to HRD most likely will not be carried out in a majority of public educational systems. In this section, guidelines are presented to facilitate the implementation of HRD in schools.

Considering Organizational Factors

Organizational factors may hinder or encourage attempts to implement HRD in schools. To assure that HRD activities are successful, it is important to minimize organizational factors that might inhibit the implementation of behavioral interventions, and to maximize factors that would help make an HRD initiative occur as planned.

In assessing the organizational context of a school system for behaviorally oriented HRD, various readiness factors should be considered to determine if implementation problems exist, to identify areas of organizational strength, and to design ways to intervene to minimize problems that have been detected. First, it is important to consider the availability of funds and personnel that can be allocated in sufficient amounts to HRD. Determining availability of funds and personnel is particularly important in situations where HRD endeavors are to occur across more than one school site or over extended periods of time, such as an entire school year. Second, the values of school staff who are to be involved in the endeavor need to be understood. If key staff members do not perceive HRD interventions as compatible with the schools' prevailing philosophy and norms, the chances of an intervention being successfully carried out may be minimal. Third, what the idea of HRD means to school administrators and staff is important to know prior to implementation. If, for example, the majority of staff view HRD as a large scale attempt at control or manipulation, the idea of HRD as a means to assist in continued staff development and improvement would have to be presented and discussed with concerned members. Fourth, if the organization in which HRD programs are to occur is not administratively stable, such as when a special services director who is supportive of HRD is about to leave the district for other employment, the circumstances for going ahead with a particular effort may not be appropriate. In contrast, a fifth factor, timing, relates to recent events or developments in the system that suggest the "time is right" for HRD, such as the availability of additional state funds to support evaluation activities.

Three other organizational readiness factors should also be considered before proceeding with the design and implementation of HRD programs. Obligation, the extent to which the school staff perceives a need for HRD and is willing to participate in activities. If staff do not feel obligated, another factor, resistance to participation, may result. A final, but most important factor, closely related to obligation and resistance, is yield, or "payoff". For example, administrators may see HRD as a positive event because meaningful staff improvement may result; others may view the endeavor as a waste of time.

Various options may be employed to assess organizational readiness relative to the eight factors mentioned. Two practical options are to interview school staff about the factors, or to administer a questionnaire to staff, such as an "organizational readiness questionnaire." Information indicating lack of organizational readiness for HRD can be used to develop interventions intended to increase readiness. For example, assessment of the organizational readiness factors might indicate insufficient funds to support a particular HRD effort. In this instance, a grant writing strategy might be undertaken to secure necessary funding from a state discretionary account. Similarly, organizational interventions can be planned and implemented for other factors considered impediments to organizational readiness (a more detailed discussion of assessing and facilitating readiness can be found in Maher, 1984).

Influencing Durability

To assure that HRD programs will be implemented as planned and will remain durable over time in a school organization, a strategic planning method can be employed. Seven factors, which can be easily remembered by using the acronym, DURABLE, describe the strategy: *Discussing, *Understanding, *Reinforcing, *Adapting, *Building, *Learning, and *Evaluating. These factors comprise an explicit, seven-step process: (a) *Discuss* the nature and scope of the HRD program with school staff; (b) *Understand* and assess the school's readiness for the program; (c) *Reinforce* school staff for participation in implementation and utilization of HRD activities; (d) *Adapt* the program to the special circumstances of the school; (e) *Build* in positive expectations about HRD; (f) *Learn* about the on-the-job needs of school staff; and (g) *Evaluate* the worth of the program for schools staff. These steps can be used by individuals involved in HRD programming.

Discussing.   The nature and scope of the HRD program is discussed with school administrators and classroom teachers. Discussion occurs at individual meetings (e.g., with the principals), small group meetings (e.g., with teachers by grade-level), and faculty meetings. The primary intent of the discussion is to enable school personnel to become aware of the HRD program and to answer their questions about the program.

Understanding.   An attempt is made to gain a more detailed view of the concerns of school staff about particular aspects of the HRD program. This kind of understanding can result from follow-up meetings with individual principals, lead teachers, or board of education members.

Reinforcing.   The intent of this step, which occurs throughout the planned change approach, is to reinforce school staff for participation in the implementation and utilization of the program. A range of reinforcers, such as verbal praise, written memos to the school principal expressing thanks for staff cooperation, and public posting (e.g., in faculty room) of data on program participation, can be used at appropriate times.

Adapting.   The purpose of this step is to adapt the program to the organizational needs and concerns of the school staff. Attempts can be made to incorporate appropriate suggestions into program operations. For example, if concerns about lack of competency in developing of IEP goals and behavioral objectives were expressed by a multidisciplinary team, several in-service training sessions could be held.

Building.   Cooperative working relationships are "built" with school staff who are to be involved in the HRD program. Strategies used to build relationships and expectations include active involvement with staff in discussing the program.

Learning.   Attempts are made to learn more about the needs of staff that might be addressed by the program.

Evaluating.   The purpose of evaluating on a regular basis (e.g., monthly) is to judge the extent to which the HRD program is worthwhile. Assessment data can be collected from written feedback from staff and by informal discussions with staff.

SUMMARY

Human resource development has been considered from a behavioral perspective and as an important aspect of school organization. Areas in which HRD may occur, school personnels' technical and interpersonal competencies, general professional areas, and personnel job satisfaction, were discussed. Supervision, consultation, organizational development, inservice training, and job design were considered approaches that can be targeted for the development of administrators, teachers, and staff. The PRICE framework and related activities were presented to describe how behavioral technology can be utilized to develop a school's human resources. In addition, how HRD approaches and behavioral interventions may be implemented in schools was discussed as an important organizational consideration.

REFERENCES

Abelson, M. A., & Woodman, R. W. (1983). Review of research on team effectiveness: Implications for teams in schools. *School Psychology Review, 12,* 125–136.

Anderlini, L. S. (1983). An inservice program for improving team participation in educational decision making. *School Psychology Review, 12,* 160–167.

Allen, C. T., & Forman, S. G. (1984). Efficacy of methods of training teachers in behavior modification. *School Psychology Review, 13,* 26–32.

Bandura, A. (1977). *Social learning theory.* Englewood Cliffs, NJ: Prentice-Hall.

Beall, M. L. (1981, April). *Communication competence and teaching: An interface.* Paper presented at the Annual Meeting of the Central States Speech Association, Chicago, IL.

Beer, M. (1976). The technology of organization development. In M. D. Dunette (Ed.), *Handbook of industrial and organizational psychology.* Chicago, IL: Rand-McNally.

Beer, M. (1980). *Organizational change and development: A systems view*. Santa Monica, CA: Goodyear.

Bergan, J. R. (1977). *Behavioral consultation*. Columbus, OH: Charles F. Merrill.

Berman, P., & McLaughlin, M. W. (1978). *Federal programs supporting educational change, Vol. VIII: Implementing and sustaining innovations*. Santa Monica, CA: Rand-McNally.

Bigelow, R. D. (1971). Changing classroom interaction through organization development. In R. A. Schmuck & M. B. Miller (Eds.), *Organization development in schools*. Palo Alto, CA: National Press.

Blake, R. R., & Mouton, J. S. (1961). *Group dynamics—key to decision making*. Houston, TX: GULF.

Blumberg, A. (1980). *Supervisors and teachers: A private cold war (2nd ed)*. Berkeley, CA: McCutchan.

Boyer, E. L., (1983). *High school: A report on secondary education in America*. New York: Harper & Row.

Brown, L. D., Aram, J. D., & Boehmer, D. J. (1974). Interoganizational information sharing: A successful intervention that failed. *Journal of Applied Behavioral Science, 10*, 533–554.

Burgio, L. D., Whitman, T. L., & Reid, D. H. (1983). A participative management approach for improving direct care staff performance in an institutional setting. *Journal of Applied Behavior Analysis, 16*, 37–53.

Caplan, G. (1970). *The theory and practice of mental health consultation*. New York: Basic Books.

Coelho, R. S. (1975, February). *Administrative team approach: Development and implementation*. Paper presented at the American Association of School Administrators Annual Meeting, Dallas, TX.

Cook, T. C., & Campbell, D. T. (1979). *Quasi-experimentation: Design and analysis for field settings*. New York: Rand-McNally.

Cronbach, L. J. (1980). *Essentials of psychological testing* (3rd ed.) *New York: Harper and Row*.

Curran, J., & Kiefhaber, A. (1980, Fall). *Mental wellness programs in industry: A survey report. Alcohol, Health, and Research World*, 54–58.

Curtis, M. J., & Yager, G. G. (1981). A systems model of the supervision of school psychological services. *School Psychology Review, 10*, 425–433.

Dunn, R., & Dunn, K. J. (1977). *Administrator's guide to new programs for faculty management and evaluaton*. West Nyack, NY: Parker.

Dyer, W. G. (1977). *Team building: Issues and alternatives*. Reading, MA: Addison-Wesley.

Fairbank, J. A., & Prue, D. M. (1982). Developing performance feedback systems. In L. W. Frederiksen (Ed.), *Handbook of organizational behavior management*. New York: Wiley.

Ferren, A. S. (1980). How teachers survive in the system. *Pointer, 24*, 39–44.

Forman, S. G. (1982). Stress management for teachers: A cognitive-behavioral program. *Journal of School Psychology, 20*, 180–187.

Formire, F., Keutzer, C., & Diller, R. (1971). Starting up a new senior high school. In R. A. Schmuck & M. B. Miller (Eds.), *Organization development in schools*. Palo Alto, CA: National Press.

Frederiksen, L. W. (Ed.) (1982). *Handbook of organizational behavior management*. New York: Wiley.

Gilbert, T. (1978). *Human competence: Engineering worthy performance*. New York: McGraw-Hill.

Goodland, J. (1984). *A place called school: Prospects for the future*. New York: McGraw-Hill.

Gorton, R. A. (1976). *School administration: Challenge and opportunity for leadership*. Dubuque, IA: Brown.

Gutkin, T. B., & Curtis, M. J. (1982). School-based consultation: Theory and techniques. In C. R. Reynolds & T. B. Gutkin (Eds.), *The handbook of school psychology*. New York: Wiley.

Harshbarger, D. D., & Maley, R. F. (1974). *Behavior analysis and systems analysis: An integrative approach to mental health programs*. Kalamazoo, MI: Behaviordelia.

Hatvany, N., & Pucik, V. (1981, Spring). Japanese management practices and productivity. *Organizational dynamics,* 5–21.

Hersey, P., & Blanchard, K. (1982). *Management of organizational behavior: Utilizing human resources.* Englewood Cliffs, NJ: Prentice-Hall.

Hinrichs, J. R. (1976). Personnel training. In M. D. Dunette (Ed.), *Handbook of industrial and organizational psychology.* Chicago, IL: Rand-McNally.

Jerrell, J. M., & Jerrell, S. L. (1981). Organizational consultation in school systems. In J. C. Conoley (Ed.), *Consultation in schools: Theory, research, procedures.* New York: Academic Press.

Jones, F. H., Fermour, W., & Carples, S. (1977). Pyramid training of elementary school teachers to use a classroom management "skill package." *Journal of Applied Behavior Analysis, 2,* 239–253.

Joyce, B., & Showers, B. (1980). Improving inservice training: The messages of research. *Educational Leadership, 36,* 379–385.

Koff, R., Laffey, J., Olson, G., & Cichon, D. (1980). Stress and the school administrator. *Administrator's Notebook, 28,* 9.

Komaki, J., Blood, M. R., & Holder, D. (1980). Fostering friendliness in a fast food franchise. *Journal of Organizational Behavior Management, 2,* 151–164.

Kratochwill, T. R., Bergan, J. R., & Mace, F. C. (1981). Practitioner competencies needed for implementation of behavioral psychology in the schools: Issues in supervision. *School Psychology Review, 10,* 434–444.

Lawrence. G. (1974). *Patterns of effective inservice education.* Tallahassee, FL: Florida State Department of Education, Florida Educational Research and Development Program. (ERIC Document Reproduction Service No. ED 176 424).

Lortie, D. C. (1975). *School teacher: A sociological study.* Chicago, IL: University of Chicago Press.

Luthans, F., Paul, R., & Baker, D. (1981). An experiental analysis of the impact of contingent reinforcement on salespersons' performance behavior. *Journal of Applied Psychology, 66,* 314–323.

MacCrimmon, K. R., & Taylor, R. N. (1976). Decision making and problem solving. In M. D. Dunette (Ed.), *Handbook of industrial and organizational psychology.* Chicago, IL: Rand-McNally.

Mackenzie, D. E. (1983). Research for school improvement: An appraisal of some recent trends. *Educational Researcher, 12,* 5–17.

Madden, N. A., & Slavin, R. E. (1983). Mainstreaming students with mild handicaps: Academic and social outcomes. *Review of Educational Research, 4,* 519–569.

McCormick, W. J. (1979). Teachers can learn to teach more effectively. *Educational Leadership, 37,* 59–60.

McDonald, R. A. (1979). *A study of the intrinsic reward structure of the classroom for the teacher.* (Doctoral dissertation, University of Toronto, 1978). *Dissertation Abstracts International, 40,* 585A.

Maher, C. A. (1980). Implementation and evaluation of behavioral, school-based special service delivery system. *Child Behavior Therapy, 1,* 32–41.

Maher, C. A. (1981a). Decision analysis: An approach for multidisciplinary teams in planning service programs. *Journal of School Psychology, 19,* 340–349.

Maher, C. A. (1981b). Time management training for school psychologists. *Professional psychology, 12,* 613–620.

Maher, C. A. (1982). A team approach for planning and evaluating personnel development programs. *Exceptional Children, 49,* 230–236.

Maher, C. A. (1984). Description and Evaluation of an approach to implementing programs in organizational settings. *Journal of Organizational Behavior Management, 5,* 69–98.

Maher, C. A. (in press). The teacher support team. *Educational Treatment of Children.*

Maher, C. A., & Bennett, R. E. (1984). *Planning and evaluating special education services.* Englewood Cliffs, NJ: Prentice-Hall.

Maher, C. A., & Hawryluk, M. K. (1983). Framework and guidelines for utilization of teams in schools. *School Psychology Review, 12,* 180–185.

Maher, C. A., Illback, R. J., & Zins, J. E. (1984). Applying psychology in schools: Perspectives and framework. In C. A. Maher, R. J. Illback, & J. E. Zins (Eds.), *Organizational psychology in schools: A handbook for Professionals.* Springfield, IL: Charles C. Thomas.

Maher, C. A., & Kruger, L. J. (1984). *The quality circle approach: Description and application to school psychological services.* Manuscript submitted for publication.

Maher, C. A., & Yoshida, R. K. (1985). *Multidisciplinary teams in schools: A review of research. In T. R. Kratochwill (Ed.), Advances in school psychology* (Vol. 4). Hillsdale, NJ: Lawrence Erlbaum Associates.

Medway, F. J. (1979). How effective is school consultation? A review of recent research. *Journal of School Psychology, 17,* 275–282.

Mertens, S. K., & Yager, S. J. (1981). *Teacher centers in action.* Syracuse, NY: Syracuse University, Syracuse Area Teacher Center.

Meyer, H. H., & Rarch, M. S. (1983). An objective evaluation of a behavior modeling training program. *Personnel Psychology, 36,* 755–761.

Miller, L. M. (1977). Improving sales and forecast accuracy in a nationwide sales organization. *Journal of Organizational Behavior Management, 1,* 39–51.

Miller, R., & Pfohl, W. F. (1982). Management of job-related stress. In R. M. O'Brien, A. M. Dickinson, & M. M. P. Rosow (Eds.), *Industrial behavior management.* Elmsford, NY: Pergamon Press.

Miller, L. G., & Swick, J. (1976). Community incentives for teacher excellence. *Education, 96,* 235–237.

National Commission on Excellence in Education. (1983). Washington, DC: United States Office of Education.

National Education Association (1980). Teacher opinion poll: Job satisfaction. *Today's Education, 69,* 8.

Neale, D. C., Bailey, W. J., & Ross, B. E. (1981). *Strategies for school improvements.* Boston, MA: Allyn & Bacon.

Negben, M. K. (1978). Conflict management in schools. *Administrators Notebook, 26,* 6.

O'Brien, R. M., & Dickinson, A. M. (1982). Introduction to industrial behavior modification. In R. M. O'Brien, A. M. Dickinson, & M. M. P. Rosow (Eds.), *Industrial behavior modification.* Elmsford, NY: Pergamon Press.

Parnes, S. J., Noller, R. B., & Biondi, A. M. (1977). *Creative action.* New York: Scribners.

Porras, J. I., & Anderson, B. (1981, Spring). Improving managerial effectiveness through modeling-based training. *Organizational Dynamics,* 60–77.

Porras, J. I., Harges, K., Patterson, K. J., Maxfield, D. G., Roberts, S. N., & Bies, R. J. (1982). Modeling-based organizational development: A longitudinal assessment. *The Journal of Applied Behavioral Science, 194,* 433–446.

Ricken, R. (1980). Teacher burnout: A failure of the supervisory process. *National Association of Secondary School Principals Bulletin, 64,* 21–24.

Riley, A. W., & Frederiksen, L. W. (1984). Organizational behavior management in human service settings: Problems and prospects. *Journal of Organizational Behavior Management, 5,* 3–16.

Rizzo, J. R., House, R. J., & Lirtzman, S. I. (1970). Role Conflict and ambiguity in complex organizations. *Administrative Science Quarterly, 11,* 233–245.

Rugus, J. F., & Martin, M. (1979). The principal and staff development: Countering the school culture. *Clearing House, 53,* 27–31.

Sampson, E. E. (1971). *Social psychology and contemporary society.* New York: Wiley.

Sanders, M. R., & Glynn, T., (1981). Training parents in behavioral self-management: An analysis of generalization and maintentance. *Journal of Applied Behavior Analysis, 14,* 223–237.

Sarason, S. B. (1982). *The culture of the school and the problem of change* (2nd ed.) Boston, MA: Allyn & Bacon.

Schloss, P. J., Sedlak, A. A., Wiggins, E. D., & Ramsey, D. (1983). Stress reduction for professionals working with aggressive adolescents. *Exceptional Children, 49,* 349–354.

Schmieder, A. A., & Yarger, S. J. (1974, November). *Teacher centers: Toward the state of the scene.* (ERIC Clearinghouse on Teacher Education).

Schmuck, R. A. (1982). Organization development in the schools. In C. R. Reynolds & T. B. Gutkin (Eds.), *The handbook of school psychology.* New York: Wiley.

Schmuck, R. A., Runkel, P. J., & Langmeyer, D. (1969). Improving organizational problem-solving in a school faculty. *Journal of Applied Behavioral Science, 5,* 455–482.

Schmuck, R. A., Murray, D., Smith, M. A., Schwartz, M., & Runkel, M. (1975). *Consultation for innovative schools: O. D. for multi-unit structure.* Eugene, OR: Center for Educational Policy and Management.

Schmuck, R., Runkel, R., Arends, J., & Arends, R. (1977). *The second handbook of organization development in the schools.* Palo Alto, CA: Mayfield.

Schwebel, M. S. (1983). *Research on cognitive development and its facilitation: A state of the art report.* Paris: United Nations Educational, Scientific, and Cultural Organization, Division of Structures, Content, Methods, and Techniques (available in English, French, Spanish).

Sergiovanni, T. J., & Starratt, R. J. (1983). *Supervision: Human perspectives.* New York: McGraw-Hill.

Sims, H. P., & Szilagyi, A. D. (1975). Leader reward behavior and subordinate satisfaction and performance. *Organizational Behavior and Human Performance, 14,* 426–438.

Skinner, B. F. (1953). *Science and Human behavior.* New York: MacMillian.

Spuck, D. W. (1974). Reward structures in the public schools. *Educational Administration Quarterly, 10,* 18–34.

Sullivan, C. G. (1980). *Clinical supervision: A state-of-the-art review.* Washington, DC: Association for Supervision and Curriculum.

Sylvester, R. (1983). The school as a stress reduction agency. *Theory into Practice, 23,* 3–7.

Trailor, C. B. (1982). Role clarification and participation in child study teams. *Exceptional Children, 49,* 529–530.

Tuttle, T. C. (1983). Organizational productivity: A challenge for psychologists. *American Psychologist, 38,* 479–480.

Van Sell, M., Brief, A. P., & Schuler, R. S. (1981). Role conflict and role ambiguity: Integration of the literature and directions for future research. *Human Relations, 34,* 43–71.

Wagstaff, L., & McCullough, T. (1973). In-service education: Education's disaster area. *Administrator's Notebook, 21,* 8.

Walton, J. M. (1981). Biofeedback: A proposed model for the treatment of teacher anxiety. *The Personnel and Guidance Journal, 60,* 59–62.

Watson, D. L., & Tharp, R. G. (1981). *Self-directed behavior: Self-modification for personal adjustment,* (3rd ed.). Monterey, CA: Brooks/Cole.

Weick, K. E. (1976). Educational organizations as loosely coupled systems. *Administrative Science Quarterly, 21,* 1–19.

Wood, F. H., & Thompson, S. R. (1980). Guidelines for better staff development. *Educational Leadership, 37,* 374–378.

Woodman, R. W., & Sherwood, J. J. (1980). The role of team development in organizational effectiveness. *Psychological Bulletin, 88,* 166–186.

Yoshida, R. K. (1983). Are multidisciplinary teams worth the investment? *School Psychology Review, 12,* 137–142.

10 Program Evaluation and Research

Thomas R. Kratochwill
F. Charles Mace
Mary S. Bissel

Evaluation of psychological and educational services is important for several reasons (Maher & Kratochwill, 1980). To begin with, there is increased accountability in public psychological and educational settings, especially in special education and related services (Barbacovi & Clelland, 1977). Second, professional standards for the practice of psychological services mandates evaluation and accountability in applied programs (American Psychological Association, 1981). Increasing emphasis on ethical and legal concerns of the quality of service necessitates some type of program evaluation in conducting psychological and educational services. Third, increasingly, individuals who provide the tax-base for services in applied settings are interested in the outcome of those services (Morrisey & Safer, 1977; see also Chapter 11). Concerns in this area reflect the allocation of resources during difficult financial times, the enactment of laws mandating certain types of educational services (e.g., PL 94–142), and the need for information by individuals in charge of special programs so decisions can be made about program improvement and development of new programs. Fourth, professionals are especially concerned about evaluating their own programs during times in which questions are being raised about the quality of services and the need for their services in applied settings (Kratochwill, 1982).

PROGRAM EVALUATION AND RESEARCH

In this chapter an overview of some program evaluation and research issues that should be considered in evaluating psychological and related educational services is provided, evaluation methodology, design issues, and some conceptual/methodological issues related to the program evaluation area are discussed. Each is discussed with various examples from the evaluation literature in the psychological field. Traditionally, program evaluation or evaluation research has been broadly conceptualized as a scientifically based activity initiated to assess the operation and impact of public policies and the action programs designed to implement these policies (Bernstein & Freeman, 1975). Some writers make a distinction between program evaluation and research. For example, Koocher and Broskowski (1977) have drawn a distinction between evaluation research, which emphasizes the standards of science, and program evaluation, which is viewed as an intrical part of program management and planning but is only secondarily designed to discover new knowledge. Nevertheless, scientific technology or the methods of scientific research can certainly be used in program evaluation. Usually, individuals assume that program evaluation must consist of compromises in the application of the methods of social science research; however, it is assumed that these methods will still be used (Weiss, 1972).

Professionals who have specific training in conventional research activities will still be able to use many of these skills in program evaluation activities. Yet, program evaluation differs from the more basic and applied research because variables in program evaluation are not necessarily carried out in an analogue context. Moreover, by the way problems are chosen and defined, how hypotheses are formulated, the degree to which inference is tolerated, and how the results are reported may differ from more well-controlled research (Rossi, Freeman, & Wright, 1979; Rossi, & Wright, 1977). When considering the distinction between program evaluation and research in behavioral psychology several important issues are worthy of consideration. The major distinction between the two activities lies in the differences in their purpose and goals (Barlow, Hayes, & Nelson, 1984). As these authors have noted, the differences lie on a continuum when considering the goals of treatment versus those of research. In pure treatment, client improvement is the primary concern; in treatment evaluation, client outcome is of primary concern, but the practitioner is interested in knowing if the client actually improved. Methods of research may be used because they provide information on client improvement. In contrast, treatment research is designed to generate scientific understanding and knowledge. Although client improvement is hoped for, it is usually or sometimes secondary to the research issues under investigation. Finally, in more "pure" research activities, client improvement may be a very low or even an irrelevant concern, such as in basic research on psychopathology, to generate data of theoretical interest. Thus, although the methods may be similar, the goals of research and program evaluation differ.

Barlow et al. (1984) state:

> There are a number of short- and long-term consequences, both for the client and the practitioner, which accrue when treatment is elevated to treatment evaluation or to treatment research. Since, in treatment research, increased client functioning is

only a side effect of the main goal of generating better organized scientific statements, treatment research would seem to decrease the probability that an individual client would be helped by participating. In treatment evaluation, however, scientific goals are subsumed under the goal of increasing client functioning. Thus, treatment evaluations seems to increase the likely benefits of treatment with little increased risk . . . treatment evaluation is a matter of adopting an empirical approach to treatment activities. Treatment evaluation is likely to make interventions more systematic, with better information supporting clinical decisions. It is hard to see how this would fail to help therapy [although this assumption has not yet itself been tested empirically.] (p. 285)

PROGRAM OUTCOME EVALUATION/RESEARCH

In the broadest context, program evaluation is a process by which the investigator obtains information about program development, improvement, and outcome (Maher & Kratochwill, 1980). In the process, the evaluator/researcher uses various assessment strategies, research designs and methods, and data evaluation strategies. In behavioral evaluation and research, a number of assessment techniques and procedures are used to conduct what is conventionally called "needs assessment" and "process evaluation"[1] It is beyond the scope of this chapter to review these issues in detail (the interested reader is referred to other Chapters of the present text and to Chapters 3, 4, 5, and 6 of Barlow et al., 1984, for a discussion of these issues in behavioral assessment).

This section of the chapter focuses on issues and strategies surrounding outcome evaluations. Outcome evaluation is a program evaluation activity that allows judgments to be made about program validity and attainment of program goals. A number of different designs and procedures have been used in program evaluation and research. The design employed is the framework through which the evaluator or researcher is able to establish the efficacy of the intervention. Of course, other factors (e.g., measurement, random assignment of subjects to conditions) are needed to achieve an evaluation of high quality. In any study in which the experimental variable is manipulated the researcher is interested in establishing a relation between the independent and dependent variable, ruling out factors that may be extraneous to the observed effect. Alternative explanations for this relation are usually referred to as threats to internal validity (Campbell & Stanley, 1963; Cook & Campbell, 1979).

---

[1]In traditional program evaluation technology, a *needs assessment* is an activity that involves identification of needs of a program on a client and the prioritization of these needs as a basis for program development. *Process evaluation* involves the judgments to be made about the manner in which a program has been implemented according to the plan established.

In program evaluation research, experimental paradigms include quasi- experimental and randomized experimental designs. Research conducted within these experimental paradigms typically involve an intervention, dependent variables, and a comparison between intervention and no intervention. Somewhat less formalized preexperimental research procedures called "case studies" are also used in an evaluation/research context. These procedures are typically conducted under conditions that may not allow the researcher to rule out threats to the internal validity of the study. Each type of research strategy is discussed and typical examples from the professional literature are presented.

The Case Study

Case study evaluation research refers to an investigation of an individual or group where the usual experimental controls are lacking (Kazdin, 1980, 1981). At the extreme of lacking experimental control, such studies are usually characterized by (a) no formal design; (b) no replication; (c) no controlled observation; (d) lack of rigorous instrumentation; and (e) subjective description of effects (Kratochwill, 1979). The usual case study is subject to almost every threat to experimental validity. Case studies were and often still are characterized by the therapist's (author's) narrative and subjective account of client (subject) behavior, the intervention used, and outcome of the "treatment." There is little or no attempt to draw comparisons, a process central to well-controlled experimental research. Varying treatment strategies often overlap, with no measures taken to differentiate between the efficacy of each component. The lack of precise and credible data sometimes has been accompanied by a claim for remarkable success of the program, a feature that undoubtedly contributes to the lack of credibility associated with these methods in contemporary evaluation methodology.

Despite these limitations, case study methods have made numerous methodological contributions (e.g., Davidson & Costello, 1969; Dukes, 1965; Kaz din, 1980, 1981; Lazarus & Davidson, 1971; Shontz, 1965). Case study investigations serve important functions in research and evaluation (Kazdin, 1980). First, case studies provide sources of ideas and hypotheses about the development of behavior. As an example, in the study of children's fears, case studies (e.g., Little Hans, Little Albert) provide the basis for development of theoretical and treatment procedures (Morris & Kratochwill, 1983). However, both psychoanalytic and behavioral approaches have tended to rely too heavily on these early cases, as has been evident in the analysis of the Little Albert study (cf. Harris, 1979). Second, they have also been the source of various therapeutic techniques and applications. Procedures discussed in case study reports are sometimes shared in professional journals, and procedures are extended by clinicians in their own work. Third, they have provided a format for the study of rare cases. In some circumstances the case study has provided information on a rare disorder (the "Three Faces of Eve," Thigpen & Cleckley, 1957, or "Dibs, in

Search of Self,'' Axline, 1964, that otherwise would have been lost to the professional community. Fourth, case studies have provided a counterinstance to acceptable intervention procedures. For example, many early therapy case studies demonstrated that it was not necessary to use trained professionals to implement programs. As these counterinstances were disseminated, the practice of using paraprofessionals became more acceptable in providing psychological and educational services.

Increasing recognition of the importance of the role of case studies in research and evaluation has prompted some writers to recommend procedures that can help promote drawing more valid inferences from case study strategies. For example, Kazdin (1981) advanced five features that, when addressed, can help make case studies more credible. First, researchers and program evaluators should try to use objective measures (e.g., direct measures of behavior) whenever possible. Second, continuous measurement, rather than prepost type measurement should also be employed. Third, past and future projections of what the dependent variable was and what it will be without intervention are important for drawing valid inferences. For example, in individual program evaluation activities, if a child has been a severe discipline problem for several months, it is unlikely that he/she will change without some type of formal intervention. An intervention that shows marked improvement would allow greater inference when the problem has been chronic. Fourth, the type of effect is important for valid inferences because a strong and immediate effect will likely be more attributable to the intervention than one that is small and delayed. Finally, both the number and heterogeneity of the subjects are important dimensions. Usually, there will be stronger inference for an intervention effect if replication occurs across several subjects; if subjects represent a diverse group (i.e., demographic characteristics), replications of the intervention across cases will provide stronger inference.

Aside from these considerations, the case study has served an important role in helping to bridge the gap between research and practice. In many situations, designing a controlled experiment or program evaluation for the sake of experimental comparison might be unethical, like in the case of a subject displaying self-destructive or violent behavior toward others. In applied settings, sophisticated methodological strategies may be impossible to implement (e.g., design and certain assessment strategies). In these circumstances the case study may be the only alternative. In addition, the case study would be valuable because it would typically be implemented under conditions that reflect the reality of applied work.

Quasi-Experiments

Several classes of designs used in research and program evaluation are regarded as quasi-experimental because they usually contain all aspects of true experiments (e.g., manipulation of an independent variable, measurement of a dependent variable), but randomization is not used to draw inferences for the intervention effect (Cook & Campbell, 1979). Thus, randomization is not used to establish the internal validity of the study. There are two general types of quasi-experimental procedures: nonequivalent group designs (e.g., one group posttest only design, posttest only design with nonequivalent groups, and one group pretest–posttest design); and time-series designs. Examples of both types of designs are presented. A more detailed treatment of time-series strategies is presented because of their frequent application to behavioral research and program evaluation.

Nonequivalent Group Designs.   Like most traditional group research and evaluation methods, the unit of analysis in nonequivalent groups designs is a group of individuals. Typically, the mean performance of subjects is examined prior to and/or following the administration of a particular intervention and subsequent conclusions are made about its effects on the dependent variables. However, nonequivalent group designs are subject to numerous threats to internal validity (Campbell & Stanley, 1963). Because group formation is not via randomization procedures, the extent to which subject characteristics of a given group interact with treatment to produce an effect is unknown. Thus, comparisons to no-treatment groups or measurement occasions are confounded by such factors as history, instrumentation, maturation, testing, statistical regression, and selection biases. Yet, for researchers forced to use these designs the outlook is not completely dim; options are available for strengthening the experimental validity of such studies (see Cook & Campbell, 1979; Kazdin, 1980).

The one-group posttest-only design involves collecting data on a single group following exposure to some intervention. No pretests or comparison groups are employed, as a result, the design has two fundamental flaws. To begin with, the absence of preintervention measures questions whether the observed effects represent a change following the intervention experience. Because there is no way to document performance without intervention, few valid inferences can be drawn. Second, there is the problem of verifying how subjects would have fared had they received no intervention at all. Without a control group, rival hypotheses, such as history and maturation, cannot be discounted. In view of these limitations it is not surprising that this design is little used in behavioral research and program evaluation.

The posttest-only design with nonequivalent groups improves on the preceeding design by including a no-intervention control group. Because intervention and control subjects are being assessed following intervention the researcher/program evaluator has some basis for comparison. Still problematic, however, is the possibility that posttest differences are due to preexisting group differences rather than or in addition to any intervention effects. In most cases, this flaw renders the design uninterpretable. However, as Cook and Campbell (1979) point out, this design can be strengthened when pretest data, other than the dependent variable under analysis, can be obtained to indicate that no substantial pretest differences were present. Greenleaf (1982) demonstrated this approach in the evaluation of a transfer or generalization training program targeting the interpersonal skill "helping others." Seventy-five "disruptive" male students were assigned to the following five experimental groups via nonrandom methods: (a) an interpersonal skill training program plus skill transfer training; (b) the interpersonal skill training only; (c) the skill transfer training only; (d) an attention control group, and (e) a brief instructions only control group. Acquisition and generalization of the interpersonal skill was assessed by means of a direct test (i.e., subject responses to vignettes provided during training) and two generalization tests (i.e., subject responses to novel vignettes and situations). Although the direct test involved pre and posttest measures, the extent to which subjects generalized to novel situations was evaluated on the basis of posttest performance only. The results of the analysis were supportive of the need to program generalization (Stokes & Baer, 1977), the subjects who received skill plus transfer training out-performed the other groups. However, because subjects were not randomly assigned to experimental conditions, confidence in the validity of these findings is limited. Fortunately, Greenleaf (1982) obtained data indicating that no significant pretreatment differences existed on subjects' classroom behavior ratings, ages, or skill pretest scores. Although not entirely compensatory, these supporting measures strengthen the conclusions drawn from the evaluation.

Like the previously discussed nonequivalent group designs, the one-group pretest–posttest design is aptly named. A single group of subjects is assessed prior to and following the administration of some intervention. This arrangement permits determination of the extent of change between measurement occasions. As noted earlier, however, omission of a control group precludes statements about the causal influence of the intervention on the dependent variable. In time-series terminology, this design is essentially an A/B configuration with a single measurement occasion in each phase. This design is also vulnerable to several internal validity threats that yield results that are, at best, difficult to interpret. Understandably, most behavioral researchers have turned to randomized group designs and time-series designs in their efforts to identify causal links between environment and behavior.

Within-Series Time-Series Designs.   In the within-series time-series design, changes are examined in a single series across time. In these designs, both simple and complex phase changes can be made. Simple phase changes include, for example, A/B/A and A/B/A/B designs. More complex phase changes can also be made, such as in the following design: A/B + C/A/B + C.

The A/B/A/B design represents one of the more common research and evaluation strategies in the behavioral field. The A/B/A/B time-series design, generally considered an improvement over the A/B/A design (from the standpoint of internal validity), examines the effect of the intervention by replicating it over time. The "A" phase serves the same purpose (prediction of future behavior in the absence of intervention) and follows the same rules (continuation until stability is established) as the "A" phase in the A/B design. The "B" phase is comparable to the same phase in the A/B design and continues until a stable level of behavior (usually, different from the baseline level) is established. At this point, as with the A/B design, the fact that the behavior change accompanied the intervention is evident, but a functional relation cannot be shown. The influences of history, maturation, and other threats to internal validity are not ruled out.

The second baseline is often referred to as a "return to baseline," a "withdrawal" phase, or a "reversal" phase. (The entire design often is called a "replication" design because the first two phases are replicated.) The second "A" phase serves several functions. If the level of behavior returns to the levels indicated in the first baseline, the predictive value of that first phase is stronger. Because only the intervention has been removed, and it is impossible to "remove" the effects of history or maturation, any change that occurred in "B" and was subsequently reversed was most likely due to the intervention rather than to either of the aforementioned threats. After the response level in the second "A" phase has been approximated, or at least shown significant return toward baseline levels, the intervention is reinstated. The desired occurrence is the resumption of behavior similar to the behavior in the first intervention phase. Inability to regain these levels would again suggest that an extraneous factor irrelevant to the intervention had caused the previous change. Barring such a finding, the behavior in the second intervention will improve, continue stable, and the experiment is concluded on an "upbeat" note, with the subject functioning in the new, improved manner.

This design also encompasses several popular variations involving modifications of the second "A" phase. The first version is useful when the target variable really cannot be reversed or when a complete withdrawal of the intervention conditions during the second "A" phase would create confusion in the subject. It consists of removing the contingency between a target behavior and environmental consequences. That is, the consequences continue; they persist regardless of the behavior exhibited by the subject.

The second variation is also valuable in the special circumstances mentioned earlier and has the further advantage of rapidly reversing behavior from the level achieved during intervention. (Some sources reserve the label "reversal design" for this particular strategy). This method consists of making consequences contingent on certain responses, except the target behavior. Other less frequently used variations include the B/A/B/A design, a design seldom used because it concludes without an intervention.

Taylor and Kratochwill (1978) employed the within-series A/B/A/B design to evaluate the effects of a program designed to change bathroom conduct of children in a preschool facility. Program administrators would be interested in the intervention because of the potential savings in staff time and costs associated with monitoring the bathroom. Figure 10.1 depicts four graphs, one for each behavior monitored. The pattern within each graph is of interest. During the 13-day baseline phase, preschool teachers and children followed their normal patterns of behavior; they were not given any instructions. The total number of target behaviors performed each day (during five observation periods) was recorded. After the 13th day, teachers were requested to enter the bathroom several times each day and give instructions and praise to the children about the target behaviors. The same behaviors continued to be monitored under circumstances similar to the baseline phase in every way except for the intervention (praise).

The first "B" phase continued for 8 school days, during that time the level of undesirable target behaviors dropped. Baseline conditions (no praise) were reinstituted for 13 more school days before the identical intervention was reintroduced for 7 days. The mean frequency of each behavior during each phase was computed and compared. It should again be noted, that had only one behavior been monitored, this would still be an example of an A/B/A/B design, but in simpler form.

Like the designs discussed previously, the A/B/A/B design has several limitations. First, an inability to retrieve baseline levels during the second "A" phase can be due to factors other than history or maturation effects. For example, even though the intervention may have been responsible for the original behavior change, other events may have taken control of the target behavior. Also, when negative or aversive procedures are used as part of an intervention to reduce target behaviors, regardless of the experimenter's manipulations during the second baseline phase, those behaviors may never return (Kazdin, 1982b). The irreversibility of some behaviors is difficult to predict. Even quick withdrawal of the first intervention does not insure that the evaluator will be able to regain baseline levels of behavior. From an ethical perspective, the A/B/A/B design may also be inadvisable if returning to baseline levels is injurious to the subject or to other persons.

The reactive effect of experimental arrangements represents a particular threat to the internal validity of this design. The manipulation of intervention and no intervention may be reactive to the subject. There are also problems in generalizing the results obtained through use of the A/B/A/B design. It is quite possible that the results can only be generalized to other situations in which repetitions and regularly spaced presentations of the intervention are possible; thus, the intervention may be more effective under these conditions than when continuously applied. If the length of each phase is not predetermined, there is also the possibility of experimenter bias affecting the timing of phase changes and, therefore, the results. Staff resistance to the reinstitution of baseline may also be a stumbling block, especially if target behaviors are particularly noxious or if staff/subject interaction is frequent. Such practical considerations, the length and

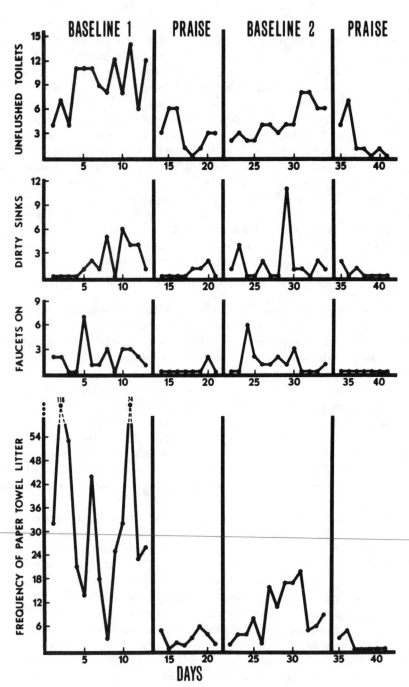

awkwardness of the strategy, and the aforementioned ethical considerations are most frequently cited issues raised in the use of the A/B/A/B design.

Complex phase changes can also be used in the within-series design. One type of complex phase change can be used with procedures called interaction designs. In these design elements the intervention component (e.g., B) is added or subtracted from another intervention component (e.g., C). Package programs may consist of several components if the interest is to add and subtract components to determine active ingredients.

Complex phase changes can also be made in a within-series design called the changing criterion strategy. The changing criterion design has been discussed in great detail in two sources (see Hall & Fox, 1977; Hartmann & Hall, 1976) and is being employed more extensively in applied settings. The changing criterion technique, like the other designs discussed in this chapter, requires baseline observations on the dependent variable of interest. Subsequently, an intervention is implemented in each of a series of phases. A stepwise change in criterion rate for the dependent variable is applied during each intervention phase; thus, each phase of the design is conceptualized as a baseline for each subsequent phase. Internal validity of the design is established through successive replication of change in the dependent variable, which changes with each stepwise change in the criterion.

An example of the changing criterion design was reported by Hall and Fox (1977), who used it to evaluate the effects of a reinforcement contingency on the division performance of a student. The student, named Steve, was characterized as disruptive; he refused to complete assignments or completed them at a relatively low rate. To establish a baseline measure of responding, Steve was provided a worksheet with nine division problems and one example. The teacher worked the example for Steve and then told him to work as many problems as he could before recess period (a 45 minute work session). The number of correct problems at the end of the session was used as the dependent variable. In the experimental phases, Steve had to compute a specified number of division problems correctly during each session. A contingency was established that involved informing the student that if he solved the problems correctly by the end of the session, he could have recess and play basketball; if he failed to complete the problems by recess, he remained in the classroom until they were correctly computed.

The criterion for each step in the design was determined by computing the mean for the baseline condition and establishing the criterion at the next highest

FIG. 10.1. Frequency of unflushed toilets, dirty sinks, faucets on, and paper towel litter for the baseline and treatment phases of the experiment. (Source: Taylor, M. J., & Kratochwill, T. R. [1978]. Modification of preschool children's bathroom behavior by contingent teacher attention. *Journal of School Psychology, 16*, 64–71. Reproduced by permission.)

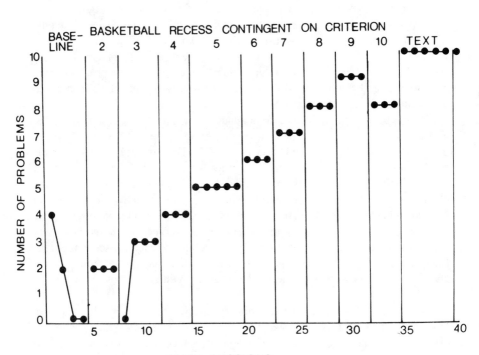

MATH SESSIONS

FIG. 10.2. A record of the number of math problems correctly solved by Steve, a "behaviorally disordered boy," during baseline; recess, and the opportunity to play basketball contingent on changing levels of performance and return to textbook phases. (Source: Hall, R. V., & Fox, R. G. [1977]. Changing criterion designs: An alternative applied behavior analysis procedure. In B. C. Etzel, J. M. LeBlanc, and D. M. Baer (Eds.), *New developments in behavioral research: Theory, method, and application.* In honor of Sidney W. Bijou. Hillsdale, NJ: Lawrence Erlbaum Associates. Reproduced by permission of the authors and publishers.)

whole problem. Following three consecutive days of performance at the specified level, the experimenter advanced the criterion by one problem. The terminal goal was to shape and maintain enough behavior to complete a textbook assignment.

Results of this study are reported in Fig. 10.2. An examination of the figure shows that Steve's rate of computing division problems dropped to 0 after only three sessions. The data also show that Steve met the criterion in a minimum number of sessions. Although he did not correctly compute the problems on the worksheet in the first session, after the criterion was raised to 3, each criterion was met successfully. Two procedures were used to demonstrate further the internal validity of the intervention. During the fourth criterion step, the criterion was held at five problems; an examination of Fig. 10.2 shows that no progressive increase was observed. During the tenth criterion step, Steve was returned to a former level of responding. Examination of the figure shows that Steve performed at that level for the minimum number of sessions and was subsequently returned to the advancing criterion sequence. Thus, Steve was essentially reintroduced to the textbook program, a procedure that he successfully continued.

The changing criterion design can be conceptualized as a series of repeated basic time-series or A/B designs, because the effect of the intervention is replicated consecutively with each criterion change. This allows criterion changes to function analogously with the sequential changes in behavior or situation to which an intervention is introduced in the multiple baseline procedure. Further discussions that relate the simiarlity of the changing criterion design to the multiple baseline design can be found in Hartmann and Hall (1976).

As was evidenced in the example of Steve, changing criterion design can be applied in situations when the researcher is interested in shaping behavior over time. The gradual criterion changes, which involve essentially a shaping component, help to assure that the subject's performance does not deteriorate, as might happen when large experimental effects are called for. Some important considerations must be attended to in the use of the changing criterion design (Hartmann & Hall, 1976). These include: (a) the length of the baseline and intervention; (b) the magnitude of criterion changes; and (c) the number of interventions or criterion changes. The baseline data series should remain stable or at least not be changing in the direction of the expected intervention effect. Thus, like other designs that necessitate a stable baseline, the researcher should continue a bseline series for several sessions to reach stability, or to eliminate trends that might militate against demonstrating treatment effects.

The intervention phases also have several considerations that the researcher must attend to. One is that although the length of each treatment phase and the number and magnitude of criterion changes are independent, they should vary as a function of the total length of treatment, the variability of the target behavior, and the difference between an anticipated terminal rate of the target behavior. It is important for each phase in the changing criterion design to be long enough to allow the rate of the target behavior to restabilize before proceeding to the next step. Moreover, the magnitude of stepwise criterion changes must be large in relation to variability or trends in the series. A final concern relates to the number of criterion changes needed for control. At least five criterion changes would be necessary in most cases; however, the researcher can establish control by maintaining the stability criterion. The researcher may also be able to return to a formal criterion for a short period of time, this was possible in the case of the application of the changing criterion design to Steve's math behavior. Overall, the changing criterion design blends into a number of practical options available to the applied researcher and program evaluator.

Between-Series Designs. The between-series time-series design compares two or more data series across time. Comparison of the two or more interventions is made between or among these series. The simultaneous or alternating treatments design provides examples of the between-series strategies. In the simultaneous treatment design (STD) the interventions are concurrently or simultaneously available; however, availability of interventions does not assure that the subject is equally exposed to each intervention. The subject may encounter each therapist/experimenter a different number of times; therefore, the intervention may not be equally represented. In the alternating treatments design (ATD), the subject is exposed to each intervention an equal number of times. The schedule of administering the interventions is predetermined and counterbalancing of times of administering the intervention is used, typically, in a Latin Square arrangement or determined through random sequencing. There are several reports of the ATD in the literature (e.g., Kazdin, 1977b; Kazdin & Gessey, 1977; Shapiro, Barrett, & Ollendick, 1980), but only one application of the STD (e.g., Browning, 1967; also described in Browning & Stover, 1971).

Shapiro et al. (1980) used an ATD to compare the relative efficacy of physical restraint and positive practice overcorrection for their effects on the reduction of self-stimulatory behavior. Three mentally retarded, severely disturbed children enrolled in a residential facility served as subjects for the study. Treatment A, physical restraint, involved a verbal warning ("No, Marcia, hands out of your mouth") and manually restraining the child's hands on a table for 30 seconds. Treatment B consisted of positive practice, it involved the same verbal warning followed by manual guidance in appropriate manipulations of the task for 30 seconds.

The researchers used the ATD across two time periods, sessions were conducted in the morning and in the afternoon each day. One therapist administered the treatment in both daily sessions throughout the investigation. Following the baseline phase, the two treatments were administered in counterbalanced order across sessions each day. A brief treatment withdrawal was also implemented. Figure 10.3, shows that physical restraint and positive practice were found to be of equal effectiveness for all children. The researchers also implemented a withdrawal of the treatment. Reinstating the treatment, resulted in reduction of the behavior to near zero levels.

The advantages and limitations of the ATD have been discussed by several sources (Barlow & Hayes, 1979; Kazdin & Hartmann, 1978). Advantages of the ATD include that several interventions can be compared in a relatively short period of time (as opposed to the length of time required for the A/B/A/B type of design); disadvantages of the reversal or withdrawal phase are usually avoided; and, although a baseline phase is often employed in an ATD, a very stable level of baseline behavior, often difficult to achieve, is not essential; a withdrawal phase may be used, as was apparent in the Shapiro et al. (1980) study, and the rapid alternation of conditions, usually within one day, provides excellent control for the history effects that often plague other designs.

However, due to the nature of the ATD strategy, multiple intervention interference may pose a problem; there are several ways to minimize this threat. First, the length of each intervention can be manipulated to maximize the subject's ability to discriminate between the two conditions. It is possible that subjects in the Shapiro et al. (1980) study did not discriminate between the two treatments. This problem is more likely when interventions have similar elements or when they share components. Second, the efficacy of one or both conditions may be a function of the rapid alternation strategy. Sidman (1960) suggests that one might simultaneously institute an A/B design using the same two interventions with another subject (the "A" phase would not be a baseline, but would represent one of the experimental conditions). The results gathered from the A/B design can then be compared to the ATD results to eliminate any possible alternation effect. Finally, juggling the rapid intervention alternations and their accompanying SDs and counterbalancing time, location, and other variables may prove quite cumbersome. In the final analysis, the evaluator must weigh the particular advantages of the design against the dexterity required in its execution.

Combined Series, Multiple Baseline Design.   Combined time-series designs make combined sets of comparisons between and within series of measurements (Hayes, 1981). The multiple baseline design falls into this category of designs. Multiple baseline designs allow evaluation of an intervention implemented across different subjects, settings, or behaviors. As in the A/B/A/B designs, several baseline observations are made prior to the intervention being introduced to the first series. The other series are maintained under baseline conditions until each successively and independently receives the intervention. Although one baseline and intervention phase (i.e., A/B) is all that is necessary for each subject, setting, or behavior monitored, the strategy can be combined with other design tactics (e.g., A/B/A/B).

The multiple baseline design provides a viable alternative to the A/B/A/B because there is no necessity to return to baseline conditions. However, because there is no within subject (behavior or setting) replications, some sources (e.g., Hersen & Barlow, 1976) contend that "slippage" in the replication process leaves the multiple baseline procedure weaker than within subject replication procedures. Although the multiple baseline strategy controls history and maturation effects, it is subject to novelty threats. However, the design has some distinct advantages over the A/B/A/B design. First, the study of multiple behaviors or settings more closely approximates naturalistic conditions in which several responses often occur simultaneously and such behaviors usually occur in a variety of settings. Therefore, the design is potentially less disrupting than the more artificial and sometimes unwieldy A/B/A/B strategy. Multiple baseline strategies can also facilitate the study of the covariance of several behaviors. Moreover, the design is useful when baseline levels of behaviors are unretrievable or when such a manipulation is considered unethical (both of these problems plague the A/B/A/B designs).

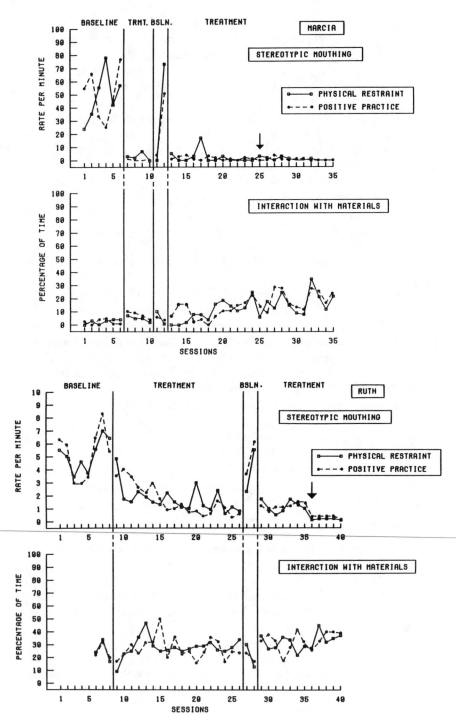

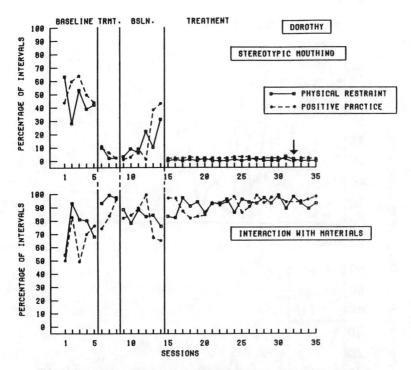

FIG. 10.3. Stereotypic mouthing and appropriate interactions with materials for Marcia (a), Ruth (b), and Dorothy (c). A 10-second, continuous interval recording procedure was used to collect data on Dorothy because a frequency count was less applicable. On-task behavior served as a measure of appropriate interaction with material for Dorothy. Arrows note when the treatment procedure was implemented unit-wide. (Source: Shapiro, E. S., Barrett, R. P., & Ollendick, T. H. [1980]. A comparison of physical restraint and positive practice overcorrection in treating stereotypic behavior. *Behavior Therapy, 11,* 227–233. Copyright 1980 by the Association for Advancement of Behavior Therapy. Reproduced by permission.)

McMahon and Forehand (1978) presented an example of the multiple baseline strategy across subjects to determine the appropriateness of a brochure (emphasizing praise and timeout) to teach mothers of preschool children to modify mealtime behaviors. Observers employed a behavioral checklist to determine the percentage of observed intervals in which inappropriate mealtime behaviors occurred; this measure served as the dependent variable. Figure 10.4 illustrates the finding with the first subject: Baseline phase (which consisted of mealtime observations during which mother and child behaved as usual) lasted for only three observation periods before the intervention (providing the mothers the brochure) was applied. The second and third subjects underwent successively longer baseline phases before an identical intervention was introduced. The intervention continued for 7 to 16 observation sessions (depending on the length of the

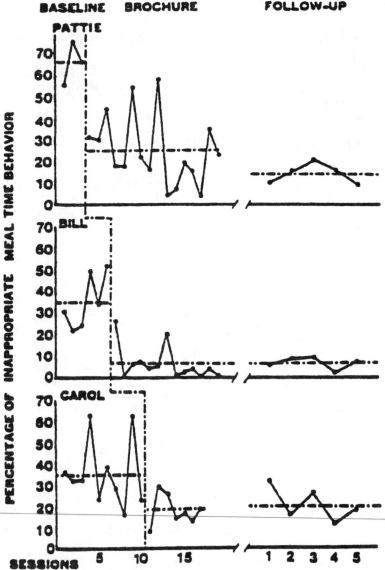

FIG. 10.4. Percentage of intervals scored as inappropriate mealtime behavior. (broken horizontal lines in each phase indicates the mean percentage of intervals scored as inappropriate mealtime behavior across sessions for that phase). (Source: McMahan, R. J., & Forehand, R. [1978]. Nonprescription behavior therapy: Effectiveness of a brochure in teaching mothers to correct their children's inappropriate mealtime behaviors. *Behavior Therapy, 9*, 814–820. Copyright 1978 by the Association for Advancement of Behavior Therapy. Reproduced by permission.)

baseline), the total number of observations for each subject remained approximately the same. The mean percentage of intervals marred by inappropriate behavior (for each subject) during baseline and during intervention were compared. The authors included a follow-up phase verifying the long-term effects of the intervention.

The previous example illustrates that the multiple baseline is quite versatile. It does, however, necessitate certain considerations and poses certain problems. As the length of the last baseline increases, the multiple baseline design is often not practical (or ethical). It is also difficult, if not impossible, to use in cases in which (due to the characteristics of the particular subjects, settings, or behaviors) a stable baseline cannot be achieved. In addition, the multiple baseline design rests on the ability of the experimenter/program evaluator to find subjects, situations, or behaviors that are truly independent of one another, and will be affected similarly by the intervention. This subtle and delicate balance is often difficult to achieve in "real life," clinical, or even in more controlled analogue situations. The unplanned interaction of subjects, or the subject's unscheduled generalization of training to new settings or behaviors before the design calls for this, is a major disadvantage of the multiple baseline program. If the investigators manage to avoid all pitfalls, they are still faced with the problem of deciding how many baselines are necessary to inspire confidence in the efficacy of the intervention. Although interventions across two subjects, settings, or behaviors are all that is essential to constitute a multiple baseline design, some noteable sources (Hersen & Barlow, 1976; Wolf & Risley, 1971) suggest a minimum of three or four inteventions for a convincing documentation.

It should be noted that the multiple baseline design and the A/B/A/B designs can be used for either single subject or group research and program evaluation. The fact that the examples used to illustrate the A/B/A/B designs involved individual subjects does not mean that the designs are limited in this manner.

Combined Designs.   Most of the time-series designs employed in behavioral research and program evaluation are pure in structure. That is, each design is easily classified as a particular type. However, combined intrasubject designs, hybrids of the more common strategies described earlier, are often used successfully. This allows the investigator to gain the advantages of the two design types and at the same time control the threats inherent to either component design.

Randomized Group Designs

As noted earlier in the chapter, randomized experiments use random assignment as a basis for drawing inferences for a treatment effect. In the typical between- and within-subject group design, some N subjects are randomly assigned to treatment and/or control groups; random assignments sometimes can be used in program evaluation research. However, it is likely that random assignments cannot be used in some applied settings for either practical or ethical reasons.

Between-Group Designs.   In their most basic form, between-groups designs refer to an experimental and control group. Between-group designs differ from the previously discussed time-series strategies in several ways. First, the average (mean) behavior of the specific groups is emphasized in the evaluation. The effect of one intervention on groups that differ on some important characteristics is often the interest of comparison. But the effect of different interventions on closely matched or randomly assigned groups is even more frequently studied. Verification that results across groups are significantly different is accomplished through a statistical comparison of the mean level of behavior exhibited by each group. The effects of the intervention(s) are evaluated by a variety of statistical tests, each test has a set of important assumptions.

Flanagan, Adams, and Forehand (1979) used a between-group design to evaluate the effectiveness of four different instructional techniques in teaching parents to use timeout procedures with their children. The 48 parents were randomly assigned to four methods: A written pamphlet, a structured lecture, a role playing exercise, and a videotape depicting a modeled example. The resulting behavior in each group was represented by three separate behavioral measures recorded by independent raters. An analysis-of-variance was performed on each of the three measures; Newman-Keul's tests indicated that all interventions groups differed significantly from the control group but not from each other. The analysis-of-variance did, however, point out several significant differences between intervention groups on each of the three specific outcome measures.

The advantage of this type of procedure is that it yields a great deal of information not only about intervention efficacy, but about the relation of the intervention to several more specific outcome behaviors. Also, inherent in the between-group design is the credibility associated with the use of many subjects, a feature that single subject time-series achieve only through repeated replication. Furthermore, if the researcher wishes to test the effect of several interventions on one behavior, avoiding the possibility of multiple intervention interference, a between-group design is useful.

A common objection to the use of group designs in program evaluation is that, whereas the investigator's main concern is the study of behavioral change as a function of environmental events, group designs often obscure important individual differences in the averaging process. Furthermore, the mean behavior of any given group is not necessarily representative of what has happened to the individuals within the group. In addition, a crucial strength of time-series designs is its ability to demonstrate the path of behavior changes across time. Most between-group studies record resultant behavior at a specific point in time. This is often unavoidable because of the practical considerations of dealing with many subjects at once.

In summary, between-group designs, like all other evaluation strategies available to the researcher, have special advantages and disadvantages. These characteristics must be evaluated in the light of program goals, type of subjects used, and practical considerations of the applied setting.

Within-Subject Designs.   In contrast to between-group comparisons, within-subject group designs achieve internal validity by using subjects as their own controls. Each subject is exposed to all experimental conditions at different points in time. Performance under each condition is assessed, typically on a single occasion, and differential effects are detected using some form of repeated measures statistical analysis. A discussion of two of the most common within-subject group designs, the crossover design and the latin square design are discussed.

The crossover design exposes two randomized groups of subjects to different sequences of intervention conditions, preceeded and followed by separate measurement occasions. To illustrate, the first group of subjects may be pretested, receive intervention A, be posttested, receive intervention B, and be posttested a second time. The resulting data may reveal differences between the two interventions and/or between the interventions and the baseline (pretest) conditions. However, the pattern of results obtained may be due, at least in part, to the order in which subjects experienced the two interventions. To control for this possibility, a second group of subjects is run through ihe sequence with the order of interventions reversed. That is, subjects in group 2 undergo intervention B prior to being given intervention A. Instead of removing order effects from the data, the procedure ensures that the effects do not operate to favor one intervention over the other.

The latin square design has the same structural characteristics of the crossover design, groups of subjects serve as their own controls by receiving each of N intervention conditions in a different sequence (Myers, 1979). A latin square procedure may be used when three or more conditions are to be compared. The term *latin square* refers to the number of interventions groups and the order of interventions being equal. Consider the situation in which three interventions A, B, and C are contrasted. A pool of subjects would be randomly assigned to three equal groups that differ solely on the basis of the order in which they receive the interventions. One possible set of sequences is ABC, BCA, and CAB for groups one through three, respectively. Although this arrangement allows for each intervention to appear once in each order position (i.e., first, second, or third), it does not satisfy the requirements of a completely balanced design in which all possible combinations of intervention sequences are accounted for (Kazdin, 1980). In our example, this would require six groups, or k factorial, where k equals the number of interventions compared.

Robinson, DeReus, and Drabman (1976) demonstrated the applicability of the latin square design in a study that examined the effects of contingent and noncontingent tutoring on disruptive classroom behavior. Sixteen, second grade students were assigned to four experimental groups. Following a baseline period, subjects were provided "happy face" tickets at the end of the day, tickets were contingent on low rates of disruptive behavior as a form of performance feedback. Superimposed on the feedback system was a different sequence of tutoring programs for each of the four groups. The four tutoring programs, Noncontingent Peer, Contingent Peer, Noncontingent College Student, and Contingent College Student, were compared. The sequencing of tutoring provided that each program appeared once and only once in each ordinal position. After receiving all four types of tutoring, subjects were returned to the feedback system alone. As might be expected, the results of the study indicated that tutoring contingent on low rates of disruption was significantly more effective in reducing the aberrant behavior than when noncontingent tutoring was provided.

The within-subject group designs, previously discussed, have some important advantages. First, fewer subjects are required to achieve a given level of statistical power than would be needed for a between-group design. This occurs because more degrees of freedom are obtained per subject and because between-subject variability can be isolated and removed from the error term used in the statistical test (see Kirk, 1968, for a detailed discussion of this issue). This is no small matter when time and/or subjects are limited. Second, situations may arise where investigation of order and/or sequence effects is an important research question that may be addressed through a within-subject design. As noted earlier, order effects refer to the influence ordinal position has on subjects' response to a particular intervention. It is quite possible, for example, that clients taught to self-monitor their dysfluent speech patterns, prior to receiving an intervention aimed at reducing dysfluencies, will be more successful after having learned to better discriminate the occurrence of these behaviors. Order effect would be reflected more in lower rates of dysfluencies than if subjects had received the intervention procedure first. A somewhat different problem, sequence effects, arises when a particular sequence of interventions produces carry over effects from one intervention phase to another. Consider two interventions for aggressive behavior, timeout and differential reinforcement of other behavior (DRO), administered to two groups of subjects in a counterbalanced order. A possible outcome, worthy of study, is that subjects experiencing DRO after a phase of timeout may fare better than those who receive DRO first, that is, the effects of timeout may carry over to result in a more effective DRO procedure.

As with any design, within-subject group strategies have limitations that are noteworthy. There is, of course, the problem of order and sequence effects discussed throughout this section. Difficulties arise when the number of conditions exceeds two because the number of groups required to achieve a completely balanced design tends to offset the power advantage inherent in these designs. Conversely, a design that is less than completely balanced can yield ambiguous results. A second problem that may be encountered with these strategies is ceiling and floor effects (Kazdin, 1980). Ceiling and floor effects occur when the degree of change in the outcome measure reaches its maximum or minimum limit. Thus, if intervention B is preceded by a powerful intervention A, there may be little room for further improvement and subsequent analysis may detect no differences when, in fact, B is a more effective intervention. The problem of ceiling effects can be attenuated to some extent by using dependent measures that have no set upper limit (e.g., rate of responding). Finally, within-subject group procedures may be contraindicated when interventions being compared require that subjects be provided conflicting information (Kazdin, 1980). For example, clients undergoing two different approaches, controlled drinking and abstinence, to the treatment of alcoholism may experience elements that are at variance with each other and that influence there responds to the second treatment.

METHODOLOGICAL AND CONCEPTUAL ISSUES IN RESEARCH AND PROGRAM EVALUATION

One of the major contributions of behavioral research and evaluation has been a strengthening of the connection between experimental psychology and practice. In addition to drawing upon laboratory findings in experimental psychology to develop interventions, there has been an emphasis on rigor and experimental evaluation of therapeutic achievement. It should be emphasized that although behavioral approaches have a scientific affiliation, other therapeutic approaches have also been evaluated. Major advances have been made in other areas of therapy in methodological and conceptual criteria (cf. Chassan, 1979). For example, in school psychology, Meyers, Pitt, Gaughan, and Friedman (1978) criticized past research in consultee-centered consultation because of inadequate description of technique and subjective criteria that were not based on directly observable behavior. They suggested that a multiple baseline strategy and attention to internal and external validity criteria would greatly improve research in this area. Likewise, Medway (1979) reviewed the results of 29 studies, published between 1972 and 1977, on the effectiveness of school consultation. Behavioral and other (e.g., mental health) consultation studies were reviewed. Suggestions were made for higher quality methodological rigor across all consultation areas. Future research, whether based on consultation or other service delivery models, will likely enhance more scientific and credible research and evaluation methodologies.

Another issue relates to the quality of research and evaluation within the behavioral field and the corresponding conclusions about the efficacy of various interventions techniques. Not all the conclusions drawn about behavioral strategies are based on empirical research and high quality program evaluation. For example, a review of behavioral research published in the *Journal of School Psychology* and *Psychology in the Schools,* in the past few years, will reveal that a number of studies employed case study methodology or designs and/or procedures that fall short of acceptable scientific rigor, in research and program evaluations. In the first author's review of the childhood treatment of selective mutism (Kratochwill, 1981), numerous treatment studies were based on case study methodology or other procedures deemed inadequate from a scientific standpoint. In this section some methodological and conceptual issues in behavioral research and program evaluation are reviewed. Special attention is given to criteria for evaluation of outcomes, generalization, and follow-up evaluation.

Criteria for Evaluation of Outcomes

Many important developments have occurred in the evaluation of program outcomes, particularly with respect to the methods used to measure the dependent variables involved. The issues involved in evaluations include experimental and therapeutic criteria, client-related criteria, and efficiency and cost criteria.

Experimental and Therapeutic Criteria.   Therapeutic research and program evaluation should not be immune from the scientific standards that must be adhered to in other forms of empirical research. Formal criteria have been proposed for data analysis in therapy research, namely, experimental and therapeutic (cf. Kazdin, 1977a; Risley, 1970; Wolf, 1978). The experimental criterion involves comparison of the dependent variable before and after the introduction of the treatment. Essentially, experimental criteria are met through the use of credible design and sometimes inferential statistical tests. Such criteria would be applied in both time-series and randomized-group designs. Some debate has occurred over the use of statistical tests in time-series research (see Kazdin, 1976; Kratochwill, 1978, 1979). Statistical analysis is sometimes perceived as an additional (redundant) criteria once a credible design has been employed and major effects are apparent through visual inspection of the data. The key issue in the controversy over the contribution of statistical analysis to experimental criteria is the use of visual inspection (sometimes called *graphical analysis*) to document program change. Some writers have noted that visual inspection may, at times, represent an unreliable method (e.g., Kazdin, 1976; Kratochwill, 1978). Critics of this position (e.g., Baer, 1977; Michael, 1974) argue that statistical analysis is redundant and unnecessary because of large therapeutic behavior change; yet, many studies do not demonstrate large effects. Consequently, debates have occurred over what type of research and evaluation methods best contribute to a scientific technology of behavior. Proponents of visual analysis have argued that large program effects will best contribute to the development of the behavioral field.

Clinical or therapeutic criteria have been proposed to increase the practical significance of therapeutic achievement. To the degree that such procedures promote large or dramatic changes in the dependent variables, they lend support to application of visual analysis. Increasingly, behavioral researchers have been concerned with determining the clinical importance of program change (Maher & Kratochwill, 1980). This has commonly been referred to as *social validation* (Kazdin, 1977a; Wolf, 1978). Wolf (1978) suggested validation on three levels:

1. The social significance of the *goals*. Are the specific behavioral goals really what society wants?
2. The social appropriateness of the *procedures*. Do the ends justify the means? That is, do the participants, caregivers, and other consumer's consider the intervention procedures acceptable?

3. The social importance of the *effects*. Are consumers satisfied with the results? *All* the results, including any unpredicted ones? (p. 207)

Kazdin (1977a) proposed two social validation procedures. In the first procedure behavior of a client is compared with the behavior of persons who have not been defined as problematic. In the second procedure, evaluations of the subject's performance are solicited by individuals in the natural environment. Change is viewed as clinically important when the intervention brings the subject's performance within socially acceptable levels determined from social judgments of significant others. If a clinical level of significance can be established, a more formal criterion is available for evaluating the intervention.

Social validation procedures are not limited for use in single case evaluation designs. These procedures can be readily adapted to more conventional research and program evaluation involving between-group and within-subject comparisons. In such cases therapeutic criteria are added to design and statistical criteria for an overall evaluation of the program. Forehand, Wells, and Griest (1982) examined the social validation of a parent training program. Based on Kazdin (1977a) and Wolf (1978), four validation procedures were employed: social comparison, subjective evaluation, social acceptability of treatment, and consumer satisfaction measures. Subjects consisted of 15 clinic-referred children and their mothers and 15 nonclinic children and their mothers. Observations in the home were conducted pre and postintervention and at a two month follow-up for the clinic group and at comparable times for the nonclinic group. Parents completed questionnaires on their own adjustment and the adjustment of their children prior to and after the intervention and at the 2 month follow-up. Consumer satisfaction and social acceptance of program measures were collected from parents in the clinic group 15 months after intervention. The program consisted of teaching parents of the clinic-referred children to use social reinforcement and timeout.

Results of the study supported the social validity of the program. The clinic children were less compliant and more deviant than the nonclinic children before intervention, but not after intervention or at follow-up. The clinic parents reported that their children were less well-adjusted than the nonclinic parents reported on their children, prior to and after the program, but not at the 2-month follow-up. The specific parent behavior measures indicated that parents of the clinic children used more positive reinforcement than the nonclinic parents after the program and at follow-up. Table 10.1 shows based on consumer satisfaction data, that parents were satisfied with the program they had received and viewed the treatment procedures as appropriate at the 15-month follow-up.

Client-Related Criteria.   The experimental criterion, whether determined on the basis of design or statistical criteria in either group or single case investigation, represents only one aspect of outcome evaluation. Four additional criteria

TABLE 10.1
Parent Consumer Satisfaction Data*

		Mean Ratings
1.	At the end of treatment, the problems of my child that were treated at the clinic were (1 = considerably worse, 7 = greatly improved).	6.1
2.	The problems of my child that were treated at the clinic are at this point (1 = considerably worse, 7 = greatly improved).	5.5
3.	How do you feel about your child in regard to the effect this treatment has had (1 = much more negtively, 7 = much more positively).	5.7
4.	I feel the approach to treating my child's behavior problems in the home by using this type of parent training program is (1 = very inappropriate, 7 = very appropriate).	5.9
5.	How confident are you in managing current behavior problems in the home on your own? (1 = very unconfident, 7 = very confident).	5.5
6.	How frequently do you use the overall group of techniques (attends, rewards, ignoring, good commands, and time-out)? (1 = never, 7 = very often).	5.2
7.	At this point, I feel that the therapists in the treatment program were (1 = extremely not helpful, 7 = extremely helpful).	6.5

*Forehand, R., Wells, K. C., & Griest, D. L. (1980). An examination of the social validity of a parent training program. *Behavior Therapy, 11,* 488–502.

can be examined in applied research and evaluation (Kazdin & Wilson, 1978). First, the importance of change or improvement in the subject(s) should be evaluated. Generally, the investigator needs to determine if the problem has been solved as a function of the program; change can be determined on the basis of the social validation procedures described earlier.

A second concern relates to the proportion of subjects who improve in a group study. As noted in the design section of this chapter, a within-subject time-series design may involve large numbers of subjects; therefore, when groups are involved concern relates to both conventional and time-series designs. In a group study it is advisable for the investigator to present data on an individual subject's reactions to the program, when possible and feasible. Consider the case in which a school psychologist is evaluating the effect of teacher consultation services across classrooms in a multiple baseline design. If the program is effective, it is likely that "effectiveness" will be presented in the average classroom performance of the subjects evaluated. A much more refined analysis of the program occurs when the psychologist determines if all students improved and to what degree. Another possibility is that some students did not improve or that some students may have become worse. Thus, the investigator must go beyond the mean performance of the group to examine individual client responses.

A third consideration relates to the breadth of changes noted in outcome measures on the subject. Although the efficacy of a program is typically evaluated on the basis of how well the original problem has been ameliorated, program effects may extend beyond the original focus or target problems. Such effects could be positive or negative for the client (Petrie et al., 1980). Petrie et al. presented the example of a school psychologist who evaluated a program in a classroom setting designed to increase time spent by students on desk activities. If this had been a research study, a number of possible effects on behaviors not directly manipulated by the evaluator could have occurred. These possibilities, depicted in Fig. 10.5, allow prediction of 162 (i.e., 3 × 2, × 3, × 3, × 3)

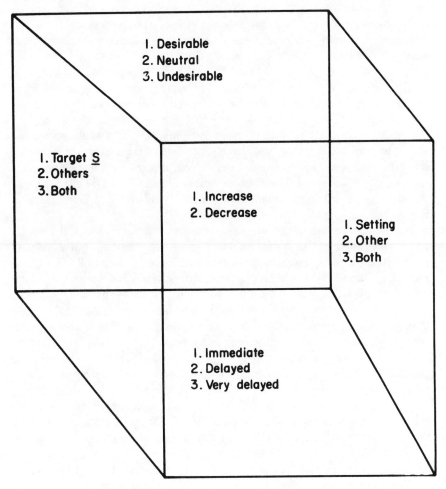

1. Desirable
2. Neutral
3. Undesirable

1. Target S
2. Others
3. Both

1. Increase
2. Decrease

1. Setting
2. Other
3. Both

1. Immediate
2. Delayed
3. Very delayed

FIG. 10.5.   Classification of various kinds of unintended effects that may occur in behaviors that are not manipulated directly by the psychologist. (Source: Petrie, P., Brown, D. K., Piersel, W. C., Frinfrock, S. R., Schelble, M., LeBlanc, C. P., & Kratochwill, T. R. (1980). The school psychologist as behavioral ecologist. *Journal of School Psychology, 18*, 222–233. Reproduced by permission.)

possible kinds of side effects. This example is presented not to advise researchers and program evaluators to evaluate all possible combinations but to alert them to the possibility of changes beyond the major dependent variable examined.

A final client-related criteria is concerned with the durability of improvements. In this criteria for evaluation of therapeutic outcomes, the investigator should be concerned with a careful follow-up to determine if the effects that occurred during treatment have maintained. Conversely, a comparison of two interventions at the end of the program may yield different results when the two are compared again several months or years later. Specific procedures will need to be programmed to ensure that program effects have been durable (see the following discussion on procedures designed to facilitate maintenance and generalization).

Efficiency and Cost-Related Criteria.   In addition to an evaluation of client outcomes, five other criteria should be considered in behavioral program evaluation (Kazdin & Wilson, 1978). First, the efficiency in duration of the program must be considered. The treatment showing the same effect as an alternative one should be preferred if it took considerably less time to implement. For example, if two forms of consultation are being evaluated, it is conceivable that the same outcome may occur in the dependent variables of interest. Yet, the one form that was the most efficient to administer would likely be preferred given the time needed to administer it.

A second and related criterion concerns the efficiency in the manner of administering the program. Can the program be administered to groups or individuals? For example, if the intervention must be administered to each child in a classroom, considerable time will be involved; if the investigator can administer the program to everyone in the class at the same time, a considerable savings in time may result. Moreover, some interventions are capable of being administered through various media, such as videotapes, films, reading. These materials can be widely disseminated, reducing time and expense.

A third criteria relates to the costs of professional expertise. For example, if the school psychologist is involved in the implementation of services, he/she has typically had extensive and costly training (e.g., from 3 to 5 years). However, many programs can be implemented by teachers or paraprofessionals, reducing the cost of professional services. Consultation is frequently cited as a form of professional school psychology services that are cost-efficient (see also Chapter 8). For example, in behavioral consultation, the consultant works through a teacher-consultee to implement services to a client (Bergan, 1977). Unfortunately, little information is available to document the cost of these professional services.

A fourth issue is multidimensional and concerns client costs (see also Chapter 11). Clients receiving services in applied educational settings typically do not pay for services because the professional is employed by the school district; however, costs extend beyond monetary issues. Costs may involve the client's physical well-being and emotional factors. For example, in a program comparing drug treatment and a behavior therapy program with hyperactive children, the investigator must be concerned about the physical side effects of the medication. Emotional costs to the client would also be a consideration when punishment procedures are employed, particularly because undesirable side effects may occur.

A final consideration relates to the cost-effectiveness of interventions. Essentially, this issue refers to how costly the program is and whether the cost for the desired outcome is justified. Certain problems may not justify spending vast amounts of time, effort, and money to effect change. This may be the case with transient problems or problems that improve with regular developmental time and with few negative consequences, without intervention.

Criteria for Generalization and Follow-up

Considerable work has gone into the development of procedures to measure and facilitate generalization in applied programs (Baer, Wolf, & Risley, 1968; Drabman, Hammer & Rosenbaum, 1979; Stokes & Baer, 1977). Although research and evaluation studies are still published without specific measures of generalization and follow-up, many journals are now requiring that these measures be included. It is recognized that demonstration of generalization is a practical concern and an ethical issue (Drabman et al., 1979). From a practical perspective, it is desirable for intervention effects to demonstrate positive effects on the individual's life; from an ethical perspective it is important to know that the program effect does not disappear when the intervention is withdrawn or discontinued.

A commonly accepted definition of generalization was provided by Stokes and Baer (1977): "The occurrence of relevant behavior under different, non-training conditions (i.e., across subjects, settings, people, behaviors, and/or time) without the scheduling of the same events in those conditions as had been scheduled in the training conditions" (p. 350). Two different conceptualizations of generalization have been presented in the literature. One is based on viewing generalization with a focus on the processes associated with generalized effects (Stokes & Baer, 1977), the other defines generalization according to the methods used and data recorded (Drabman et al., 1979). A discussion of each perspective follows.

Programming Generalization.   Stokes and Baer (1977) conceptualized generalization as an active process and technology. Based upon their review of the literature, nine general categories of generalization were identified: train and hope, sequential modification, introduce to natural maintaining contingencies, train sufficient examplars, train loosely, use indiscriminable contingencies, program common stimuli, mediate generalization, and train to generalize. Various

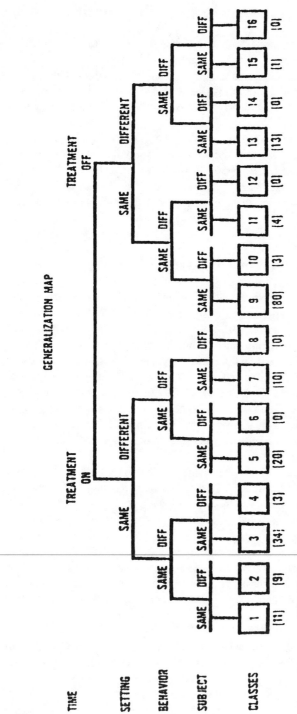

GENERALIZATION MAP

FIG. 10.6. The generalization map depicting the 16 different classes of generalized treatment effects. The numbers in parentheses indicate the number of studies found that illustrate a particular class of generalization (Source: Drabman, R. S., Hammer, D., & Rosenbaum, M. S. [1979]. Assessing generalization in behavior modification with children: The generalization map. *Behavior Assessment, 1,* 203–219. Copyright 1979 by the Association for Advancement of Behavior Therapy. Reproduced by permission).

studies that build on this technology continue to be published in the behavioral literature.

Assessment of Generalization.   Drabman et al. (1979) presented a conceptual framework for various classes of generalization. Their "Generalization Map" (see Fig. 10.6) provides an assessment guideline that encompasses 16 distinguishable classes of generalization. Within this framework there are essentially four major categories of generalization. In the first, variously labeled generalization across time, response maintenance, or follow-up, behavior change is assessed in the intervention setting following the withdrawal of the program. In this form of generalization assessment one must note if the intervention is formally continuing or was discontinued. An issue that emerges in follow-up assessment is how long and how frequent the assessment should be. Although this will depend on the type of problem involved and on practical considerations, a general rule is to be generous with these measures (e.g., 6 to 12 months, or longer). The more frequent the measures and the longer they are taken, the more that can be said about the effects of the program.

A second type of generalization involves measurement across settings. Generalization refers to change in behavior in settings separate from the specific environment in which intervention occurred. Drabman et al. (1979) note that the criterion for a new environment is established by the presence or absence of salient discriminative stimuli that were present in the intervention environment. For example, a more obvious change in environment would occur if the researcher assessed behavior across school and home environments.

Generalization across behaviors, the third type of generalization involves a change in a response not specifically programmed for change during the program. Generalization would be assessed by determining if the behavior said to be generalized can be defined independently of the definition of the target behavior. For example, if the investigator has implemented a treatment program to increase academic responding (e.g., math units completed), generalization would be said to occur on improved classroom conduct (not part of the original definition).

The final category of generalization is assessed by measuring the change in behavior of nontarget subjects. Thus, generalization to a different subject is recorded when a nontarget subject (to whom no contingencies are applied) demonstrates a behavior change following implementation of the intervention. An example of this type of generalization would occur when the researcher finds that a peer demonstrates positive change when the intervention is applied to a target child.

SUMMARY AND CONCLUSIONS

In this chapter we provided an overview of some major aspects of research and program evaluation methodology in the behavioral field. The behavioral field is an area of psychological investigation in which applied research and program evaluation have been useful in theory building and in the development of applied knowledge. Psychology and education have much to gain through the application of findings from behavioral research and evaluation. Moreover, investigators in the applied field will find that the methodology in behavioral research and evaluation provides a useful format in the conduct of applied investigation.

Following some of the perspectives of Barlow et al. (1984), it was suggested that the goals and purposes of program evaluation and research are different. Although the primary goal of research is to make better scientific statements and generate knowledge for the field, the primary goal of treatment is to improve the client. Nevertheless, through some of the strategies of research treatment evaluation may be possible and is even desirable, but the primary goal will be improved client functioning. Single case studies and time-series strategies were advanced as alternatives for the treatment evaluation activity. Studies from the applied literature were presented as general examples of evaluation strategies.

Some applied research and evaluation designs were also discussed. After presenting an overview of the advantages and limitations of case study methodology, quasi-experimental group and within-series, between-series, and combined-series time-series designs were discussed. It must again be emphasized that time-series designs have been used rather extensively in behavioral research and evaluation, but work in the field is by no means limited to this approach. Examples of the application of between group and within subject designs and some advantages and limitations of these approaches were also presented.

The discussion of some specific designs was followed by a review of some methodological and conceptual issues involved in applied research and evaluation. Specifically, some criteria for evaluations of outcome of applied investigation, including experimental and therapeutic criteria, client-related criteria, and efficiency and cost-related criteria were discussed. This was followed by a discussion of some criteria for generalization, including procedures for programming generalization. Adherence to methodological and conceptual issues can improve greatly research and evaluation in applied settings.

Many of the basic designs and evaluation strategies employed in the behavior field are being used increasingly across a variety of problems and disorders. A major contribution of the time-series approaches is that they have been used to evaluate treatments applied to an individual subject. However, as noted earlier, they are not limited to this approach, a group can compose an experimental unit in virtually any of the strategies.

There is another issue that should be emphasized in discussing time-series tactics. In some instances, the use of the single case time-series design has been recommended as a model for merging the role of the scientist and practitioner (Barlow et al., 1984). Individuals who adhere to the scientist/practitioner model have frequently suggested that this approach may provide one of the best ways to merge the role. Yet, the use of this type of single case time-series design in clinical practice may prove problematic (Kratochwill & Piersel, 1983). Indeed, there are certain features that have been associated with time-series research that we have tried to elucidate in this chapter. First, time-series research is by no means limited to one subject; groups of subjects can be employed. Second, program outcome measurement is becoming an increasingly sophisticated strategy. In most cases, strategies require considerable sophistication and a great deal of effort to implement by the researcher/program evaluator. Third, the design, including those that are even the most basic strategies in the field, such as the A/B/A/B tactics, require considerable time and sophistication to implement. Thus, in many cases the strategies represent as difficult a tactic to implement in applied settings as any other design, such as between-group research methodologies.

The application of evaluation methodology of any kind extends beyond the issues raised earlier and includes the readiness of schools, as organizations, for data-based decision-making approaches. Especially salient in this activity are the following issues: (a) capability of staff to engage in research and evaluation, especially their knowledge and appreciation of when to seek consultation on technical matters; (b) sanctions that may be needed to move forward with evaluation efforts; (c) need for improvement and support of staff in data collection routines; and (d) importance of availability of funds needed to support research and evaluation activities.

The researcher/program evaluator must take an active role in offering staff preservice and inservice training on matters of evaluation, tools of evaluation, and when to seek consultation. Moreover, it is essential that the evaluator have support and sanctions from administrators in the conduct of all program evaluation efforts, and that staff are supportive of involvement in data collection and other technical aspects of their role in evaluation. Finally, the costs of program evaluation in time and money are high. Funds must be made available to support the implementation of program evaluation materials, supplies, and staff time. Without the availability of funds to adequately support the entire evaluation process, it is doubtful that a case can be made for the efficacy of evaluation in decision-making.

Most research strategies discussed in this chapter will probably not be adopted if service is the primary objective of the evaluator. On the other hand, certain features of case studies or even basic elements of time-series strategies may be used in program evaluation efforts. Certainly, many school psychologists whose primary function and role is generation of research or program evaluation will use these strategies. To this end, we hope that we have provided an overview of the advantages and limitations of research and program evaluation options. School psychologists will find these methodologies as difficult and challenging as any other strategy in program evaluation. These design strategies will be used by individuals in applied settings whose primary interest is in generating applied research. This research would answer questions that have been raised over the empirical basis of effectiveness of practice. Most likely, individuals using the approaches outlined in this chapter will be researchers, individuals who have a special interest in answering applied therapeutic issues essential for the practice and development of psychology and education as a scientific field. We hope we have stimulated an interest in researchers and program evaluators to use these approaches to develop that knowledge base.

ACKNOWLEDGMENT

The authors would like to express their sincere appreciation to Ms. Karen Kraemer for word processing the manuscript.

REFERENCES

American Psychological Association. (1981). Specialty guidelines for the delivery of services by school psychologists. *American Psychologist, 36*, 670–681.

Axline, V. M. (1964). *Dibs: In search of self.* New York: Ballantine books.

Baer, D. M. (1977). Perhaps it would be better not to know everything. *Journal of Applied Behavior Analysis, 10*, 167–172.

Baer, D. M., Wolf, M. M., & Risley, T. R. (1968). Some current dimensions of applied behavior analysis. *Journal of Applied Behavior Analysis, 1*, 91–97.

Barbacovi, D. R., & Clelland, R. W. (1977). Special education in transition. *Public Law*, 94–142.

Barlow, D. H., & Hayes, S. C. (1979). Alternating treatment design: One strategy for comparing the effects of two treatments in a single subject. *Journal of Applied Behavior Analysis, 12*, 199–210.

Barlow, D. H., Hayes, S. C., & Nelson, R. O. (1984). *The scientist practitioner: Research and accountability in clinical and educational settings.* Elmsford, NY: Pergamon Press.

Bergan, J. R. (1977). *Behavioral consultation.* Columbus, OH: Charles E. Merrill.

Bernstein, I. N., & Freeman, H. F. (1975). *Academic and entrepreneurial research.* New York: Russell Sage.

Browning, R. M. (1967). A single-subject design for simultaneous comparison of three reinforcement contingencies. *Behavior Therapy, 5*, 237–243.

Browning, R. M., & Stover, D. O. (1971). *Behavior modification in child treatment.* Chicago: Aldine-Atherton.

Campbell, D. T., & Stanley, J. C. (1963). Experimental and quasi-experimental design for research and teaching. In N. L. Gage (Ed.), *Handbook of research on teaching.* Chicago: Rand-McNally.

Chassan, J. B. (1979). *Research design in clinical psychology and psychiatry* (2nd ed.). New York: Irvinton.

Cook, T. D., & Campbell, D. T. (Eds.). (1979). *Quasi-experimentation: Design and analysis issues for field settings.* Chicago: Rand-McNally.

Davidson, P. O., & Costello, C. G. (1969). *N = 1: Experimental studies of single cases.* New York: Van Nostrand-Reinhold.

Drabman, R. S., Hammer, D. C., & Rosenbaum, M. S. (1979). Assessing generalization in behavior modification with children: The generalization map. *Behavioral Assessment, 1*, 203–219.

Dukes, W. F. (1965). N-1. *Psychological Bulletin, 64*, 74–79.

Flanagan, S., Adams, H. E., & Forehand, R. (1979). A comparison of four instructional techniques for teaching parents to use time-out. *Behavior Therapy, 10*, 94–102.

Forehand, R., Wells, K. C., & Griest, D. L. (1982). An examination of the social validity of a parent training program. *Behavior Therapy, 11,* 488–502.

Greenleaf, D. O. (1982). The use of structured learning therapy and transfer programming with disruptive adolescents in a school setting. *Journal of School Psychology, 20,* 122–130.

Hall, R. V., & Fox, R. G. (1977). Changing criterion designs: An alternative applied behavior analysis procedure. In B. Etzel, G. M. LeBlanc, & D. M. Baer (Eds.), *New developments in behavioral research: Theory, method, and application* (pp. 151–166). *In honor of Sidney W. Bijou.* Hillsdale, NJ: Lawrence Erlbaum Associates.

Harris, B. (1979). Whatever happened to little Albert? *American Psychologist, 34,* 151–160.

Hartmann, D. P., & Hall, R. V. (1976). A discussion of the changing criterion design. *Journal of Applied Behavior Analysis, 9,* 527–532.

Hayes, S. C. (1981). Single-case experimental design and empirical clinical practice. *Journal of Consulting and Clinical Psychology, 49,* 193–211.

Hersen, M., & Barlow, D. H. (1976). *Single-case experimental designs: Strategies for studying behavior change.* Elmsford NY: Pergamon Press.

Kazdin. A. E. (1976). Statistical analyses for single-case experimental designs. In M. Hersen & D. H. Barlow (Eds.), *Single-care experimental designs: Strategies for studying behavior change.* Elmsford, NY: Pergamon Press.

Kazdin, A. E. (1977a). Assessing the clinical or applied significance of behavior change through social validation. *Behavior Modification 1,* 427–452.

Kazdin, A. E. (1977b). Methodology of applied behavior analysis. In T. A. Brigham & A. C. Catania (Eds.), *Social and instructional processes: Foundations and applications of a behavior analysis.* New York: Irvington/Narbury-Wiley.

Kazdin, A. E. (1980). *Research design in clinical psychology.* New York: Harper & Row.

Kazdin, A. E. (1981). Drawing valid inferences from case studies. *Journal of Consulting and Clinical Psychology, 49,* 183–192.

Kazdin, A. E. (1982a). Methodology of psychotherapy outcome research: Recent developments and remaining limitations. In J. H. Harvey & M. M. Parker (Eds.), *Psychotherapy research and behavior change: The master lecture series* (Vol. 1). Washington, DC: American Psychological Association.

Kazdin, A. E. (1982b). *Single-case research designs: Methods for clinical and applied settings.* New York: Oxford University Press.

Kazdin, A. E., & Geesey, S. (1977). Simultaneous-treatment design comparisons of the effects of earning reinforcers for one's peers versus for oneself. *Behavior Therapy, 8,* 682–693.

Kazdin, A. E., & Hartmann, D. P. (1978). The simultaneous-treatment design. *Behavior Therapy, 9,* 912–922.

Kazdin. A. E., & Wilson, G. T. (1978). *Evaluation of behavior therapy: Issues, evidence, and research strategies.* Cambridge, MA: Ballinger.

Kirk, R. E. (1968). *Experimental design: Procedures for the behavioral sciences.* Belmont, CA: Brooks/Cole.

Koocher, G. P., & Broskowski, A. (1977). Issues in the evaluation of mental health services for children. *Professional Psychology 8,* 583–592.

Kratochwill, T. R. (Ed.). (1978). *Single subject research: Strategies for evaluating change.* New York: Academic Press.

Kratochwill, T. R. (1979). Intensive research: A review of methodological issues in clinical, school, and counseling psychology. In D. C. Berliner (Ed.), *Review of research in education.* Itasca, IL: F. E. Peacock.

Kratochwill, T. R. (1981). *Selective mutism: Implications for research and treatment.* Hillsdale, NJ: Lawrence Erlbaum Associates.

Kratochwill, T. R. (1982). Advances in behavioral assessment. In C. R. Reynolds & T. B. Gutkin (Eds.), *Handbook of school psychology* (pp. 314–350). New York: Wiley.

Kratochwill, T. R., & Piersel, W. C. (1983). Time series research: Contributions to empirical clinical practice. *Behavioral Assessment, 5,* 165–176.

Lazarus, A. A., & Davidson, G. (1971). Clinical innovation in research and practice. In A. E. Bergin & S. L. Garfield (Eds.), *Handbook of psychotherapy and behavior change: An empirical analyses* (pp. 196–213). New York: Wiley.

Maher, C. A., & Kratochwill, T. R. (1980). Principles and procedures of program evaluation: An overview. *School Psychology Monograph, 4*(1).

McMahon, R. J. Forehand, R. (1978). Nonprescription behavior therapy: Effectiveness of a brochure on teaching mothers to correct their children's inappropriate mealtime behaviors. *Behavior Therapy, 9,* 814–820.

Medway, F. J. (1979). How effective is school consultation? A review of recent research. *Journal of School Psychology, 17,* 275–282.

Meyers, J., Pitt, N. W., Gaughan, E. J., Jr., & Freidman, M. P. (1978). A research model for consultation with teachers. *Journal of School Psychology, 16,* 137–145.

Michael, J. (1974). Statistical inference for individual organism research: Mixed blessing or curse? *Journal of Applied Behavior Analysis, 1,* 647–653.

Morris, R. J., & Kratochwill, T. R. (1983). *Assessment and treatment of children's fears and phobias.* Elmsford, NY: Pergamon Press.

Morrisey, P., & Safer, N. (1977). Implications for special education: The individualized education programs. *Viewpoints, 53,* 31–38.

Myers, J. (1979). *Fundamentals of experimental design.* Boston: Allyn & Bacon.

Petrie, P., Brown, D. K., Piersel, W. C., Frinfrock, S. R., Schelble, M., LeBlanc, C. P., & Kratochwill, T. R. (1980). The school psychologist as behavioral ecologist. *Journal of School Psychology, 18,* 222–233.

Risley, T. R. (1970). Behavior modification: An experimental-therapeutic endeavor. In L. A. Hammrlynck, P. O. Davidson, & L. E. Acker (Eds.), *Behavior modification and ideal mental health services.* Alberta: University of Calgary.

Robinson, S. J., DeReus, D. M., & Drabman, R. S. (1976). Peer and college student tutoring as reinforcement in a token economy. *Journal of Applied Behavior Analysis, 9,* 169–177.

Rossi, P. H., Freeman, H. E., & Wright, S. R. (1979). *Evaluation: A systematic approach.* Beverly Hills, CA: Sage.

Rossi, P. H., & Wright, S. R. (1977). Evaluation research: An assessment of theory, practice and politics. *Evaluation Quarterly, 1,* 5–52.

Shapiro, E. S., Barrett, R. P., & Ollendick, T. H. (1980). A comparison of physical restraint and positive practice overcorrection in treating sterotypic behavior. *Behavior Therapy, 11,* 227–233.

Shontz, F. C. (1965). *Research methods in personality.* New York: Appleton-Century-Crofts.

Sidman, M. (1960). *Tactics of scientific research.* New York: Basic Books.

Stokes, T. F., & Baer, D. M. (1977). An implicit technology of generalization. *Journal of Applied Behavior Analysis, 10,* 349–368.

Taylor, M. J., & Kratochwill, T. R. (1978). Modification of preschool children's bathroom behavior by contingent teacher attention. *Journal of School Psychology, 16,* 64–71.

Thigpen, C. H., & Cleckley, H. M. (1957). *Three faces of Eve.* New York: McGraw-Hill.

Weiss, C. H. (1972). *Evaluation research: Methods of assessing program effectiveness.* Englewood Cliffs, NJ: Prentice-Hall.

Wolf, H. M., & Risley, T. R. (1971). Reinforcement: Applied Research. In R. Glaser (Ed.), *The nature of reinforcement* (pp. 310–325). New York: Academic Press.

Wolf, M. M. (1978). Social validity: The case for subjective measurement or how applied behavior analysis is finding its heart. *Journal of Applied Behavior Analysis, 11,* 203–214.

11 Legal and Ethical Issues

Susan L. Graham-Clay
Daniel J. Reschly

Behavior change programs are becoming increasingly popular in schools. Indeed, a variety of techniques and procedures are extremely attractive because of their demonstrated effectiveness in changing the academic and social behavior of children (O'Leary & O'Leary, 1977). However, lack of formalized legal and ethical guidelines specifically designed for use in schools, the underlying philosophical rationale for behavioral approaches that is often at variance with the causation of human behavior accepted by school personnel, and the need for schools to deal with the deviant behavior of students quickly and effectively, have served to make schools susceptible to neglect of the legal and ethical issues involved in implementing behavioral programs (Martin, 1975a). Compared with the behavioral interventions used with clinical populations in closed settings, less careful scrutiny has been afforded behavioral procedures in schools, a trend not likely to last (Harris & Kapche, 1978).

In recent years, a growing concern has developed concerning the legal and ethical issues surrounding behavior change programs and procedures. Concern has stemmed from several sources. Misconceptions of behavior modification as "mind control" (Wherry, 1983), and misunderstanding of approaches that do and do not constitute legitimate behavioral techniques (Stolz, Wienckowski, & Brown, 1975) have aroused public unrest.

The potential for misapplication of behavioral procedures and programs is real, and may lead to exaccerbation of inappropriate behavior. Thus, for school applications, O'Leary and O'Leary (1977) have stressed the need for teacher and parent involvement to safeguard against possible misuse. The "heightened sensitivity" of the general population to ethical issues and the increasing demand for accountability (Harris & Kapche, 1978) have also directed attention toward the use of behavior change programs in schools. Public school personnel are beginning to be held responsible for the behavioral interventions they carry out in schools (Gast & Nelson, 1977; Wherry, 1983).

Clearly, there is need for everyone involved with, and who has concerns about children in our schools, to address legal and ethical issues in implementing any kind of behavioral change strategy in schools. This chapter focuses on general legal and ethical guidelines that have been developed in recent years and the application of these guidelines to the specific stages involved with behavioral interventions.

LEGAL AND ETHICAL GUIDELINES

The influence of the law over the lives of school personnel has expanded in recent years (Reschly, 1983). Various legal principles and ethical guidelines from professional organizations represent efforts to assure that the rights of clients or students are protected and that effective services are provided by competent professionals. The dual purposes of legal and ethical guidelines (i.e., to protect clients' rights and to ensure competent services) are reflected in a variety of sources including legislation, litigation, and professional standards.

Legal Influences

Legal influences exist in two general forms: *Constitutonal* provisions refined through case law; and *Legislation*, refined and implemented through case law, rules, and regulations.

Constitutional Provisions and Case Law.   Education is primarily a state governmental function. The framers of the United States Constitution viewed education as a residual function of the states. However, over the past three decades the federal government and the federal courts have become, usually reluctantly, increasingly involved in state and local educational activities. Court decisions and federal legislation have profoundly changed schools and markedly expanded the rights of students. These changes, although peripheral in some ways, have important implications for behavioral interventions.

The Fourteenth Amendment to the United States Constitution contains two phrases that have been applied by federal courts to educational issues. The *Equal Protection* clause prohibits states (recall that education is a state function) from denying " . . . to any person . . . equal protection of the laws." This provision has been part of the basis for desegregation orders, remedies to overrepresentation of minorities in special education classes, and mandates to serve handicapped students. The equal protection clause does not have direct application to behavioral interventions. The only application we can anticipate would occur in a situation in which a group is unfairly or unjustifiably placed in or is exposed to behavioral intervention programs. An equal protection claim might arise if the program unfairly limited educational opportunities. These circumstances are highly unlikely, but we need to be sensitive to possible issues concerning bias or discrimination. These concerns arise if there is disproportionate representation of a minority group in a special program, a circumstance that might occur with certain kinds of behavioral interventions.

Due Process.   The most relevant legal concept to behavioral interventions is due process, especially the informed consent component. Due process is part of the Fourteenth Amendment and appears in various state and federal statutes. Due process protections have been prominent in several recent court opinions concerning the rights of students.

A good synonym for due process is procedural fairness in decision making. The important elements of due process (i.e., prior notice, written consent, access to records, right to appeal decisions, right to add information, and impartial hearing) are described thoroughly in several publications (Abeson, Bolick, & Hass, 1975; Bersoff, 1978; Buss, 1975).

The various due process procedures, including the need for informed consent, often seem excessively bureaucratic until applied to a personal example. Imagine that a significant decision was about to be made about you or your children, and that this decision would influence your (their) educational opportunities or call negative public attention to you (them), for example, seclusion time out (see later section of this chapter). If that kind of decision is to be made, you would want to be informed, exercise consent rights, and so forth. Personalizing the situation is a good way to resolve the instances in which legal or ethical requirements for informed consent are unclear, which is more often the case than not.

Informed Consent.   *Informed consent,* a legal term, has been described as an "ethical imperative" in the practice of behavior therapy (Wilson & O'Leary, 1980). A client has the right to consent or refuse to participate in a proposed treatment program, a decision that should be based on knowledge about what will be involved. True informed consent consists of three components: knowledge, voluntariness, and competency (Friedman, 1975). *Knowledge* refers to information about the program and program goals, understanding of the nature of treatment, facts about treatment alternatives, knowledge of the right to decline or withdraw at any time, and an understanding of the potential risks and benefits involved. *Voluntariness* involves a freely-entered-into agreement by the client, in the absence of coercion or duress of any kind. *Competence* implies the ability to make a well-reasoned, responsible decision based on an understanding of the information provided.

Special problems arise in ensuring informed consent with a school-aged population. It is not likely, for example, that many children would consent to receive punishment (Glenn, 1980). The capacity to give consent implies sufficient age to make sound decisions and to act on one's own behalf. Children are not considered to have such a capacity (Martin, 1975b). As informed consent pertains to children, the basic problem is one of comprehension (Martin, 1975b). As it pertains to behavior change programs in schools, the legal and ethical issues are reflected in the following questions: When is informed consent required? and Who should give it?

An important (and debatable) issue involves the extent to which informed consent is required in specific manipulations or interventions in the classroom (Martin, 1975a). Ambiguity exists if behavioral manipulations are in keeping with normal teacher expectations and behavior, such as varying the quality and/or quantity of teacher praise. As the intervention involves increasingly obvious changes in how an individual is being treated, the need for informed consent becomes more salient. In discussing discipline in the classroom, Overcast and Sales (1982) emphasized that a "general standard of reasonableness" must prevail. These authors also noted that the courts give educators a rather wide latitude in imposing discipline, including corporal punishment, as long as the criterion of "reasonableness" is met.

There are no straightforward, unequivocal legal guidelines about whether informed consent is required. In special education placement informed consent is "triggered" by two general circumstances: (a) an alternative educational placement and program is about to be considered; or (b) when the student is being treated differently in a way that is obvious to a casual observer and/or in a way that is clearly atypical or unusual in comparison to conventional classroom practices. Usually, this is interpreted to mean that counseling or other individual work with students outside of the classroom should be preceeded by informed consent (Bersoff, 1982). The need for informed consent is far less clear if the intervention is carried out by the teacher in the regular classroom. In this situation, consideration should be given to the expected duration of the program, the degree of departure from the normal classroom routine, and the degree to which the individual is singled out and treated differently by others in the classroom. Admittedly, these considerations do not lead to easy resolution of issues concerning informed consent. However, these considerations along with personalizing the situation, "what would I want if . . .," provide a good framework for analyzing these issues.

A related issue is, From whom should informed consent be obtained? Because children are presumed not to have the capacity to consent for themselves, consent must be obtained from the individuals responsible for them. Glenn (1980) has suggested that a compromise between a "child's right to self-determination and a child's status as a minor" (p. 615) involves "informed forced consent." In the case in which a child is not capable of mature and responsible decision making, the child is informed of the reason for the intervention and what is hoped will be gained as a result of the intervention; the child is not actually given a choice to participate. Glenn's (1980) notion of informed forced consent reflects a common practice in the implementation of behavior change programs in schools. However, the age of the child may be a critical variable.

Glenn (1980) interpreted the *Kremens v. Bartley* (1977) Supreme Court case, which pertained to the legal rights of institutionalization, to imply that informed forced consent may be used until a child is 14 years of age. This would suggest that increased legal rights are forthcoming to adolescents in regulating their own involvement in treatment; there are also implications for informed consent. It should be noted that problems exist in applying judicial decisions to school-based policies and procedures. Most decisions are gleaned from other settings, such as mental health and mental retardation, and implications for the classroom are unclear and may be tenuous.

Informed consent is a procedural right (Wherry, 1983) that is highlighted in Principle 6 of the "Ethical Principles of Psychologists" (APA, 1981). In practice, "consent is often given on behalf of the incompetent client by parents or guardians—an arrangement which is fraught with many moral and legal entanglements" (Woods, 1982, p. 35). Indeed, the legal and ethical requirements of informed consent, as it relates to behavior change programs in schools, are difficult to resolve. Perhaps the underlying issue (or "near nonissue" according to Kicklighter, 1983) is that the "real" client has yet to stand up. Are we here for the kids or for the parents? Kicklighter (1983) suggested that, in the majority of cases, "when we serve one, we serve the other" (p. 120).

It would seem that legal and ethical safeguards entail seeking out rather than avoiding informed parental consent (O'Leary & O'Leary, 1977). Parents deserve a clear explanation of a proposed intervention program. Alternatives should be presented and discussed, the benefits of the proposed approach expressed, and the risk/benefit ratio weighed. The right to withdraw from the program must be understood, and voluntary consent given. If possible, efforts should also be made to obtain permission from the student (O'Leary & O'Leary, 1977). At the very least, students should be informed of the proposed behavior change program at a level they can be expected to understand and appreciate, and to the degree that their abilities allow. By sharing in the selection of preferred incentives, and even in the selection of the approach to be used, children can make a meaningful contribution to a behavior change program (Stolz and Associates, 1978).

Legislation and Rules and Regulations.   A second general source of legal influences is legislation and the rules and regulations formulated to implement legislation. Legislation is enacted at the state and federal level. Legal statutes (i.e., actual laws passed) are usually comparatively brief and general, and reflect the overall intent of the legislative body. Laws passed by legislative bodies are almost always implemented through a set of rules and regulations that provide specific definitions of terms and more precison regarding compliance with the law. The general trend is that laws are seldom repealed or amended; but rules and regulations are changed or refined more frequently. Usually, rules and regulations are formulated by a department in the executive branch of government. Depending on the nature of the law and other customs, rules and regulations may be changed easily with little or no subsequent legislative review.

Over the past decade there has been a cycle of litigation, legislation, and further litigation concerning the educational rights of handicapped students (Bersoff, 1982). The first phase was litigation based on the constitutional principles of equal protection and due process. In the second phase state and federal legislation was passed that established and extended the educational rights of handicapped students. The third phase, which has continued during the 1980s, is further litigation based on state and federal legislation. This dynamic process in which legal concepts are refined and extended precludes the development of a permanent, definitive list of legal guidelines. Guidelines have undergone many changes in the past, and are likely to continue to evolve throughout our professional careers.

The basic principles concerning education of handicapped students reflect the litigation–legislation–litigation cycle. These principles also have implications for behavioral interventions in school settings. The principles are as follows: (a) appropriate educational services at public expense based on the individual's needs and abilities; (b) educational programming in the least restrictive (i.e., most normal) environment that is feasible; (c) individualized educational program; (d) due process procedural protections; and (e) protection in evaluation procedures provisions. To illustrate the litigation-legislation cycle, consider the first principle, appropriate education at public expense. This principle was established in two landmark court cases in the early 1970s (PARC, 1972; Mills, 1972), and was based, in large part, on the constitutional principles of equal protection and due process. The principle was refined and extended in legislation passed in almost every state and by the United States Congress by the mid-1970s. The rules and regulations implementing the federal law (*Federal Register,* 1977) provided a set of requirements about this and other principles concerning education of the handicapped. Now, there are tens, if not a hundred or more, cases in the federal courts that concern the meaning of the legislation and the accompanying rules and regulations. A specific question currently before the courts in several states is whether an appropriate education for severely handicapped students, guaranteed by legislation, must be "year round" (i.e., 12 rather than the traditional 9 month school year). Several courts have affirmed the concept that in retrospect is a far journey from the first litigation phase when courts were asked to determine whether the severely handicapped even had the right of access to the public schools.

We suspect that there will be similar refinements in other key concepts, including the crucial notion of informed consent. The implications of these legal principles for behavioral interventions are extremely important. For example, the free, appropriate education guarantee led directly to far greater numbers of severely and profoundly handicapped students in the schools. Although still only a small percent of the overall population, these students required use of more fundamental and more finely sequenced behavioral interventions, many of which were seldom if ever used previously in the schools. Procedures for teaching very basic self-help skills (e.g., toileting and feeding) and for controlling and suppressing self-injurious behaviors have become part of the educational program for some students. At the same time, legal and ethical concerns associated with some of these intervention strategies, addressed some years before in "closed" institutional settings, have become increasingly important issues in the schools. Now, persons working in the schools need to be concerned about guidelines and policies regarding the use of aversive procedures, or exclusion techniques. Another important concept, related by analogy to least restrictive environment, is least drastic alternative. Although more of an ethical then legal guideline, least drastic alternative suggests use of less intrusive, more natural strategies whenever possible (see later discussion).

Summary. Legal guidelines are not static. There have been enormous changes in this realm, a trend that is likely to continue. Persons educated today in legal concepts and guidelines will be, if the trends of the past two decades continue, far out of date within a few years. Continuing education in this area is imperative.

Professional Standards

Standards developed by scientific and professional associations are another mechanism in which the dual goals of protecting client/student rights and ensuring competent professional personnel are pursued. A variety of standards concerning ethics, graduate program acreditation, licensing or certification, and professional competencies have been developed by various scientific/professional associations. The professional/scientific associations that are most important for our work are the American Association for Counseling and Development (AACD), the National Association of Social Workers (NASW), the American Psychological Association (APA), the National Association of School Psychologists (NASP) and the Association for the Advancement of Behavior Therapy (AABT). The codes of ethics and other standards developed by these organizations can be obtained at the addresses listed in the references to this chapter. Readers are encouraged to acquire and to become familiar with the codes of ethics and standards of their respective associations.

Knowledge of and commitment to uphold professional standards, especially ethical standards, are essential attributes of everyone in the helping professions. Standards usually help us to become sensitive to potential problems and raise our consciousness concerning likely conflicts. These outcomes are critical to competent and humane professional work. Moreover, in particularly troublesome areas where there are no unequivocal guidelines or standards, knowledge of the general ethical standards for one's profession, and conscientious efforts to apply these standards to the specific problematic situation at hand, meet the case law criterion of "reasonable" behavior. In the absence of specific legal or professional guidelines, conscientious effort to apply general ethical concepts is the only way one can proceed.

As implied in this discussion, there are many difficulties with professional standards. These difficulties are discussed briefly (a more detailed discussion was provided in Reschly, 1980). A major problem is that professional standards are usually written at a general level that, more often than not, fails to indicate specific courses of action or methods to resolve competing interests. Bersoff (1975) provided several examples in which even the most conscientious application of APA or NASP codes of ethics would not provide sufficient guidance to the individual professional. There are many other problems, such as ineffective enforcement mechanisms, reluctance to report violation of standards, ignorance of existing standards, and so on.

Summary.   The leading figures in behavioral interventions research and development have been sensitive to the need for professional standards, especially ethical codes (Gambrill, 1977). In comparison to other professional orientations, behavioral proponents have long recongized the potential ethical conflicts associated with deliberate application of learning principles to change behavior (Bandura, 1969). Approaches to counseling or therapy, including those that claim to be "nondirective", involve, at a minimum, social influence processes that produce changes in clients/students. The behavioral approach, perhaps more than other approaches, has reflected concerns for protecting clients/students' rights at all stages of the intervention process. In subsequent sections of this chapter, legal and ethical concepts are applied to the key stages in behavioral interventions. The legal and ethical issues described are, for the most part, described in the context of individual treatment programs. However, it should be noted that consideration of these issues applies equally to interventions carried out with small groups of children, entire classrooms, or interventions instituted at the organizational level.

STAGES OF BEHAVIORAL INTERVENTIONS

The behavioral consultation model developed by Bergan (1977) is used to provide an overall framework within which legal and ethical issues are discussed (see also Chapter 8, Behavioral Consultation). According to Bergan's (1977) model, a behavioral change program can be divided into a number of separate, but not necessarily discrete, stages or phases. The first stage, *problem identification,* focuses on specification of the target child and target behavior(s) of concern. The collection of baseline data and a review of the data to document the existence of a problem is a must. The *problem analysis* stage involves a careful assessment of the identified problem behavior(s) and an attempt to determine the controlling events in the school and, more specifically, the classroom setting. An intervention strategy is then devised, incorporating procedures to assess performance continuously through the intervention phase.

Plan implementation involves carrying out the selected behavioral change procedure. It includes assigning "implementation roles" and developing "implementation skills" through training as necessary (Bergan, 1977). The program must also be given adequate monitoring with subsequent revision of intervention procedures if required. The *problem evaluation* stage incorporates an evaluation of the degree to which the program goals have been met, and an assessment of the effectiveness of the treatment plan. A review of the data is essential in the evaluation process. Also, post-implementation planning must occur to provide for maintenance and generalizaton of the behavior(s) and for follow-up procedures. The importance of these two components has been highlighted by Kratochwill (1982).

Although interventions sometimes entail a preventive rather than the remedial or treatment focus implied earlier; an intervention aimed at prevention is not necessarily inconsistent with the stages just described. Bergan (1977) recognized the preventive function and the role of behavioral consultation at several levels. Thus, in keeping with Bergan's (1977) stages, behavioral interventions that have a preventive goal must identify a *potential* problem, determine appropriate alternative behaviors, devise an intervention strategy, monitor effectiveness and so on.

PROBLEM IDENTIFICATION

The first step in any behavioral intervention is to determine the specific nature of the concern (see also Chapter 2). Thus, the primary focus is to define the target client(s) and target behavior(s), and to verify the existence of a problem (or identify a potential problem). From the beginning, however, ethical questions arise: When is a problem *really* a problem? In other words, how significant is the behavior and who sees it as a concern?

Sulzer-Azaroff and Mayer (1977) suggested that a real problem exists when one or more of the following occur: several independent requests for assistance involving the same student (or students) are received; a student's level of functioning is significantly discrepant from peers; and/or a dramatic change in behavior is observed. In addition, consideration should be given to whether the behavior significantly interferes with the learning or development of the identified child and/or his/her peers. Adherence to these guidelines should provide appropriate ethical safeguards in the identification of a true problem behavior.

Legal safeguards involve documentation of the existence of a problem (Martin, 1975b), preferably through the use of behavioral observations not only of the target child's behavior but also the behavior of the child's peers (Harris &

Kapche, 1978). If baseline data are consistent with peer data, the existence of a problem must be questioned (perhaps there is another problem correlated with the referral?). If a behavior can be tolerated, then a behavioral intervention may not be justified (Martin, 1975b).

Once the existence of a problem is documented, selecting an appropriate target behavior and behavioral objectives are perhaps the most difficult, yet important steps in the process. "The behavior modification approach provides a set of rather well-defined procedures to change behavior, but the procedures do not spell out the goals or the behaviors which *ought* to be taught or changed" (O'Leary, 1972, p. 509). Basic philosophical questions underlie the extent to which society (or a subset of society) can define a behavior as undesirable and then set about to change it (Woods, 1982). Value judgments become necessary in changing behaviors and selecting more appropriate behaviors (Martin, 1975a). In effect, who is to decide what behaviors are desirable in the classroom, or whose values should be represented in the choice (Harris & Kapche, 1978; O'Leary & O'Leary, 1977; Winett & Winkler, 1972)?

Behavior modification has been accused of supporting rather than changing the *status quo* in schools. A survey study by Winett and Winkler (1972) suggested that behaviors most frequently targeted in the classroom reflected the norms of "silence and lack of movement" (p. 501) or "be still, be quiet, be docile." Although this study has been challenged, it did highlight the fact that anyone involved in implementing a behavior change program in the classroom should seriously consider the behavior that is to be changed (O'Leary, 1972).

External criteria to guide the selection of appropriate target behaviors and goals are, for the most part, unavailable (Stolz, 1978). Certainly, behaviors should be selected that will be of short and long-term benefit to the child, and that will continue to be supported and reinforced naturally, both in and out of school. The long-term utility of the behavior (Harris & Kapche, 1977; Hawkins, 1975) and the social validity or social significance of the goals must be addressed (Van Houton, 1979; Wolf, 1978). Ethical selection of target behaviors and goals requires knowledge or hypotheses about the behaviors that "should" be present (Hawkins, 1975) balanced against the "right" of the child to exhibit or not to exhibit these behaviors. The selection of target behaviors must be sensitive to variables, such as age, sex, culture, and socio-economic status, tempered by a liberal definition of what is considered to be or tolerated as acceptable behavior (Woods, 1982). Often the question of whether to select academic rather than other school behaviors must be considered. Recognition of the need to target an appropriate "alternative" behavior is essential.

When all parties involved agree to the necessity and direction of a change, then perhaps appropriate safeguards have been taken. If total agreement is not the case, an ethical dilemma exists (Martin, 1975a). Questions about who is the real client, and to whom does the therapist owe first allegiance become critical (Winkler, 1977). Depending on the source of the referral and the nature of the problem, the "real" client may be the child, the parents or the teacher. In the end, the therapist must be bound by allegiance to his/her own values and consideration of community norms. It would be of questionable ethical practice to be involved in implementing a behavior change program if one had concerns about the appropriateness of the target behavior, or the proposed goals of treatment.

PROBLEM ANALYSIS

The problem analysis stage incorporates two broad phases (Bergen, 1977). The first phase involves identification of factors that might influence the behavior(s) of concern; the second phase involves selection of a behavioral change strategy to solve the problem. The selection and subsequent implementation of school-based behavior change techniques are replete with legal and ethical issues. General policies and safeguards must be considered in conjunction with special issues that relate to specific procedures or techniques. In this section, the general legal and ethical guidelines are presented, followed by considerations pertaining to a number of specific behavioral approaches.

General Guidelines

Legally, perhaps the major impetus for the use of behavioral techniques have been "substantive rights," such as the right to treatment and the right to an education (Wherry, 1983). A number of court cases have addressed these basic rights. (For a detailed presentation of specific judicial proceedings and their implications for use with behavior change programs in schools, consult Wherry, 1983). Fundamental requirements, such as the right to an "adequate treatment" and an "individualized treatment plan" have also been identified in the courts (Wherry, 1983).

Legal implications and ethical standards suggest that behavioral procedures should be selected on the bases of demonstrated effectiveness (in short and long-term effects) (Harris & Kapche, 1978). The "efficacy and efficiency" of a treatment must be considered (Wilson & O'Leary, 1980) in accordance with a client's right to receive the best possible validated treatment (Davison & Stuart, 1975; Woods, 1982). Indeed, therapeutic endeavors should not only be subjected to rational and empirical validation (Davidson & Stuart, 1975) but to practical validation as well (Woods, 1982). The area of social validity (Van Houten, 1979; Wolf, 1978) is a positive step forward in the identification and assessment of the appropriateness of procedures and "real-life" significance of goals.

Court decisions have also emphasized the "use of the least intrusive and restrictive intervention, the most benign, practical and economical in implementation" (Wexler, 1973, in Stolz and Associates, 1978, p. 22). Implications for the classroom suggest that behavior change programs lie on a continuum in terms of intrusiveness or the degree of external control exerted, the type of reinforcer used (i.e., similarity to normal contingencies), and the setting in which the program is carried out (e.g, regular vs. special class placement). Less intrusive methods should be applied first, and should be shown to be ineffective prior to the implementation of a more intrusive procedure. Therefore, the need for a hierarchical guide or strategy for the selection of intervention procedures is apparent. Thus, soft reprimands would be used prior to overcorrection that would be a less intrusive intervention than seclusion time out (Stolz and Associates, 1978). Broadly speaking, this principle also favors the development of positive alternative behaviors over the reduction of undesirable behaviors (Wilson & O'Leary, 1980).

However, strict adherence to this sequencing principle may, on occasion, produce an ethical dilemma. In an urgent and/or serious situation (such as self-injurious behavior), the selection of a less intrusive intervention might prove less effective than the use of a more potent technique. Intervention choices must be guided by consideration of the risk/benefit ratio, potential for negative side effects, and fully informed consent. The least possible risk and discomfort must be weighed against the greatest possible expected benefit (Davison & Stuart, 1975).

Most would agree that positive reinforcement should be used before an aversive or punishment procedure. However, because positive reinforcement is often a less obvious form of control, there has been a tendency to disregard the ethical issues involved (Martin, 1975a). Natural rewards, such as social reinforcement, should be used before tangible rewards. A practical reinforcement hierarchy proposed by Christian (1983) suggested a continuum of reinforcers ranging from concrete rewards (such as food and toys) to more abstract reinforcers (such as praise and self-reinforcement). The goal is to enter the hierarchy at the highest possible level of abstractness, and work toward the most abstract reinforcers possible. Thus, the long-term goal should always be to decrease the need for tangibles and maintain behavior on the basis of social praise and internal self-reinforcement (Christian, 1983; O'Leary & O'Leary, 1977). There has been a trend away from the use of tangible rewards toward the use of more natural reinforcers, such as free time, extra recess, special activities, available in most every classroom (Stolz and Associates, 1978).

Finally, the least restrictive environment is another principle that has been highlighted by the passage of PL94-142. Efforts should be directed at maintaining a child in the least restrictive (i.e., "normal") setting possible given the nature and extent of the problem. Thus, depending on the referral problem, a behavior change program carried out in the regular class *may* be a less intrusive and less restrictive alternative that should be tried prior to consideration of a special educational program.

Special Procedures

There are a myriad of behavioral techniques that can be applied appropriately and effectively in the classroom. It is beyond the scope of this chapter to discuss these techniques in depth. However, in this section the authors attempt to high-light some of the legal and ethical issues to be considered when using some general behavioral approaches. It should be noted that, for the most part, behavioral procedures in schools have not been specifically litigated, and legal implications are often "gleaned from cases in other settings" (Wherry, 1983, p. 50).

Token economies. Token economies have been a widely used behavioral procedure in classrooms (see also Chapter 4). They involve an explicit aim to change behavior and, as such, have been viewed as bribery by some (O'Leary & O'Leary, 1977). Token economies should not be considered as a "panacea for all problems" (Harris & Kapche, 1978) and careful consideration must be given as to whether such a program is indicated. Specific issues to be addressed include maintenance or generalization of behavior beyond the token economy, and the need to consider appropriate reinforcers (Harris & Kapche, 1978). Caution must be exercised to ensure such a program is properly implemented and that any type of coercion or pressure is avoided.

Group Contingencies. A variety of group contingency procedures are possible (see also Chapter 4). Typically, a whole group of students (e.g., an entire class) is treated as a unit (Sulzer-Azaroff & Mayer, 1977). Receipt of group reinforcement is dependent on the behavior of the group. The "Good Behavior Game" (Barrish, Saunders, & Wolf, 1969) is an example of a group contingency technique. The game involved the recording of out-of-seat and talking-out be-haviors of students in a regular fourth grade class who were divided into two teams. The game was played during specified class times, and rule violations were recorded, the team that committed a violation received a mark on the board. Reinforcement was provided to the team that received the fewest marks by day's end, or to both teams if neither received more than a criterion number of rule violations. The reinforcers used were natural to the classroom (early recess, lining up early for lunch, or special projects).

Group contingency programs have been criticized because of the pressure exerted on an individual by a group, if nonproblem students are used to influence target individuals (Stolz and Associates, 1978). Ethical considerations involve the potential effects these programs may have on the overall social climate of the classroom, in addition to bullying or ridicule of specific students whose behavior may cause their team to lose. These programs have also been questioned legally (Stolz and Associates, 1978). The concern expressed involves the peer pressure of the group that may interfere with the "psychological well-being" of the individual student. However, Wherry (1983) has noted that the Consent Decree of *Ross v. Saltmarch,* 1980, may have provided some impetus for the use of group contingency procedures in schools.

Home-based contingency systems. These programs involve the administra-tion of back-up reinforcers at home based on information received from school (see Broughton, Barton, & Owen, 1981 for review; see also Chapter 7). Home-based systems include parents in their child's educational team and provide for a much broader and potentially more potent array of reinforcement and/or punishment alternatives. Indeed, the greater involvement of parents in the discipline process has been recommended by the courts (Wherry, 1983).

However, home-based contingency systems present several ethical considerations. For a program to be effective, parents must apply contingencies in a consistent, cooperative manner; programs should not be implemented if parents are unwilling or unable to comply. The amount of parent training required is also an unresolved issue. There is the potential for unstable parents to allow such a program to justify abuse or humiliation of their child (Lahey, Gendrich, Gendrich, Schnelle, Gant, & McNees, 1977). It would be of questionable ethics to institute a home-based behavior change program without supplying sufficient safeguards to insure the child's safety and the correct application of the procedure (Broughton, Barton, & Owen, 1981).

Punishment.   Punishment techniques have the greatest potential for misuse and harm to a child (Harris & Kapche, 1978; see also Chapter 4). A continuum of aversive procedures exist, again it is suggested that the least aversive procedure be used prior to a more aversive procedure. This caveat is not only an ethical rule-of-thumb, but one that has been sanctioned by the courts in suggesting that corporal punishment should never be employed first, and should be attempted only after behavior change efforts have been attempted through alternative means (*Baker v. Owen,* 1975 as discussed by Wherry, 1983). The right of public school officials to use corporal punishment was affirmed by the U.S. Supreme Court in *Ingraham v. Wright,* (1976). However, school personnel must exercise "prudence and restraint" in the use of corporal punishment. It must not be cruel nor excessive, it must be proportional to the seriousness of the offence, and consideration must be given to age, size, sex, and physical strength of the student (Overcast & Sales, 1982).

Repp and Dietz (1978) point out that target behaviors that may be considered appropriate for the use of punishment would include self-injurious behavior or aggressive behavior that is physically damaging to another student. In deciding whether punishment should be used, the available data on the efficacy of the technique with the particular population and behavior problem should be considered (Stolz & Associates, 1978). O'Leary and O'Leary (1977) have pointed out that although spanking in schools has been legitimized through Supreme Court rulings, no behavioral research has been conducted evaluating spanking. On the other hand, some aversive techniques have been shown to be effective. For example, in the treatment of self-injurious behavior in autistic children, punishment produces rapid cessation; more positive procedures would take longer to effect the behavior, and thus, expose the child to a longer period of self-injury. With all behavioral programs, but especially when aversive procedures are used, it is essential to document the need for intervention, to try more positive and less intrusive procedures first, to document program implementation and effectiveness, and to set a goal for program termination.

Time Out. Time out is a behavioral strategy that has frequently been addressed in the literature (see also Chapter 4). It is often used in schools, but is considered to be a high-risk intervention that must be individualized (Gast & Nelson, 1977). Time out is subject to misapplication because a number of parameters must be considered for the procedure to be used properly. For example, verbal explanation, warning, location, duration, schedule, and release procedures are all factors to be identified (Gast & Nelson, 1977). In addition, there are different degrees of time out, ranging from contingent observation to exclusion to seclusion time out. The mildest form that can be appropriately used should be the technique that is employed first.

The use of time out has also been addressed by the courts, and the following guidelines have been proposed by Wherry (1983):

1. Time out should be used where the behavior of the student creates "substantial disruption."
2. Duration of time out should not exceed one hour.
3. Books or school work should be provided during time out.
4. Exclusion should be from privileges and not from substantive rights.
5. Time out should be closely and directly supervised (p. 49)

SUMMARY

The target behavior(s) identified, the behavioral goals of treatment, and the selection and implementation of a behavior change program are intimately related. In addition, consideration of the technique to be used, how, in what setting, for how long, and so on, combine to create a complex multidimensional framework, which provides a host of potential choices and alternatives. It is the responsibility of the behavior change agent to select the strategies and carefully implement the procedures that reflect thoughtful consideration of the legal and ethical precautions involved.

PLAN IMPLEMENTATION

Once a behavioral change procedure has been selected and the specifics of the plan worked out, implementation of the proposed treatment plan involve assigning intervention roles and ensuring the competence of the individuals who must carry out the plan.

The issue of training and competence is an important one in the entire field of behavior therapy (see also Chapter 9). "Adequate competencies" (Harris & Kapche, 1978) on the part of anyone who designs and implements behavior change programs are required, however, specification of appropriate training, knowledge, and skills is difficult. Agras (1973) has described the competent behavior therapist as someone who: "must have knowledge of the principles underlying behavior modification, experience in the application of such knowledge to human behavior problems, and experience in the experimental analysis of deviant behavior, both for research purposes and as an approach to the ongoing evaluation of clinical care. He must also, however, demonstrate certain less well-defined characteristics, usually referred to as general clinical skills" (p. 169). Others have identified the need for guided practice, field experience, direct observation and feedback, and consultative follow-up (Harris & Kapche, 1978; Rosenfield, 1979; Stein, 1975). Whether certification of the behavior therapist is required is controversial (Agras, 1973). Indeed, it has been suggested that the procedures should be certified rather than the people who use them (Risley, 1975).

Training and competence as it relates to implementation of behavior change programs in schools is a particularly sensitive and pertinent issue, because schools deal with minors who have little or no control over the behavioral program in which they participate. Also, school-based behavior change programs often involve the participation of one or several nonprofessionals in the field of behavior therapy (e.g., teachers, teacher-aides, parents). Thus, inadequate training and skills can be compounded with the potential not only to seriously undermine the effectiveness of an intervention, but to produce unexpected side effects as well.

Who should design and implement behavioral change programs in schools? To date, this question has not been answered by the courts. In practice, teachers are often identified as the primary behavior change agents, usually, under the direction of a consultant (e.g., school psychologist).

Ethical safeguards suggest a team approach to a behavioral intervention. Everyone involved must be aware of and willing and capable of complying with the specifics of the intervention. It is the responsibility of the consultant to supervise the program, to ensure that appropriate data is collected and to monitor progress to assess program effectiveness. It is also the responsibility of the consultant to anticipate problems so that difficulties relating to unforseen circumstances are minimal. Adequate ongoing supervision and consultation are essential ingredients to ensure the quality of a behavioral program.

If a teacher or behavior therapist is unwilling or unable to invest the time and energy involved in carrying out a behavior change program, or if the training or competence of either is questionable, implementation of a behavioral program might be legally suspect, and would be ethically inappropriate and unwise.

PROBLEM EVALUATION

It has been noted previously that, more and more, public school personnel are being held accountable for the behavior change programs they institute in the classroom (see also Chapter 10). The move toward accountability is compatible with the philosophy of behavior therapy committed to the continuous measurement and evaluation of the specific effects of treatment (Wilson & O'Leary, 1980). The observation and documentation of behavioral changes allows for the evaluation of program effectiveness and makes accountability possible and necessary. Indeed, the ethical responsibility to evaluate treatment effects is recognized most clearly by behaviorists.

The concern for evaluation is evident in the data collection and record keeping that occurs throughout all stages of a behavioral change program. This is critical not only in identifying when a problem is significantly discrepant from peers, but also in the ongoing monitoring and evaluation of the effectiveness of the program. The confidentiality of data is assumed, as is the sharing of data and relevant information with the parties involved (Harris & Kapche, 1978).

Despite the accepted need for evaluation of treatment effects, specific evaluation strategies are left to the discretion of the change agent. How much of a change is considered socially valid? How long should an intervention continue before it is deemed ineffective, and a new strategy pursued? What behaviors other than the target behavior(s) should be monitored to assess the side effects of treatment? These are realistic questions for which there are no definitive answers. However, trends toward the standardization of visual inspection criteria in charted data (Parsonson & Baer, 1978) and toward procedures to establish social validity (Van Houten, 1979) are just two of the ways that evaluation procedures can be expected to improve in the near future.

The issue of social validity should be emphasized. It is becoming widely recognized that behavioral changes must be assessed on their social usefulness and importance. Wolf (1978) suggested three levels of social validation: (a) the social significance of the goals of behavioral interventions; (b) the social appropriateness of the procedures used; and (c) the social importance of the effects. Procedures to assess the social validity of a behavior change have included social comparison and subjective evaluation (Van Houten, 1979). These methods are helpful in selecting appropriate target behaviors and in identifying when to terminate an intervention. According to Van Houten (1979) appropriate termination of treatment involves determination of the "optimal range" of the target behavior, which is best done through social validation procedures.

In keeping with this is the need to provide for generalization experiences. Generalization refers to the transfer of changes in behavior across situations, across behaviors, and across individuals. For example, the social skill of verbally complementing others taught in a group setting might be expected to transfer to the classroom setting. However, "It is increasingly recognized that generalization is not a passive phenomenon and usually must be specifically programmed" (Kratochwill, 1982, p. 345). Thus, generalization must be planned for and evaluation procedures must consider the generalized effects of a behavioral program.

"Evaluation is not complete, however, until follow-up assessments of behavior change have been conducted to demonstrate its maintenance and generality" (Sulzer-Azaroff & Mayer, 1977, p. 474). Follow-up must be planned in advance so that the environment will be structured to provide for maintenance of the behavior change, and procedures to enhance generalization will be provided. Those who design and carry out behavior change programs in schools should be ethically bound to evaluate the long-term effects of the behavioral program for which they are responsible.

The monitoring and evaluation of intervention effects may be easy to disregard in schools, because children have little potential for countercontrol (Krapfl, 1975). There may be little overt pressure for behavior change agents to analyze what they are doing, who is benefitting from the intervention, how much and at what cost. However, the need to assess program effectiveness is an ethical must. Likewise, documentation and record keeping through the entire behavior change programs process should make behavior change in schools better able to withstand the scrutiny of the courts.

FUTURE DEVELOPMENTS

As noted earlier, concern about legal and ethical matters has advanced rapidly in recent years; this trend is expected to continue. All professionals in this and related areas are likely to find that merely keeping up with these developments will be challenging.

A great deal of the research anticipated by authors of other chapters will have implications for legal and ethical guidelines. For example, the research pertinent to social validity will increasingly identify the domains of functioning and the specific behaviors that do, indeed, make a difference. As these crucial behaviors are identified, along with the subject and setting variables that almost certainly will also be important, we can expect better, more useful specification of target behaviors. This will contribute to the resolution of the perennial questions of what behaviors? Decided on by whom? For what purposes? Many other research advances discussed in other chapters will have analogous effects on legal and ethical considerations.

One area of research, fascinating to us, but largely ignored so far, is the question, At what age can students exercise informed consent rights? Bersoff (1982) was a major influence on our thinking about this question. We believe that various kinds of studies could be carried out to address this question. An initial stage might be simulations of informed consent transactions involving different kinds of problems and students of varying ages. Another step might be to compare the decisions and reasoning of parents and students. Comparison could involve, with carefully designed protections, actual cases. The real life question, of course, is not whether some or most students of a certain age can wisely exercise informed consent rights, but rather whether students who are referred or otherwise become the participants in behavioral interventions can exercise these rights.

Research in these and related areas will undoubtedly influence legal and ethical principles. These principles, dynamic and complex as they are and must be, represent the best efforts of professionals in several disciplines to ensure competent practices and protect participants' rights and interests.

REFERENCES

(AABT) Association for the Advancement of Behavior Therapy, 420 Lexington Ave., New York, NY 10017.

Abeson, A., Bolick, N., & Haas, J. (1975). *A primer on due process.* Reston, VA: Council for Exceptional Children.

Agras, W. S. (1973). Toward the certification of behavior therapists? *Journal of Applied Behavior Analysis, 6,* 167–173.

American Psychological Association. (1981). *Ethical principles of psychologists.* Washington, DC: Author.

(APA) American Psychological Association, 1200 Seventeenth St. NW, Washington, DC 20036.

(AACD) American Association for Counseling and Development, 5999 Stevenson Ave., Alexandria, VA 22304.

Bandura, A. (1969). *Principles of behavior modification.* New York: Holt, Rinehart, & Winston.

Barrish, A. H., Saunders, M, & Wolf, M. M. (1969). Good behavior game: Effects on individual contingencies for group consequences on disruptive behavior in a classroom. *Journal of Applied Behavior Analysis, 2,* 119–124.

Bergan, J. R. (1977). *Behavioral consultation.* Columbus, OH: Charles E. Merrill.

Bersoff, D. N. (1975). Professional ethics and legal responsibilities: On the horns of a dilemma. *Journal of School Psychology, 3,* 359–376.

Bersoff, D. N. (1978). Procedural safeguards. In L. Morra (Ed.), *Due process: Developing criteria for evaluating the due process procedural safeguards provision of Public Law 94-142* (pp. 63–142). Washington DC: U.S. Office of Education, Bureau of Education for the Handicapped.

Bersoff, D. N. (1982). The legal regulation of school psychology. In C. R. Reynolds & T. B. Gutkin (Eds.), *The Handbook of School Psychology.* New York: Wiley.

Broughton, S. F., Barton, E. S., & Owen, P. R. (1981). Home-based contingency systems for school problems. *School Psychology Review, 10,* 26–36.

Buss, W. (1975). What procedural due process means to a school psychologist: A dialogue. *Journal of School Psychology, 13,* 298–310.

Christian, B. T. (1983). A practical reinforcement hierarchy for classroom behavior modification. *Psychology in the Schools, 20,* 83–84.

Davison, G. C., & Stuart, R. B. (1975). Behavior therapy and civil liberties. *American Psychologist, 30,* 755–763.

Federal Register. (1977, August 23). Regulations implementing Education for all Handicapped Children Act of 1975 (Public Law 94-142), (p. 42474–42518). Author.

Friedman, P. R. (1975). Legal regulation of applied behavior analysis in mental institutions and prisons. *Arizona Law Review, 17,* 39–104.

Gambrill, E. D. (1977). *Behavior modification: Handbook of assessment, modification, and evaluation.* San Francisco: Jossey-Bass.

Gast, D. L., & Nelson, C. M. (1977). Legal and ethical considerations for the use of timeout in special education settings. *Journal of Special Education, 11,* 457–467.

Glenn, C. M. (1980). Ethical issues in the practice of child psychotherapy. *Professional Psychology, 11,* 613–619.

Harris, A., & Kapche, R. (1978). Behavior modification in schools: Ethical issues and suggested guidelines. *Journal of School Psychology, 16,* 25–33.

Hawkins, R. P. (1975). Who decided that was the problem? Two stages of responsibility for applied behavior analysts. In W. S. Wood (Ed.), *Issues in evaluating behavior modification* (pp. 195–214). Champaign, IL: Research Press.

Kicklighter, R. H. (1983). Clients all. *Journal of School Psychology, 21,* 119–121.

Krapfl, J. E. (1975). Accountability for behavioral engineers. In W. S. Wood (Ed.), *Issues in evaluating behavior modification* (pp. 219–236). Champaign, IL: Research Press.

Kratochwill, T. R. (1982). Advances in behavioral assessment. In C. R. Reynolds & T. B. Gutkin (Eds.), *The handbook of school psychology* (pp. 314–350). New York: Wiley.

Kremens, V. Bartley (1977). *United States Law Week, 45,* LW 4451.

Lahey, B. B., Genrich, J. G., Genrich, S. I., Schnelle, J. F., Gant, D. S. & McNees, M. P. (1977). An evaluation of daily report cards with minimal teacher and parent contacts as an efficient method of classroom intervention. *Behavior Modification, 1,* 381–394.

Martin, R. (1975a). The ethical and legal implications of behavior modification in the classroom. In G. R. Gredler (Ed.), *Ethical and legal factors in the practice of school psychology* (pp. 53–66). Harrisburg, PA: Pennsylvania Department of Education.

Martin, R. (1975b).*Legal challenges to behavior modification.* Champaign, IL: Research Press.

Mills vs. Board of Education, 348 F. Supp. 866 (D.D.C. #1972).

(NASP) National Association of School Psychologists, 1511 K. Street NW, Washington, DC 20005.

(NASW) National Association of Social Workers, 1425 H Street, NW, Washington, DC, 20005.

O'Leary, K. D. (1972). Behavior modification in the classroom: A rejoinder to Winett and Winkler. *Journal of Applied Behavior Analysis, 5,* 505–511.

O'Leary, S. G., & O'Leary, K. D. (1977). Ethical issues of behavior modification research in schools. *Psychology in the Schools, 14,* 299–307.

Overcast, T. D., & Sales, B. D. (1982). The legal rights of students in the elementary and secondary public schools. In C. R. Reynolds & T. B. Gutkin (Eds.), *The handbook of school psychology* (pp. 1075–1100). New York: Wiley.

(PARC) Pennsylvania Association for Retarded Children vs. Commonwealth of Pennsylvania, 343 F. Supp. 279 (E. D. Pa. 1972).

Parsonson, B. S., & Baer, D. M. (1978). The analysis and presentation of graphic data. In T. Kratochwill (Ed.), *Single subject research: Strategies for evaluating change* (pp. 101–165). New York: Academic Press.

Repp, A. C., & Dietz, D. E. (1978). On the selective use of punishment—suggested guidelines for administration. *Mental Retardation, 16,*250–254.

Reschly, D. (1980). Assessment of exceptional individuals: Legal mandates and professional standards. In R. Mulliken & M. R. (Eds), *Assessment of children with low incidence handicaps* (pp. 8–23). Washington, DC: National Association of School Psychologists.

Reschly, D. (1983). Legal issues in psychoeducational assessment. In G. Hynd (Ed.), *The school psychologist: Contemporary perspectives* (pp. 67–93). Syracuse, NY: Syracuse University Press.

Risley, T. R. (1975). Certify procedures not people. In W. S. Wood (Ed.), *Issues in evaluating behavior modification* (pp. 159–181). Champaign, IL: Research Press.

Rosenfield, S. (1979). Introducing behavior modification techniques to teachers. *Exceptional Children, 45,* 334–339.

Stein, T. J. (1975). Some ethical consideration of short-term workshops in the principles and methods of behavior modification. *Journal of Applied Behavior Analysis, 8,* 113–115.

Stolz, S. B., & Associates. (1978). *Ethical Issues in behavior modification.* San Francisco, CA: Jossey-Bass.

Stolz, S. B., Wienckowski, L. A., & Brown, B. S. (1975). Behavior modification: A perspective on critical issues. *American Psychologist, 30,* 1027–1048.

Sulzer-Azaroff, B., & Mayer, G. R. (1977). *Applying behavior-analysis procedures wi!h children and youth.* New York: Holt, Rinehart, & Winston.

Van Houten, R. (1979). Social validation: The evolution of standards of competency for target behaviors. *Journal of Applied Behavior Analysis, 12,* 581–591.

Wherry, J. N. (1983). Some legal considerations and implications for the use of behavior modification in the schools. *Psychology in the Schools, 20,* 46–51.

Wilson, G. T., & O'Leary, K. D. (1980).*Principles of behavior therapy.* Englewood Cliffs, NJ: Prentice-Hall.

Winett, R. A., & Winkler, R. C. (1972). Current behavior modification in the classroom: Be still, be quiet, be docile. *Journal of Applied Behavior Analysis, 5,* 499–504.

Winkler, R. C. (1977). What types of sex-role behavior should behavior modifiers promote? *Journal of Applied Behavior Analysis, 10,* 549–552.

Wolf, M. M. (1978). Social validity: The case for subjective measurement or how applied behavior analysis is finding its heart. *Journal of Applied Behavior Analysis, 11,* 203–214.

Woods, T. S. (1982). Procedures and policies for regulating fieldbased behavioral technology. *Behavioral Disorders, 8,* 32–40.

Author Index

Freeman, H. F., 254, *286*
Freidman, M. P., *288*
Friedenberg, P., 121, *128*
Friedman, P. R., 275, 291, *308*
Frinfrock, S. R., *69*, 279, *288*
Fry, B. L., 49, *73*
Furukawa, M. J., 93, *107*

G

Gagné, R. M., 19, 20, 30, *36*
Gallagher, J. D., 138, *149*
Gallahue, D. L., 132, *150*
Gallessich, J., 200, *217*
Galloway, C. G., 51, *73*
Galvin, G. A., 103, *105*
Gambrill, E. D., 296, *308*
Gannaway, T., 116, *128*
Gant, D. S., 159, 160, 162, *179,* 302, *308*
Garber, S., 164, *177*
Garlick, B. J., 122, *130*
Garten, K. L., 48, 53, *71*
Gast, D. L., 290, 302, *308*
Gaughan, E. J., Jr., 275, *288*
Geesey, S., 266, *287*
Gelfand, D. M., 84, 88, *105*
Gendrich, J. G., 159, 160, 162, *179,* 302, *308*
Gendrich, S. I., 159, 160, 162, *179,* 302, *308*
Gentile, A. M., 138, *149*
Gerler, E. R., Jr., 126, *128, 129*
Gershaw, N. J., 93, 94, *105*
Gersten, R., 116, *129*
Gesten, E., *108*
Gilbert, T., 231, *249*
Gintis, H., 39, *71*
Glass, G. V., 191, *217*
Glenn, C. M., 292, 293, *308*
Glynn, E., 87, 88, *105*
Glynn, T., 55, *68,* 239, *252*
Goety, E. M., 135, *149*
Gold, M. W., 122, *129*
Goldfried, M. R., 14, 15, 24, *36,* 116, *129,* 171, *178,* 184, 188, *217*
Goldhammer, K. A., 112, *129*
Goldstein, A. P., 85, 93–95, *105,* 188, *217*
Goldstein, E. O., 169, *178*
Goodenough, F. L., 14, 15, *36*
Goodland, J., 231, *249*
Goodman, H., 142, *149*
Goodman, J., 57, *72*
Goodwin, D. L., 16, *36*

Gordon, 24
Gorton, R. A., 226, *249*
Gottman, J. M., 191, *217*
Graham-Clay, S., 9
Graubard, P. S., 55, *69*
Graves, A. W., 43, 54, *70, 71*
Gray, 22
Graziano, A. M., 154, *177*
Green, D. R., 171, *179*
Greenan, J. P., 112, *129*
Greenleaf, D. O., 85, 95, *105,* 259, *287*
Gresham, F. M., 9, 166, 167, 173, *178*
Grieger, R. M., 78, *105,* 196, 197, 200, *217*
Griest, D. L., 23, *36,* 277, 278, *287*
Grimm, L. G., 188, *217*
Grise, P., 2, *10*
Groden, J., 90, *104*
Guidubaldi, J., 153, *178*
Guillion, M. G., 155–56, *179*
Guppy, T. C., 50, 51, *72*
Gutkin, T. B., 67, 228, *249*

H

Haas, J., 291, *307*
Haas, K., 52, *71*
Haimes, 24
Haisch, L., 45, *70*
Hall, G., 141–42, *151*
Hall, G. E., 30, *36*
Hall, R. V., 51, *69,* 193, 199, *217,* 263–65, *287*
Hallahan, D. P., 43, 52, 54, 59, *70, 71*
Halpern, A., 119, *129*
Halsdorf, M., 171, *177*
Hamblin, R. L., 41, *70*
Hammer, D. C., 281–83, *286*
Hammill, D. D., 24, *35*
Hanawalt, D. A., 125, *129*
Hansen, C. L., 46, 47, 61, *70*
Harges, K., 234, *251*
Haridman, S. A., 135, *149*
Haring, N. G., 61, *70*
Harris, 34
Harris, A., 289, 297–98, 299, 301, 302, 304, 305, *308*
Harris, B., 256, *287*
Harris, F. R., 77, 79, *104, 105,* 134, *150*
Harris, V. W., 58, *70*
Harshbarger, D. D., 223, *249*
Hart, B. M., 77, 79, *104, 105*

Muller, S., 91, *106*
Murphy, A., 82, *107*
Murray, D., 236, 237, *252*

N

Nadolsky, J., 113, 115, *130*
Nagle, R. J., 166, 167, *178*
Naisbitt, J., 111, *130*
Nay, W. R., 27, *37*
Neale, D. C., 225, 229, 231, *251*
Neff, W. S., 113, 115, 116, *130*
Negben, M. K., 239, 240, *251*
Neisworth, J. R., 168, *179*
Nelson, C. M., 290, 302, *308*
Nelson, R. O., 3, 4, 6, *10, 11*, 14–16, 18, 23, *36, 37*, 42, *70*, 244, 254, 284, *286*
Neumann, A. J., 193, 197, *216*
Newell, K. M., 134, 137, *150*
Noller, R. B., 224, *251*
Noonan, J. R., 122, *130*
Norman, J. E., 52, 53, *70*

O

O'Brian, F., 135, *150*
O'Brien, R. M., 243, *251*
O'Connor, R. D., 94, *106*
O'Dell, S., 154, *179*
Oden, S., 94, *106*
O'Hara, C., 49, 53, *71*
O'Leary, 58
O'Leary, K. D., 82, 88, *105, 106*, 143, *150*, 155, 171, 172, *179, 180*, 187, 197, *218*, 289, 291, 293, 298–300, 303, 305, *308, 309*
O'Leary, S. G., 143, *150*, 187, *218*, 289, 293, 298, 300, 303, *308*
Olexa, D. F., 96, *107*
Ollendick, T. H., 84, *107,* 266, 267, 269, *288*
Olson, D. H. L., 171, *177*
Olson, G., 239, *250*
Orlick, T., 133, *150*
Ossip, D., 140, *149*
Overcast, T. D., 292, 302, *308*
Owen, P. R., 302, *307*

P

Pacquin, M. J., 48, 59, *72*
Padawer, D. D., 92, *107*
Paluska, T., 50, *68*

Parker, F. C., 79, *107*
Parnes, S. J., 224, *251*
Parra, E., *216*
Parsons, R. D., 184, *218*
Parsonson, B. S., 305, *308*
Pate, R., 131, 139, *150*
Patterson, G. R., 155–56, 164, 169, *179*
Patterson, K. J., 234, *251*
Patterson, M. R., 26, *36*
Paul, R., 243, *250*
Paulson, T. A., 195, *217*
Pavlov, I. P., 7, *11*
Pearce, E., 123, *128*
Pease, G. A., 88, *107*
Peckham, P. D., 34, *37*
Peed, S., 164, 169, *178, 180*
Perlmutter, L., 122, *128*
Perry, C., 145–47, *149, 150*
Perry, M. J., 93, *107*
Perry, R., 192, *216*
Persons, S., 79, *108*
Peterson, A. C., 145, *149*
Peterson, D. R., 24, 25, *37*
Peterson, R., 103, *105*
Petrie, P., 279, *288*
Pfohl, W. F., 238, *251*
Phelps, L. A., 112, *129*
Phillips, E. L., 165, 171, *177, 179*
Piersel, W. C., 8, 45, 48, 50, 67, *72*, 184, 185, 195, *218*, 279, 285, *288*
Pine, A. L., 121, *128*
Pisor, K., 164, *177*
Pitt, N. W., 275, *288*
Pless, I. B., 169, *180*
Poggio, J. P., 193, 198, *219*
Polefka, D. A., 166, *179*
Pollack, M. J., 168, *180*
Popham, W. J., 21, 30, *37*
Poplin, M., 154, *180*
Porras, J. I., 234, 240, *251*
Porterfield, J. K., 84, *107*
Posovac, E. J., 6, *11*
Powell, K. E., 131, 132, *150*
Powers, M. A., 84, *104*
Pratt, R., 142, *149*
Pree, M. M., 48, *71*
Premack, D., 78, *107*
Presbie, R. J., 141, *150*
Presnall, D., 119, *128*
Pressey, S. L., 242
Pressley, M. P., 97, *107*

Subject Index

325